DAY by DAY

THROUGH THE BIBLE

DAY by DAY

THROUGH THE BIBLE

Edited by

KEN TOTTON

PRECIOUS SEED PUBLICATIONS

© Copyright Precious Seed Publications 2015
Pitcot Farm, Pitcot Lane, Stratton on the Fosse,
Radstock, BA3 4SX, UK.

First published September 2015

ISBN 978 1 871642 80 3

This is the sixteenth book in the Day by Day series.

The others are:

Day by Day through the New Testament
Day by Day through the Old Testament
Day by Day in the Psalms
Day by Day Moments with the Master
Day by Day in Prayer
Day by Day with Bible Characters
Day by Day Christ Foreshadowed
Day by Day Bible Promises
Day by Day Divine Titles
Day by Day Bible Commands
Day by Day Paradise to the Promised Land
Day by Day Bible Pictures and Parables
Day by Day Bible Questions
Day by Day Living in the Promised Land
Day by Day Christ and His Apostles

Printed in the UK

Contents

Preface

The Day by Day series seeks to promote the daily enjoyment of the Bible. The original volume, *Day by Day through the New Testament,* was published in 1979, and this sixteenth volume supports reading through the Bible in one year. Each contributor has been asked to give a balanced coverage of the passages allotted to him, and the highlighting of the biblical reference in bold at the top of each page indicates the focus of the meditation.

God's perfect Servant testified, 'The Lord God hath given me the tongue of the learned, that I should know how to speak a word in season to him that is weary: he wakeneth morning by morning, he wakeneth mine ear to hear as the learned', Isa. 50. 4. May we follow His delightful example, and be able to truly say with the prophet, 'Thy words were found, and I did eat them; and thy word was unto me the joy and rejoicing of mine heart', Jer. 15. 16.

This production was once again a real team effort. John Bennett conceived the concept, compiled the daily passages, and provided valuable advice and encouragement at every stage. John Scarsbrook, Brian Clatworthy, Richard Collings, Howard Barnes, and Michael Sparkes assisted with checking and proof reading.

Typesetting was carried out by John Bennett, while the cover design is the work of Barney Trevivian. All are deserving of our thanks for their valued expertise, commitment, and contribution.

On behalf of the Precious Seed Committee,
Ken Totton July 2015

Glossary

ESV English Standard Version
JND   New Translation, J N Darby
KJV   King James Version
NASB   New American Standard Bible
NKJV   New King James Version
RV   English Revised Version
YLT Young's Literal Translation

The Contributors

Wesley Ferguson	N. Ireland	Jan 1 – 15
David Newell	Scotland	Jan 16 – 31
Richard Collings	Wales	Feb 1 – 14
Stephen Arbuthnot	Scotland	Feb 15 – 28
Ken Totton	England	Mar 1 – 16
Bert Cargill	Scotland	Mar 17 – 31
Mark Kolchin	USA	Apr 1 – 15
Jack Hay	Scotland	Apr 16 – 30
Rutherford Rabey	England	May 1 – 16
Stephen Grant	Scotland	May 17 – 31
Randal Amos	USA	June 1 – 15
Phil Coulson	Scotland	June 16 – 30
Roy Hill	England	July 1 – 16
Colin Lacey	England	July 17 – 31
Alan Gamble	Scotland	Aug 1 – 16
Brian Gunning	Canada	Aug 17 – 31
John Bennett	England	Sept 1 – 15
Keith Keyser	USA	Sept 16 – 30
Ken Rudge	England	Oct 1 – 16
Tom Wilson	Scotland	Oct 17 – 31
Gordon Stewart	England	Nov 1 – 15
Alistair Sinclair	Scotland	Nov 16 – 30
David McAllister	Ireland	Dec 1 – 16
Malcolm Davis	England	Dec 17 – 31

Biographies of the Contributors

Wesley Ferguson is an elder in the assembly in Antrim in Northern Ireland. He is the author of numerous magazine articles. He authored Genesis in the Ritchie series *What the Bible Teaches*. He was previously a teacher and a schools' inspector.

David Newell is in fellowship in the assembly at Eastpark Gospel Hall, Glasgow, Scotland.

Richard Collings is in fellowship in the assembly at Caerphilly, Wales and is a committee member of the Precious Seed Trust.

Stephen Arbuthnot lives in Glasgow and is a member of the assembly meeting in Avenuepark Street, Maryhill, Glasgow, where he gives help in Bible teaching. He is married with two daughters.

Ken Totton is an elder in the Roseford assembly, Cambridge, England. Following a career in telecommunications, he now engages in Bible teaching in the UK. He is also Publications Editor for Precious Seed Publications. He is married to Kate and has two sons.

Bert Cargill has had a lifelong involvement with the assembly in St. Monans. He was a chemistry lecturer for over 30 years. Latterly, with early retirement, he has written and edited books and articles for the UK and abroad. Married to Isobel, they have six grandchildren.

Mark Kolchin, along with his wife Cynthia, was commended to the Lord's work in 1993 by the assembly in Toms River, New Jersey, USA. He engages in an itinerant Bible teaching and conference ministry, and maintains an evangelistic and Bible teaching web site, www.knowtheword.com. He has written on a variety of topics in the Christian life.

Jack Hay is in fellowship in the assembly at Perth, Scotland. He is a commended full-time worker preaching the gospel and teaching the word throughout the UK, North America, and the Far East. He is also the author of numerous magazine articles.

Rutherford Rabey is in fellowship in Wylam assembly in Northumberland, England. He is married to Rachel and has two daughters, Elspeth and Miriam.

Stephen Grant is in fellowship in the assembly at Bridge of Weir, Scotland. He is a commended full-time worker involved in preaching the gospel and Bible teaching. He has written the book *Of no reputation*, published by John Ritchie Ltd. He is married with a family.

Randal Amos has, by the grace of God, been answering the call to 'preach the word' for the past 35 years with his wife Sylvia being a faithful help. He is commended by Linwood Gospel Chapel in New Jersey and Northgate Bible Chapel in Rochester New York and is now in the assembly at Oregon City, Oregon.

Phil Coulson and his wife Rachel were commended to a full-time preaching and teaching ministry by the Forres assembly in 1999. Since then, Phil has moved widely amongst the assemblies in the UK and abroad, particularly in Asia. Phil and Rachel have two children and five grandchildren, all living in Forres, Scotland.

Roy Hill is in fellowship in the assembly at Pensford Gospel Hall, near Bristol, and is well known as an international Bible teacher. He is married with five children and thirteen grandchildren. Roy spent his working life in the printing industry and was chairman of the Precious Seed Trust for many years.

Colin Lacey was headteacher of a large secondary school. He is married to Alison, and has two sons and six grandchildren. Now retired, he lives in Bath and meets with the believers in Manvers Hall. He travels throughout the UK teaching the word of God. He is the author of the commentaries on Judges and Nehemiah in the John Ritchie *What the Bible Teaches* series.

Alan Gamble is in fellowship in the assembly at Bethesda, Linthouse, Glasgow, Scotland. He is active in Bible teaching in the UK and North America. He serves as a trustee of Interlink, a missionary service group. He is married to Elizabeth, and they have three adult children and three grandchildren. His professional background is in law.

Brian Gunning is in fellowship in the Brockview assembly in St. Catherines, Ontario, Canada. He is an elder in the local assembly, editor of *Counsel* magazine, and director of Gospel Folio Press. He has an active itinerant preaching ministry throughout North America.

John Bennett is an elder at the Gospel Hall, Kirkby-in-Ashfield, Nottinghamshire, England. He is active in ministry in England and has written numerous articles for assembly magazines. He became a trustee of Precious Seed in 2002, publications editor in 2004, and ministry articles editor in 2010. He is married to Rachel and has three children, one of whom is married.

Keith Keyser is a commended full-time worker and is in fellowship in the assembly meeting at Gilbertsville, Pennsylvania. He ministers throughout North America and spent some time in Spain. He also regularly writes material for assembly magazines.

Ken Rudge is an elder in the assembly at St. Austell, Cornwall. A former primary school headteacher, he is active in Bible teaching and local evangelism. A former editor of Precious Seed, he retired from the Trust in 2009.

Tom Wilson is an elder in the Springburn assembly in Glasgow and ministers the word throughout Scotland. He was for many years editor of Believer's Magazine, and is a retired principal of a specialist college in Glasgow.

Gordon Stewart is in fellowship with an assembly in Wallingford, Oxfordshire. He is married, with four children.

Alastair Sinclair is in fellowship with the assembly at Crosshouse, Ayrshire, and is active in oral ministry throughout the UK. He writes regularly for assembly magazines and is married with a family. He works in the IT industry.

David McAllister and his wife Priscilla were commended to the work of the Lord by the Parkgate assembly, Belfast. They worked in Zambia for eighteen years, and are now in Donegal, Ireland. They have four children.

Malcolm Davis, together with his wife Ruth, is in fellowship at Harehills Gospel Hall, Leeds. A retired academic librarian, he has authored volumes on the books of Joshua, Isaiah, Ezekiel, Daniel, Zechariah, and Revelation. He has contributed many articles to various Christian magazines.

Acknowledgements

The Publishers acknowledge the kind permission of the copyright owners, John Ritchie Ltd, for the use of the readings taken from *The Yearly Bible Calendar* by Henry Groves, which form the basis of each day's readings within this book.

We also acknowledge the support of Gospel Folio Press, who use these readings to form the basis of their Bible reading plan in the *Choice Gleanings Calendar*.

January 1st

Genesis 1. 1 – 2. 3; Job 1. 1 – 2. 10; Matthew 1

IN THE BEGINNING GOD

The Bible is given to us by God. Its record spans the history of the universe until there will be a new heaven and a new earth. Outside of that created universe stands the eternal Maker, Controller, Redeemer and Lord of all, God Himself. He is before all things and by Him all things are sustained. He is worshipped as 'God Most High', 'Possessor of the heaven and the earth', Gen. 14. 19 ESV.

The record in Genesis chapters 1 and 2 shows the universe formed progressively by an orderly mind. Godly scientists of a past generation studied the universe to develop their understanding of the mind of God. They believed, with the psalmist, that 'the heavens declare the glory of God; and the firmament sheweth his handywork', Ps. 19. 1. Modern science continues to add to our understanding of the wonders of the universe, in particular how complex it is, especially the nature of organic creation.

The godly may be tempted to doubt, even despair, because of the chaos in the world at large. We need not fear that God has lost control. At the centre of earth's history stands the story of the in-carnation, when God took human flesh. A holy child, God's Son, was born of a human mother to redeem fallen humanity. His life on earth ended when He was crucified. Some thought then that He had been defeated, and they jeered. Others were appalled that He was dead. But He triumphed in His death, having finished His work of redemption.

After He arose from the dead the preachers of the gospel proclaimed to His enemies, concerning God's Son, 'this Jesus, delivered up according to the definite plan and foreknowledge of God, you crucified and killed by the hands of lawless men. God raised him up, loosing the pangs of death, because it was not possible for him to be held by it', Acts 2. 23-24 ESV.

God stands supreme throughout history. He was before all things, and His purposes cannot be thwarted. He will be gloriously supreme when redeemed human beings sing His praise and that of His Son eternally. His people can conquer even if they are slain.

January 2nd

Genesis 2. 4-25; Job 2. 11 – 3. 26; **Matthew 2**

MIGHTY KING, WEAK PEOPLE

Matthew's Gospel depicts Christ as the Great King over all. His genealogy is traced in chapter 1, back to David, who was God's kind of king.

It is fitting, therefore, that chapter 2 tells of sages who came from the east to pay tribute and do homage to an infant king, whose birth was blazoned on the heavens for those whose eyes were opened to read the signs. It is not surprising that the same chapter tells of king Herod's alarm at the birth of a king in his own kingdom. Those were sad days in Israel, when a man of Herod's character, without lineage or character to commend him, ruled, and even rejoiced to be called 'Herod the Great'.

Humanly speaking, the prospect of Jesus' surviving, not to speak of reigning, was slim. The brutality of Herod stands in stark contrast to the seeming weakness and mildness of the holy family. The vital factor in the clash between Herod and the infant Christ is the fact that God can use the weak to achieve His purpose. The weak family had a message in a dream from God bidding them to flee. They were central to divine plans which could not be thwarted by any king, however great. Then, later, they had a message through an angel telling them of Herod's death. 'There shall come forth a shoot from the stump of Jesse', said the prophecy in Isaiah chapter 11 verse 1 ESV. This prophecy was about to move towards fulfilment.

The history of the church abounds with examples of how God used men and women of limited social standing or intellect to achieve great things for mankind. Godless organizations may glorify strength or intelligence. Every humanly devised civilization has had its 'stars' and supermen. Each generation poses as being more 'advanced' than its predecessor. Each wave of fashionable scientific theory becomes obsolete. Yet during all these phases of human self-glorification there have been simple men and women of God who have lived to serve God and their fellows and left a great spiritual legacy. The weakest saint, depending on God, is stronger than the most brutal enemy of God. 'If God be for us, who can be against us?'

January 3rd
Genesis 3; **Job 4-5**; Matthew 3
INTEGRITY TESTED BY GOD
The book of Job records the experience of a great man of God whose integrity is severely tested by God and proved to be genuine. God has allowed Satan to subject Job to a most harrowing set of circumstances. Yet God is still in control.

Job has lost his animals, his equipment, his servants and his family. His wife is unsympathetic and without understanding. His health is gone. Now his friends have come and show some tact in sitting silent for a week. At this point Job curses the day he was born and longs for death.

Eliphaz tries to help. His advice is frank but lacks understanding of Job as a person. He speaks of the holiness of God. He reminds Job of better days which are now past. Then he draws conclusions which sound logical, but which are wildly off the mark. Blind to the severity of his friend's suffering, he wounds when he seeks to heal. He merely adds to Job's sorrow.

We know from the reading of the complete story that, as Job had earlier enjoyed the confidence of God, he still enjoys it at the end. God is happy to refer to 'my servant Job' – chapters 1, 2 and 42.

Meanwhile Job continues to examine his conscience as he had done while he was healthy and prosperous. He knows that God is good and just, but he yearns to understand why He has chosen now to afflict him so sorely. His friends merely add to his distress.

Many believers have endured disablement or other suffering and come to terms with it in their communion with God. We are edified by their testimonies as to the ways of God. Amy Carmichael, who suffered severe illness, brought great deliverance to girls in India and wrote devotional testimonies. But not all suffering believers achieve this level of victory through patient endurance. How do we approach a suffering believer? Can we enter into their sorrow? Sometimes a silent embrace and a few tears of sympathy are the best medicine. They may need to express their bewilderment without interruption. 'What I do thou knowest not now, but thou shalt know hereafter', John 13. 7.

January 4th
Genesis 4-5; Job 6-7; Matthew 4
WHERE IS THY BROTHER?

God breathed the breath of life into man's nostrils and man became a living soul. Life was God's gift. When Adam sinned mankind came under the sentence of death, for sin brings death. Adam hid from God; he was afraid because sin broke his communion with God. God called, 'Where art thou?'

But the break in communion did not cease to affect Adam's race at that point. The next phase is introduced by another question, 'Where is thy brother?' for Cain slew Abel, who became the first person who died after sin began its deadly work. He died at his brother's hand. Sin separates us from other men as surely as it separates us from God.

By faith Abel offered to God an acceptable sacrifice, Heb. 11. 4, and he heads the list of the faithful in that chapter.

The long list of Adam's descendants in these chapters of Genesis is punctuated by the refrain, 'and he died'. This is still the lot of mankind, Heb. 9. 27, for death came upon all the race.

Romans chapter 1 describes the stages by which sin spread to affect all humanity. First there was a denial of God as Creator. Then people began to worship mere creatures below them in dignity. This was followed by a loss of understanding of men and women as complementary to each other. Then there follows the disintegration of human society in quarrelling and disputing. The Epistle to the Romans gloriously declares how salvation can provide for people to be at peace with God and with their fellows.

The term 'brother' is one which links us with all mankind. It presupposes the debt that we owe to show affection and co-operation. It speaks of our responsibility to show care for others, to respect others. When we sin against our brother or sister, we should consider the question, 'Where is he or she?', and remember how we broke a divinely established bond. Romans chapter 1 tells of the Creator denied, and it ends with a description of society bitterly and violently divided. This division may be on the basis of family, nationality, or race. It leads inevitably to a denial of what we owe to our fellow human beings. 'Where is thy brother?'

January 5th
Genesis 6-7; Job 8; **Matthew 5. 1-20**

A GOOD KING: WHAT KIND OF SUBJECTS?

Matthew chapter 4 tells us how the Lord preached the gospel of the kingdom. But what kind of people would its citizens be? Here in chapter 5 the Lord describes them.

He pronounces nine beatitudes. The first and the eighth beatitudes describe aspects of the character of the citizens and declare that 'theirs is the kingdom of heaven'. The overall picture presents to us people who have a character which shows that they are genuine. They are not acting a part to impress but living according to conviction.

The key question is, 'What are our real values?' The Lord expects us to have an influence on our community, an influence for good. Salt is a valuable substance to fight corruption. Is our influence on our community wholesome, morally healthy, or does it exude a nasty smell of corruption? In other words, are we *salt*?

Salt also makes food more tasty and digestible if used judicially. Do our attitudes and behaviour foster a pleasant atmosphere amongst those with whom we rub shoulders?

If salt is well used the person using it is aware of the taste of what is being eaten. 'Salty' people improve the wholesomeness of the society they move in, but will not be concerned to draw attention to themselves or to be noticed and admired.

The kingdom is also marked by light, the light of truth and righteousness. Are our dealings with others honest and such as to give the gospel a good name? We need to be living the truth before we are qualified to preach it. We remember the order of the expressions in the clause, 'all that Jesus began to do and to teach'. In Ephesians chapter 4 Paul describes how Christians should act as a body, manifesting truth and love. After this basic truth is stated he gives examples. One weighty item is the exhortation, 'Speak every man truth with his neighbour', v. 25. *Telling* the truth is a vital basis for *teaching* the truth. Many Jewish religious leaders in New Testament times lived greedy lives and showed little regard for integrity. These were not true citizens of a heavenly kingdom; they showed none of the features of disciples of 'the way, the truth and the life', John 14. 6.

January 6th

Genesis 7. 11 – 8. 19; **Job 9-10**; Matthew 5. 21-48

A MEDIATOR BETWEEN GOD AND MEN

In these chapters Job is in a quandary: how can a mere man be right in the sight of God? God is Creator of heaven and earth and we are His puny creatures. He is all-powerful, absolutely holy; He knows our every thought and He cannot be faced in a confrontation. Our only hope is to have a mediator who could 'lay his hand upon' God and man to bridge the gulf between us. But Job knows of no such mediator, and the result is total frustration, for he is not aware of any particular wickedness in himself to call down such misery as he is now experiencing. His problem is how to make his case before God.

We accept Job's description of the awful holiness and absolute power of God. We agree that it is to be expected that He will be absolutely just in His dealings with mortals. How marvellous that we can agree with Job as to the greatness and justice of God! We can, however, understand and wonder how there is someone who can 'lay his hand on' God and on us mortals. A Mediator has been found: 'There is one God, and one mediator between God and men, the man Christ Jesus; who gave himself a ransom for all', 1 Tim. 2. 5-6.

From all eternity He is the divine Son of God, so He can 'lay His hand' on God. Taking human flesh He did not cease to be truly God. Yet He was the Son of Mary, a human offspring. He was truly David's royal Son, yet David's Lord, Ps. 110. 1.

He gave Himself a ransom for us all on the cross. He paid our debt. What heaven demanded for our redemption, heaven paid. This is the glorious ground of our eternal hope, praise God! Job's problem is solved by God, for none other could have solved it.

He was absolutely holy, God manifest in flesh. The world, for the first time, was confronted with a true man who lived an absolutely holy life. The purpose of His coming was 'that he by the grace of God should taste death for every man', Heb. 2. 9.

One Mediator, throned above,
Bears witness God is light and love;
None but the Son sets sinners free,
'Come now', he saith, 'Come unto me'. HANNAH K. BURLINGHAM

22

January 7th

Genesis 8. 20 – 9. 29; Job 11-12; **Matthew 6. 1-18**

YOUR FATHER SEES AND KNOWS

Nowadays many people are keen to advertise the good things they have done and conceal their vices. The society in which the Lord Jesus lived was very similar to ours. Men of religion were anxious that people should see them praying, or donating to temple funds, or engaging in good works. They put great effort into ensuring that everyone saw, or at least knew, what these activities were.

The Lord Jesus confronts this superficial, often cynical approach. His emphasis is on what God the Father *sees* and *knows*. If we are truly serving the Lord we should not let ourselves be diverted into activities for which we seek public applause.

We can learn a great deal about ourselves from His teaching on this subject. Do we ensure that as many people as possible know when we donate to popular good causes? By contrast, *our Father* sees secret good deeds, v. 4. That is the important thing; not that other people see them. If we succeed in getting credit from other people for our deeds, this is our reward, which is not as important as our Father's approval. We need also to remember that public applause may be fickle and short-lived.

Do we make our religious activities as public as possible, to be seen by others, and gain their approval? Remember, when you pray in secret your Father sees. That is enough.

Do we make elaborate prayers in public to impress other people? Your Father knows what your prayer means, however short or plain it may be. The sample prayer given to the disciples by the Lord acknowledges God as Father and expresses a desire to submit to His plans and desires for us. We notice the emphasis in the prayer on our acknowledgement of the Father's will.

Go, labour on, 'tis not for nought;

Thine earthly loss is heavenly gain;

Men heed thee, love thee, praise thee not;

The Master praises – what are men?   C. WESLEY

Let us seek to leave appreciation of our service to the Lord. He sees. He knows. That is enough.

January 8th
Genesis 10. 1 – 11. 26; Job 13-14; **Matthew 6. 19 – 7. 6**
SERVING GOD OR MAMMON?

The Lord Jesus had warned His hearers that seeking credit and praise from others for what they regarded as charity may gain their praise, but not God's. Their short-lived reward would be in public opinion.

There is another danger: we may seek security in possessions and investments, but they may fail and leave us destitute. The Christian's true values are found in investing in heaven. Do we expend time and energy and resources in doing what will please God?

If our hearts are set on wealth ('Mammon'), can they at the same time be true to the God whom we serve? Where do our priorities lie? Is there much difference between hoarding money and spending large amounts on material possessions? Both activities show an unhealthy preoccupation with material things.

Are we careful not to overspend on clothing? God decks out the flowers and shrubs with colours which we cannot match. He clothes even the humblest creatures, again with colours which we cannot match. Are we careful about what we spend on fine foods? We must remember that God feeds even the humblest of His creatures. Are we not more important to Him than they are?

Some of the earliest scriptures declare the wisdom of God as Creator. They show the splendour of plants and animals in their glorious colours and their skilful search for food. These things are the gifts of God to them as creatures. Yet they have a short life on earth and then they are gone. God feeds them, and we are of greater value to God than they are, for we are made in His image and we have the promise of life beyond our earthly stay.

Society lavishes care on those things which 'quality' newspapers feature each week. But these are things which occupy the minds and hearts of people who have no eternal hope! 'For after all these things do the Gentiles seek', Matt. 6. 32.

'Your heavenly Father knoweth . . .' Christian history testifies to the faithfulness of God to provide for our needs as we serve Him. He even enables us to help others also. That is our privilege. People whom we help by our aid are also valuable to Him.

January 9th
Genesis 11. 27 – 12. 20; Job 15; Matthew 7. 7-29
I WILL BLESS THEE

This short passage of Bible history is of immense importance. A single family in the city of Ur in Mesopotamia 'served other gods' rather than Jehovah, Josh. 24. 2, the true God and Creator of all. God, 'the God of glory appeared to . . . Abraham', a member of that family, Acts 7. 2, and His purpose in calling Abraham out of Ur is of tremendous import. The ultimate outcome of this call will be worldwide blessing through Abraham's family, especially that member whom we know as Jesus, our Lord.

Abraham's life was changed. He left all that Ur stood for or boasted. He believed God's promises and went out, not knowing where he was going, Heb. 11. 8, except that he was conscious that God was with him. He left the 'other gods' and built an altar to the one true God. This would always be the most solid and lasting thing he would ever build. Many of his relatives disappear from the Bible story. His nephew Lot follows Abraham, but without Abraham's vision of God's purpose. Sarah, Abraham's wife, is with him; she is a vital part of God's plan to bless.

There is a famine almost at the start of the story, and Abraham escapes into Egypt, with Lot and Sarah. His actions there are sad to relate; but this story is told, not to glorify Abraham, but to tell of God's grace, and they did return from Egypt.

Every Christian is on a journey with God. We came to trust Him when we answered His call in the gospel. We accepted His invitation through the call of Christ, 'Come unto me', Matt. 11. 28. This involves leaving behind a way of life which is false and which ends in death. Without Christ we must suffer eternal loss.

All Christians at some points in life make wrong decisions; we all fail in some respects. But our firm foundation is our 'altar' – our worship of God as the One who is true and to be trusted. We need to learn that we follow the Lord, not His servants; for they can all fail, but He cannot. He will bless us. Abraham was tested throughout his life for God. God had said, 'I will bless thee', and He still blesses those who trust Him for salvation and for all that it entails. He cannot fail.

25

January 10th
Genesis 13-14; Job 16-17; Matthew 8. 1-27

LIFT UP NOW THINE EYES

Genesis chapters 13 and 14 outline for us two possible ways of planning our lives. Abraham and Lot set out together on a journey. Abraham went at God's bidding, trusting in God; Lot, his nephew, merely followed him. God prospered both of them. Their flocks became so large that, though they were in harmony – 'brothers', as Abraham put it – they had to arrange to seek separate pasture. Lot chose grazing lands on the basis of appearance, thinking of financial gain. Abraham, giving Lot first choice, let God choose for him. Lot 'lifted up his eyes' to see profit; God bade Abraham to lift up his eyes to see the generosity of His provision for him.

Lot saw grazing potential, but he could not see a corrupt and corrupting society, a moral cesspool in Sodom. God promised Abraham a spiritual inheritance for himself and his great posterity. His descendants would be a blessing to mankind, while Lot's gain was short-lived, for war left him a helpless prisoner. Abraham, concerned for his nephew, set out and rescued him.

Abraham was weary after his victory and unaware of a subtle but dangerous approach by the king of Sodom. But Abraham was trusting God, and God knew what Abraham did not know. He timed Abraham's support against the approach by the king of Sodom perfectly.

King Melchizedek of Salem, sent by God, met Abraham with food and drink to refresh and strengthen him. Melchizedek worshipped God the Creator and his intervention was most timely for Abraham's need. We know little of this king, but the Bible shows him as providing the kind of timely help which those who worship God can now receive through the risen and glorified Christ. He is our Great High Priest after the order of Melchizedek.

Abraham and Lot serve to provide for us examples of two ways of life. We can judge by appearances when making choices, and without thought for long-term results; or else we can rely on God's protection, seeking always to keep within the path of His choice. 'Thy word is a lamp unto my feet, and a light unto my path', Ps. 119. 107.

January 11th
Genesis 15-16; Job 18-19; Matthew 8. 28 – 9. 17

HAS GOD PROBLEMS WHICH WE NEED TO SOLVE?

Genesis chapter 15 is a pivotal chapter in the story of Abraham's walk with God. Twice we read that 'the word of the Lord came unto Abraham', and the basic message was, 'Fear not!' God repeated His promises to him of progeny and a land.

The ritual described here is a covenant sworn to Abraham unilaterally by God. Abraham's part was to fend off from the ceremony the predatory birds. The terms of the covenant told of a long delay before full ratification.

Chapter 16 introduces the episode of Sarah's attempt to help the Lord out of the difficulty which she imagined was posed by her barrenness. She arranged that Hagar, her Egyptian maid, would bear a child to Abraham. It would be counted, she said, as Sarah's, and so the promise of a succession would be fulfilled. But her thinking was misguided, for she was unaware that nothing is 'too hard for the Lord', Gen. 18. 14. The record of this plan makes it clear by repetition that Ishmael was 'the child that *Hagar* bore', not Sarah's. This was a humanly devised solution to a problem which was no problem at all to God. In the end it solved nothing.

God's promises to us are not always fulfilled as quickly as we want. Sometimes they are fulfilled in ways we had never expected. Abraham must 'walk before the Lord' and wait.

The later history of Ishmael's descendants has borne out the truth of the high level of tension and strife forecast here. God told Hagar that her son's descendants would dwell over against [their] kinsmen', Gen. 16. 12 ESV. Little did Sarah know the unexpected consequences that would arise from her device. God asks us to leave issues to Him:

O will that willest good alone,

Lead thou the way, thou guidest best;

A little child I follow on,

And trusting lean upon thy breast. G. TER STEEGEN

The beauty of a tapestry is hidden until the work is completed and the plan of the skilful craftsman is then fully displayed.

January 12th

Genesis 17; Job 20; **Matthew 9. 18-38**

THE HAND OF FAITH AND THE HAND OF POWER

Today's reading is about two hands; our empty hand receiving blessing from the Lord, and His hand giving hope to the hopeless.

The two people on whom the two stories focus were a woman who had a serious ailment for twelve years, and a little girl of twelve years of age who was past human aid because of a recent illness. The little girl's story is interrupted to introduce the woman's; so that in effect the two stories become one. Taken together they tell us basic truths about God's salvation.

The woman's ailment rendered her unclean according to the law of Moses, a sensitive problem. Human help was unavailing. She decided that she must seek discreet contact with the Saviour, for she had heard of His power – maybe just a touch of His clothing would be sufficient. He went beyond her expectation, explaining that her faith in touching Him was a vital link to heal her. Her hand was the link. Her faith was proved by her outstretched hand. The word 'made whole' in His address to her is the word usually translated 'saved'. She was saved by faith. A sinner's faith saves him or her, as a link to the Saviour, not as a merit.

But this woman's story is told inside the story of the little girl who was utterly helpless, unable even to stretch out a hand. People thought the Saviour was wasting His time bothering about the girl, for she was totally helpless. She could not touch Him, but He could touch her. Though she could not hear the voices of people around her, she could hear the voice of the Saviour. He said on another occasion, 'The dead shall hear the voice of the Son of God, and they that hear shall live', John 5. 25. Every conversion is marked by a person responding to the Saviour's call. It is His power which lifted the girl, and today also lifts those who respond to His call.

People were astounded: 'It was never so seen in Israel'. People about whom we have despaired can be saved because of His power and willingness to save. He sees people as 'sheep without a shepherd', Matt. 9. 36; and He can save those for whom we are praying. Therefore pray, for He can hear us when we call.

January 13th

Genesis 18; Job 21; Matthew 10. 1-23

ANYTHING TOO HARD FOR THE LORD?

Our Genesis passage opens with Abraham sitting in the entrance to his tent. He was approached by three strangers and received them hospitably. Suddenly, one of them who seemed to be the spokesman, asked where Sarah, Abraham's wife was.

The stranger proceeded to repeat the promise which God had previously made, that Sarah would bear a child. By this time in her life she was too old to bear a child. She laughed to herself at the promise. The spokesman by this time can be identified as 'the Lord'. The Lord knew that He was able to make good the promise. God is the Author of life, so He can overcome barrenness. 'Is anything too hard for the Lord?' the stranger asked.

The other two men then left and Abraham, we read, 'stood yet before the Lord'. So we find Abraham aware of his visitor's identity. Amazingly, we read that God felt that He must tell Abraham about the judgement soon to fall on Sodom.

Aware that Lot by this time was living in a house in Sodom, Abraham was alarmed for Lot's sake. He felt that the situation was difficult, if not impossible, for God. How could He, the righteous Judge of all the earth, destroy the righteous along with the wicked? So Abraham interceded with God to spare Sodom because of the righteous people in it. Abraham could not see how God could avoid acting unjustly if He destroyed Sodom. But God was not in any difficulty. Two angels would take four people by the hand out of Sodom. Maybe the rescued people were not keen to leave the city, but God 'remembered Abraham and sent Lot out', Gen. 19. 29.

Genesis chapter 18 teaches us that God can make good His promises and can execute just vengeance, according to His own will and character. We should beware of acting in difficult circumstances in ways which are of dubious integrity. We know that our attempts to move God's will along often causes negative results, and therefore we should exercise patience as we wait on Him to work out His purposes in grace. The fallout from our clumsy schemes to 'make things easier' for Him may well be catastrophic, and leave a trail of bitterness.

29

January 14th

Genesis 19; Job 22; **Matthew 10. 24 – 11. 1**

ABLE TO KILL, BUT NOT THE SOUL

It is a sobering thought to realize that the Lord Jesus was preparing His disciples in this section of Matthew's Gospel for martyrdom. In fact, most of the Twelve were martyred. In recent years concentrated hatred and violence against genuine Christians have risen noticeably, so this passage is very timely.

The Lord reminds His followers that their persecutors' power is limited. He was going to be taken out and crucified, and He reminded His disciples that they would also be subjected to violence and might even be killed. But remember that He rose victorious from the dead!

Hostility starts with slander and verbal abuse – 'called the Teacher . . . Beelzebub'. But the enemy is not content with this. They must be prepared for actual martyrdom. How, then, shall they prepare for that? He bids them remember that their Father cares even for mere sparrows, the least of birds. Are we not more important in God's sight than sparrows? Why, even the very hairs of our head are numbered!

Hostility is to be expected even from relatives; the Lord foretold it. Whom do we love more, the Lord or earthly friends and relatives? As He carried His cross toward Calvary, are we ready to follow? 'He that loseth his life for my sake shall find it', v. 39.

Verse 42 adds the fact that caring for others who are faithful to the Lord and in need will not go unrewarded. This is the time for sacrifice: the rewards will assuredly follow.

Governments may oppose the reading of, or possession of the Bible. They may oppose the teaching of the Bible to children. They may insist that all religions are of equal validity, or that children should be instructed in atheism to enable them to 'make intelligent decisions' about moral and spiritual issues.

We should be thankful for what freedoms we have. We should also be exercised about the Christians who are persecuted and marginalized for their faith. The cup of cold water will be rewarded. Today the sacrifice, tomorrow the rich reward.

January 15th

Genesis 20-21; **Job 23-24;** Matthew 11. 2-30

HE KNOWETH THE WAY THAT I TAKE

The book of Job opens with a challenge made by God, twice issued, on behalf of one whom He describes as 'my servant Job'. The book ends with God rebuking Job's 'comforters', 'Ye have not spoken of me the thing that is right, as my servant Job hath', Job 42. 7. Here, in the middle of the book, Job longs to know where he might find God. He longs to understand his suffering. Yet he cries out, 'But he knoweth the way that I take', 23. 10.

It is important to note the next verse, 'When he hath tried me, I shall come forth as gold'. He is confident that in the end God will vindicate him. He is repeating his earlier assertion, in chapter 19 verse 25, 'I know that my redeemer liveth'; that is, to vindicate him. He has now risen above the temptation merely to bitterly resent the mistaken criticisms levelled at him by his 'friends'. God 'knows' the way that he takes in the same sense as we read in Psalm 1 verse 6: 'For the Lord knoweth the way of the righteous'. This is more than knowing *about* their way; it virtually means 'approves of it'. God acknowledges the genuineness of Job's uprightness. We admire 'the patience of Job', Jas. 5. 11.

It is sobering for us to read of Job when we are surrounded by friendly Christians. If everyone misunderstands us and accuses us of error, or in some cases lays false charges against us, can we, like Job, call God to witness our integrity? If we can honestly do this, it is a possession to treasure beyond price. May we seek God's praise.

The sorrows of the daily life,
 The shadows o'er my path which fall,
Too oft obscure the glory's light,
Until I rise above them all.
Alone with Thee, O Master, where
The light of earthly glory dies;
Misunderstood by all, I dare
To do what Thine own heart will prize.   ANON.

January 16th
Genesis 22; Job 25-26; Matthew 12. 1-21

HERE AM I, MY SON

This chapter, so memorable for its foretaste in picture form of the atoning death and glorious resurrection of God's beloved Son, is also a powerful testimony to Abraham's excellence as a parent. In God's command, Isaac's question, and Abraham's response we find a model of what good fathers ought to be.

In the instruction to 'take now . . . thine only son Isaac, whom thou lovest', v. 2, we learn of Abraham's **fatherly tenderness**. He doesn't speak of his love for Isaac but God, who alone knows the wellsprings of the human heart, does. Unlike the domestic hatred to be seen in the coming tribulation, when 'the brother shall betray the brother to death, and the father the son', Mark 13. 12, Abraham was a pattern of genuine affection. This truth colours the rest of the narrative. It must have been long obvious to Isaac for, without resistance, he submitted himself to his father's intention to offer him as a sacrifice. He did not know what lay behind Abraham's action but he trusted his father's love.

The effectiveness of **fatherly training** is demonstrated in Isaac's clear understanding of spiritual exercise. Father and son would 'go yonder and worship', v. 5, the son, obviously a young man well able to handle heavy loads, carrying the necessary equipment. Isaac, we may be sure, had done all this before. His question, 'Where is the lamb?' v. 7, reveals a knowledge of the divine requirements for a burnt offering. Fathers are responsible to teach their children biblical principles and to exemplify the public responsibilities of the males in assembly gatherings. Silent fathers usually produce silent sons.

The third point is the easiest to overlook. Abraham's **fatherly nearness** is evident in his prompt reply to Isaac's appeal; he was as quick to respond to his son as he was to heed his God, vv. 1, 7, 11. A biblical family consists of mother, father, and offspring. A father constantly away from home may not be there in the moment of crisis to answer his son's questions. In the same way, assembly elders, who are likened to fathers, 1 Tim. 5. 1, need to be on hand to deal with the problems and anxieties which arise in the lives of the saints. May we all be where we ought to be.

January 17th

Genesis 23; **Job 27-28**; Matthew 12. 22-50

WHERE SHALL WISDOM BE FOUND?

Chapters 27 and 28 of Job are part of the patriarch's final extensive response to his three friends. Though noted for their profound wisdom, not one of them has been able to explain the terrible circumstances which have so suddenly engulfed this righteous man. All they have done is to insist, wrongly, that all the time he must have been a secret sinner to merit such calamities.

But Job longs for the understanding to comprehend God's ways with him. Although a man who 'feared God', 1. 1, he has to admit that God has 'taken away my judgment; and the Almighty . . . hath vexed my soul', 27. 2. Chapter 28 makes best sense read in a modern translation which brings out his poetically graphic description of the physical risks men take when mining the bowels of the earth for precious ore. Man quests ceaselessly for silver and gold. But wisdom, the greatest of treasures, defies human endeavour. It cannot be uncovered by mere hard work, v. 14, nor purchased with money, v. 15, for its price is 'above rubies', v. 18.

The answer is that God is the source of true wisdom. Only the Creator, whose omniscience 'looketh to the ends of the earth, *and* seeth under the whole heaven', v. 24, is able to fathom it, because He is in Himself the originator of all things. What men cannot grasp, God fully comprehends. For the believer, it is the greatest of consolations to know that human experience in this world, which so often seems anarchic and random, is in reality governed by the infallible wisdom of God. The New Testament goes further and locates that wisdom specifically in the person of Christ, 1 Cor. 1. 24. Though the child of God may not always know the 'why' of God's dealings with him, he certainly knows the 'who': the same One who died for our sins supervises our steps day by day.

Since God is sovereign, it is therefore the believer's wisdom reverently and humbly to submit to His ways, however inscrutable, for 'the fear of the Lord, that *is* wisdom; and to depart from evil *is* understanding', v. 28. And if we feel our spiritual ignorance, we have only to pray in accordance with James's instruction: 'If any of you lack wisdom, let him ask of God, that giveth to all *men* liberally, and upbraideth not; and it shall be given him', Jas. 1. 4-5.

33

January 18th
Genesis 24; Job 29-30; **Matthew 13. 1-23**
HE THAT HEARETH THE WORD
By means of stupendous miracles and incomparable teaching, the Saviour's earthly ministry announced to the people of Israel the kingdom so often spoken of by the prophets. His miracles proved His power to establish that glorious messianic era; His teaching set out the solemn entrance requirements. And yet few Israelites responded positively. To help the disciples understand the apparent failure of His preaching, the Lord revealed secrets about the kingdom which were not disclosed in the Old Testament. He started with the parable of the sower. Although in context it relates to the message about the inauguration of Messiah's righteous reign over the earth, its principles apply to the proclamation of God's word today.

In categorizing four distinct reactions to the preached word, the Lord Jesus underlined what it really means to listen. The first hearer, from whose heart the word was snatched away, illustrates the importance of the **understanding**, v. 19. God's word is not to be treated like 'a very lovely song of one that hath a pleasant voice, and can play well on an instrument', Ezek. 33. 32. Its teaching is not a mindless entertainment but a solemn message from heaven to be received intelligently into the head and diligently into the life.

The second response highlights the necessity of **endurance**, vv. 20-21. The rocky ground listener grasped something of the meaning of the word, for he laid hold of it with joy, but it was all superficial. Come trial or tribulation he reverted to his old ways, because the scripture was never truly rooted deeply in his heart.

For the third audience, associated with thorny ground, it was not so much persecution which stumbled him as the routine temptations of daily life, 'the care of this world, and the deceitfulness of riches', v. 22. Real conversion will display enduring **continuance** through thick and thin.

Finally we meet the genuine believer, marked by **fruitfulness** for God, reproducing in his life glimpses of the character of the Lord Jesus who taught His disciples that 'Herein is my Father glorified, that ye bear much fruit', John 15. 8.

January 19th
Genesis 25; Job 31; Matthew 13. 24-43
AND ISAAC INTREATED THE LORD FOR HIS WIFE
Genesis 25 includes in quick succession two of the important structural formulae which hold the book together: 'these are the generations of', vv. 12, 19. The expression, which might be paraphrased 'this is what became of', here introduces the history of two major figures, but the less significant person is disposed of first. Therefore Ishmael, although Abraham's firstborn, is got out of the way before attention turns to the elect seed, Isaac, through whom God had promised blessing for the earth. The same pattern can be seen in chapters 36 verse 1 and 37 verse 2. 'He taketh away the first, that he may establish the second', Heb. 10. 9. First Cain, then Abel; first Ishmael, then Isaac; first Esau, then Jacob; first Saul, then David; first Adam, then Christ. Our natural birth cannot satisfy God – that is why we must be born again, John 3. 7.

It is no surprise that the brief section about Ishmael says nothing of his spiritual life, for the New Testament sums him up as a 'profane person', Heb. 12. 16, one with no real interest in the things of God. The story of Isaac, on the other hand, highlights a lovely feature of his marriage. In anxiety and bewilderment, both husband and wife consulted the Lord. Because their union was childless and because the promise to Abraham was that Isaac's seed would enrich the world, 'Isaac intreated the Lord for his wife . . . and the Lord was intreated of him, and Rebekah his wife conceived', v. 21. The guarantee of God's covenant promise by no means stifled his **intercession.** Indeed, he could be assured that his supplication was in harmony with God's will.

The next problem arose when his prayer was answered and Rebekah found herself bearing antagonistic twins. In her confusion she went to the Lord with her **inquiry**. 'And the Lord said unto her, Two nations are in thy womb, and two manner of people shall be separated from thy bowels; and *the one* people shall be stronger than *the other* people; and the elder shall serve the younger', vv. 22-23. The information that God's election was settled on the younger son should have influenced the conduct of the parents but, alas, faith gave way to favouritism. Let us be sure that we give due heed to the Lord's answers to our prayers.

January 20th
Genesis 26; **Job 32-33**; Matthew 13. 44 – 14. 12
I AM YOUNG, AND YE ARE VERY OLD
The first thing we learn about Elihu, who unexpectedly intrudes into the Job debate at this point in the narrative, is that he is angry. Four times in five verses the word 'wrath' is used of him. The second thing we note is that he is significantly younger than the previous speakers, 32. 4, 6. That, of course, does not make him a mere novice, for his discourse is both intelligent and confident. Nevertheless there is obviously an age gap of which he is very conscious. That, he tells us, is why he restrained himself from speaking until this moment.

Even Eliphaz, presumably the eldest of the three original visitors, had earlier pulled rank on Job in order to underline the importance of the triumvirate: 'With us are both the grayheaded and very aged men, much elder than thy father', 15. 10. And of course age should have its advantages in terms of accumulated experience, wisdom, and sympathy. Rehoboam's elderly counsellors were far more astute in their advice than the young king's contemporaries, 2 Chr. 10. 6-11. But, as Elihu remarks, 'Great men are not *always* wise: neither do the aged understand judgment', 32. 9. Mere seniority in years does not guarantee the possession of spiritual understanding, for it is possible to be physically and even intellectually advanced and yet spiritually stunted. On the other hand, we may feel that the young Elihu himself is perhaps a little intemperate in his peppery self-assurance.

In every local assembly there should be young and old functioning peaceably together in the service of God. Because it is in the nature of youth to become impatient and hot-headed, Peter gives the instruction, 'Likewise, ye younger, submit yourselves unto the elder', 1 Pet. 5. 5. And because weight of years sometimes generates intolerance, Paul urges the Corinthian saints, 'If Timotheus come, see that he may be with you without fear: for he worketh the work of the Lord, as I also do. Let no man therefore despise him', 1 Cor. 16. 10-11. The young have to respect the old, while the old must endeavour not to intimidate the young. John's First Epistle addresses fathers, young men, and little children. In our local assembly may we minister together in family harmony.

January 21st
Genesis 27; Job 34-35; **Matthew 14. 13-36**
BUT JESUS SAID

Matthew's crisp record of two stupendous miracles contains five utterances by the Lord Jesus. His spoken words, though brief, are, as always, memorable and instructive.

'They need not depart; give ye them to eat', v. 16. The disciples were worried. The hour was late, the people many, and their homes far distant. In answer to their honest awareness of a genuine need the Lord indicated that those who perceive a problem should themselves seek to remedy it. In the local assembly it is all too easy to act as a 'back-seat driver' who tells others what to do without lifting a finger to help.

'Bring them hither to me', v. 18. Five loaves and two fish seemed laughably insufficient. But it is when we confess our total bankruptcy that the Lord graciously takes the little we have, however feeble, and consecrates it for His service. He has the power to make much of our meagre resources.

'Be of good cheer; it is I; be not afraid', v. 27. He who could come to His disciples' aid in the midst of a raging tempest, walking serenely on the surface of the water, can certainly draw near to His people today in their trials. His gracious presence gives us every reason for cheer because of who He is – the sovereign Creator of the universe, the Saviour of sinners, the Shepherd of the sheep. Paul enjoyed that special closeness during his final imprisonment when many had deserted the Apostle: 'No man stood with me, but all *men* forsook me: . . . Notwithstanding the Lord stood with me, and strengthened me', 2 Tim. 4. 17.

'Come', v. 29. This, one of the most compact commands in the Bible, is the order to step out in faith, an order given not to anyone but to a disciple who had specifically requested the opportunity. We shouldn't be surprised when God answers our prayers.

'O thou of little faith, wherefore didst thou doubt?', v. 31. Peter started out well but like so many of us he became distracted by his immediate circumstances. What was it he doubted? The word of Christ, who had instructed him to come! Faith is practical confidence in God's energizing word; when the Lord calls He also graciously imparts the power to fulfil His command.

January 22nd
Genesis 28; Job 36-37; Matthew 15. 1-28

THE LORD IS IN THIS PLACE

Jacob's journey from his family home in search of a suitable wife was an arduous one. But God wonderfully strengthened him for future trials by manifesting Himself at Bethel.

We first of all meet the **place**: 'And he lighted upon a certain place . . . And Jacob awaked out of his sleep, and he said, Surely the Lord is in this place; and I knew it not', vv. 11, 16. It is possible to be in a privileged position and not appreciate it. Sleep fled from Jacob as he suddenly became aware of the awesomeness of the God who had made Himself known. Naming the spot Bethel, v. 19, he confessed that it was God's house and required of him the utmost reverence. The house of God today, the local assembly, is not a social club for religious people but a gathering of saints in the presence of the Lord of glory, 1 Tim. 3. 15.

Second, we note the **pillows** which assured Jacob's night's sleep: 'he took of the stones of that place, and put them for his pillows, and lay down in that place to sleep', v. 11. No feathers on which to rest his head but hard stone, and yet this uncomfortable setting brought Jacob into a personal encounter with the Lord which he seems to have lacked in his parental home. Sometimes it is when we have to move out from the cosy security of our background that we learn more about God.

Third, we hear God's gracious **promise**: 'behold, I am with thee, and will keep thee in all places whither thou goest, and will bring thee again into this land', v. 15. God undertook to accompany him, guard him, and restore him to the land of his inheritance. Such a pledge must have solaced the heart of a man separated from his loved ones and estranged from his brother. Christians rejoice in a Saviour who has guaranteed that 'I will never leave thee, nor forsake thee', Heb. 13. 5, and 'I will come again, and receive you unto myself', John 14. 3.

Finally, we see Jacob erect a memorial **pillar**. The same stones on which he had rested his head now became a standing testimony to God's dealings with him, v. 18. We do not set up monuments today; instead, believers are meant to be living witnesses of God's saving grace, shining as 'lights in the world', Phil. 2. 15.

Genesis 29; **Job 38–39**; Matthew 15. 29 – 16. 12

WHO IS THIS?

This is the moment for which every reader of Job has long been waiting. After three rounds of wearisome argument, in which Job has loudly protested his innocence while his friends have persisted in accusations of gross wickedness, both camps have fallen silent. Only Elihu has continued the hostilities, offering a fresh perspective on the controversy and (unknowingly) paving the way for a divine intervention. He has just drawn Job's attention to the rumble of distant thunder: 'God thundereth marvellously with his voice; great things doeth he, which we cannot comprehend', 37. 5. His own words have been increasingly drowned out by the gradual approach of a tumultuous storm: 'Out of the south cometh the whirlwind', 37. 9. But this is just the prelude.

Now, 'out of the whirlwind', 38. 1, Jehovah speaks and man is instantly silenced. Completely bypassing the friends, the Lord addresses Himself exclusively to Job, asking two unexpected questions: 'Who is this?', v. 2, and 'Where wast thou?', v. 4.

The first question focuses on Job's **imprudence**. He, the outstandingly godly man of his day, has dared to question God's ways, and his challenge has had the effect of obscuring the wonders of divine wisdom. Believers, especially those facing severe trials, have to exercise tight control over their lips lest they say things that cause others to think ill of God. Asaph, deeply perturbed by the prosperity of the wicked, restrained his tongue from uttering what his heart thought, because 'If I say, I will speak thus; behold, I should offend against the generation of thy children', Ps. 73. 15. Better remain silent than stumble the saints of God.

The second question highlights Job's **ignorance**. Where was he when God's creative energy brought planet earth into existence in all its beauty, variety, and complexity? If Job couldn't fathom the beginnings of things how could he hope to grasp the present outworking of God's ways with His creatures? Believers are shut up to the wisdom and goodness of a God who cannot fail, assured that they were individually chosen in Christ 'before the foundation of the world', Eph. 1. 4.

January 24th
Genesis 30; Job 40-41; **Matthew 16. 13 – 17. 13**

WHOM DO MEN SAY THAT I THE SON OF MAN AM?

We tend, understandably, to focus our attention upon Peter's marvellous answer to the second of the Lord's questions: 'Thou art the Christ, the Son of the living God', 16. 16. That grand confession, combining messianic dignity and deity, was immediately endorsed by the Saviour Himself and shortly afterwards by the Father's voice out of heaven, affirming that 'This is my beloved Son, in whom I am well pleased; hear ye him', 17. 5.

But it would be a mistake to overlook the first question. In their response, the disciples offered a digest of contemporary opinion about the Lord Jesus, which identified Him with John the Baptist, Elijah, Jeremiah, 'or one of the prophets', 16. 14. Why did people mention such names? Quite obviously, the Saviour must, in certain ways, have reminded them of past spiritual celebrities.

The most recent, John the Baptist, was noted for the unwavering consistency of his **witness**. The Lord had described him as 'the lamp that burneth and shineth', John 5. 35 RV, for nothing save death could dim his earnest testimony. But the Lord Jesus is far greater as the ultimate 'faithful witness', Rev. 1. 5, and the 'true Light, which lighteth every man', John 1. 9.

Elijah was remarkable for the sensational **wonders** which accompanied his labours in the breakaway northern kingdom of Israel. In the face of Ahab's apostasy, his prayers caused drought and downpours, his words multiplied meal and oil, and brought about resurrection. But how much grander were the Saviour's miracles! He did in Israel 'the works which none other man did', manifesting power over disease, demons and death, and yet at the end of His ministry He had to indict the nation because they had 'both seen and hated both me and my Father', John 15. 24.

Jeremiah, writer of Lamentations, was celebrated for his tender-hearted **weeping** over Jerusalem's suffering at the hands of the Babylonian invaders. 'Behold, and see if there be any sorrow like unto my sorrow . . . wherewith the Lord hath afflicted me in the day of his fierce anger', Lam. 1. 12. But how much more did the Saviour sorrow as He endured God's wrath against our sins on Calvary? In every way He has the pre-eminence.

40

January 25th
Genesis 31; Job 42; Matthew 17. 14 – 18. 14

MY SLEEP DEPARTED FROM MINE EYES

Jacob's description of his service as herdsman for the duplicitous Laban, vv. 38-41, is a testimony to a good shepherd's care. Assembly elders can learn much. For a start, the true shepherd must be **resident** with the flock. Jacob could not do his job from a distance. Come wind and weather he had to be on the spot where he was needed. That is why Peter speaks of elders being 'among' the saints in a local assembly, 1 Pet. 5. 1. It is impossible simultaneously to be a faithful elder and a globe-trotting Bible teacher. As a consequence, the godly elder is unlikely to become famous down here because his sphere of activity is restricted. He will, however, gain God's approval, which is all that matters, 1 Pet. 5. 4.

Jacob tells Laban he was 'twenty years in thy house', v. 41. The shepherd is to be **persistent** in his work, for his is no short-term service. He cannot run off to pastures new, or accept other offers, but must stick doggedly to his task even though the flock may be small and the rewards few. David's brother jeered about 'those few sheep', 1 Sam. 17. 28, but in God's eyes numbers are not everything. A mere eight were saved in the ark, yet Noah was not criticized for failure. Our God looks not primarily for success but faithfulness even 'in a very little', Luke 19. 17.

Third, the shepherd must be **vigilant**, his eye constantly alert to the specific needs of the flock. At lambing time when urgent assistance might well be required Jacob obviously paid scrupulous attention to 'thy ewes and thy she-goats', v. 38. Individual sheep may stray, or contract disease, or be mauled by the attacks of predators. In one of the great pastoral chapters of the Old Testament Israel's religious leaders are charged with negligence in their duty: 'The diseased have ye not strengthened, neither have ye healed that which was sick, neither have ye bound up that which was broken, neither have ye brought again that which was driven away, neither have ye sought that which was lost', Ezek. 34. 4. Invert that verse and you have a description of what a genuine shepherd should be doing: watching carefully over the flock, providing encouragement, correction and guidance where needed. It's tough to be a real elder. Such men need our prayers.

January 26th
Genesis 32. 1 – 33. 17; **Psalms 1-3**; Matthew 18. 15-35
BLESSED IS THE MAN
To launch a book with the word 'blessed' is a powerful inducement to read on! Indeed, each of the first three psalms includes a special beatitude.

We learn first that there is an abundant blessedness in spiritual **separation**, in being able to say 'No' to what is wrong: 'Blessed is the man that walketh not . . . nor standeth . . . nor sitteth', 1. 1. The psalmist uses a plural word so that the first verse may be rendered, 'O the happinesses of the man!' This may seem strange to a world which accentuates the positive, but before the believer can truly grow in grace he is responsible to lay aside 'all malice, and all guile, and hypocrisies, and envies, and all evil speakings', if he genuinely thirsts for 'the sincere milk of the word', 1 Pet. 2. 1-2. Only after the three negatives do we hear of the godly man's active delight in the law, 1. 2. May we be diligent to remove anything that damages our appetite for the scriptures!

There is also a particular blessing in biblically informed **expectation**. 'Kiss the Son, lest he be angry, and ye perish from the way, when his wrath is kindled but a little. Blessed are all they that put their trust in him', 2. 12. The word rendered 'trust' is translated 'hope', Prov. 14. 32, for genuine faith always has an eye on the future. Despite man's hostility, Messiah's promised reign from Zion is assured, 2. 6. There are therefore only two possible responses: either we shall be marked by opposition, like the foolish kings of the earth, vv. 2-3, or by humble submission as recommended in v. 12. Though he may be out of step with a godless society, the believer basks even now in the sunshine of divine favour as he looks ahead to Christ's coming glory.

Finally, the psalmist reminds us of the grand blessing of **salvation**: 'Salvation belongeth unto the Lord: thy blessing is upon thy people', 3. 8. Jonah must have memorized this psalm because he quotes from it in his distress, yet its truth transcends all circumstances. From first to last salvation is of God: whether physical or spiritual, He alone devises, provides and applies it. David, fleeing from Absalom, knew his preservation, like Israel's national welfare, rested wholly on the Lord. So does ours.

January 27th
Genesis 33. 18 – 34. 31; Psalms 4-6; **Matthew 19. 1-15**
LET NOT MAN PUT ASUNDER
Raised in a culture which permitted divorce, the Pharisees used the well-known controversy between two rabbinical traditions as a trap with which to snare the Lord Jesus. Presumably they expected Him to agree either with the strict camp (which limited divorce to sexual infidelity) or the looser camp (which allowed it for almost any trivial reason). The Lord, however, spiked their guns by doing neither; instead, He took them right back to the beginning for a lesson in the **importance of marriage**. Because it was instituted by God Himself, it was to adhere to His rules.

The Genesis creation record, He demonstrated, included no allowance for divorce, for 'he which made them at the beginning', v. 4, 'said, For this cause shall a man leave father and mother, and shall cleave to his wife: and they twain shall be one flesh', v. 5. Answering their appeal to the directions built into the law, the Lord revealed that Moses had later permitted divorce simply because of human hard-heartedness. Nevertheless, 'from the beginning it was not so', v. 8. The disciples' astonished response, that 'If the case of the man be so with his wife, it is not good to marry', v. 10, indicates that they understood Him to be affirming nothing less than the absolute **indissolubility of marriage**, apart from death. Their horrified conclusion, that to marry without an ejector seat made bachelordom preferable, underlines His startlingly emphatic teaching.

In the light of the clear-as-crystal statements in the parallel passages, Mark 10. 1-12, Luke 16. 18, and in Paul's instructions, 1 Cor. 7. 10-11, the contentious exception clause, 'except for fornication', v. 9 RV, is perhaps best viewed as relating exclusively to the Pharisees' question about divorce rather than the matter of remarriage. That is, although separation may be permissible under certain circumstances, remarriage never is.

Believers living in a society which has turned its back on divine standards need to hear afresh that biblical marriage is strictly heterosexual, involving 'male and female', v. 4, and monogamous, with one man cleaving faithfully to 'his wife', v. 5, for the whole duration of his pilgrimage on this earth.

43

January 28th
Genesis 35; Psalms 7-8; Matthew 19. 16 – 20. 16
AND ISAAC GAVE UP THE GHOST, AND DIED

This is a chapter of funerals: Deborah, Rebekah's nurse, v. 8; then Rachel, as she gave birth to Benjamin, vv. 18-19; finally Isaac, v. 29. God takes away an aged family servant, a mother, and a patriarch, for 'The Lord killeth, and maketh alive', 1 Sam. 2. 6.

We do not know the age of **Deborah**, but she must have been advanced in years when she transferred her valuable service to Jacob's growing family. That her death is recorded testifies to the affection in which she was held, the name of the burial place meaning 'oak of weeping'. Every death causes tears, but the New Testament believer will 'sorrow not, even as others which have no hope', 1 Thess. 4. 13, because he possesses the glad anticipation of Christ's coming.

Rachel was, of course, Jacob's favoured wife, even though in the sovereignty of God it was Leah who became the mother of the priestly and kingly tribes of Israel, v. 23, and through whom the Messiah came. God's purposes sometimes override our own preferences. The account of her death is given in some detail: 'And it came to pass, as her soul was in departing, (for she died) that she called his name Benoni: but his father called him Benjamin', v. 18. It is both sad, because of the name she gives her last child ('son of my sorrow'), and yet positive, because we are reminded that death is more than bodily dissolution, for it involves the departure of the soul. At death the Christian's body goes to the grave, awaiting resurrection, while the spirit departs into the immediate presence of the Lord Jesus where it is 'absent from the body, and . . . at home with the Lord', 2 Cor. 5. 8 RV.

As might be expected, the death of **Isaac** gets greatest prominence in the chapter. Similar language is used of Abraham's passing, Gen. 25. 8, and the phrase 'gathered to his people' implies a reunion with deceased relatives in the place of departed spirits which the Old Testament calls Sheol. But the full prospect of joyous reunion is a distinctly New Testament revelation, grounded on the atoning death, resurrection and return of Christ: living believers will be caught up together with saints who have been raised from death 'to meet the Lord in the air', 1 Thess. 4. 17.

January 29th
Genesis 36; **Psalms 9-10**; Matthew 20. 17-34

THE LORD ALSO WILL BE A REFUGE FOR THE OPPRESSED

The Psalms overflow with testimonies to God's greatness and grace, testimonies often arising out of perilous circumstances.

In Psalm 9 we learn about Jehovah's **righteousness**: 'he shall judge the world' and 'minister judgment to the people in uprightness', v. 8. Old Testament writers did not live in some fantasy utopia but knew only too well the failures of their own people, despite all their privileges, and the wickedness of the nations round about. Nevertheless, under inspiration they were able to look ahead in the confidence that Jehovah's purposes would be fulfilled in the establishment of His just reign over the earth. The New Testament supplements this by specifying that the Lord Jesus will be the divine king, for when God 'will judge the world in righteousness', it will be 'by that man whom he hath ordained; whereof he hath given assurance unto all men, in that he hath raised him from the dead', Acts 17. 31. The resurrected man of Calvary will become the ruling man.

Before that day dawns, however, the Lord provides for His beleaguered people the practical shelter they need in a hostile environment, for 'the Lord also will be a **refuge** for the oppressed, a refuge in times of trouble', v. 9. The Hebrew word here twice rendered 'refuge' is elsewhere translated 'high tower', 2 Sam. 22. 3, and 'place of defence', Isa. 33. 16. God Himself becomes the military garrison to safeguard His feeble saints.

In case any reader should wonder if Jehovah could be counted upon to keep His pledges, David added a word of encouragement: 'They that know thy name will put their trust in thee: for thou, Lord, hast not forsaken them that seek thee', v. 10. David knew from experience that the God of scripture is unfailing in His **reliability**. To know His name is to be intelligently aware of all that He is in the glory of His ineffable person. After all, He is the 'Lord', the self-existent, self-sufficient I AM who has 'neither beginning of days, nor end of life', Heb. 7. 3. No wonder we read that 'the name of the Lord is a strong tower: the righteous runneth into it, and is safe', Prov. 18. 10. There is no securer place for the weary believer than nestling in God's faithfulness.

January 30th
Genesis 37; Psalms 11-14 **Matthew 21. 1-32**
ALL THE CITY WAS MOVED, SAYING, WHO IS THIS?
It was a good question. Never had anyone entered Jerusalem in so strange a manner and to such loud acclaim.

Matthew answers the citizens' bemused query in several ways. By the normative use of the simple name 'Jesus', v. 21, his narrative insists upon the **genuine humanity** of the Lord Jesus Christ. There could be no doubt that the one who gave practical instructions, v. 2, purged the temple precincts, v. 12, engaged in verbal debate, v. 16, lodged in Bethany, v. 17, hungered, v. 18, and taught, v. 23, was a real man.

But in sending His disciples apparently to appropriate somebody else's property the Saviour significantly referred to Himself as 'Lord', v. 3, for in His **undiluted deity** He possessed absolute authority over the whole of creation. When Christians call Christ Lord they are not only affirming that He is the living God of the universe but also testifying to His right to tell them what to do.

His entrance into Israel's capital was strikingly unusual because He who had hitherto walked the roads of Palestine on foot now chose to ride the short distance between Bethphage and the city, 'sitting upon an ass, and a colt the foal of an ass', v. 5. The reason is spelled out in the carefully selected quotation from Zechariah's prophecy, v. 5. There the arrival of the long-promised messianic king is announced, Zech. 9. 9. The Lord Jesus deliberately set out to fulfil that prediction to the letter and in so doing gave public notice of His **inherent majesty**. The multitudes and the local youngsters picked up the identification by heralding Him as 'son of David', vv. 9, 15. Yet the following verse in Zechariah 9 awaits His glorious return for its fulfilment. As often in the prophets the first and second comings of Christ are compressed so that only in retrospect can one see the great stretch of time which separates them.

The parable which concludes this section, vv. 28-32, hints at His **faithful ministry**. The two sons in the story were both imperfect – one was a prevaricator, the other a penitent. But the Lord Jesus was the Son who promptly, uncomplainingly, and flawlessly did His Father's will. Such a person deserves our worship.

January 31st
Genesis 38; Psalms 15-16; Matthew 21. 33 – 22. 14

SHE HATH BEEN MORE RIGHTEOUS THAN I

Genesis 38 is hardly a chapter to strike the reader as a roll call of righteousness, and yet it is included in the scriptures of truth for our learning. In its honest account of the appalling failings of Judah, his sons, and his daughter-in-law, it offers vital lessons in godly living.

Judah's marriage to a local Canaanite woman illustrates, in negative fashion, **the significance of separation**. 'Judah went down from his brethren', v. 1, to engage himself in an unequal yoke, whereas the great commendation of Joseph is that he was 'separate from his brethren', Gen. 49. 26. The believer is meant to be set apart from the self-indulgent lifestyle of a godless world so that he can please the Lord.

Judah's caddish behaviour also illustrates **the dangers of deception**: as he tricked his daughter-in-law, with the false promise that his son would take her to wife in fulfilment of the levirate custom, so she tricked him into incest. It is not a savoury story. But Judah was treading the same pathway as his father Jacob, for the biblical principle of recompense is inescapable: 'as thou hast done, it shall be done unto thee: thy reward shall return upon thine own head', Obad. 1. 15. Believers should remember that 'if any man destroyeth the temple of God, him shall God destroy', 1 Cor. 3. 17 RV. What I do to my local assembly God will do to me.

One of Handel's great oratorios is entitled *The Triumph of Time and Truth*. This could form a fitting caption to the entire chapter for, in God's sovereign purpose, all the chicanery was eventually brought to light. In a scene reminiscent of a Shakespearean drama Tamar produced the proofs of Judah's guilt, vv. 24-25, drawing from him a reluctant confession of his own culpability, v. 26. Because our God is still on the throne **the triumph of truth** is assured at the glorious return of Christ.

Finally, the whole sordid tale astonishingly magnifies **the grace of God**. Judah's incestuous relationship with his pagan daughter-in-law resulted in the birth of Pharez, v. 29, whose name, along with his mother's, is incorporated into the Messiah's genealogy, Matt. 1. 3. Only God can bring good out of evil!

February 1st
Genesis 39; Psalm 17; Matthew 22. 15-46

FROM POTIPHAR TO THE PRISON

There are a number of Old Testament personalities who displayed lovely features that would later be manifested in all their fullness in the life of our Lord Jesus. Others passed through experiences that would be foreshadowings of what the Lord endured during His earthly life. Few, if any, more reflected the winsome ways of Christ and suffered similar underserved rejection and betrayal than did Joseph.

From being the much-loved son in his father's house he was discarded by his brothers and sold for twenty pieces of silver. Taken down into Egypt he became a servant. There in the home of Potiphar he faced temptation and eventually, due to the false accusations made by Potiphar's wife, Joseph languished in prison. Despite this hatred, opposition, and injustice he retained his moral purity and there is no record of any blemish in Joseph's life. These admirable characteristics reflect the perfections that were resident in God's Son and in these ways the life of Joseph presents many similarities and comparisons with the life of our blessed Saviour.

However, there is one matter concerning Joseph which stands in total contrast to the experience of Jesus. The two lowest points in Joseph's life are recorded for us in Genesis chapter 39. The first was when he was taken down into Egypt and was sold as a slave. We read of this in the first verse of the chapter. The second incident is detailed for us in verse 20 when Joseph was put in prison for a crime he had not committed. It was recorded that at these two despairing moments 'the Lord was with Joseph', vv. 2, 21. When everything was against him and circumstances were most adverse, Joseph was not alone, the Lord was with him.

The writer to the Hebrews refers to the 'contradiction of sinners against Himself' that Jesus experienced. As unimaginably difficult as this was, it does not equate nor compare to the depths of suffering and loss He felt during the three hours of darkness at Calvary. There, He who knew no sin was made sin **for us,** 2 Cor. 5. 21, and at the time of His greatest crisis, when He needed God most, He was abandoned by Him, Matt. 27. 46.

February 2nd
Genesis 40; **Psalm 18. 1-29;** Matthew 23.

THE LORD IS MY ROCK

Based on the information given in the heading of this psalm it is probable that David wrote these words were some time after his military exploits recorded in 2 Samuel chapter 8 and before the sad events detailed in chapter 11. At the time of writing he was at a highpoint in his life. He had subdued the Philistines, conquered the Moabites, and defeated the Syrians. He reigned unchallenged over all Israel administering judgement and justice to all his people.

If he was to reflect on his earlier life he would have remembered his slaying the lion and the bear in the wilderness, and his triumph over the Philistine giant Goliath in the valley of Elah. What an illustrious character David was! Few, if any, had excelled above what he had achieved. From his present exalted position it would have been easy for him to think that he had achieved so much by means of his own strength and ingenuity. Even if he recalled the times that Saul had tried to kill him, or thought back to his exile in the cave of Adullam, he might have been tempted to attribute his preservation to his personal resourcefulness.

However, David does not succumb to self-adulation and he is most careful to ensure that the credit for his personal deliverance and present stability is given to the Lord who is his rock. He recognizes that the Lord is the source of his *strength,* v. 1, his *security,* v. 2, and his *salvation*, v. 3. He is painfully conscious that in those days of adversity his morale was at a very low ebb, for he refers to his sorrows, fears, and distress. He was fully aware of the power of those that opposed him, describing it as the 'floods of ungodly men', v. 4.

In Psalm 50 verse 15 we read, 'Call upon me in the day of trouble: I will deliver thee, and thou shalt glorify me'. Those words, written by Asaph, are an apt summary of the psalm we are considering today. David informs us that he called upon the Lord in his distress, v. 6, and in verse 17 he says, 'He delivered me from my strong enemy, and from them which hated me'. As a result David glorifies God, saying, 'I will call upon the Lord, who is worthy to be praised', v. 3.

February 3rd

Genesis 41. 1-49; Psalm 18. 30-50; **Matthew 24. 1-28**

WHEN AND WHAT

In the week leading up to the momentous events that took place at Calvary our Lord spoke on two occasions to the disciples about His second coming. The first occasion is recorded in Matthew chapter 24 and is generally referred to as the Olivet Discourse; the second occasion is detailed in John chapter 14 and is often described as the Upper Room ministry. To have a right understanding of these two chapters it is vital that we note several contrasts between them.

At the beginning of Matthew chapter 24, the Lord leaves the temple and He sits on the Mount of Olives, two locations that are very much linked with Israel. In John chapter 14, He is in an upper room with the disciples, but we have no indication as to its specific location. In Matthew the Lord sets out a number of events that have to take place *prior* to His return. He refers to wars, rumours of wars, persecution of believers, earthquakes, carnage, and unparalleled tribulation. He speaks about false Christs, the gospel of the kingdom, Judaea, Daniel the prophet, the Holy Place, and the Sabbath.

Two days later in the Upper Room the Lord is with the same men and once more He talks about His coming, but this time He doesn't refer to any preceding signs. He does not mention the Sabbath, the temple, Old Testament prophets or any tribulation. Very tenderly He offers words of comfort and reassurance and simply says, 'I will come again and receive you unto myself'.

We may well ask, 'Why does the Lord use such different styles in His teaching?' The answer is connected to the disciples. In Matthew chapter 24 the disciples were representative of that future remnant of the nation of Israel that will be looking for the coming of their Messiah as the great tribulation reaches its climax. That's why the Lord speaks about the Sabbath, the Holy Place, and Judea, etc. In John chapter 14 those same men are representative of the church, for as apostles they are going to be the founder members of that church. Many believers today fail to distinguish between the Lord's coming to the *air* for the church and His coming to the *earth* for Israel. These two chapters reveal the distinctions.

February 4th

Genesis 41. 50 – 42. 38; **Psalm 19**; Matthew 24. 29-51

THE HEAVENS DECLARE THE GLORY OF GOD

We live in a day of unprecedented rejection of divine truth, and no truth is more open to ridicule and denial than that of creation. Learned men have become vain in their imaginations, and professing themselves to be wise, they have become fools. As the children of God the eyes of our understanding have been opened so that 'through faith we understand that the worlds were framed by the word of God, so that things which are seen were not made of things which do appear', Heb. 11. 3.

In just ten words Moses sums up the mighty work of creation: 'In the beginning God created the heaven and the earth', Gen. 1. 1. On the second day of the creation week God made the firmament and on the fourth day he bedecked it with lights to divide the day from the night, to be for signs, seasons, days, and years and to give light on the earth. 'And God made two great lights; the greater light to rule the day, and the lesser light to rule the night, Gen. 1. 16.

From then onwards the sun has been consuming about 600 million tons of hydrogen every second, no wonder it is called a 'great light'. God also made the moon, which compared to the sun is much smaller in size and lesser in density, but it still has sufficient power to have a controlling influence on the tidal patterns of the earth's seas.

Finally, having made the sun to rule the day and the moon to rule the night God did one more thing on that fourth day. In an absolute masterstroke of understatement verse 16 ends 'he made the stars also'. Five words are used in the King James Version to describe this immense act, but two of those have been inserted by the translators so the verse should end: 'the stars also'.

In the firmament hang billions of galaxies, each star is unique and all of them are suspended on nothing, but are kept in place by the Son of God. Whilst no man can compute the total number of stars, '*He* telleth the number of the stars; he calleth them all by their names', Ps. 147. 4. Truly 'the heavens declare the glory of God and the firmament showeth his handywork. Day unto day uttereth speech, and night unto night sheweth knowledge'.

February 5th
Genesis 43; **Psalms 20-21;** Matthew 25. 1-30.

THE KING SHALL REJOICE

The two psalms in today's readings probably refer to two different periods in David's life. In that respect they are not chronological but the Spirit of God has set them next to each other for there is a definite link between them. Psalm 20 is *anticipative* for it foresees a day of trouble, v. 1. Battles lie ahead and help will be required, and so David and his people look to the Lord to supply the needed resources. Although he was a proven warrior, the psalmist acknowledges that victories will not be achieved in his own strength. Others might place their confidence in chariots and horses but Israel would remember the name of the Lord their God and so their prayer ascends, 'Save, Lord', v. 9.

There is a practical lesson here for each of us to consider. Maybe we can recall times when we have acted in our own strength, believing that we were equal to the task that needed to be done instead of trusting in the Lord. With impetuosity and self-confidence we have attempted to so something for God, only to quickly learn how foolish such actions were. We ought to heed the exhortation 'Trust in the Lord with all thine heart; and lean not unto thine own understanding. In all thy ways acknowledge him', Prov. 3. 5-6.

In Psalm 21 David is *reflective*. The conflict has taken place, the battle is over, victory has been won, the blessings of that triumph are being enjoyed, and there is a note of praise ringing through the verses. The prayers of the previous psalm have been answered, so David can write, 'Thou hast given him his heart's desire, and hast not withholden the request of his lips', v. 2.

Once more there is a practical application we need to observe. A feature of the last days is that men will be 'unthankful' but this ought not to be true of us. Whilst it is a privilege to carry everything to God in prayer we need to ensure that we present our requests with thanksgiving and acknowledge His gracious answers to our supplications.

The psalm also has a prophetic anticipation that will be fulfilled in the Lord Jesus' second advent when honour and majesty will be His, v. 9ff.

February 6th
Genesis 44; **Psalm 22**; Matthew 25. 31-46

THE SUFFERINGS OF CHRIST

It is appropriate that Psalm 22 precedes Psalm 23 for there David says that the Lord was his shepherd. That relationship was only possible because of the sacrifice that was made by the person David is writing about in the psalm before us today. Although the introduction to Psalm 22 informs us that David was the penman, he is writing of the circumstances of another, for he describes things that he never knew in his own experience.

In Peter's First Epistle we read the phrase 'the sufferings of Christ and the glory that should follow', 1 Pet. 1. 11. This verse supplies for us an apt summary of the contents of Psalm 22, for in verses 1 to 21 we read of the sufferings of Christ, and from verse 22 to the end we read of the glory that will be His. The sufferings presented in the opening section begin with those inscrutable agonies endured by our Lord in the three hours of darkness that elicited that heartrending cry 'My God, my God, why hast thou forsaken me?'

In respect of the order of events at Calvary, the psalm moves in reverse order to that which occurred. Each of the Gospel writers begin with the sufferings men heaped on our blessed Lord at Gabbatha and then at Golgotha, before informing us of the hours of darkness when Jesus was forsaken by God. However, Psalm 22 opens with the forsaking and then works backwards detailing the physical abuse that men inflicted. There may be a number of explanations for this deliberate order, but one thing is certain. Our salvation does not rest on what men did to Christ, but depends entirely on what transpired in those three hours that are described in verse 2 as being in the daytime yet in a night season.

There are two principal passages in the Old Testament that present the sufferings of Christ prophetically, this Psalm and Isaiah chapter 53 and both end in a similar way. Isaiah says that 'he shall see his seed, he shall prolong his days, and the pleasure of the Lord shall prosper in his hand. He shall see of the travail of his soul, and shall be satisfied', vv. 10-11. Psalm 22 concludes 'A seed shall serve him . . . they shall come and shall declare his righteousness'. Well do we sing, 'Thou art worthy, Jesus, Lord'.

February 7th

Genesis 45; **Psalms 23-24**; Matthew 26. 1-30

THE SHEPHERD PSALM

David, the author of Psalm 23, is described in 2 Samuel as 'the sweet psalmist of Israel', and of the many psalms he wrote this is undoubtedly the most well known and oft-repeated. Although he was a shepherd, David portrays himself in these verses as one of the flock, and writes about his relationship with the shepherd. In Psalm 80 Asaph refers to God as the 'Shepherd of Israel', but our reading today opens with David declaring, 'The Lord is *my* shepherd'.

Because he knew that the Lord was his shepherd, David was confident that he would lack nothing. His shepherd would provide **rest**, v. 2, **recovery,** v. 3, **reassurance,** v. 4, **refreshment,** v. 5 and a **residence,** v. 6.

You may have noticed that the Psalm starts in a field and it ends in a house, but in between there is continual movement, for the sheep are being taken on a journey. This journey follows a pathway that begins in green pastures, moves alongside still waters, and crosses over a valley before arriving and terminating at the house. Some of that journey is very pleasant and serene, but the tranquillity of verses 2 and 3 gives way to adversity. We could understand David wanting to lie down in green pastures and walk beside the still waters. How lovely it would be to put time 'on hold' in those scenes of blessing and peacefulness, but life is not like that, and so the pathway descends into the valley of verse 4.

The one place none of us would want to remain in is the valley of the shadow of death, and thankfully we will not have to. It is reassuring to observe the language David uses, for he says, 'Yea though I walk *through* the valley', he's not going to remain in it. He is confident that he will come out at the other end. In this life neither tranquillity nor adversity are constants, they come and go. The only constant in the Psalm is the presence of the Lord, for even in the valley David could say, 'Thou art with me'.

Five times David uses the words 'he' or 'his', vv. 2-3, for he is talking *about* the shepherd. In verses 4 and 5 the language changes and five times he uses the words 'thou' or 'thy' for he is talking *to* the shepherd, but at the end David is *with* the shepherd.

February 8th

Genesis 46. 1 – 47. 27; Psalm 25; **Matthew 26. 31-56**

THE GARDEN OF GETHSEMANE

At the dawn of human history a man stood in a garden and, in effect, he said to God, 'Not thy will but mine be done'. Despite being placed in the most congenial of environments Adam deliberately transgressed the commandment of God. The impact of that first man's action has been universal and catastrophic, for 'as by one man sin entered into the world, and death by sin; and so death passed upon all men, for that all have sinned', Rom. 5. 12.

As a result of Adam's actions God cursed the ground for his sake. No longer able to yield its full harvest it was going to produce thorns. Henceforth, work would not be a pleasure for Adam; it was going to be a chore, and it would be by the sweat of his face that he was going to eat bread. Communion between God and Adam was severed, and ultimately Adam would die. Thus, from one act of disobedience in paradise there was brought into the human vocabulary such words as thorns, sweat, and death.

Adam was the first man, but thankfully there is another man. He is called the 'last Adam' and He too was in a garden. As He entered Gethsemane the forces of darkness were being marshalled against Him. Judas was about to betray him; the city of Jerusalem would soon call for Him to be crucified; and in the hour of His deepest agony Peter, James, and John would be sleeping.

Leaving those three, Jesus went a little farther and falling on His face He prayed, 'O my Father, if it be possible, let this cup pass from me: nevertheless not as I will, but as thou wilt', v. 39. His prayer was the complete opposite to that of Adam, yet He was to endure all the consequences of Adam's rebellion. It was probably a cold night, yet He sweated profusely, and the next day He was going to be crowned with thorns, and, at some point after the ninth hour, He was going to die.

Three times Jesus prayed in Gethsemane. Years later the Apostle Paul prayed three times in respect of his 'thorn in the flesh'. The response he got was, 'My grace is sufficient for thee: for my strength is made perfect in weakness', 2 Cor. 12. 9. The Lord understood Paul's need, and out of His own personal experience He could act as a compassionate High Priest.

Genesis 47. 28 – 48. 22; Psalms 26-27; Matthew 26. 57-75

BY FAITH JACOB

There is an interesting comparison between the first and last occurrences of the name Jacob in the scriptures, particularly in relation to his hand. The first time we encounter Jacob's name is in Genesis chapter 25, where we have the record of his birth. His mother, Rebekah, was carrying twins, and Esau was delivered first followed by Jacob. However, in the process of being born Jacob's hand took hold of Esau's heel.

We know from other scriptures that there was a spiritual significance to the order in which the twins were born. In addition, the incident just described is referred to by Hosea as being an evidence of Jacob having power with God, Hosea 12. 3. However, this strange action by Jacob also revealed that there was a devious side to his character, a feature that would manifest itself on a number of occasions in his later years. Not without some degree of justification, Esau said of Jacob, 'Is not he rightly named Jacob? for he hath supplanted [i.e., displaced] me', Gen. 27. 36.

The last reference to the name Jacob is found in Hebrews chapter 11 verse 21: 'By faith Jacob, when he was a dying, blessed both the sons of Joseph; and worshipped, leaning upon the top of his staff'. What a lovely epitaph to the life of this now aged patriarch! There may have been several unseemly actions in Jacob's past, but the divine record closes with a testimony to his faith and links it to the events detailed in Genesis chapter 48.

If Joseph had had his way Manasseh would have received the special blessing from Jacob, for he guided his son to Jacob's right hand and he led Ephraim to Jacob's left hand. However, despite the fact that his eyes were dim so that he could no longer see, Jacob deliberately crossed his hands so that the privileges of the firstborn were conferred upon the younger son. This once perverse supplanter completes his pilgrimage as a man of faith and a worshipper of God.

Many have started out well on the Christian pathway but, for various reasons, they have been sidetracked before the end. May we make it our goal to finish our days like Jacob, in faith and worshipping God.

February 10th
Genesis 49; Psalms 28-29; **Matthew 27. 1-26**

I HAVE BETRAYED THE INNOCENT BLOOD

Even in these days when spiritual things are being disdained in today's Western culture, the name Judas is still synonymous with treachery and betrayal. Very few mothers when naming a son are prepared to call them by that name, since there is a stigma attached to it.

Just a few days prior to the events that unfolded on the night of the Saviour's betrayal, Judas had visited the chief priests and captains and asked how much they would give him to betray Jesus. Luke says that they 'covenanted to give him money', Luke 22. 5 suggesting that some form of bartering went on. Eventually Judas felt he had secured a reasonable deal, settling for thirty pieces of silver. That was Judas' estimation of the value of Christ. How paltry this was compared to Mary's estimation. She brought a pound of spikenard, which was very costly, to anoint the feet of Jesus.

Maybe for twenty-four hours or so Judas held in his feverish clasp that meagre sum, but on seeing Jesus being condemned to death he 'repented himself' and returned to his paymasters. In deep anguish he confessed, 'I have sinned in that I have betrayed the innocent blood'. Having achieved their objective in capturing Jesus, Judas was no longer of any use to the chief priests and they abandoned him as though he was just a dispensable commodity.

Alas the dastardly deed was done, there was no way back for Judas and forlornly he threw the pieces of silver on the floor of the temple, all thirty of them. Leaving that building he went out into the night and ended his life. What a tragedy, he was a man who just hours earlier had kissed the door of heaven but went down to a sinner's hell.

The hypocrisy of the chief priests beggars belief. They were willing to kill Jesus because of envy, knowing that He was innocent. Yet they had the audacity to say of the money strewn across the temple floor that it would not be lawful to put it into the treasury, as it was the price of blood. Where had this money come from originally? From these very same men and, in all probability, it had been taken from the offerings that had been put into the treasury!

February 11th
Genesis 50; Psalm 30; **Matthew 27. 27-44**

A MAN OF CYRENE

From the spitting and crowning with thorns in the Praetorium, verses 27-31, we come to 'a place called Golgotha' where Jesus is stripped and crucified by the soldiers, scorned by the chief priests, reviled by those that passed by, and ridiculed by the two thieves. Mockingly the elders and scribes said, 'He saved others; himself he cannot save'. The first part of their statement was blessedly true for He did save others, but their implication was that He was on the cross as a helpless victim, forced by the whim of Pilate to be crucified.

There was someone who was at Calvary reluctantly, but it wasn't Jesus – it was Simon of Cyrene. He had to be pressed into service; Matthew says he was 'compelled' to bear the cross, and Luke states that they 'laid hold on him'. In contrast to this reluctance, our blessed Saviour went out to die willingly. It was Jesus who said in the Upper Room, 'Arise let us go hence', and even in the Garden of Gethsemane He said, 'Rise, let us be going'. There were more than twelve legions of angels ready to move at His call, but 'as a sheep before her shearers is dumb, so he openeth not his mouth', Isa. 53. 7.

The Gospel writers tell us very little about Simon. We know his name, that he had two sons, and that he came from Cyrene in north Africa. Cyrene was a thriving metropolis and a centre of learning. How unlike Jesus this is, who came from a lowly place, a rural backwater of no repute! We can say that Simon was an ordinary man from an extraordinary place, whereas our Saviour was an extraordinary Man from an ordinary place.

An examination of the Synoptic Gospels makes it clear that it was merely by chance that the soldiers happened to bump into Simon, there was nothing premeditated about his being at Calvary. In total contrast to that, our Saviour was 'delivered by the determinate counsel and foreknowledge of God', Acts 2. 23. Peter tells us that He 'was foreknown before the foundation of the world', 1 Pet. 1. 20 ESV.

Although Simon carried the cross, it is never called the cross of Simon, but it is called 'the cross of Jesus', John 19. 25.

February 12th
Exodus 1. 1 – 2. 22; Psalm 31; **Matthew 27. 45-66**

WHY?

The verses in today's meditation begin at midday on the fourteenth day of the first month, when an untimely darkness covered the whole land, and they conclude at some point on the fifteenth day with the sealing of the sepulchre by the chief priests and the Pharisees.

Many supernatural events occurred during that period. Jesus died, the veil of the temple was rent in two from the top to the bottom, the earth quaked, rocks shattered, and graves burst open. Amidst the callous indifference of the soldiers, tender-hearted women stood at a distance observing what was taking place. In fulfilment of Isaiah chapter 53 our Lord was not buried in the common grave that pitiless men had prepared for Him, but was gently laid in Joseph's new tomb, for He was to be 'with the rich in his death'.

Despite the fact that a raging thirst caused His tongue to cleave to His jaws, Jesus spoke on seven occasions as He hung on the middle cross at Calvary. Matthew and Mark record just one of His sayings: 'My God, my God, why hast thou forsaken me'. Of this, A. W. PINK wrote, 'The crucifixion of the Lord of glory was the most extraordinary event that has ever happened on earth, and this cry of the suffering one was the most startling utterance of that appalling scene'.

Here we have just nine words in English (and less than half that in the original language), yet who can explain them? In asking this question we get a glimpse of the severity and bitterness of our Saviour's sufferings. The Lord was forsaken in **Gethsemane** by His disciples. At **Gabbatha** He was forsaken by His nation, but at **Golgotha** He was forsaken by His God. Men hid their faces from Him, the disciples had forsaken Him, and the sun withdrew its light from Him, but the most grievous agony He endured was that His **God** forsook Him.

We note that it was at the *ninth* hour that Jesus uttered this cry. The darkness has lifted and He is no longer forsaken, but He is reflecting on the infinite horrors contained in those hours of darkness, and so He asks: 'Why hast thou forsaken me?'

February 13th
Exodus 2. 23 – 3. 22; Psalms 32-33; Matthew 28
MOSES, MOSES!
While Aaron and the people of Israel were suffering under the lash of Egyptian taskmasters, Moses was being pampered as though he was the son of Pharaoh's daughter. There in the palace he would have been trained in all the wisdom of the world and was, no doubt, being groomed for a high place in society. What a bright future lay ahead of this Israelite! It was his for the taking.

Although he had been separated from his people, the instruction Moses had received from his own mother, as she acted as the 'childminder' for Pharaoh's daughter, must have made an enduring impressions on him. He may have been trained to be Egyptian in his ways, but he was very much a Hebrew at heart, and the credit for that must be given to the godly influence of Jochebed. Perhaps you are a mother and are reading this little meditation to your family today? May you be encouraged to continue with this invaluable work that has immeasurable potential!

If the first forty years of Moses' life were spent in a palace learning that he was a 'somebody', the next forty years were going to be spent in the western fringes of a wilderness where he would discover that without God he was actually a 'nobody'. There in that lonely place, at eighty years of age, God called to him out of the burning bush, 'Moses, Moses!' This double call places Moses in a very select group of people. Only four persons in the Old Testament and three in the New Testament were addressed by God in this manner. This was God's initial call to Moses for a work that was going to occupy him to his dying day.

Had Moses continued in the palace, or remained in the wilderness looking after Jethro's sheep, we would not have heard about him. Had God accepted the variety of excuses he made for not rising to the challenge of leading Israel, his name would have meant little or nothing to us. The reason why we know about him, and for his prominence throughout the scriptures, is because he did *respond* to the call of God and *chose* to serve Him rather than to enjoy 'the pleasures of sin for a season', Heb. 11. 25. That same challenge and choice has not gone away for it still confronts each of us today. What choice will I make?

60

February 14th
Exodus 4; Psalm 34; Acts 1
EXCUSES, EXCUSES!
By the time we reach the end of chapter 3 we would have expected to read that Moses was raring to go. He had heard God's call, witnessed the unique sight of a burning bush that was not consumed, and had been the recipient of very specific revelations of God. In addition God made definite promises that He would be with Moses, so there was no need for any further delay. Regrettably, the chapter we are considering makes disappointing reading, for Moses resorts to making excuse after excuse.

In verses 1 to 9 Moses uses the *people* as an excuse, assuming that they would not believe him. This was an audacious excuse and totally contradicted what he had been told by God. How amazingly patient and merciful God was! In chapter 3, He had assured Moses that the people *would* hearken to his voice and yet the opening words of chapter 4 are, 'But, behold, they will not believe me, nor hearken unto my voice'. Instead of chiding with Moses, or even giving up on him, God graciously provided two miracles which were designed to reassure His reticent servant. The incident with the rod was to assure him that he had delegated *authority* from God to lead Israel. The miracle of the leprous hand was to remind Moses of *God's omnipotence* which he could depend on in his service before the people.

In verses 10 to 12 Moses referred to his *lack of eloquence* but this was not only a feeble excuse but it contradicted the two miracles that had just taken place. The ability to lead Israel and their deliverance from Egypt was going to depend on God's power and authority, not Moses' oratory. Finally, in verse 13 Moses in effect said to God, 'Send someone, but please do not let it be me'. At this point God became angry with His servant. In measure He agreed to what Moses asked and provided him with Aaron to act as his mouthpiece, but it was not what God initially wanted.

In our meditations yesterday and today we have noted that God had called, prepared, and equipped Moses for the task – a task he began well but which he could not finish due to failure later in his life. Thankfully, we can think of another servant of God, of whom He could say, 'He shall not fail'. Isa. 42. 4.

February 15th
Exodus 5. 1 – 6. 13; **Psalms 35-36**; Acts 2. 1-21
OPPOSITION
The psalmist of Psalm 35 is a man of God. Therefore, he suffers persecution. In this he is typical of believers in all dispensations. His words also foreshadow what the Lord would experience to a greater degree than any. He would truly be hated 'without a cause', v. 19, and know what it was for 'false witnesses', v. 11, to rise against Him.

But the psalmist is not a Christian! His requests that God should take forceful punitive action against those who are against him are quite contrary to the attitude of believers of this dispensation. We would pray for the salvation of any who persecute us and set themselves up as our enemies.

However, he is not wrong in how he reacts. He is in keeping with the dispensational current of his day when God was in judgemental mode in respect of nations round about Israel. In fact, God used Israel to clear their Promised Land of its inhabitants, as His punishment of those nations because their iniquity had reached its fullness. The people saved during the tribulation by believing the gospel of the kingdom will similarly call for God to take vengeance on their enemies. The Lord Jesus will respond to their requests, by pouring out unparalleled judgement against the unrepentant prior to establishing His kingdom.

The psalmist does, however, give a good example which Christians should readily follow, in that he resorts to thanksgivings and praise to God, v. 18, not only as an individual but also in a congregational setting. So we today in every type of circumstance should never give up worshipping our God, both privately and in the fellowship of our local assembly. It should also be the prime purpose of Christians to magnify the Lord, v. 27, in every way we can.

Psalm 36 brings before us a delightful collection of divine characteristics which should thrill our hearts: mercy, faithfulness, righteousness, loving-kindness. Since we have been born of God, we should be manifesting these ourselves and also enjoying the 'fatness of thy house', v. 8, which for us is God's spiritual provision in our local assembly.

February 16th
Exodus 6. 14 – 7. 25; Psalm 37; **Acts 2. 22-47**
LOCAL ASSEMBLY FELLOWSHIP
At the start of this chapter the baptism in the Holy Spirit has taken place, that begins the history of the church, comprising all believers from the Day of Pentecost to the rapture, 1 Cor. 12. 13. In this closing section we now see the commencement of local church fellowship: baptized believers in a locality assembling together in order to share in spiritual privileges and responsibilities, v. 42.

Peter has been boldly preaching the good news about the Lord Jesus the rejected Messiah, but now the risen, exalted, victorious Saviour at God's right hand. The crowds listening may have included some that had cried 'Away with him', John 19. 15, but those who believed what Peter said were certainly taking the opposite stance to the Jewish leadership's view of Christ. Instinctively they knew they had to come together and form a body of people bound by a common acceptance of the apostles' teaching.

Christian fellowship ever since has been doctrinally based, which includes all the apostolic writings of the New Testament. The weekly *breaking of bread* is an act of primary importance for believers, meeting weekly, to remember their crucified yet risen Lord. These early believers showed great courage in openly identifying themselves with Christ in such a hostile environment, so nothing trivial or avoidable should ever keep us away from the Lord's supper. This is also why we must be in local church fellowship, as it is the only context in which we can break bread. It is an expression of fellowship with Christ and His people. We must engage in prayers individually, but this passage clearly intimates that *collective prayer* is a divinely appointed necessity for Christians. Missing the prayer meeting for no good reason is something we should never even begin to contemplate.

There will doubtless come a time in our lives when due to illness or infirmity we just can't get to meetings any longer. But let us seek to ensure that until that time comes we are continuing 'stedfastly' with God's people in a local assembly which, because of His presence, is a foretaste of the great gathering in the air when the He comes to take us home, 1 Thess. 4. 17.

February 17th
Exodus 8; Psalms 38-39; Acts 3

PURPOSE AND POWER

Everything that God is has to be declared. What He is in His power and majesty is manifested in the heavens. But what He is in His purpose and character only fully comes out in his dealings with men. As Christians we know Him in the riches of His grace. The Egyptians were to get to know Him through His government.

Nothing is random with God, or accidental, or unexpected. In Exodus, the Lord has already intimated His intention to take His people out of Egypt. This, He said, would be opposed by Pharaoh whose heart He would harden, Exod. 3. 19; 4. 21. The Lord is in control of everything and works out His purpose according to His will. God will also get glory, whether through government and despite the wrath of man, or through grace and despite the inability of men to merit salvation. God even raises up wicked men like Pharaoh in order to display what He is, and that all the world might know Him, 9. 16.

The plagues were not random. They specially targeted the false deities of the Egyptians, 12. 12. For example, in our chapter today, some scholars suggest that the plague of frogs was against Heqet, the goddess of birth, who had a frog's head. The lice represented Set, the god of the desert. The flies were because of the god Uatchit, possibly represented by a fly. Every plague would be a message to the Egyptian people that the living God of the Hebrews was infinitely greater than their fictitious gods. In those judgements, God was in fact being gracious towards them so that they might come to know the truth! Although, in sending the plagues, God was acting in the interests of His people, the judgements were neither arbitrary nor undeserved.

In the plagues also we have an amazing display of God's mighty power, particularly in the precise control He can exercise over creation, so that which caused the Egyptians to really suffer was sometimes, as with the flies, kept entirely away from His people. God has the same precise care over His people today. Moreover, we can rejoice that before judgements much worse than the plagues come upon our world in the great tribulation, we will have been safely raptured out of the way, 1 Thess. 1. 10.

February 18th

Exodus 9; **Psalms 40-41;** Acts 4. 1-31

CHRIST PRESENTED

These two Psalms contain good examples of how in Old Testament verses which are close together the Lord Jesus can be presented to us in three different ways. Firstly, there are those verses which are clearly about the Lord Jesus because they are directly *quoted* of or by Him in the New Testament; then there are those which although not quoted about Him are words which were *fulfilled* by Him, or which *could be said* about Him; then lastly there are those words which most definitely are *not* about Him, because He couldn't say them as they wouldn't be true, or because His behaviour contradicted them.

For example, Psalm 40 verses 6 to 8 have words which are quoted directly about Christ in the Letter to the Hebrews. Indeed they could only be about the Lord, for none but the pre-existent One could truly say, 'Lo, I come to do . . . '. Also, only the Lord fully did the will of God and had it written in its completeness within His heart. Then in verse 10 we have words which could have been said by Him: 'I have not concealed thy loving kindness and thy truth'. The Lord Jesus manifested both these in His words and deeds. But in verse 12 we have words which He most definitely could *not* say: 'Mine iniquities have taken hold upon me'. Indeed He said instead, 'Which of you convinceth me of sin?' Then again, Psalm 41 verse 9 is used by the Lord Himself about Judas. The question of verse 5, though not recorded in the New Testament, well sums up what the Pharisees could have been saying as they plotted to kill Him. But the confession of verse 4 could never come from the lips of our sinless Saviour. This is one of the wonders of Scripture that there can be such variety within the same passage. This provides us with a real focus for our meditation, particularly in the personal Psalms, as we look for Christ in all the scriptures.

We must also let the words speak to our own spiritual condition. Psalm 40 verse 2 reminds us of what God has done to change us. Psalm 41 verse 12 speaks of what God is doing for us now, while verse 13 gives us some responding language of worship which should never be far from our lips.

February 19th
Exodus 10; Psalms 42-43; **Acts 4. 32 – 5. 11**

LOVE AND LYING

In Acts chapter 2 we read how Christians were joined together because of commonly believed doctrine and shared spiritual exercises. However, it should not surprise us that the bonds so established extended into the realm of personal and practical needs. After all, a key feature of the Lord's teaching before returning to heaven was that His disciples should love one another. So now we see this love in action as those who had property sold it in order to meet the needs of others. Their doctrinal assertions about the resurrection of Christ were accompanied by practical displays of the love of Christ, who though He was rich yet became poor to meet the needs of those who had absolutely nothing. Grace was needed by those who had property in order to sell it, and then be willing to give away the entire proceeds, and also by those in need to be willing to receive from others. Human selfishness and pride were rendered inoperative. Even the worldly mindset of the financial advisor who might advise, 'Don't sell your capital assets', was completely ignored! Albeit this did mean that in the future poor saints in Jerusalem would need help from other places, Rom. 15. 26.

Alas, however, the flesh soon reared its ugly head! Whilst Ananias and Sapphira may be an example of how a married couple should act as one, sadly it was in an entirely wicked way. They committed a most serious sin by telling a lying to the Holy Spirit. The Lord Jesus had taught that lying is satanic, John 8. 44, and thus early on in the church age it would be established by apostolic discipline that Christians had to live lives wherein lying had been put away, Col. 3. 9. This passage is so important because it not only shows that the assembly was to be a sphere of moral discipline, it would also emphasize to all Christians that our daily lives are lived in the sight of the living God, and that the Holy Spirit who graciously dwells within is aware of all that we do, think and purpose in our hearts. That the Holy Spirit is a distinct divine Person is clearly shown by Peter's words in chapter 5 verses 3 and 4 where He is spoken of as One who is called God and can be lied to.

February 20th
Exodus 11. 1 – 12. 20; Psalm 44; Acts 5. 12-42
SLAUGHTER AND SACRIFICE
So here it comes, the ultimate plague: the targeted slaughter of all the firstborn in Egypt without any class discrimination. Who does this dreadful thing? The God of Israel. How do the Hebrews escape it? By just being Israelites? No! They need a sacrifice. Something must die; blood must be shed. The blood must be seen by God. Obey God's word, and they'll be safe and ready to escape from Egypt and Pharaoh. Through this dramatic episode we learn lessons for all time. Because of God's holy character, divine judgement is absolutely necessary and inevitable. It will be severe and unavoidable for those who will not accept His prescribed way of deliverance. God's way of deliverance must be by blood sacrifice. The experience of the Egyptians and Israelites is a wonderful picture for us of the only possible way of escape from divine punishment. And escape most certainly must be provided for us by God Himself.

But in His judgement God also displays mercy! He restricts His judgement to the firstborn in order to punish Pharaoh for enslaving Israel His 'firstborn', Exod. 4. 22. Such is the Lord's power, it could have been many more in each family who died or indeed all the Egyptians. God will always temper His judgements in time, such is His justice and longsuffering. The time for no mercy at all awaits the eternal fires of hell.

The lamb could only ever be a picture of our Saviour: 'Christ our passover is sacrificed for us', 1 Cor. 5. 7. He was absolutely sinless and undeserving of any judgement, yet willing to bear what was due to us. We did not kill Him directly, but it was our sins that necessitated His death if we were ever to be saved. And we can never forget it. A collective memorial is given to us in the breaking of bread, one of the privileges and duties of Christians as commanded by the Lord. But in heaven we'll see forever the marks of Calvary in His hands, feet, and side.

God has seen the blood of His Son shed for us and therefore can righteously pass over us for judgement. The sacrifice will never need to be repeated, as its infinite value will be undiminished through all eternity. What a wonderful Saviour we have!

February 21st
Exodus 12. 21-51; **Psalms 45-46**; Acts 6

CHRIST AND COMFORT

Psalm 45 brings before us many of the beautiful features of the Lord Jesus which are all balanced in perfect harmony. He is 'mighty', yet His might is exercised in 'grace'; He possess essential 'majesty', but this is expressed through 'meekness'; He rides 'prosperously' but never at the expense of 'truth' and 'righteousness'; the 'terrible things' are directed towards His 'enemies' and not His people. It is in the way that He maintains seemingly contrasting characteristics that He brings out the fullness of His personal glories.

But then there is also His deity and His kingship. Verses 6 and 7 are used by the writer to the Hebrews to prove the absolute and infinite superiority of the Son to angels. The Son is *God*! And as such He is the Eternal King. What a reign His will be! He will govern by absolute righteousness, not just for the sake of it, but because of His *love* of it. No greater incentive could there be for Christians, as those who are subject to His Lordship now and will share with Him in His future reign over earth, to be marked by a resolute love at all times for what is right, and a perpetual hatred of what is wrong.

Once we appreciate something of the glories of Christ from Psalm 45, the comfort of Psalm 46 will mean so much more to us. All that God was to the godly Jew comes to us through the person of our Saviour. It's the personal nature of His strengthening ministry for us that's so evident. He does not only provide a 'refuge' but He himself *is* that 'refuge'. He personally is in the 'midst' and gives 'help'. The fact that we can say He is 'with us' is not a cause of boasting, but rather that which should drive us to our knees in humble thanksgiving for His grace. It is the truth of His deity that is the ultimate guarantee of our peace and safety, because He is supreme over all things that may trouble us. So we truly can 'be still', knowing that He is the God who loves us.

We can also rejoice in the worldwide peace that Psalm 46 verse 9 anticipates, when the Lord Jesus vanquishes all the forces of the world which have been set against Him, and against the faithful Jewish remnant at the end of the tribulation period.

February 22nd
Exodus 13. 1 – 14. 4; Psalms 47-48; **Acts 7. 1-29**
PROMISE, PRESENCE, PROVIDENCE
Stephen is responding to the allegation that he had blasphemed against Moses and God. To do this he traces God's dealings with His people, beginning with the selection out of the world population of Abraham of Ur of the Chaldees as the father of God's special nation. The God who made the choice is the 'God of glory', the only real God that there ever has been, or could be, and thus immediately honours Him as the One to whom all glory uniquely belongs. Stephen will show that it is his accusers who are in the wrong, because of their murder of the 'Just One'.

So, with Abraham, the dispensation of promise began. 'Abraham believed God, and it was accounted to him for righteousness'. He moved solely on the basis of divine statements, orally given. We have to live according to the words that God has graciously given to us in His unchanging word. Things might seem to be going wrong – four hundred years in slavery might have sounded as if the plan was going to fail – but for Israel (and us) all is foreknown and controlled by the God who calls.

Joseph maybe thought things were BADLY awry when he was taken down into Egypt. There, however, he knew the unfailing presence of the God of Jacob, who never lets His people down. Joseph had maybe little idea of what God had in store for him, but the meaning of his dreams became clear in God's way and time. Though our pathway may be sometimes unclear, and what is round the next corner is hidden from us, we too must just rest in the goodness of God who is always present with us in our earthly pathway.

Moses would be accused of murder by some. If he'd been apprehended by the Egyptian authorities it would have been the end of any hopes he might have had of doing anything to help his people. But God looked after him and ensured that he was protected and prepared for the work He wanted him to do. That's providence. God will always overrule in the interests of His purpose, which will also always be in the best interests of His people, even though they may go aside from the remit He has given and act independently of Him. That's grace!

February 23rd
Exodus 14. 5-31; Psalms 49-50; Acts 7. 30 – 8. 4
POWER, PURPOSE AND PRESERVATION

To have been one of the charioteers of Pharaoh's chosen six hundred must have been one of the greatest honours of the world of their day. They probably felt invincible compared to other nations round about. But on the day of this passage they would learn, albeit with no future benefits for them, that there was a power greater than them all – the God of the Hebrew slaves. The Lord would demonstrate His mighty power by holding back the sea to let His people through, then by sending it rushing back to drown the Egyptian forces with not even one able to escape. The recently released Israelites would see their pursuers dead on the sea shore, never to trouble them again. But the power of God would also be shown in a more subtle way. He would harden Pharaoh's heart, thus securing the Egyptians' change of mind and their total defeat that would bring great glory to His name. This mighty act would become the measure of His power for generations to come. For us, the measure of it is the resurrection of our Lord Jesus Christ, Eph. 1. 19, 20.

God never uses His power on a whim or in a random fashion. He always acts according to a purpose. Two great aspects of it are in this story. First and foremost, there is His honour and glory. Then, there is the deliverance of His people. He will act for them, even though they display distrust of Him! God's purpose reaches its fullest point in the glorious exaltation of His Son, subsequent to His victory over every possible enemy there could be. Through this purpose, His people also will be preserved. The Israelites had already been preserved from His direct judgement through the blood of the Passover lamb displayed as instructed. Now they are saved from going back to Pharaoh's slavery by His power over the sea. The all-powerful, purposeful, and preserving God of the Hebrews, is the same God today of all those who have simply received His Son as their Saviour. They grasp that Satan, and the world under his control, have been finished for them as a controlling power in their lives by the blood shed on Calvary's cross. Let us resolve never to go back to our 'Egypt' – the godless ways of this world – but rather to remain true to our great Deliverer.

February 24th
Exodus 15; **Psalm 51**; Acts 8. 5-40
CONFESSION AND CLEANSING
The 'sweet psalmist of Israel' committed adultery and murder! Who would have thought it? Who would have thought there would be a full disclosure of his wicked deeds in the divine record for all to read? Yet it is there, and most surely recorded for us that we might take heed, be warned, and learn from his mistakes.

David shines so brightly in this psalm because he freely confesses his sin, with no attempt to mitigate it, or pass the blame on to anyone else. He shows that he knows the *seriousness* of what he has done by the terms 'transgression', 'iniquity', 'sin', 'evil', and in relation specifically to the murder, 'bloodguiltiness'. He takes full *responsibility* by using the words 'my' and 'mine'. He teaches us that sin is primarily an act of rebellion against God by asserting it's against Him, and Him alone, that he had sinned, v. 4. This does not mean that he discounted at all how much he had wronged Uriah and his family. David shows he felt the *filthiness* of his sin by using the words 'wash', 'cleanse', 'purge', 'clean'.

But David also wonderfully shows us how God is able and willing to forgive him completely for his actions. In confessing, he shows contrition and casts himself upon God's mercy and loving-kindness, attributes of God's character essential for forgiveness. Then, David also shows spiritual intelligence by calling for 'hyssop', not meaning that he believed herbal remedies could deal with sin, but rather indicating the need for the application of the value of the blood of sacrifice, Exod. 12. 22. We are reminded that our sins can only be forgiven because of the price paid by the Lord Jesus through the shedding of His blood at Calvary.

This psalm beautifully demonstrates the grace of God towards His people when they sin. But scripture also faithfully records the government of God towards David through the words of Nathan, 2 Sam. 12. This shows that there is a price to be paid by believers, here and now, for sins wilfully committed. If we sin we must be marked by confession and contrition, and thereafter enjoy the blessedness of forgiveness. But we should also be prepared for repercussions in practical ways which will be far from pleasant. We reap what we sow. Let us heed the warning!

February 25th

Exodus 16; Psalms 52-54; **Acts 9. 1-31**

CONVERSION

While Saul's conversion experience has aspects which are unique to him, there are also many points about it which are common to every believer. A light shines from heaven. Everyone who believes does so as a result of God shining within them by His Spirit to give illumination as to His glory seen in the person of Christ. A voice is heard. When we call upon the name of the Lord it's because He is calling us in accordance with His purpose and grace. The title 'Lord' is used immediately by Saul. Instructions are given, because living is now about doing His will instead of his own. Ananias is sent by God to speak to Saul. God will use other Christians to help those who have newly believed. Saul prays – as never before! Praying is an immediate evidence of divine life. No prayer life means there has been no salvation.

Then, God speaks of the service Saul will fulfil, a very special service indeed for him of which Gentile believers are the beneficiaries. However, all Christians have been 'saved to serve'. Paul gets baptized. The biblical examples show us that every believer should ideally be baptized right after conversion. Then, he is 'with the disciples'. Christian fellowship is essential for every believer. We have to resist isolationism and realize God has directed that we grow in grace, in fellowship with others. Later on, Paul never set himself up as a one man mission or teaching centre. He worked in fellowship with other servants and assemblies, and established assemblies which were dependent on the Lord, not on him. Then, he starts preaching! He gets straight into it, because God gives the abilities His people need to do the work He wants them to do. So he grows spiritually, as we all must do right throughout our pilgrimage on this earth. The opposition comes – as it will to some degree for all – from the world, maybe from friends and family, and certainly from within. Saul's life will never be the same again. He has been completely turned around. The chief opponent of the gospel has become its foremost proponent. And for us all, trusting Christ was what changed us, not only for eternity, but for the whole course and character of our life in this world. Conversion is real; let's live the reality today!

February 26th
Exodus 17; Psalm 55; Acts 9. 32-43
WATER AND WARFARE
Two great pictures are given for the education of Christians in this chapter. The water from the rock speaks clearly of the supply of the Holy Spirit given freely to all who believe in the Lord Jesus, John 7. 39. The war with Amalek pictures the spiritual struggle within the believer between the new nature and the old sinful nature, which was not removed at conversion, Gal. 5. 17.

Even the first verse of the chapter prompts thoughts of principles that will be fully developed in New Testament teaching for believers today. We read of the 'congregation'; this anticipates the vital need for believers to assemble together in their localities, and not remain isolated. Then the Israelites are called 'children of Israel' just as we today are simply and wonderfully the children of God. They 'journeyed', and Christians too are ever travelling heavenwards and homewards, and should be marked by purposeful spiritual growth on the way. Israelites were in the 'wilderness', reminding us of the spiritual emptiness of this wicked world through which we journey. They had 'commandments', as we have, through the Lord's direct teaching and also by the apostolic writers, that we'll be glad to obey if we love Him.

The rock which yielded the water had to be smitten. This is a simple yet powerful picture of how the blessing of spiritual life which is brought to us through the indwelling Spirit of God was secured by the sufferings of the Lord Jesus under God's rod of justice on Calvary. The cost paid by the Lord should be a great motivation to us to live daily according to the desires of the Spirit, and not those of the flesh. Amalek attacking Israel pictures the assaults which will come upon us from the enemy within. The flesh will attack us quickly from the day of our conversion, and throughout our Christian lives. We must never become complacent and think we are beyond its reach, for it is ever near. The Holy Spirit within is given to enable us to apply the sharp sword of the word of God to gain victory over the evil desires of the flesh, and to live according to the dictates of holiness as taught and encouraged by scripture, Gal. 5. 16.

February 27th
Exodus 18; **Psalms 56-57**; Acts 10. 1-23

FEAR AND FAITH

These two psalms are very helpful to those facing physical persecution. For those of us who know little or nothing of that, they still have a ministry. The language to express distress is applicable to various difficulties that we may have to face throughout life. For example, many things may make us 'afraid', like the threat of unemployment or the loss of good health, and it is at least a kind of encouragement to know that a man like David had times of fear. Various types of unpleasant circumstances may result in our feeling oppressed, and that all is 'against' us. Some experiences may even be called 'calamities' which threaten to 'swallow' us up because they seem so overpowering. God in His kindness has inspired the psalmist to guide us in to how we should respond or act when such difficult times arise. First and foremost, we must be resilient in our trust in God and His abounding mercy. We must not forget that God is for us, even when things seem to be against us. The permanent proof of that is, of course, our Lord's sufferings in our stead on Calvary. In times of trouble we must never hesitate to cry out to Him, nor indeed be ashamed of our tears. This psalm and others like it prove that God does not expect us to be super-persons who don't have ordinary human reactions to painful experiences. In fact, we could do ourselves damage if we try to resist them and employ an approach, which is actually rooted in the pride of the flesh, that pretends we are above being affected by them.

Despite the difficulties of David, he is yet to be found praising God, and in particular 'his word'. This is perhaps the most important help for us in the psalm. It is through the 'truth' in the scriptures that God, by His Spirit, will be able to minister to us the strength we need to cope with difficult times. If we have neglected His word in the past, then that ministry will not be what it could be for us in the trial; and in the trial the golden rule must be – do not neglect the Bible! To do so would be to shut off the voice of God at the time we need it most. Neither should we cut ourselves off from fellow believers, as it is often through them that God meets us in our need, Heb. 10. 25.

74

February 28th
Exodus 19; Psalms 58-59; **Acts 10. 24-48**

GOD AND THE GENTILES

God's purpose that Gentiles should come into blessing is clear from the earliest statement of the Abrahamic covenant in Genesis chapter 12. The prophet Isaiah also has many delightful promises of blessings on Gentile peoples. However what was nowhere disclosed in Old Testament times was that a new body would be formed consisting of Jews and Gentiles on an equal footing, namely, 'the church, which is [Christ's] body'.

Indeed it must have been one of the hardest things for Jewish Christians to come to terms with that, after the Day of Pentecost, they no longer had any special place among the peoples of the world, but were to enjoy the blessings of God exactly as the Gentiles were going to do through believing the gospel of their Messiah! Yet, God in His kindness towards Israel did special things to encourage them to accept the new situation. Among these were the giving of the 'sign gifts', miraculous abilities manifested for a temporary period of time to provide evidence to the Jews that the blessing of Gentiles was truly God's purpose. It is seen in the section before us today. Peter, of all people, was a zealous Jew. There was nothing wrong with that, but his whole mind-set had to be changed. So he was given the vision of the sheet and the unclean animals to teach him that God had made a change so that there was now no longer any difference between Jew and Gentile. Both, being guilty of sin before God, Rom. 3. 23, could be cleansed through the blood of Christ. The meeting with Cornelius did not result in a re-run of Pentecost, for the descent of the Holy Spirit as recorded in Acts chapter 2 was an unrepeatable event when all Christians were baptized 'into one body'. But the same gift of speaking in foreign languages, neither known through upbringing or previously learned, was given to convince the Jewish observers that the Gentiles had been blessed with the same gift of the indwelling Spirit as they had been. We today do not have any of such sign gifts, having instead the complete revelation of the God in the scriptures. But we can still fully rejoice that God turned to Gentiles in order to bring us into the fullness of blessing through simple faith in the Lord Jesus.

March 1st
Exodus 20. 1-26; Psalms 60-61; Acts 11. 1-18
THE TEN COMMANDMENTS

Paul stated that one of Israel's outstanding privileges was 'the giving of the law', Rom. 9. 4. The great objective of deliverance from Egypt was that Israel should become God's *holy people*, Exod. 19. 6, hence the opening words of the chapter, 'I am the Lord thy God, which have brought thee out of the land of Egypt, out of the house of bondage', 20. 2. In the context of the faith of Israel, the law sets out the standards expected of those who have *already entered into covenant relationship* with God. Love motivates obedience, v. 6. The Victor of the exodus has every right to impose His standards on His ransomed people. Israel's elders had accepted His offer without questioning what He might demand, 19. 8. The terrifying phenomena of thunder and lightning, fire and earthquake on Mount Sinai herald God's unutterable holiness. Lest we Christians should think such considerations outdated, the writer to the Hebrews exhorts us, 'Let us have grace, whereby we may offer service well-pleasing to God with reverence and awe: for our God is a consuming fire, Heb. 12. 28-29 RV.

These 'Ten Commandments' form the fundamental legislation for Israel; the legal codes which follow in the Pentateuch derive from these. The first three draw out the implications of God's redemptive actions. No rival God is to be countenanced. Any representation of God is sure to degrade Him. A spurious invocation of God's name must carry His condemnation. Work is part of God's creatorial design for humanity, Gen. 3. 17-19, but so is rest after labour. The fifth commandment is explicitly reaffirmed in the context of the Christian household, Eph. 6. 2-3.

The final five commandments show us that our relationship with God must regulate all our *human* relationships. The rich young ruler in his blind naivety thought that he had kept the commandments from his youth, Luke 18. 21, but the Lord Jesus radicalized them, drawing out their spiritual essence, Matt. 5. The lustful look and murderous anger are alike condemned by this code. How precious, therefore, to be accepted by God through faith in Christ, and for the righteous requirement of the law to be fulfilled in us by the power of the indwelling Spirit, Rom. 8. 1-4.

March 2nd
Exodus 21; Psalms 62-63; **Acts 11. 19-30**
CHRISTIANS AT ANTIOCH
The reading describes a most encouraging advance of the gospel – the establishment of a church at Antioch in Syria. In turn, this would become a centre for the evangelization of the Roman world. Significantly, Luke traces the beginning of the work to the dispersion of God's servants through *persecution* at the time of Stephen. Take heart: our merciful Saviour God can make even the wrath of man to praise Him, Ps. 76. 10.

It is to be noted that this major expansion took place *directly under God*, vv. 21, 23, rather than being orchestrated by the church at Jerusalem. That said, those at Jerusalem were delighted to send Barnabas to greet and help them. He, like Stephen, was full of the Holy Spirit and faith, cp. 6. 5, and amply justified his name 'son of encouragement', for he exhorted the converts that with determination they should cleave to the Lord. How refreshing to see believers truly rejoicing in a new work of God in which they had had no part! No wonder that the showers of blessing fell, as many were added to the Lord, 11. 24, cp. Ps. 133.

It is to Barnabas' credit that he saw an opportunity for the outstanding gifts of Saul in the instruction of this diverse and growing church. May we be delivered from blinkered independence and be prepared to recognize and profit from the differing gifts of others. One can imagine the rich and intensive coverage of 'the whole counsel of God' during that precious year, v. 26. Bible teaching needs to be orderly and systematic if saints are to be fitted for their ministries in the body of Christ. These new believers – saved Jews and Gentiles united on an equal footing – were dubbed 'Christians' – a new name for the people of God. Progressively in Acts we learn the distinctive characteristics of the church of God and its separation from Judaism.

The Holy Spirit's warning of coming famine prompted a beautiful spontaneous action. As those of Antioch had benefited from the *spiritual* input of Barnabas, they respond with *material* gifts to the poor saints of Jerusalem, a vital principle in supporting the work of God, Rom. 15. 27. We can learn practical brotherly care from this. Thanks be to God for His unspeakable gift!

March 3rd
Exodus 22. 1 – 23. 9; Psalms 64-65; **Acts 12**
PRINCIPLES ILLUSTRATED
The opening verses well illustrate a sad scenario that that has often been repeated throughout the centuries – powerful religious authorities enlisting the powers of the state to persecute a religious minority. In this case it is Herod and the Jews. Herod (whose character seems to be all of a piece with his forebears) moves against the church and finds that it delights the Jews.

1. The sovereignty of God

The fact that James is martyred and that Peter and John survive causes us to wonder why? And really we have no answer to such questions – not down here, that is, 'For now we see in a mirror, darkly . . . but then shall I know even as also I have been known', 1 Cor. 13. 12. Hebrews chapter 11 teaches us that faith is no less evidenced in the case of those who are killed, sawn asunder, etc, than in those who 'escape the edge of the sword'.

2. Resting on God's promises

How is it that Peter could be found fast asleep, knowing that he could be taken out to execution in the morning? Could it be related to the fact that the Lord had spoken of his one day being old, John 21. 18? Peter would not have been very old at this time, so he clearly understood that his work for the Lord was not yet complete.

3. The value of prayer

There are more than thirty references to prayer in the Acts of the Apostles. The infant church was characterized by poverty, piety, power, but, above all, *prayer.* What do we often find among Christians in the Western world? Worldliness and weakness, and also comparative *prayerlessness.* Surely this is a timely word to us all. Wouldn't it be good for all of us to rediscover the priority of prayer?

4. The law of recompense

We see this clearly illustrated in the terrible fate that befalls Herod. He appears one day in his royal regalia, makes a great oration, and the people spontaneously accord him divine honours. And Herod loves it! However, judgement falls. God is not mocked: for whatsoever a man sows, that shall he also reap. And yes, the principle applies to Christians too!

March 4th

Exodus 23. 10-33; **Psalms 66-67**; Acts 13. 1-25

COME AND HEAR . . . WHAT HE HAS DONE FOR MY SOUL

This psalm celebrates a recent national deliverance, and it has been suggested that it may have been composed for Judah's King Hezekiah by the prophet Isaiah, cp. Isa. 38. The *collective* praise of God, vv. 1-12, gives way in the latter part to an *individual's* response and testimony to God's mercy, vv. 13-20.

The whole earth is summoned to praise Israel's glorious God, vv. 1-4. Subjugated enemies are forced to come cringing before Him. We look forward to the day when every knee shall bow and every tongue confess that Jesus Christ is Lord, Phil. 2. 10-11.

This sovereign God is awe-inspiring in His interventions in human affairs, vv. 5-7. The exodus passage of the Red Sea and the crossing of Jordan together showcase His invincibility and saving power. The Christian sees the power and glory of God supremely demonstrated in the resurrection of the Lord Jesus, which at the same time serves notice to the world that God will judge it in righteousness, Acts 17. 31.

The psalmist continues to bid the nations praise God for more recent deliverances of His people. As in the times of the judges, He still permits terrible trials and oppressions to overtake them, often on account of their sins. Yet, amidst it all, they are *upheld* by God in life, v. 9, *refined*, v. 10, and, in the end, brought out into a wonderful '*place of abundance*', v. 12 ESV. As Christians, we regularly experience the disciplinary hand of our Father, but we can endure it in faith knowing that His ultimate goal is our spiritual wealth and blessing, Heb. 12. 7-11.

In some dire extremity, the psalmist made pledges to God which he now faithfully fulfils by various sweet savour offerings and sacrifices, vv. 13-15. The Christian is eternally obligated to God for His mercies; the only appropriate response is to 'present your bodies a sacrifice – living, sanctified, acceptable to God – your intelligent service', Rom. 12. 1 YLT.

The joyful experience of God's intervention in answer to his prayer moves the psalmist to testify to all who fear God, vv. 16-20. All praise belongs to the faithful God, who has not removed His mercy ('steadfast love' ESV) from him.

March 5th
Exodus 24; Psalm 68; Acts 13. 26-52
THE COVENANT SEALED

At the invitation of God, Moses and his associates along with seventy elders of Israel ascend Mount Sinai, for the solemn covenant ratification ceremony. Only Moses as mediator is bidden approach the Lord; the mass of the people must remain distant, v. 2. Moses constructs an altar fully representative of the twelve tribes, for this covenant unites the people in obedience to God. The 'words', v. 3, recall the Ten Commandments; the 'judgements' refer to the resulting stipulations, chs. 21-23. Ancient covenants were ratified by the shedding of blood, hence Moses applies half of the blood to the altar, and the other half he sprinkles on the people who pledge their obedience, vv. 3, 7. Symbolically, God and His people are thus united, and this is attested by a fellowship meal involving both parties, v. 11. Part of the covenant blessing is the enjoyment of a vision of God, though the reference to feet suggests that this may be all that they see, cp. 33. 21-23. The remarkable fact is recorded that they survive this awe-inspiring encounter with God unscathed.

There are instructive parallels here with the new covenant commemorated weekly in the Lord's supper. Echoing verse 8, the Lord Jesus declared on the night of His betrayal, 'This is my blood of the covenant, which is poured out for many for the forgiveness of sins', Matt. 26. 28 ESV. As one with Christ, we rejoice before God in appreciation of the Saviour's person and work, Deut. 27. 7. As regards obedience, we are 'elect according to the foreknowledge of God the Father, through sanctification of the Spirit, *unto obedience* and sprinkling of the blood of Jesus Christ', 1 Pet. 1. 2. Similarly, under the new covenant, God pledges: 'I will put my laws *into their minds*', Heb. 8. 10. The new covenant is not written externally on tablets of stone, but on the fleshy tables of believing human hearts; through the miracle of new birth God implants within us *the desire* to obey Him, cp. Rom. 8. 3-4.

Run, John, and work, the law commands,
Yet finds me neither feet nor hands,
But sweeter news the gospel brings,
It bids me fly and lends me wings!   JOHN BERRIDGE

80

March 6th

Exodus 25; **Psalm 69**; Acts 14

I HAVE BORNE REPROACH

David is in deep and prolonged trouble from which he has been pleading for deliverance, but without relief, vv. 1-5. It's like sinking in overwhelming mire, about to be swept away by a raging torrent. Many powerful enemies are bent on destroying him, hating him without any basis whatsoever. At several points the experiences transcend those of David, and find their deepest fulfilment in the unparalleled sufferings of Christ, Rom. 15. 3.

David acknowledges his sin and guilt before God, vv. 5-12. He has a crushing sense that God is dealing with him punitively on account of sin, cp. v. 26. He has been especially zealous for God and 'his house'; thus, he has become a focus for the abuse the ungodly would otherwise have directed at God, cp. 2 Tim. 3. 12.

But the psalmist appeals to God for deliverance at what he considers an opportune time, vv. 13-18, a time when God is near to save, Isa. 55. 6. He appeals to God's covenant faithfulness. Deep waters threaten, the depths, the pit. God seems so distant; why doesn't He intervene? He appeals to God to be his Avenger, his Kinsman-redeemer.

Then comes a heightened appeal, vv. 19-21; he feels utterly bereft of sympathy and comfort; enemies pile on their wicked abuse; gall for food, vinegar for drink – metaphorical for the psalmist, bitterly literal in the case of the Lord Jesus. He is facing a tidal wave of shame and scorn, vv. 7, 12, 20-21.

Righteousness demands that the ungodly must be repaid for their vicious and gratuitous abuse, vv. 22-28. They have aggravated the misery of one under divine judgement, so the psalmist wants them struck out of the book of the living; death must be their portion, and the desolation of their house, cp. Rom. 11. 9.

A renewed prayer from the depths is followed by a switch to praise, vv. 29-36, in the conviction that his prayer will be answered. Heart worship is superior to formal sacrifice and ceremonial v. 32, contrast v. 6. God finally vindicates His captive people. The concluding verses broaden out in perspective: God will visit Zion and Judah, and will re-establish and vindicate His oppressed people – events of truly worldwide significance.

March 7th
Exodus 26. 1-30; Psalms 70-71; **Acts 15. 1-21**
GUARD THE GOSPEL!

A previous meditation noted the blessings of happy interdependence between the Christians at Antioch and those at Jerusalem. Satan was sure to challenge such brotherly harmony, and we read that 'certain men' from Judaea arrived and declared, 'Except ye be circumcised after the manner of Moses, ye cannot be saved', v. 1. This struck at the very heart of the gospel of grace. By implication the atoning work of Christ was insufficient for salvation – it had to be supplemented by human effort. Moreover, as *Galatians* spells out, such circumcision involves a commitment to keep the whole law – a retreat from justification by faith. We each need to be crystal clear on what constitutes the gospel of the grace of God. Beware of all 'Christ plus' errors: 'Christ supplemented is Christ supplanted'. As the error had come from Judaea, to Judaea the apostles must go to confer with the Jerusalem leadership.

Following much debate on the contentious issue, Peter emerges to set out plainly how *God* had graciously and emphatically directed the salvation of Gentiles, vv. 7-9. The lessons of the home of Cornelius had been well learned by this 'living stone'! One does not need to become a Jew in order to be saved.

Barnabas and Paul then continue with the report of the 'signs and wonders *God had done* through them among the Gentiles', v. 12, cp. v. 4. God had sealed this major gospel advance with undeniable signs.

James' summary and conclusion again emphasizes God's initiative in Gentile inclusion, v. 14, in fulfilment of His purpose to bless Gentiles prophesied through Amos, v. 17. In Christ risen and glorified, the fortunes of the dynasty of David are eternally restored, signalling the gathering of the Gentiles to the name of the Lord. James' inspired counsel, therefore, is that Gentile believers need add no meritorious works to faith in Christ. The only provisos, each negative, were intended to respect the conscience of Jewish fellow-believers, and thus protect gospel unity, vv. 20-21.

This is a practical outworking of the law of love. May we ever guard the clarity, purity, and freedom of the gospel, but, at the same time, be careful as to our responsibilities.

March 8th

Exodus 26. 31 – 27. 19; **Psalm 72**; Acts 15. 22-35

OF HIS KINGDOM THERE SHALL BE NO END

This glorious messianic psalm celebrates the rule of David's successors as God's representatives on the throne of Israel. It is entitled 'for Solomon', and there are several allusions to his distinguished reign. At the same time, as C H SPURGEON aptly commented, 'a greater than Solomon is here', and both Jewish and Christian interpreters have recognized a pen picture of God's ideal ruler, Messiah Himself. How refreshing that after all man's corruption and misrule it will yet be triumphantly proclaimed: 'The kingdom of the world has become the kingdom of our Lord and of his Christ, and he shall reign forever and ever', Rev. 11. 15 ESV.

In verses 1 to 7, we see that this reign is founded on the essential qualities of righteousness, justice, and equity. He is the ready champion of the needy and the oppressed. Righteous Himself, the effect of His reign will be refreshing, regenerating, and righteousness affirming, with its resultant and enduring peace.

Verses 8 to 14 describe no parochial ruler, but rather that His kingdom will extend to the uttermost parts of the earth. The echoes of Solomon's reign are evident here, cp. 1 Kgs. 10. 1ff., but the geographical and spiritual scope is far greater. Meditating on this Psalm, ISAAC WATTS penned his famous hymn 'Jesus shall reign'. Today we rejoice in the worldwide spread of the gospel and that God is visiting the nations to take out of them a people for His name. In view of this, how concerned are we to support missionary endeavour in every way possible? Beyond this age, however, we confidently await the millennial reign of Christ when all His enemies will be subjugated and universal tribute will be paid to God's King.

Verses 15 to 17 are to be taken as prayers, cp. ESV, for the wellbeing of the king, v. 15; for the blessing of His people and land, v. 16; and for the eternal perpetuation of His name amidst worldwide blessings, v. 17, cp. Gen 12. 3. Very appropriately the closing doxology for Book 2 of the Psalms magnifies the Lord's unique hand in all this, vv. 18-20. Every devout heart must surely respond, 'Even so, come, Lord Jesus', Rev. 22. 20.

March 9th
Exodus 27. 20 – 28. 14; Psalm 73; Acts 15. 36 – 16. 15

THE LAMP OIL AND THE PRIESTHOOD

The directions for the provision of olive oil to fuel the lampstand are instructive. There must be no darkness in the sanctuary, for God is the source of light and life. There is to be 'no night there', cp. Rev. 22. 5. The constant shining of the lamps, silently fed by the pure oil, powerfully symbolizes the mighty yet gracious ministry of the Holy Spirit, Zech. 4. 6. Amidst the challenges and difficulties of bearing witness to Christ, how encouraging this is for us as individual believers and assemblies alike!

Directions for the Aaronic priesthood follow, ch. 28. Aaron is to be attired in garments for glory and beauty. The fabrics and the colours identify him as a man of the sanctuary. By contrast, our Lord Jesus needs no ornate vestments to distinguish Him, His glories are intrinsic; His atonement perfect and final; and His ministry is in the heavenly and eternal 'tabernacle', Heb. 9. 24.

Consequently, as believers, we have a divinely-provided fitness to enter God's presence, and to function as holy priests, 1 Pet. 2. 5.

Israel's high priest was a *representative* man; in Aaron every Israelite was presented before God. The ephod is the archetypal garment of priesthood, and its details are most instructive. In particular we may note that the name of each tribe is engraved on onyx stones, set in the shoulder pieces of the ephod. The *shoulder* suggests strength and safety, Isa. 9. 6; Luke 15. 5. Each tribe is equally named in an orderly manner, irrespective of size or spiritual track record. The names are not simply painted on, but *engraved*, Exod. 28. 9, 11, suggesting God's unchangeable commitment to His people. Later, through Isaiah, God reassures Israel: 'Yet will I not forget thee. Behold, I have graven thee upon the palms of my hands; thy walls are continually before me', Isa. 49. 16. Are you a sanctuary person? Are you careful to be *inclusive* in your intercessions for God's people?

My name from the palms of His hands eternity will not erase;
Impressed on His heart it remains, in marks of indelible grace.
Yes, I to the end shall endure, as sure as the earnest is giv'n;
More happy, but not more secure, the glorified spirits in heav'n.

AUGUSTUS M. TOPLADY

March 10th

Exodus 28. 15-43; Psalms 74-75; **Acts 16. 16-40**

A COLONY OF HEAVEN IN A COLONY OF ROME

Luke introduces Philippi informing us that it was a proud Roman colony, with distinctive privileges, laws, and customs – an outpost of Rome in that part of Macedonia. Later, writing to the Philippians, Paul alludes to their *higher citizenship*: 'Our citizenship is in heaven, and from it we await a Saviour, the Lord Jesus Christ', Phil. 3. 20 ESV. Are you marked out as a heavenly citizen in the midst of a 'crooked and perverse generation', 2. 15?

The orthodox male Jew routinely thanks God that he was not born a slave, a Gentile, or a woman, yet, interestingly, members of each of these categories enjoy blessing at Philippi.

The slave girl was in the bondage of an evil spirit, and her ability to predict brought her heartless masters financial gain. Far from accepting free publicity from such a tainted source, Paul was grieved, and, there and then, exorcized the demon in the name of Jesus Christ, v. 18. We note the *principle of integrity*. God's work cannot be promoted by unclean agents; the end does not justify the means. The girl was rendered useless to her masters, who then turned upon the servants of God. Lives changed by the power of the Holy Spirit will not be universally welcomed.

The Philippian church was born amidst sufferings, and we see the *principle of adversity* in the submission of the apostles to the hardships of flogging and imprisonment. How much inconvenience are we prepared to accept in the service of Christ? Nor was this mere stoical resistance! The golden thread of prayer and praise pervades this chapter, vv. 9, 13, 16, and transforms even the darkest hour, v. 25. Is it at all surprising that God sent an earthquake to move the ruthless jailer to conversion? As with Lydia, faith in Christ revolutionized his attitude and behaviour, and was attested in baptism, vv. 15, 34. Moreover, salvation extended to the jailer's household, family members and servants. What a demonstration of the power and grace of God!

Citizenship recurs as a theme, and, finally, Paul and Silas informed the magistrates that their Roman citizen rights had been violated. This was not to retaliate, but rather to protect the infant church from future harassment by the authorities, vv. 35-39.

March 11th
Exodus 29. 1-37; **Psalms 76-77**; Acts 17. 1-15
GOD OUR HELP IN AGES PAST

Psalm 77 opens with the poet in deep despair, yet it closes with his animated recounting of God's great deliverances. The psalmist speaks in the singular, and it is clear that he feels the low fortunes of his people keenly and personally. He is overwhelmed by dark despondency.

In his extremity he appeals to God in prayer, 'My hand was stretched out in the night', v. 2 RV. Like Jacob bereft of Joseph, his soul refused to be comforted, Gen. 37. 35. Sleep eludes him, yet, in his lonely night vigils, he ponders the history of Israel and wonders if now God has finally abandoned His people, vv. 4-9. Has He changed His character? Will He ever again be merciful? His perplexity tumbles out in six pointed questions, each expecting the answer 'No'.

Verse 10 marks the beginning of the second section of the psalm, and renewed confidence in God, 'Then I said, "I will appeal to this, to the years of the right hand of the Most High"', ESV. What is the recipe for this spiritual tonic? Firstly, God's power is unrivalled and undiminished. Secondly, that power is put forth for the deliverance of His people, 'Thou hast with thine arm redeemed thy people', v. 15. God's people are designated sons of Jacob and Joseph, to stress on the one hand God's care for all the tribes, cp. Obad. 18, and, on the other, to evoke memories of God's tender providential care of the Israelites under Joseph, and later whilst slaves in Egypt.

The recollection of redemption from the slavery of Egypt and Pharaoh sets the backdrop for a poetic description of God's sovereignty, power, and glory displayed at the exodus, vv. 16-20. As WILLIAM COWPER memorably put it, 'He plants His footsteps in the sea and rides upon the storm'. The sea flowed back where Israel had passed over on dry ground, with no visible trace of God's triumphant march, v. 19. Through such convulsions of nature the great Shepherd of the sheep led His flock by the hand of His appointed leaders. We can exclaim with that same Moses: 'The eternal God is thy refuge, and underneath are the everlasting arms', Deut 33. 27. Yet, there is an even greater victory, Heb. 13. 20!

March 12th

Exodus 29. 38 – 30. 10; Psalm 78. 1-31; **Acts 17. 16-34**

PREACHING TO INTELLECTUALS

Writing to the Corinthians, Paul stated, 'Ye see your calling, brethren, how that not *many* wise men after the flesh . . . are called', 1 Cor. 1. 26. Fortunately he wrote '*many*', not '*any*', for God delights to save in all walks of life. This passage is highly relevant to our present situation, witnessing for Christ amidst a godless and biblically illiterate population.

Finding himself in Athens, Paul's spirit is stirred as he sees the city 'wholly given to idolatry', v. 16. The philosophers and intellectuals had received a garbled report that Paul was setting forth some new and strange deities – Jesus and 'the resurrection'. Invited to address this intellectual élite, Paul the consummate evangelist discovers a ready point of contact with his audience: an altar 'to the *unknown God*', v. 23. This is a real attention-grabber, yet, at the same time, a damning admission of the ignorance of Athens' idolaters.

Pagans in the ancient world worshipped a whole pantheon of false deities. Establishing the *truth* about God is, therefore, a vital first step. Paul explains in simple language the reality of the one true and living God. He identifies Him as the transcendent Creator and Sustainer of all, vv. 24-26. Moreover, He is sovereign in the affairs of nations, with gracious designs for all men.

The apostle communicates *scriptural truths*, but uses selected extra-biblical sources to make his points – poems which resonate with his audience. Evangelism often requires bridges to be established from the thought-world of the audience to biblical truth.

Paul's preaching is pointed and deeply challenging; this is no mere take-it-or-leave-it lecture. To summarize: 'their idolatry is unthinkable; their ignorance is intolerable; their judgement is inevitable', R. LUCAS. The ultimatum delivered by Christ's resurrection is compelling: all men everywhere must repent. Praise God, there were results, even at the Areopagus, v. 34!

Let us beware of 'writing off' the cultured and educated: they too need the gospel. Paul shows us the way, with his bold demolition of their idolatry and challenging presentation of the truth about the one true and living God.

March 13th
Exodus 30. 11-38; Psalm 78. 32-72; Acts 18. 1-23
REDEMPTION, WASHING, ANOINTING, AND INCENSE
Although, at first sight, this chapter brings together a disparate set of instructions, a clear logical and spiritual order is discernable.

The half-shekel **atonement money** was required of every Israelite who was numbered amongst the congregation. The amount paid was the same, irrespective of means and the small sum ensured affordability. We recall Peter's words, 'ye were not redeemed with corruptible things, as silver and gold . . . but with the precious blood of Christ', 1 Pet. 1. 19.

The next item encountered is the **laver**, vv. 17-21. It is emphasized that the priests must use this vessel in their approach to God 'that they die not'. This reminds us of the unutterable holiness of the God of Israel and the need for both initial and continual cleansing on the part of those who engage in His service. Accordingly, every believer has experienced 'the washing of regeneration and renewal of the Holy Spirit', Titus 3. 5 ESV.

Following cleansing with water, the priest could then be anointed with the holy **anointing oil,** vv. 22-33. Directions are given for its production according to a unique formula. Tabernacle vessels as well as priests were to be anointed. Note that holiness was a positively *fragrant* thing, not merely a matter of the removal of pollution. So for us, whilst we reject the 'works of the flesh', there must also be the positive fruit of the Spirit – the fragrance of Christ's character formed in the believer, Gal. 5. 19-23.

Finally, **sweet incense** was to be prepared, vv. 34-38. Again, this was produced to a special recipe, with imitations expressly prohibited. By beating the incense the exotic fragrances would be released, and this was to be placed in front of the ark, v. 36, the place where God and man could meet. Incense is frequently associated with prayer in scripture, Ps. 141. 2; Rev. 5. 8. It is wonderful to know that our prayers come before God in all the acceptability of His beloved Son, 1 Pet. 2. 5.

What great encouragement, then, to draw near with a true heart in full assurance of faith, having our hearts sprinkled from an evil conscience, and our bodies washed with pure water! Heb. 10. 22. Thus fitted for His presence, God will never turn us away.

March 14th
Exodus 31; **Psalms 79-80**; Acts 18. 24 – 19. 20

A CRY FOR RESTORATION

The psalms speak concerning all of the earthly circumstances of Israel. Psalm 80 contemplates the people in exile and the land at the mercy of surrounding enemies, v. 13. The psalm is punctuated by the refrain 'Turn us again O God . . . and we shall be saved', vv. 3, 7, 19, cp. v. 14. Most crushing to the Hebrew mind is the thought that God Himself is alienated from His sinful people, v. 4. There's many a Christian testimony, both individual and corporate, languishing in such a state today, and the psalm speaks directly to this situation. Do we not grieve as we ponder the fragmentation of the church's witness to Christ in this world?

The poet begins with an appeal to Israel's Shepherd. No parochial Judahite, he has a heart for the totality of the Twelve Tribes – Joseph, Ephraim, Benjamin, Manasseh, vv. 1-2. The nation has experienced dark days aplenty, and he yearns for God to dispel the gloom and shine forth from His sanctuary. Similarly the saint today yearns for the coming of the Lord. Despite such depressing conditions, faith in God remains intact. The repeated prayer highlights that only God can restore His people.

The nation has shed copious tears, and has been derided by their enemies, vv. 5-6. Memories of past blessings and the unique role assigned to Israel in the purpose of God, pictured by the vine, only serves to accentuate present despair, vv. 8-11. The vineyard is derelict, the Gardener has abandoned it, and foes desecrate it, cp. Isa. 5. 5-7. Yet in spite of it all, Israel occupies a unique place in God's affections – His flock, His people, His vine, vv. 1, 4, 8. Surely God will not cast away the people He foreknew? Similarly, the Christian knows that God will graciously bring to completion the work He has begun in us, Phil. 1. 6.

When Benjamin was born, his dying mother Rachel named him Ben-oni, 'son of my sorrow', but Jacob in his deep emotion renamed him Benjamin, 'son of my right hand'. Accordingly, the closing appeal is that the Lord would replace His firm hand on Israel, and once again make it strong on His behalf, v. 17. The fullest version of the refrain reminds us that the Lord combines covenant faithfulness with limitless power, cp. Jer. 32. 17.

March 15th
Exodus 32; Psalms 81-82; Acts 19. 21-41

REBELLION AND INTERCESSION

Before Moses returned to the camp, Israel had broken the first two, and probably the seventh commandments. This profoundly grave outbreak of idolatry indicated a swift departure from the ways of God, v. 8. Moses had been hidden from sight up the mountain, and his delayed return proved too great a test for a people so recently escaped from the idolatry of Egypt. We may discern a parallel in the idolatry, superstition, and sheer paganism of many sections of Christendom whilst our Lord's return is awaited. It is also solemn to read of Aaron's feeble capitulation to the desire of the people, probably in a misguided attempt to limit the damage by linking the worship of the bull-calf to that of Jehovah. Alluding to such appalling scenes, Paul warned the Corinthians (and us), 'Let him that thinketh he standeth take heed lest he fall', 1 Cor. 10. 12. Religious activities which appeal to the senses still have the capacity to entice the Lord's people, should we lose our grip on spiritual and eternal realities, cp. Heb. 11. 27b.

This crisis proved a stern test of the leadership of Moses. God disowns His people, labelling them 'thy (Moses') people', and proposes a fresh start with Moses as a new Abraham, v. 10. To his credit, Moses appeals to God's recent redemption of *His* people, His reputation in the eyes of the Egyptians, and His covenant promises to Abraham, buttressed by divine oath. The statement that 'the Lord repented', v. 14, reflects a triumph of Moses' integrity and leadership, cp. John 6. 6. When serious failure overtakes God's people, how do we react? Such circumstances should drive us to humiliation and prevailing intercession.

Debased notions of God inevitably lead to debased treatment of fellow human beings, vv. 6, 25. The situation demanded swift remedial action, irrespective of family loyalties. The Levites had remained faithful to God, and by their resolute intervention were commended, for Moses had said, 'Consecrate yourselves to day to the Lord, even every man upon his son, and upon his brother; that he may bestow upon you a blessing this day', v. 29. Fidelity to our holy God must outweigh our commitments to errant family members and friends. It is profoundly sad when it is otherwise.

March 16th

Exodus 33. 1 – 34. 3; **Psalms 83-84**; Acts 20. 1-16

LONGING FOR THE COURTS OF THE LORD

Psalm 84 pulsates with deep emotions and the intense desire of the psalmist to be present in the temple of God at Jerusalem. More specifically, he seeks *God Himself.*

Yearning for the temple, vv. 1-4. Weary with surrounding idolatries, the psalmist's whole being – heart, soul, and flesh – is longing to be in the presence of the living God in His temple. It is his spiritual *home*, resounding with praise and prayer. He envies the birds who can migrate there at any time, and the Levites whose continual service is there, vv. 3, 4. How much does 'the church of the living God' mean to us, 1 Tim. 3. 15? Surely it is far more wonderful than any material temple.

Marching upward to Zion, vv. 5-8. Most Israelites lived at some distance from the temple, and would make a regular pilgrimage to be there, perhaps at a major festival. This would be a joyful procession in company with other devoted worshippers. Yet the journey had its dangers and trials. The secret was to find all necessary strength in God, and to have an undivided heart committed to the pathway of pilgrimage, v. 5. Dry arid valleys such as Baca (lit. 'weeping') must be traversed, but in fellowship with God even such an adverse experience is transformed into a well of spiritual resources. And nearing Zion strength is renewed, and a safe arrival in the presence of God is assured, v. 7.

Communion with God, vv. 9-12. The temple was a magnificent building, but the surpassing attraction was *the presence of God.* In this section the psalmist's heart goes out to God in praise and intercession; note the rich variety of designations of God. Specifically, he prays for blessing upon the anointed king, whose stable rule preserves ready access to Zion. Similarly, we are exhorted to pray for those in authority that we might lead a peaceful and quiet life, 1 Tim. 2. 2. To the psalmist, a day in the courts of the Lord is the best of days; the humblest role in the house of God is far better than any association with 'the tents of wickedness'. The writer concludes the psalm 'lost in wonder, love, and praise'. The Lord is the source of all light, health, protection, favour, honour, and every good gift. Can you truly concur with verse 12?

March 17th
Exodus 34. 4-35; Psalms 85-86; **Acts 20. 17-38**
WATCH AND REMEMBER!

This last message of Paul to the assembly at Ephesus ends with an emotional farewell on the shore. They would see his face no more! Where would they turn for help now? God and the word of His grace would be their unfailing resource, and it is ours also.

Paul leaves them with a lot to think about. First he reminds them of his own **integrity** as a servant of the Lord among them: his humility of mind, the faithfulness of his stewardship, the thoroughness of his teaching, and his courage facing a dangerous future. His ambition was to finish his course with joy. Do you think that God's people will remember these things about us? Are these features evident in our lives now?

Then, he warns them about **dangers ahead** in their own circles. It was not going to be plain sailing on calm seas. Grievous wolves would get in among the flock; perverse words and ways would come from those they thought they could trust; deception and subtlety would fragment the assembly. What a prospect! And it happened – and it has been repeated through the centuries!

How can we face such dangers? By watching and remembering. 'Watch and pray', said our Lord Jesus. The enemy is still so active. Turn often to the scriptures and stir up your minds by way of remembrance! Be steadfast and strong in the Lord.

Finally, he commends them to the God who would never fail them. The word of His grace would build them up and never fail to comfort them. He recalls the **words of the Lord Jesus** (not recorded elsewhere) how it is more blessed to give than to receive. That is what the Lord showed and taught while here on earth, and so, as His people, we are called to support the weak and minister to others. The Lord Jesus even said that as we do it to others we do it to Him and for Him, Matt. 25. 40.

So this passage leaves us with a lot to think about – our own integrity, humility and fidelity; our courage in facing dangers in the path of duty and service for the Lord; our opportunities to serve others, rather than looking for others to serve us; to give rather than to receive. This is true blessedness.

Let us watch and remember!

March 18th
Exodus 35; Psalms 87-88; Acts 21. 1-16
A HEART MATTER
The real work of building the tabernacle can now begin in earnest after the interruption caused by the tragic events of chapter 32. The commands of the Lord through Moses again challenge the people and call them to work. The great task required willing hearts first, skilled hands next, and true spiritual exercise in shared responsibilities. Nothing less is required of us today.

It had to begin in their hearts. So we read first about **willing hearts to bring and to offer**, v. 5. That is also the message in 2 Corinthians chapter 8 verse 12, 'first a willing mind'. In Egypt it was forced labour, hard and painful, now it is to be devoted labour willing and giving, motivated by a heart of love for the Lord. Is this behind our giving and our work for Him today?

Then, we read of **wise hearts to come and to make**, v. 10. These beautiful and precious objects and furnishings would not appear from nowhere! Human effort and God-given abilities would change basic materials into things of beauty and glory, which speak to us of Christ. So also in the assembly today all our gifts and contributions are to be brought and used so that Christ might be glorified and exalted among us.

We further read about **hearts that stirred them up,** v. 21. They seemed to catch the vision and accept the challenge, and what enthusiasm followed! Peter stirred up the saints to spiritual growth and activity, 2 Pet. 1. 13, while Paul told Timothy to 'stir up the gift of God' in him, 2 Tim. 1. 6. We often need stirring up like this, but not as in Proverbs chapter 28 verse 25.

Another important thing which this chapter highlights is how **everyone got involved** – no one opted out! The word 'every' occurs many times. It was 'both men and women', v. 22, 'every man' v. 23, 'all the women, vv. 25-26, 'every man and woman whose heart made them willing', v. 29. What unity of purpose and fellowship of effort.

Each person's work is different but everyone's is necessary. This is the teaching of 1 Corinthians chapter 12 and Ephesians chapter 4. Every member is necessary, none is redundant, each is different – all for the good of the body, and the glory of the Head in heaven.

March 19th
Exodus 36; Psalm 89. 1-18; Acts 21. 17-40
MORE THAN ENOUGH!

HUDSON TAYLOR, the pioneer missionary to China, said, 'God's work done in God's way will never lack God's supply'. We see in Exodus chapter 36 how true that is. What huge amounts they brought and what a variety! And it was not only on one day, but 'every morning'! The liberality and enthusiasm of these people seemed to know no bounds. They had to be stopped from bringing. What a blessed situation to be found in.

One day the Apostle Paul was able to say something similar, 'I have all, and abound', Phil. 4. 18. There was no hint that the Philippian assembly should send more! The gift they had sent him was a great help and encouragement to him, but it was also credit to their account, and it brought glory to God. We should keep these principles in mind when we give to the Lord and His servants. It is a spiritual exercise to glorify God.

The people were motivated and willing-hearted, the work was spiritual and shared, and two specially gifted and commissioned men headed it up. These were particularly filled with 'wisdom of heart', 35. 35, and Aholiab had a 'heart that he may teach', v. 34. This is always God's way to expand and continue His work, 2 Tim. 2. 2: 'faithful men who shall be able to teach others also'.

The Lord called them by name, Exod. 35. 30; they were 'chosen vessels'. He filled them with His Spirit, v. 31. He put wisdom in their hearts, and also He required their complete obedience to all that He commanded, 36. 1. They would not miss anything out, nor would they add anything extra – something else from this chapter for us to keep in mind. Aholiab and Bezaleel are remarkably like Stephen, of whom we read in Acts chapter 6.

In the rest of Exodus 36 no other names are credited with making the curtains and the clasps to join them, the boards and their silver sockets and bars, the beautifully embroidered vail the colourful door curtain, and the pillars for each. But we may be sure that when the Lord's people saw the completed structure, they would be so glad that they had contributed to it. Will we have cause to rejoice in the day of Christ, Phil. 2. 16, because of what we contributed in our day of opportunity here?

March 20th
Exodus 37; Psalm 89. 19-52; Acts 22. 1-21

SHITTIM WOOD AND PURE GOLD

To construct the four things detailed in Exodus chapter 37 and to be placed inside the tabernacle itself, only two materials were selected – shittim (or acacia) wood and pure gold. Note the two descriptors, for just any kind of wood or any type of gold would not do. It is generally agreed that acacia wood is resistant to decay and durable for centuries. Pure gold has great value and beauty. On a practical level, it is pliable and can be worked into shape quite easily.

These four items of tabernacle furniture were not only to be functional but also to be beautiful. They point us to Christ, so the construction materials were selected by God Himself to remind us of the deity and humanity of our Lord.

But now let us say further that the ark with its mercy seat shows us the basis of our communion with God, and the accessibility of His throne for us to find grace to help in time of need, Heb. 4. 16. Similarly the table can represent our fellowship with Him and with each other when we feed upon Christ from the scriptures, 1 John. 1. 3. The seven-branched lampstand can signify our light in a dark world, Phil. 2. 15. The incense altar, the place for the blood of atonement, points us to Calvary, Luke 23. 33. For the believer, all of these things are **durable and precious**, for a lifetime on earth, and in greater measure for eternity.

Aholiab's and Bezaleel's materials were durable and precious. This is the type of material we should use in our work for the Lord. It can be Godward or manward, our priesthood is both holy and royal, but whatever it is, we must be careful what we build with. 1 Corinthians chapter 3 reminds us that in the local assembly the foundation of all true spiritual work is Christ, secure, durable, precious, and beautiful. The challenge is, 'Let every man take heed how he buildeth thereupon', v. 10.

So are we building with gold, silver, precious stones? Are our contributions spiritually beautiful, valuable, and durable? That is what is needed for adorning the house of God, for helping and encouraging the saints, for reaching the lost with the gospel.

March 21st
Exodus 38; **Psalms 90-91**; Acts 22. 22 – 23. 11

YEARS AND DAYS

Psalm 90, written by Moses, may be the oldest one in the book. The first verse notes our ancestry, then verse 2 takes us back to pre-creation and then to eternity. It is a psalm about *man who is mortal* and his *God who is eternal*. Our seventy or eighty years pass so quickly, v. 10. We say, 'How time flies!' But for God even a thousand years are as nothing, v. 4.

This psalm is first about our **years and their brevity.** Think about them passing! The years which measure our life on earth are likened to a night-time sleep over by morning, v. 5; a crop of grass mown down by evening, v. 6; and a tale that is told, v. 9. WILLIAM SHAKESPEARE took this one up and said it was like 'a tale told by an idiot, full of sound and fury, signifying nothing'! How tragic if that were to describe any of us!

So let's ask three questions about the story of our lives:

(1) Is it worth reading and is it well written? People do read us every day! We are an 'epistle of Christ', 'known and read of all men', 2 Cor. 3. 2-3.

(2) Does it have a serious meaning – are we living consistent Christian lives in the light of eternity, or are we imposters?

(3) How long is it? We have no control over this one, but we know that short stories are sometimes better than long ones. However long or short it is, what really matters is: how it will end? Will we 'finish our course with joy'? Acts 20. 24.

All these years are made up of **days and their opportunity.** Think about their potential! We must 'number [them and] apply our hearts unto wisdom', v. 12. They may be days of gladness, v. 14, or days of affliction, v. 15, but each one comes with its potential for good or bad, for success or failure, to be used or wasted. And they don't come our way again.

Every day the Master is looking for labourers to work in His vineyard, for shepherds to tend His flock, and for sons who will be about their Father's business. These days of ours are days of opportunity and responsibility, preceding a great day of accountability, a day of recompense and reward. Will you give account with joy and not with grief, Heb. 13. 17?

March 22nd

Exodus 39; Psalms 92-93; **Acts 23. 12-35**

GREAT DANGER, GREAT RESCUE

God has just given a welcome reassurance to His beleaguered servant, in danger of being torn to pieces by an angry Jewish mob: 'Be of good cheer, Paul, you must bear witness also at Rome'. That is God's purpose for him and nothing can thwart it.

But now this purpose is threatened. A desperate plot is hatched to kill Paul. More than forty fanatical Jews bind themselves by a curse, neither to eat nor drink until they have killed him in an ambush. In hindsight we wonder if they starved to death! However, a curious young lad overheard their plot.

Think about this lad, a teenager perhaps, Paul's nephew who must have cared about his uncle – in the right place at the right time! God has His servants everywhere, sometimes the smaller they are the better so that their size does not obstruct their work! So we notice first how God uses someone small and weak to confound many who are mighty and arrogant, 1 Cor. 1. 27. A similar thing happened when Gideon's 300 men defeated the mighty host of Midian, Judg. 7.

But next we see how God is going to use something large and powerful to protect Paul. We might even think it was excessive – four hundred soldiers and seventy cavalrymen to guard one man! Forty Jews would not stand a chance against them! And he will have the care and comfort of a beast to ride on. Similarly, Elisha was able to show his servant besieged in Dothan a 'mountain full of horses and chariots of fire', 2 Kgs. 6. 17.

So a day of plotting, of potential danger and defeat, is followed by a night of careful preparation for Paul's complete safety, and free transport to Caesarea. In two days time he was there.

Thus would be brought about the first stage of Paul's journey to Rome, as God had promised. The Lord would provide lodgings for him in the security and relative luxury of Herod's Praetorium, the official residence of the governor Felix. He would later provide free transport for him on a ship to Rome.

For us in dangerous or threatening situations, what is God's promise? 'The angel of the Lord encampeth round about them that fear him, and delivereth them', Ps. 34. 7.

March 23rd
Exodus 40; Psalms 94-95; Acts 24. 1-23
A BLESSED NEW YEAR'S DAY

The first year of the wilderness journey had been eventful, to say the least! But at the start of their second year, something wonderful and beautiful was now happening, recorded at the end of this book of Exodus.

A great work of construction was completed: 'the tabernacle was reared up', v. 17, and every part of it, great and small, was 'as the Lord commanded Moses'. Count how many times this phrase occurs in this and the previous chapter! Then 'the glory of the Lord filled the tabernacle', v. 34, and this glory cloud would lead the nation all the way to the fair land of promise. What a blessed way to start a year! What a blessed way to live every day of the year – obeying the Lord's commands in all we do, enjoying the Lord's presence each step of the journey home!

For yet a third time, although much more briefly and tersely, the Lord tells Moses how everything must be done in preparing a dwelling place for Him in the midst of His people. The instructions never altered! God never changes His mind! Even at the very end of the Old Testament when things had gone from bad to worse, the call is still, 'Remember the law of Moses my servant', Mal. 4. 4. No changing the original word of God to accommodate a new way of life!

Only when it is all done in the way that God commanded, in every prescribed detail, do we read that 'Moses finished the work', v. 33. In some respects he is like another great servant of the Lord who said, 'I have finished my course, I have kept the faith', 2 Tim. 4. 7. '*Then* a cloud covered the tent', v. 34. God set His seal of approval of all that Moses and the children of Israel had done. It is God's 'Well done' spoken in a cloud of glory.

On this occasion Moses could not enter the tabernacle because of the glory which filled it. At the call of God, he had entered the glory of God's presence on Mount Sinai some months before this. When he came down his face shone with the radiance of a reflected glory which the people could not bear to look at. But, here, all we see is the glory of God filling the tabernacle, for 'every whit of it uttereth His glory', Ps. 29. 9 KJV mg.

March 24th
Leviticus 1; Psalms 96-98; Acts 24. 24 – 25. 12

OFFERINGS OLD AND NEW

In Exodus chapter 40 verse 29 we read that Moses offered for the first time on the newly constructed brazen altar 'the burnt offering and the meat offering'. Leviticus will now give the details of these, and describe many other ceremonies, sacrifices, and offerings which from then on would be expected from the redeemed and sanctified people of God.

We come first to a description of, and a prescription for, the burnt offering, for God's requirements are precise because they are meaningful. This one in particular would be referred to as a 'continual burnt offering', first in Exodus chapter 29 verse 42, then several times in Numbers chapter 28. Also we read that priests would offer 'oftentimes the same sacrifices which can never take away sins', Heb. 10. 11. So what was the point of all the repetition? The Epistle to the Hebrews tells us.

For them, these offerings did two things: (1) They enabled godly Israelites to show their gratitude to God, not by duty or compulsion, but by freewill. The first three offerings described in Leviticus were of this type. God is always glorified in His people's frequent acts of gratitude. (2) They ensured that God's people would not remain estranged from Him because of their sin. The sin and trespass offerings were obligatory, designed to demonstrate the grace of God along with His holiness.

For us, these sacrifices also do at least two things: (1) They help us to worship God and rejoice in Christ, for He is the perfect fulfilment of all that these offerings mean. For example, He is the perfect 'burnt offering', the One whose strength and purpose, whose inward motives and outward actions were entirely pure and for the glory of God. These offerings are 'figures', 'patterns', 'shadows' of better things to come, indeed of Him who was to come, Heb. 9. 9, 23; 10. 1. We can now, and we often should, come right into the heavenly sanctuary and offer our better sacrifices, the fruit of our lips, praising His name, 13. 15. (2) They show us the superiority of the sacrifice of Christ, that one sacrifice once offered to take away sins, 10. 12. By His one offering He has perfected us for ever, v. 14. Blessed be His name!

March 25th
Leviticus 2; **Psalms 99-101**; Acts 25. 13-27

HOW IS YOUR SINGING?

Have you noticed how many of these psalms we are reading this week are about singing? So how is your singing? It's not a question of how good a singer you are or want to be, but rather why, and how, and when, and where, and what do you sing.

Psalm 99 focuses on the fact that God is great and holy, so it is at His footstool and at His holy hill we worship Him with reverence and praise Him in awe. In Psalm 101 the subject is God's mercy and judgement, and so the singer wants to match his behaviour to his song, 'in a perfect way'.

In Psalm 100 there is a threefold call, vv. 1-2, to 'make a joyful noise', to serve with gladness, and to sing. The reason for this is the intelligent realization that **the Lord is God, our Creator**.

All that we are physically and mentally, individually and unitedly, has come from Him. In no sense are we self-made: we did not make ourselves, v. 3. Elsewhere, David said, 'I will praise thee, for I am fearfully and wonderfully made', Ps. 139. 14. It is nonsense to think that we evolved from nothing by a long unplanned chain of random events. No, we are His people and He loves us; we are the sheep of His pasture and He feeds us.

In verse 4 there is another threefold call: to thank Him, to praise Him, and to bless Him. The reason is that **the Lord is good, our Redeemer** whose mercy and truth are everlasting.

We can and should sing and praise Him individually wherever we are. He even 'gives songs in the night', Job 35. 10. But, in verse 4, the call is to 'enter His gates', 'into His courts', surely a reminder that we should *gather with others* to unite in our songs of worship and thanksgiving. Isn't it wonderful to blend your voice with others in the local church? When the praise reaches His ear in heaven, how good to know that you have contributed to it. God's ancient people were exhorted to appear before Him three times in the year, and none were to come empty-handed, Deut. 16. 16. So be sure to come and contribute to the singing, 'with the spirit and with the understanding also', 1 Cor. 14. 15.

Soon we'll be singing in heaven, better than ever, but for the same reasons – He created us; He redeemed us, Rev. 4. 11; 5. 9.

March 26th
Leviticus 3; **Psalm 102**; Acts 26. 1-18

A DAY OF GRIEF AND YEARS OF GLORY

Psalms 22, 69, and 102 each describe prophetically 'the sufferings of Christ, and the glory that should follow', 1 Pet. 1. 11. In Psalm 102 we can see how earnest prayer gives way to eternal praise, how a lonely day of trouble and weeping leads on to years of joy and praise in the great company of all the children of God.

This is one of five psalms entitled 'a prayer'. A few before this have been songs, the next few will be praises. We would have had no songs or praises had our Lord Jesus not experienced the weeping, the real sufferings and sorrows described in this prayer.

On the cross it was all so real for Him: Psalm 22 reminds us how He was forsaken and brought into the dust of death; Psalm 69 how far down He sank under the floods of God's judgement; this psalm how keenly He felt the loneliness of these hours when 'his own self bare our sins in his own body on the tree', 1 Pet. 2. 24; alone in all His grief and pain, with none to take pity, no one to share that awful load, as a 'sparrow alone upon the housetop'.

The Psalm can be read under three headings:

Prayer of the Suffering Saviour – His grief at Calvary;

Praise of His Gathered Servants – His glory in Zion;

Permanence of His Chosen Seed – His greatness through eternity.

Calvary's grief is described in a prayer, vv. 1-11; a dark day of unfathomed sorrow. The Psalm tells of 'days' that are 'troubled', 'consumed', 'reproached', 'withered', 'shortened'. There never was a day like it for Christ – days like a declining shadow, v. 11.

God's favour to Zion and its people is described, vv. 12-22. The Lord is now appearing in His glory, v. 16, in the height of the sanctuary, v. 19. The time of divine favour has arrived, and the praise is loud and long. For Israel, that time is future, but we can enjoy it today, and should already be praising Him all the more.

Then *eternity's bliss* is described, vv. 23-28; His greatness endures forever. He is the same. His chosen seed is established. As we read again, 'his servants shall serve him; and they shall see his face', Rev. 22. 3. What a wonderful eternal future is ours because a lonely, dark day of sorrow was His!

March 27th
Leviticus 4. 1-26; **Psalm 103**; Acts 26. 19-32
BLESS THE LORD, O MY SOUL
Reading Psalm 103 brings to mind JOHNSON OATMAN'S familiar hymn, 'Count your blessings', and the less orthodox but entirely correct version which continues, 'name them by the score, and it will surprise you there are millions more'.

At the beginning and end of this psalm we call upon our souls to 'bless the Lord'. The reasons are numerous and precious. We can bless (i.e., thank and praise) Him only because He has first so abundantly blessed us. Similarly, 'We love him because he first loved us', 1 John 4. 19. The psalm starts and finishes by being personal and individual, but expands to be congregational and universal, so abundant and widespread are God's blessings.

His individual benefits are to be remembered, vv. 1-5. The pronoun is 'my' or 'thy'. Here are six wonderful benefits which God in His amazing grace has bestowed upon each one of us. These are both temporal and eternal, physical and spiritual, for God cares about everything we need. We have even been renewed, v. 5, 'a new creation in Christ Jesus', 2 Cor. 5. 17.

His shared mercies are to be recalled, vv. 6-18. The pronouns are 'us' and 'our', and extending to 'them that fear him'. First, these mercies deal with our sins, removing them from us as far as east is from west, an immeasurable distance, even as the height (or depth) of His mercy cannot be measured, v. 11. After that we learn about His compassionate mercies for our feeble and frail frames which are but dust, yet crafted and sustained by His mighty power and wisdom, mortal, but precious in His sight. Because of this we should be those who 'fear him', and 'remember his commandments to do them'.

His universal dominion is to be recognized, vv. 19-22, with the pronoun 'his' ten times. It's all about the Lord. We read of His stable, heavenly throne, and His earthly and universal kingdom; of His strong angels and His obedient seraphim; of adoring hosts above and servants everywhere who are willing to do His pleasure. All His works in all places are now summoned to bless the Lord, everyone, everywhere. But finally, may this praise never be silent within our souls!

March 28th

Leviticus 4. 27 – 5. 13; Psalm 104; **Acts 27. 1-26**

DANGERS ON THE DEEP

Here begins the longest part of Paul's journey to Rome, as 'a prisoner of Jesus Christ'. Julius is one of several kind and helpful centurions we read of in the New Testament.

The voyage begins at Caesarea in a ship which would take them past Cyprus to Myra on a promontory of Lycia, the route being decided by the expected direction of the autumn trade winds. At Myra they transfer to a corn supply vessel bound for Rome from Alexandria, and set sail for Crete. What a surprise lies ahead of that ship's company of 276 persons!

Ignoring Paul's advice to remain in Crete for the winter, and lulled into a false sense of security by a fine southerly wind, out they go. Then disaster strikes! Fierce Euroclydon sweeps down upon them, tearing sails and shrouds, threatening the integrity of the wooden ship, making them jettison cargo, and eventually resign themselves to their fate. How realistically it is described – an eyewitness account by Luke!

Onto the heaving deck of this apparently doomed ship someone steps forward. It's a prisoner who takes command! They won't ignore Paul this time. Here is a man with a word from God! He rebukes their stubbornness, but doesn't stay there.

His message has three strands, v. 25. Firstly, it is **encouragement,** 'Be of good cheer!' Then it is about **trust,** 'I believe God'. Finally it is a message of **hope,** 'It shall be even as it was told me' – there will be no loss of life. The storm wasn't over, but here was a message to hold on to as long as the storm lasted!

What do we do in the storms of life? What can we hold on to? Anchors can drift, cables can snap, sails can tear, and ships can leak and sink. All human resources can falter and fail.

But we have a hope, an anchor of the soul, sure and steadfast, fastened 'within the veil', Heb. 6. 19. The Lord Jesus Himself, 'the Forerunner' has entered heaven for us. Look to Him for the **encouragement** you need. **Trust** in Him whose word never fails. He is our **hope** – for present grace and future glory.

When you find others in deep trouble or despair, that's the kind of message you should take to them, too.

March 29th
Leviticus 5. 14 – 6. 7; Psalm 105; **Acts 27. 27-44**

SAFE AT LAST ON MALTA

If you had never read this story before, you would be on the edge of your seat, wondering what was going to happen next! It is so graphically described by Luke as he relives it, maybe some months later. He never mentions himself, but for him too it was a marvel of divine providence and protection.

There are fourteen more days and nights of seething tempest. Then, at midnight, experienced seamen with their uncanny ability detect a critical change: land is near, and with it the possibility of total shipwreck. No matter how dangerous it is out on the sea, most ships are wrecked on the shoreline.

Again Paul takes the lead, first to foil an attempt by the sailors to abandon ship and leave all the others to their fate. Then, at daybreak, he encourages them all with a further confirmation of their safety. He advises them to eat some food, backing this up by his own example, and giving thanks to God 'in the presence of them all'. This was more than 'grace before meat'. Can you imagine what he said as his voice rang out above the howling wind and crashing waves?

Stronger daylight showed a possible landing place on an unknown shore. St Paul's Bay in northeast Malta is traditionally the place – at least that's for today's tourists! But here were no tourists, and the swim to the shore was no keep-fit exercise. Those on boards were not surfing for a thrill – it was survival mode!

The ship broke up, such was the violence of the huge breakers, but no one was hurt. The proposal to kill off the prisoners was given short shrift, thanks again to that good centurion Julius. And 'they escaped all to land'.

Isn't it wonderful how God works out His own plans? He uses people when He wishes, but can work without any. When our Lord was here, He alone calmed a severe storm on the Sea of Galilee, bringing His scared disciples safe to land, comfortable and dry, marvelling at the greatness of His power. In this instance, He used several people and circumstances to bring these folk safe to land, but cold and wet and hungry! Watch what He will do for them next, and who He will use to do it!

March 30th

Leviticus 6. 8 – 7. 10; Psalm 106; **Acts 28. 1-16**

ON TOWARDS ROME

'We came to Rome' is the climax of our story in v. 16. But what a journey it has been – at least 1600 miles by sea and land with no short cuts, rather detours! It's perhaps a picture of the journey of life: the onward course unexpected and uncharted, but the destination sure!

This last stage on Malta is full of interest and instruction. 'The present rain and the cold', v. 2, would stretch the endurance of already wet and miserable survivors coming out of the surf. Making a fire on the beach was going to give some temporary comfort, and Paul wasn't too preoccupied to join in the effort and contribute his bundle of sticks. But then a viper came out of the fire and fastened on Paul's hand – was that going to defeat him at last? Many of them thought so! Would it be the last straw?

No! Neither tempest nor cold, neither natural serpents nor the Evil One himself (pictured in that viper), could thwart God's purpose for His servant. Reading 2 Corinthians chapter 11 verses 25–27 we note how Paul would recall such perils and why.

The people of Malta showed great kindness to these strangers – that was real 'hospitality', Heb. 13. 2. But, in return, many of these heathen folk received a blessing. Paul graciously brought healing and help to them, one whom they had thought was a murderer, a god, or just a strange prisoner who had survived a terrible storm. No doubt they would hear the gospel too – seed was sown that would bear fruit later perhaps.

After three months, the voyage resumed in another ship and, after two more ports of call, it brought them all to Puteoli, 'where we found brethren', 28. 14. Then, more brethren came to meet him at Appii Forum, and Paul 'thanked God, and took courage'. Isn't it always a great encouragement to meet fellow Christians?

It is important to minister to others, to bring help and courage to the weak, to use every opportunity to spread the gospel, but, in addition, the company of brothers and sisters in Christ is special – and indispensible on the journey home. This is true wherever we are. Even when they meet for the first time, Christians have that special bond of love and fellowship which others don't have.

March 31st

Leviticus 7. 11-38; **Psalm 107**; Acts 28. 17-31

OH THAT MEN WOULD PRAISE THE LORD!

'In everything give thanks', says Paul, 1 Thess. 5. 18, and in Hebrews chapter 13 verse 15 we read, 'By him [Christ] therefore let us offer the sacrifice of praise to God continually'.

Psalm 107 states this in different and specific ways. Praises follow answered prayers – or they ought to, for here we read four times, 'Oh that men would praise the Lord for his goodness, and for his wonderful works to the children of men'.

There can be no doubt in our minds that the Lord is good, v. 1, and that 'his mercy endureth for ever'. But do we remember to 'say so'? And to say so *often*? That is our challenge today, for we too have been redeemed and gathered, vv. 2-3, redeemed out of sin's slavery and gathered to His precious name. How we ought to thank and praise Him at all times, whether on our own, in our homes, or in our assembly gatherings!

This psalm, perhaps, follows the varied experiences of the *nation of Israel* – from Egypt to Canaan, later into captivity and dispersion, then at the end into millennial blessings. But we can find in it at least four reasons why we should often praise the God of *our* salvation, for it contains our spiritual history too.

Our wanderings have **ceased**, vv. 4-9. We have been delivered from our distresses. Our longing souls are now satisfied with His gracious provision. We are filled with all *the goodness of God*. Praise Him for all that!

Our bondage has been **broken**, vv. 10-16. We have been brought out from the shadow of death. When there was no one to help we were freed by the *power of God*. Praise Him for that!

Our afflictions are **healed**, vv. 17-22. When we stumble, His word reaches, corrects, comforts, and strengthens us. We rejoice at the ongoing *work of God* in our lives. Praise Him for that!

Our dangers are **averted**, vv. 23-32. Storms often come while we 'do business' on the sea of life. At our wit's end, we cry and He comes, and we receive *the peace of God*. Praise Him for that!

So it's about praises for answered prayers, for mercies that are new every morning, for blessings temporal and eternal, for Christ who saves and satisfies! Oh give thanks unto the Lord!

April 1st
Leviticus 8; Psalm 108; **Mark 1. 1-20**
THE PREACHING AND PRIORITIES OF THE KINGDOM

Mark begins his narrative of Christ very differently from the other Gospel writers. It is the quick-paced, straight-forward, action-packed record of the perfect Servant, doing His perfect work. Absent is a noble genealogy, such as is found in both Matthew and Luke. The 'beginning' in verse 1 refers to the commencement of His earthly ministry, and stands in contrast to the lofty description of the eternal Son who was in the beginning with God, John 1. 2. There is no long introduction, no angelic display, and no glorious pronouncements. Instead, we are immediately immersed in the activities of the Messiah and His messenger John, who prepares the way for Him who 'came not to be served but to serve and to give His life a ransom for many', Mark 10. 45 ESV.

The importance of preaching is evident in this chapter. First, John gives a message of repentance to prepare the hearts of his audience in acknowledging their sin, 1. 4. He does not accommodate them; they go out to him, v. 5. This truth should challenge every generation of preachers to keep the same high standard and to examine the content of their message. That episode is followed by preaching that extols the worthiness of the One who alone could meet their need, vv. 7-8. Afterwards, the Lord preaches a similar message of repentance, v. 15. It is always good when our words are in line with His! Here we find preaching in the wilderness, preaching in Galilee, v. 14, and later preaching in the synagogue of the Jews, v. 39. The preaching of the word should be everywhere and to everyone.

The baptism of our Lord and His temptation in the wilderness are also recorded in this account. He identifies with His own, sin apart, 2 Cor. 5. 21. His baptism underscores the importance of this priority in public testimony for all true believers. The voice from heaven, v. 11, heard later on the mount, Luke 9. 35, and echoed again prior to the cross, John 12. 28, signified the Father's approval. The dove, a symbol of the Holy Spirit, foreshadowed His ministry of reconciliation and offer of peace with God. The passage concludes with a call to discipleship and a commitment to evangelism, further priorities for us in our service for Him.

April 2nd

Leviticus 9; **Psalms 109-110**; Mark 1. 21-45

A CRY FOR GOD'S INTERVENTION

Psalm 109 portrays the anguish of heart that the psalmist experienced when vilified by his adversaries. Though standing for righteousness, he was falsely accused, v. 2, engulfed by hateful words, v. 3, and rewarded evil for good, v. 5. In response to his love, v. 4, his character was maligned, his heart wounded, v. 22, and his soul condemned, v. 31. But despite the mistreatment he received, and its physical consequences, vv. 23-24, he did not take matters into his own hands, but rather gave himself to prayer. He called for divine retribution in proportion to the measure dealt to him, vv. 17-18. His cry was for vindication, v. 21. This cry for God's vengeance has been echoed by the righteous who have been persecuted for righteousness' sake by those who despise God and His people. By contrast, our Lord clearly teaches a very different approach towards our enemies – love, Matt. 5. 44.

But this Psalm also foreshadows the multitude of injustices suffered by our Lord during His earthly ministry. He too was maligned, falsely accused, and rewarded evil for good. He was compassed about with words of contempt, Luke 23. 33-43, cp. Ps. 22. 16, fought against without a cause, John 8. 46; 19. 6, and betrayed by Judas, whose days would indeed be few and his office filled by another, Ps. 109. 8, Luke 22. 48. Like the psalmist, He gave Himself to prayer, but how different a prayer it was! 'Father, forgive them for they know not what they do' was His cry. With it, He opened a final 'city of refuge', where the sinner can find a safe haven from the punishment that his actions deserve, Heb. 6. 18.

When it comes to persecution, our natural inclination is to retaliate. Like James and John, we want to call down fire from heaven upon those who do not side with us, Luke 9. 54. But, instead of taking this path, we should follow the steps of our Saviour who did not threaten or revile, but rather commit our souls unto Him who judges righteously, 1 Pet. 2. 21-23.

Psalm 110 verse 1 tells us that God will make His enemies His footstool when He judges the world in righteousness by the Man He has ordained, Acts 17. 31. Until then, let us pray for our enemies that we may glorify God and win them for Christ.

108

April 3rd

Leviticus 10; Psalms 111-112; **Mark 2. 1-22**

GOD'S WORK IN SALVATION

In our reading today, we notice two different ways in which God brings about salvation. In verses 1 to 12, He uses those who are available and willing to serve as His instruments. In verses 13 to 17, we see how He draws people to Himself through the power of His word. One takes place in a building; the other takes place at a tax booth. Both however affirm the efficacy of His call. These calls are witnessed by many and bear fruit to the glory of God.

When the Lord entered Capernaum, it was not long before a crowd gathered to hear His words. Such was the character of the early years of the Lord's earthly ministry. There was a favourable audience at this stage. How different it would be later at Calvary, Luke 23. 33-39! The fact that He preached the word to them, Mark 2. 2, again highlights the importance of sharing the scriptures whenever the opportunity is provided. The message to the helpless paralytic carried by four friends was one of forgiveness. It was offered in response to an observable faith, v. 5, exhibited on their part by diligence in overcoming the obstacles to bring their friend to Christ, and exhibited by the paralytic in that he would walk away, bed in hand, v. 12. The word spoken to the sceptical scribes that 'the Son of Man has power on earth to forgive sins', v. 10 NKJV, not only conveys the truth that forgiveness is available through Him alone, but also that He has power to forgive only while they are on earth. Salvation is never attainable after death, Rev. 22. 11. The entire account should therefore speak to us of the cooperative effort we should make in helping others come to Christ before it is too late.

In the case of Levi, conversion came as a result of a simple, yet powerful call, 'Follow Me'. There was no coercion and no coaxing. There was no drawn out debate or conversation. Neither were there friends to assist. Instead, the change was accomplished privately in the heart, yet it effected great outward results. Levi had his 'connections' – the lower echelons of society, desperately in need of the Physician, v. 17. His provision of a feast evidenced a true change of heart and demonstrates that a wider mission field is often opened with every conversion experience.

April 4th
Leviticus 11; Psalms 113-115; Mark 2. 23 – 3. 12

THE CLEAN AND THE UNCLEAN

This chapter, like Deuteronomy chapter 14, lays out the dietary regulations established by God for the nation of Israel. It classifies what is clean and unclean into four main groups: living things on the earth, vv. 1-8; in the water, vv. 9-12, in the air, vv. 13-19, and insects, vv. 20-23. The second half of the chapter deals with the laws regarding defilement and its remedy. The purpose of this highly detailed chapter is summarized in the last two verses: that Israel may distinguish between the holy and unholy, v. 47, a theme that continues for the next four chapters.

God's purpose in calling Israel from among the nations was to demonstrate the blessing of following the one true God. At Sinai, He declared that He had brought them to Himself to be a peculiar treasure above all peoples, Exod. 19. 4-5. It was to reinforce in their thinking that they were different and expected to live by a higher standard than the nations around them. When Balaam was hired by the King of Moab to curse Israel as they approached the Promised Land, all he saw was a people dwelling alone, not 'reckoned among the nations', Num. 23. 9. Instead of cursing, he blessed, and what he blessed he could not reverse, v. 20. Israel indeed was different. Of no other nation could it be said that God found them, led them, instructed them, and kept them as the apple of His eye, Deut. 32. 10. By establishing these dietary laws, He was teaching, in clear terms, what constituted for them the clean and the unclean, partly for purposes of health and hygiene, but even more so for unquestioning obedience to His word.

But there are other spiritual lessons that emerge from this chapter. The nations deified and worshipped many of these creatures more than the Creator, Rom. 1. 25. These laws helped Israel to remain separated. Believers are not to live by the standards of the world. Instead, like that which is clean, they should feed on the word of God, lifting their thoughts above the filth of this world. Further, Peter's vision of unclean animals on the white sheet let down from heaven portrays the way that God has cleansed through the blood of Christ that which is unclean by nature, Acts 10. 15; cp. Rev. 1. 5.

April 5th

Leviticus 12. 1 – 13. 23; **Psalms 116-117**; Mark 3. 13-35

LOVE FOR THE LORD

Here is the expression of a heart overflowing with thanksgiving for deliverance from a life-threatening situation, v. 1. Most attribute these words to David, though some see in it the experience of Jonah, as words in verse 18 reflect those of the runaway prophet, Jonah 2. 9. It relates the gratitude of one of God's own, who narrowly escaped the jaws of death, to utter the praises of the Lord. It describes the psalmist's agony and ecstasy – the agony of a frightening near-death experience, v. 3, and the ecstasy and joyful exhilaration of divine help, vv. 12-14.

The reason for the writer's affliction is not directly stated; reasons for the trials we go through often are not revealed. Some trials may be *punitive* as with Jehoshaphat, 2 Chr. 19. 2, and others *corrective* as with Job. Whatever the situation may have been here, there was some measure of doubt in the psalmist's heart, who, in the midst of his distress, called all men liars, v. 11. Numerous doubts may surface as we go through the valley of the shadow of death. But the fiery trials that threaten to overwhelm us can result in a deeper conviction, v. 10, a reaffirmation of relationship, and a new-found liberty, v. 16. Trials can loosen our bonds, deepen our faith, and heighten our resolve. Daniel's friends discovered this truth in the fiery furnace, and so did Paul who drew upon the psalmist's brush with death to teach the lessons of faith to the Corinthians, 2 Cor. 4. 13-17. As harrowing as they may be, these 'light afflictions' work for us a far more exceeding and eternal weight of glory, a glory that will be revealed at the appearing of Jesus Christ, 1 Pet. 1. 7. The result is joy now, honour and praise then.

The writer declares his four unswerving 'I wills', as should we, when we come through our trials. He steadfastly asserts: 'I will walk before the Lord', v. 9; 'I will take the cup of salvation', v. 13; 'I will pay my vows', vv. 14, 18; 'I will offer to thee the sacrifice of thanksgiving and will call upon the name of the Lord', v. 17. It is the praise He desires from everyone, as Psalm 117, the middle chapter of the Bible, affirms. God's merciful kindness is great toward all and His truth endures forever. Praise the Lord!

April 6th

Leviticus 13. 24 -59; **Psalm 118**; Mark 4. 1-20

I SHALL NOT DIE BUT LIVE

This is the sixth and last of the Egyptian Hallel Psalms that were sung by Israel with the celebration of the Passover. It is quite possible that our Lord sang this Psalm with His disciples on the night of His betrayal, Matt. 26. 30. It clearly prefigured the events leading to Calvary, the full display of the builders' rejection of the Stone of Israel, Gen. 49. 24. It is decidedly messianic in its overtones, and very helpful for those who have stared death in the face, Ps. 118. 17.

As with many of the Psalms, a summary statement declaring the goodness and grace of God begins the writer's thoughts. It is an unwavering call to Israel and to all those 'who fear the Lord' to praise our God, vv. 1-4. What follows is the reason for such action: to highlight the Lord's intervention amidst the circumstances that caused such alarm. The psalmist was compassed about by his enemies and targeted in order that he might fall, suggesting the experiences of David, but Moses also, as God's appointed deliverer of His people. Prophetically it describes the travail of the Son of God. Each one called out in their distress, and each one was convinced they would ultimately prevail with God's help, vv. 6-13, though the Saviour's experience was on a higher plane with deeper purposes to accomplish, Ps. 22. 1, 30. He it was who humbled Himself and stooped to allow His creatures to treat Him so. The pattern is put before us so that we may follow His steps and learn to put our confidence in God and not in man. Paul could have boasted of his confidence in the flesh, but instead he was quick to affirm that his rejoicing was in Christ Jesus alone, Phil. 3. 3. Whether it is Moses or David or you or me, the question remains: where have we placed our hope and confidence?

The bigger picture in this Psalm however is the rejection of the Stone which the builders refused. He came unto His own and His own received Him not. It was a miscarriage of justice, but marvellous in the Lord's eyes and ours, v. 23. The sacrifice was bound to the horns of the altar, v. 27, the Lord laying on Him the iniquity of us all. As a result of these great events we may say, 'This is the day . . . let us rejoice and be glad in it', v. 24.

April 7th
Leviticus 14. 1-32; Psalm 119. 1-40; Mark 4. 21-41
CONTAMINATED NOW CLEAN

When the Lord Jesus instructed the ten lepers to show themselves to the priests in Luke chapter 17 verse 14, it was in accordance with the words that are found in today's reading. Whether this was accomplished before this time is debatable, but, if it was, it was never recorded in scripture.

The law of the cleansing of the leper was not the process by which a leper was healed, but rather a declaration that healing had *already taken place*. It was the means by which the leper was ceremonially cleansed, restored and brought back into the congregation. That process involved being brought to the priest, v. 1, who would then go outside the camp to examine and verify the claim of healing, v. 3. Next, followed a ritual that involved one bird being killed over running water, v. 5, and its blood sprinkled seven times over the leper, vv. 5-6. The other bird, which had also been dipped in blood, was let loose to fly freely in the open field. Afterwards, the leper was washed, shaved, and allowed into the camp for seven days, but not inside his tent, vv. 7-9. On the eighth day, at the door of the tabernacle, two male lambs and one ewe lamb were sacrificed and their blood, along with oil, was applied to the leper's right ear, right thumb, and big toe of the right foot, vv. 14-20. A similar procedure took place for poor lepers also, vv. 21-32. Wonderfully, God had made provision for them to be healed, cleansed, and rescued from their miserable situation.

Marvellous are the pictures of salvation and restoration brought before us in this passage. The leper portrays the sinner brought to our great High Priest who applies the blood to the one in need. The first bird pictures the death of Christ; the other bird, His resurrection, Rom. 6. 6-11; 2 Cor. 4. 11. The redeemed sinner, with blood applied, and cleansed through the washing of regeneration, is seen as having died with Christ yet united in His resurrection to listen to, work for, and walk in the ways of God, as depicted by the blood on the ear, thumb, and toe. It is the same outcome for the sinning believer who, through the ministry of our High Priest is also healed, cleansed, and restored to live fully for Christ. Once contaminated, now clean!

April 8th

Leviticus 14. 33-57; Psalm 119. 41-72; **Mark 5. 1-20**

THE MAN OF GADARA

Having exhibited His power over the natural realm in Mark 4, the Lord Jesus now demonstrates His power over the supernatural. The tempest that beset the disciples on the Sea of Galilee now raged in a different way in the soul of this man from Gadara. Despite the intensity of each, both disciple and demoniac were calmed by the hand of the One who had power and authority over death, disease, and the demons. He rules over all.

Coming ashore to the land of the Gadarenes, the disciples were immediately confronted by this individual with an unclean spirit, v. 2. It would not be the last time for them that a difficulty emerged following a fearful experience, Luke 9. 34-40. Trials often come in droves – all the more reason to stay close to the Lord as we travel through this world, Ps. 63. 8. The scene presents death and self-destruction: a helpless, hopeless incorrigible, dominated by evil influences, unchained and untamed, running among the tombs. Some of the devil's subjects operate undetected for a time, Mark 1. 21-28; others, like this man, are visible to all and instil fear, even from a distance.

The gripping scenes of this narrative bring before us the remedy for such a pitiful condition. The power of darkness, though strong is not stronger than the Lord, John 1. 5. With just a word, the demons flee to the swine, a new source of uncleanness and a new object of their destructive influence. The man who previously had been naked and deranged is now found sitting clothed and in his right mind, clear evidence of the great reversal that took place in his life. Delivered from what was surely 'so great a death', cp. 2 Cor. 1. 10, he now had a 'so great salvation', Heb. 2. 3. It is ironic that the townspeople, after witnessing the strange events that occurred that day, pleaded to have the Lord leave the region, Mark 5. 17. It is testimony to the darkness of men's hearts that they collectively sought to drive away the Lord of life. In contrast, the man begged to stay with Him, v. 18, and, later, headed home to his friends to publish his testimony, its transforming effect later confirmed, 7. 31-37. Only Christ can change a life so dramatically!

April 9th
Leviticus 15; Psalm 119. 73-112; Mark 5. 21-43
GOD'S REQUIREMENT FOR HOLINESS

Leviticus chapter 15 pictures for us the requirement of holiness in every aspect of the believer's life. Whether in leisure or in labour, vv. 5, 9, or in public, v. 10, or private, v. 16ff., there is always the need for personal vigilance to maintain the standard that God declares. In our sin-stained world in which uncleanness is so easily excused, God's holy word holds high the standard for every generation. So aptly Isaiah proclaimed this sad reality: 'I am a man of unclean lips, and dwell in the midst of a people of unclean lips', Isa. 6. 5. He knew it well, though it seems the people did not, hence the reason why God chose him to go. Anyone moving more closely toward the Lord will always sense their own inadequacy and will cry out in utter despair for cleansing. It is the place that the Lord would have us to be if we would tap into His power and enjoy His presence.

Whether for salvation or sanctification, this chapter reminds us of the need to receive cleansing from sin. The Corinthians upon faith in the Lord Jesus were washed, 1 Cor. 6. 11, as is every blood-bought child of God, Rev. 1. 5. Firstly, however, must be the understanding that all our righteousnesses are as filthy rags, Isa. 64. 6. Personal sin needs to be properly dealt with. Necessary steps must be taken according to God's way. If not, the sinner will die in their sins, a truth to which the self-righteous Pharisees were blind, John 8. 24, 9. 41. Once God's way is taken, the person will be cleansed and can then 'draw near with a true heart in full assurance of faith', Heb. 10. 22. There is no doubt that, clothed with His righteousness, no suspicion will lurk as believers are 'clean every whit' in His presence.

But there is also the need for ongoing personal holiness. Believers have been given all things that pertain to life and godliness, 2 Pet. 1. 3. If there is failure, there is still a pathway to purity. The young man can cleanse his way, Ps. 119. 9, and so can the older man, like Jacob who headed back to Bethel, the place of his spiritual beginnings, Gen. 35. 1-3. Action must be taken to disinfect the contagion of our inner lives that can so easily contaminate our work, and those with whom we come in contact.

April 10th
Leviticus 16; Psalm 119. 113-144; Mark 6. 1-29
ISRAEL'S DAY OF ATONEMENT
The opening verse of this momentous chapter provides the background to the events included in this deep and highly typical portion of God's word. It deals with the Day of Atonement and the procedures ordained by the Lord to deal with the sins of His people. The immediate context was the offering of profane fire upon the altar by Nadab and Abihu. It was so that Aaron would know that he could not come 'at all times into the holy place', v. 2. It emphasized the barrier that restricted entrance into God's presence and the need to approach God through means established only by Him. The fact that the work was done by the high priest alone symbolizes the work of the Lord Jesus who had by Himself purged our sins, Heb. 1. 3.

Firstly, Aaron was instructed to wash before putting on holy garments, highlighting the need for purity in the life of the high priest who made the offering. Afterwards, two goats were taken for the sin offering and a ram for the burnt offering. A bull was offered up to atone for the sins of the high priest and those of his house, Lev. 16. 6, and the blood was sprinkled seven times on the mercy seat of the ark of the covenant in the Most Holy Place. Then, presenting the two goats at the door of the tabernacle, lots were cast. The one upon which the Lord's lot fell was offered up; the other, the scapegoat, was released into the uninhabited wilderness, representing atonement for the sins of the people.

The Lord Jesus is our great High Priest. He is the only One qualified to enter God's presence, absolutely pure, inside and out; yet, because of Him His people can enter also.

If the types in this chapter are tremendous, grander still are the differences. The Lord has no need to be washed as did Aaron, and no need to put on special garments since His are already scented with myrrh, aloes, and cassia, Ps. 45. 8. Like the high priest, He offered blood, but not every year and not with that of another, Heb. 9. 25. It was His own blood, Acts 20. 28, offered *once* at the end of the ages to bear the sins of many, Heb. 9. 28. Not merely covered, they are *put away* forever, to be seen no more.

April 11th

Leviticus 17-18; Psalm 119. 145-176; **Mark 6. 30-56**

LOAVES AND FISHES, WIND AND WAVES

Three scenes supply snapshots of the life and ministry of our blessed Lord. One is in a desert place; another is in a grassy area; the third is on the sea. Varied are the venues of our Saviour's helping hand.

The lesson in the first is all too common: too much work and not enough time to rest and reflect on the ways of the Lord. This marked the ministry of the disciples, and often marks ours as well, hence the need to come apart. They were to set aside those legitimate things that had occupied them – a good example to us in our modern, technology-driven world. Another lesson is that of doing, then teaching, v. 30. In this, they were following the pattern of the Master, Acts 1. 1, and the same for Paul and his companions, 1 Thess. 1. 6. It is a lesson we need to learn also.

The next episode is the feeding of the five thousand. Apart from the resurrection, this is the only miracle that is repeated in all four Gospels. Despite being in the wilderness, the Lord was pursued by the multitudes. Moved with compassion, v. 34, the Great Shepherd did what He does today – fed His flock like a shepherd, Isa. 40. 11. Unlike the faithless shepherds in the days of Ezekiel, He is the Shepherd who sought out His sheep, delivered them, gathered them, and brought them out, Ezek. 34. 1-23. While He was feeding the company, He was also teaching His disciples the principles of effective ministry. Firstly, there was *leadership*: 'Give ye them to eat', v. 37. The disciples wanted to send the crowd away, v. 36, but leadership is action-orientated and demands involvement if lives are to have an impact for Christ, vv. 39-40. *Relationship* is needed to bridge the gap between those in need and those who can help. It was the little lad who provided the loaves and fishes, and not the disciples, John 6. 9. Verse 42 demonstrates the mutual blessing when we give our lives to serve others. The fragments collected underscore the lesson of *stewardship.* Nothing is to be wasted in the work of the Lord.

In all, we see His gracious work in bringing His people through the storm; coming in the night, in a time of trial; and comforting with words of reassurance to strengthen their faith, vv. 50-51.

April 12th
Leviticus 19-20; **Psalms 120-123;** Mark 7. 1-23
FROM THE BOTTOM TO THE TOP

Psalms 120 to 134 are designated 'songs of degrees', literally 'ascents'. Probably they were sung in connection with the celebration of the feasts of Jehovah. During Solomon's day, they might have been sung corresponding to the fifteen steps that led to the temple mount. They may have also been sung as the captives were approaching Jerusalem returning from their Babylon captivity where they had long hung their harps, Psalm 137. In every situation we may experience the presence of God.

In Psalm 120, verses 1 and 2, the psalmist cries out to be delivered from the one who defamed his character. He took his distress to the Lord and then directed his words to the slanderer, v. 3. Verse 5 records the 'woe is me' syndrome that often characterizes us in the throes of self-pity, similar to Joshua upon his defeat at Ai, Josh. 7. 7. The psalmist relates how difficult it was to patiently wait for the Lord to act without retaliating, when evil is returned for good, v. 7, something that Peter exhorts us to do when following in the steps of the Lord, 1 Pet. 2. 23. Our low points are what make us look up in the time of trouble as the next Psalm brings out.

Psalm 121 reminds us that when matters are more than we can handle, we should look away from ourselves to Him who is our help. 'I lift up my eyes to the hills. From where does my help come?' v. 1 ESV. Our help is certainly not from the hills, but beyond them to the Lord 'who made heaven and earth', v. 2. Our problems should change our perspective and lift our eyes to heaven, a place far away, but always near for our defence.

Psalm 122 joyfully anticipates standing within the walls of Jerusalem again. No doubt it dealt with the time of David's rejection and absence from His beloved city. As then, so now should the prayer go up to 'Pray for the peace of Jerusalem'.

Psalm 123 reminds us again to lift our eyes to the One who dwells in the heavens. As Jehoshaphat prayed when he was surrounded by His enemies: 'Neither know we what to do but our eyes are upon thee', 2 Chr. 20. 12. We wait expectantly, as a servant does with his master, for help to come, Ps. 123. 2.

April 13th
Leviticus 21; **Psalms 124-127**; Mark 7. 24 – 8. 10

OUR TRUST IN THE LORD

Once again, we hear the familiar refrain: 'Our help is in the name of the Lord, who made heaven and earth', Ps. 124. 8. It is the confession of the redeemed, forged upon the anvil of life's experience. Since God has made the heavens and the earth, He can be relied upon to deliver us from those who rise against us and from the 'snare of the fowlers', vv. 6-7. God is bigger than our problems, and all is not lost even when the waters are rising and the streams and proud waters are about to go over our soul, vv. 3- 4. Hope is renewed at His intervention. He is the God who promises to bring us through, Isa. 43. 2, even when the floodwaters threaten. As STUART HAMBLEN wrote: 'It is no secret what God can do, what He's done for others, He'll do for you'.

The theme of trust is continued in the next song of degrees. The firm image of Mount Zion, fixed and immoveable provided the perfect parallel of what our trust is like when we put it fully in the Lord, 125. 1. The protection of the mountains that surrounded Jerusalem corresponds to the protection afforded His people, v. 2. How important to keep this in mind when 'all around our soul gives way', EDWARD MOTE, and shakes, Heb. 12. 26. 'He shall never suffer the righteous to be moved', Ps. 55. 22. Those that turn aside unto the crooked ways forfeit the life of blessedness and will be led forth with the workers of iniquity, 125. 5, even as those who walk, stand, and sit with those who do not love the Lord, 1. 1.

How encouraging are the verses found in Psalm 126! But when deliverance comes, what joy, what singing, what praise! They that sow in tears shall reap in joy, v. 5. The tears that water our couch, 6. 6, and have been our food day and night, 42. 3, God will keep in His bottle, 56. 8. It does not miss His register but becomes the means of watering the precious seed that doubtless yields a joyful spiritual harvest, 126. 6.

The benefits and heritage of the life of faith extends to work and family also. 'Without me, ye can do nothing', the Saviour reminded His disciples the night before His death, John 15. 5. Whether it is building a house, guarding a city, working all night, or raising a family, 127. 1-3, we need Him in everything we do.

April 14th
Leviticus 22; Psalms 128-131; Mark 8. 11-26
SUITABLILITY IN THE SERVICE OF GOD
Together, Leviticus chapters 21 to 23 emphasize important regulations concerning the priests in their official capacity as ministers of the Lord. The former chapter speaks mainly of the need to be free from defilement. The latter chapter gives the details of properly observing the seven Feasts of *Jehovah*, later described as 'of the *Jews*', John 5. 1. The middle chapter underscores the requirement for personal separation and what constituted an acceptable sacrifice, vv. 17-33. All were necessary for service that was pleasing to God.

Only those who were born into the tribe of Levi and into the line of Aaron were qualified as priests. It was their responsibility by *birth*. Any who evidenced the defects listed in chapter 21 were excluded from spiritual service. They were also disqualified through contact with unclean things as Leviticus chapter 22 verses 1 to 16 brings out. They were still numbered among the nation, but hindered in their service. For the Christian, we too have the privilege of access and ministry to Him through the *new birth*, having been born again by the word of God. We are exhorted to 'come out from among them, and be ye separate . . . and touch not the unclean thing', 2 Cor. 6. 17. We are directed to offer up spiritual sacrifices acceptable to God through Jesus Christ, 1 Pet. 2. 5. Cognizant of these and other promises, we are to 'cleanse ourselves from all filthiness of the flesh and spirit, perfecting holiness in the fear of God', 2 Cor. 7. 1. It is when this is true that our deeds are 'well-pleasing in his sight', Heb. 13. 21.

All this highlights the moral perfections of our Great High Priest. He had no defects, and He perfectly fulfilled the requirements for priesthood, though He sprang from the tribe of Judah. He 'did no sin', 1 Pet. 2. 22; 'knew no sin', 2 Cor. 5. 21; and there was 'no unrighteousness . . . in him', John 7. 18. He was never tainted by sin, and was as the blessed man of Psalm 1, who always set the Lord before Him, Ps. 16. 8. He was 'holy, harmless, undefiled, separate from sinners and made higher than the heavens', Heb. 7. 26. He is indeed the perfect Priest and the perfect Sacrifice. 'Praise the Saviour, ye who know Him', THOMAS KELLY.

April 15th
Leviticus 23. 1-22; Psalms 132-134; **Mark 8. 27 – 9. 13**
PETER'S CONFESSION OF CHRIST
When the Lord brought His disciples to the area of Caesarea Philippi, He was bringing them to a citadel of rampant paganism. Carved into the mountain niches were the visible evidences of man's innate rebellion against the one true God, represented by vain images of the world and its religion. But the steps of good men are ordered by the Lord, Ps. 37. 23, and so it was for His disciples. What seemed to be an unnecessary excursion away from the crowds became an important lesson in the school of faith. May we always see the value of the twists and turns of the Saviour's leading.

The question asked was meant to test their understanding and allegiance to Him. Against this backdrop of unbelief, came the penetrating question, 'Who do men say that I am?' Their answer was correct but lacked conviction. The Lord drove home the point personally by asking, 'But who do *you* say that I am?' v. 29. What followed were four important revelations of the Lord's Person and work. They were: the Christ, v. 29, the cross, v. 31, the cost of discipleship, v. 35, and His coming in glory, v. 38 – four components of the gospel message.

In the account of the transfiguration in chapter 9, there is an expansion of these four components. After six days, the Lord took Peter, James and John to a mountain where they would have a dramatic encounter with Moses, Elijah, and the transfigured Lord Jesus. It has often been referred to as the account of three men, two men, and one Man. The Lord revealed a glimpse of His future kingdom glory. After He had prayed, Moses and Elijah, representing respectively the law and the prophets, appeared to them speaking of His 'decease (exodus) which he was about to accomplish', Luke 9. 31 NKJV. A surprising way to refer to His impending death! But it was truly His work to finish. The perfect Servant had come to do the Father's will and be obedient unto death, Phil. 2. 8. After the cloud overshadowed all three, the voice came out of heaven, reaffirming the pre-eminence of Christ and He is seen standing alone. 'Jesus takes the highest station', THOMAS KELLY, and He does so eternally.

April 16th
Leviticus 23. 23-44; Psalms 135-136; **Mark 9. 14-32**

FAILURE ADDRESSED

The Lord Jesus had been on the mountain-top with three of His disciples. For them, the experience was memorable, a little picture of those seasons when believers gather around Him, and are 'eyewitnesses of His majesty', 2 Pet. 1. 16. As always, while we are occupied with Him, there is still tremendous human need down in the valley, and that day, the other disciples just could not cope.

The need centred on a demon-possessed boy. This evil spirit was particularly malicious, vv. 18; 22, and the boy's condition was of long standing, v. 21. Such was the unusual ability of the spirit, that the Lord Jesus labelled it, 'this kind', v. 29. Not long before this He had given His disciples authority over '*all* devils', Luke 9. 1, this one included, and yet, so far, they appeared powerless. He attributed their ineffectiveness to their spiritual condition, Mark 9. 29, a solemn lesson for Christian service today.

On His arrival, the Saviour had found the scribes badgering His disciples, v. 14, and, as ever, the Good Shepherd stepped in to protect His own sheep, v. 16. He did it whenever they experienced a verbal assault, for example, in Matthew's home, Mark 2. 16-17, or in the cornfields, vv. 23-28. 'He loved them unto the end', John 13. 1. It is encouraging that His care for His own is still constant.

From the perspective of the public, the disciples' failure reflected on their Master. Almost reproachfully, the distressed father spoke to the Lord Jesus about '*thy* disciples', v. 18. Remember that our failures affect His reputation. David's sin gave 'great occasion to the enemies of the Lord to blaspheme', 2 Sam. 12. 14.

'Bring him unto me', v. 19; as ever the Lord was in control with power to meet the need, but the father's '*if* thou canst', v. 22, epitomized the general unbelief that so distressed the Saviour, v. 19. Beware! A pessimistic attitude is infectious, as is illustrated in the negative influence of the ten rebellious spies, Num. 13. 27-33.

It is to the credit of the disciples that they wanted to review the incident, and to pinpoint their failure: 'Why could not we cast him out?' v. 28. It would do us good if, in the privacy of prayer, such enquiries were made, rather than ignoring failure and pretending that all is well. Prayer will resolve many issues.

April 17th
Leviticus 24; Psalms 137-138; **Mark 9. 33-50**
DISPUTE RESOLUTION

The dispute among the disciples centred on 'who should be the greatest', v. 34. Fresh from their thrilling experience on 'the holy mount', 2 Pet. 1. 18, perhaps Peter, James, and John saw themselves as prime candidates. The recent failure of the other nine probably confirmed their feelings, but their whole mind-set was in complete opposition to the attitude of their Master, the One of whom scripture says, 'he humbled himself', Phil. 2. 8. Self-promotion and the craving for position should be foreign to the believer in Christ. Modesty must be the keynote.

The undignified squabble was aggravated by the fact that it was 'by the way', v. 33, in full view of the public. Joseph knew the quarrelsome nature of his brothers and their appetite for recrimination, so he warned them, 'See that ye fall not out *by the way*', Gen. 45. 24. It is so sad when conflict among believers is in the public domain. The disciples had to be censured, but the Lord reserved the rebuke for 'in the house', v. 33. It was not administered in public, reinforcing the lesson that some matters should never be aired openly. The need for the rebuke was urgent, administered immediately He entered the house, and before He sat down, vv. 34-35, but He waited until the door was closed.

The Lord then taught them that the pathway to greatness was to be 'servant of all', v. 35. Considering the human ego, it is a hard lesson to learn. Most of us see ourselves as deserving attention, with the world owing us something. True greatness sees every one else as being due our interest and service, even those such as children who are generally regarded as less important than their seniors, v. 37. The disciples felt duly chastened.

John broke the embarrassing silence with an irrelevant statement. It was likely a ploy to take the heat off them; change the subject quickly, just as the woman at the well did when the Lord pinpointed her sin, John 4. 17-20. We are all experts at wriggling out of issues. It was a bit rich that the twelve had rebuked a man for doing what they had failed to do! The Lord indicated that we should never meddle with those who ostensibly are serving Him, but neither does He give a mandate to join them in their activities.

April 18th
Leviticus 25; Psalm 139; **Mark 10. 1-31**
ATTITUDES

These verses record a number of wrong attitudes. The Pharisees asked a barbed question about family life and social order; their motive was to tempt Him, v. 2. Their approach trivialized a practice that destroys lives, damages children, and debases society. For them it was only a debating point, and sadly it can still be raised carelessly in that vein around a supper table. In His response, the Lord reaffirmed the divine ideal of a permanent one-man one-woman relationship, vv. 6-9. He amplified His teaching to the disciples, explaining that remarriage after divorce creates an adulterous relationship, vv. 10-12.

The disciples' attitude to children now comes under scrutiny, vv. 13-16. They had forgotten how precious they were to the Saviour, 9. 36-37, and regarded them as a nuisance. The Lord Jesus saw in children the simple trust that is necessary for a place in the kingdom. When He was a child, a man had taken Him up in his arms, Luke 2. 28; He now takes children into *His* arms, v. 16. God had been manifested in the flesh; the One who had dwelt in light unapproachable had come so close that children nestled in His arms! Let us all see great spiritual potential in children, and wisely facilitate their coming to Him, v. 14. Never hinder them.

In the ruler who came running there are obvious attitude problems. There was within him the innate desire to *do* something to secure eternal life, v. 17, coupled with a smug self-righteousness that made him feel adequate, v. 20. Loved by Christ and faced with the challenge of following Him, his miserly selfish attitude hindered him from blessing; he was among those who trusted in riches, v. 24. Trusting in himself that he was righteous, Luke 18. 9, and trusting in his riches combined to exclude him from the kingdom; he was still not 'saved', Mark 10. 26.

By contrast, the disciples had 'left all', v. 28. The fact that Peter 'began to say' perhaps indicates that the Lord interrupted him. Graciously the Saviour responded to a potential boast by promising rich recompense for such sacrificial devotion, not only here and now, but eternal life 'in the world to come', v. 30. Like these men, let us make the right choices in life.

April 19th
Leviticus 26; Psalms 140-141; **Mark 10. 32-52**

EMOTIONS

The emotions of astonishment and fear swept over the disciples when they saw that the Lord Jesus was determined to go to Jerusalem, v. 32. Was He unaware of His danger? His response was to disclose the precise details of His imminent sufferings, right down to the spitting and the scourging, but culminating in resurrection. Paul went to Jerusalem, '*not knowing* the things that [would] befall [him] there', Acts 20. 22. The Lord knew in advance every blow that would fall and every wound that would be inflicted.

> No unforeseen event
> E'er took Him by surprise;
> Toward the Cross with fixed intent
> He moved with open eyes.   I. Y. EWAN

The next section features irritation as a major emotion, v. 41. James and John were ambitious for prominence in the coming kingdom. It is to their credit that they took the Lord at His word; He had promised that the apostles would sit on twelve thrones judging Israel in His future administration, Matt. 19. 28. However, their bid for major honours annoyed their fellow-disciples, v. 41. 'Blessed are the peacemakers', and the greatest of all peacemakers poured oil on the troubled waters: 'Jesus called them to him', v. 42. This time, there was no child as an object lesson in humility. The great Exemplar Himself was their model, v. 45. He came to minister; He came to give His life; there was their pattern. Aspiring to greatness demands being a 'minister' (servant, deacon), v. 43. Reaching the top means being a 'servant (slave) of all', v. 44. He said, 'I am among you as he that serveth' (deacon service), Luke 22. 27. He 'took upon him the form of a servant' (bondslave), Phil. 2. 7. What was demanded of them was expressed practically by Him. He is now 'far above all', Eph. 1. 21!

The emotions that gripped Bartimaeus were expectation, conviction, and determination. Hearing about the visitor to Jericho he anticipated 'mercy', for he held the belief that Jesus was the 'son of David', the long-promised Messiah. The outraged crowd rebuked him, but, undeterred, he acknowledged Christ's Messiahship still; being wonderfully blessed, he became a follower.

April 20th
Leviticus 27; Psalms 142-143; **Mark 11. 1-26**

FREED TO SERVE

'The Lord hath need of him', v. 3. Jerusalem beckoned, and the King's arrival was the subject of Bible prophecy: 'riding upon an ass, even upon a colt the foal of an ass', Zech. 9. 9 RV. Joseph rode in a chariot, Gen. 41. 43; Mordecai was led in honour mounted on a steed from the king's stables, Esther. 6. 11; Israel's judges had white asses, Judg. 5. 10; the sons of Jair and Abdon all had their 'ass colts', Judg. 10. 4; 12. 14; and each of David's sons had his mule, 2 Sam. 13. 29. This Son of David possessed no mule; 'he became poor', 2 Cor. 8. 9. No one gave Him a chariot or a horse. This 'Judge of Israel' had no white ass to call His own. To fulfil scripture, He borrowed the colt.

'Loose him', v. 2. Unflattering though it is, there are parallels between Bible donkeys and our experiences. The 'firstling of an ass' had to be redeemed 'with a lamb', a substitute to *loose* it from the threat of death, Exod. 13. 13. Donkeys could be *lost* or *laden*, Exod. 23. 4-5, depicting the sinner's plight; but the *sentenced* donkey of Exodus chapter 13 can become the *serving* donkey of Mark chapter 11. Once 'loosed' from sin's burden, bondage and penalty, we come under a new authority: 'Being then made free from sin, ye became the servants of righteousness', Rom. 6. 18.

The two disciples were dispatched to commandeer the ass, v. 2, and the whole procedure was carried through 'as Jesus had commanded', v. 6. The lesson is *implicit* obedience. As far as the animal's owner is concerned, the lesson is that of *instant* obedience; '*straightway* he will send him hither' v. 3. Let us ask ourselves whether our obedience is as unquestioning and as prompt.

The incident demonstrates the Lord's right to requisition His people's property. He used Peter's boat, and an unnamed disciple's upper room. Matthew made his home available, and Joseph donated his new tomb. The word 'stewardship' is often used as the umbrella term for the fact everything that we possess is held in trust for Him. David had grasped the truth of it: 'all things come of thee, and of thine own have we given thee', 1 Chr. 29. 14. May we all be as conscientious, as we administer what has been entrusted to us!

April 21st
Numbers 1; Psalms 144-145; Mark 11. 27 – 12. 17

THE WARRIORS

The book of Numbers commences with Israel located 'in the wilderness of Sinai' in the early days of their trek to Canaan, Num. 1. 1. It ends with them encamped 'in the plains of Moab' in sight of their goal, 36. 13; Numbers is clearly the book of the wilderness.

Warfare was anticipated *en route*, and so numbering the fighting forces was deemed a priority; consequently, in chapter 1 we have the *warriors*. Subsequent chapters will focus on the *workers*, the Levites who had responsibility for the tabernacle. A small section is devoted to *the worshipers*, 3. 1-4, the priests who ministered to the Lord. Christians fulfil all three roles! There is a call for us to be 'good soldiers of Jesus Christ', 2 Tim. 2. 3-4, enduring the hardships of the *war* zone, unimpeded by the distractions of civilian life. An appeal is made for us to be 'always abounding in the *work* of the Lord', 1 Cor. 15. 58. As 'an holy priesthood' we *worship*, offering up 'spiritual sacrifices', 1 Pet. 2. 5.

This army would not comprise boy soldiers, for the qualifying age was twenty, v. 3. A level of maturity was necessary to engage the enemy. The devil is designated 'an enemy', Matt. 13. 39, and undoubtedly he will attack those who are young in the faith and vulnerable, but there are areas of conflict from which the young can be shielded. This is illustrated by God refusing to take His newly redeemed people too close to Philistine territory; they were too inexperienced to be exposed to warfare, Exod. 13. 17.

Although Moses and Aaron had ultimate responsibility for this census of the troops, v. 3, a prominent member of each tribe of Israel was to accompany them, v. 4. It is an illustration of the old maxim that not only should things be done properly, but they have to be *seen* to be done properly. Paul always made his arrangements transparently 'that no man should blame us', 2 Cor. 8. 20.

The Levites were not included among the soldiers, v. 47. Their remit was to 'bear the tabernacle', v. 50. Their tents encircled the sanctuary, v. 53, convenient for the work to which they were called. Do our domestic and employment arrangements suitably accommodate our responsibility to the house of God?

April 22nd
Numbers 2; Psalms 146-147; Mark 12. 18-44
ENCAMPED AROUND THE TABERNACLE
'Let all things be done decently and in order', 1 Cor. 14. 40. God never operates haphazardly; He is a God of order. When He liberated Israel from Egypt, 'they went up harnessed', 'in orderly ranks', Exod. 13. 18 NKJV. As they travelled through the wilderness, there was structure to their encampment. The tabernacle was central, but with its badger skin exterior, it was a very unimposing sight, a type of Him in whom men saw 'no beauty that they should desire him', Isa. 53. 2. Believers appreciate His worth and gather to His name, Matt. 18. 20. Let the house of God be central to our lives, and our association with it as scripturally ordered as was the camp of Israel.

Previously we observed that the Levites were in proximity to the tabernacle, convenient for their work. Surrounding them were the myriads of Israel with three tribes situated at each cardinal point of the compass. They had no liberty to choose their location; God allocated their position. Let us all be as submissive to God's direction for our lives, not only as to *what* we do, but as to *where* we do it. The Holy Spirit who had gifted Barnabas and Saul also dictated where that gift should be deployed, Acts 13. 1-4. Let us be equally sensitive to His guidance for our lives.

The sight of the camp was impressive, the symmetry such that from a vantage point Balaam had to acknowledge, 'How goodly are thy tents, O Jacob', Num. 24. 5. They were arranged like lined-up trees, v. 6. People scrutinise our lives as Balaam spied on Israel. Do they observe godly order, holiness, righteous conduct, and Christ-like qualities? What impression do we make?

On the march, the tabernacle was central, with six tribes preceding it, and six behind, v. 17, illustrating the fact that the Lord and His interests should take prime place in our lives. In different ways, some were more vulnerable than others. Simeon was linked with Reuben and Gad, two tribes who would not enter Canaan. Simeon was uninfluenced; we should be like him and never bow to peer pressure. Those under Dan's standard went 'hindmost'; earlier, those located there had been attacked by Amalek, Deut. 25. 18. We need to keep up, and to be constantly vigilant.

April 23rd
Numbers 3; Psalms 148-150; Mark 13
THE LEVITES
A short paragraph is devoted to '**the sons of Aaron**', v. 2. It is sad that two of those sons never functioned because 'they offered strange fire', v. 4. The lesson is that activity that is unsanctioned by God can never find favour with Him. HUDSON TAYLOR spoke about 'doing God's work in God's way', a principle that we should always keep in mind. Unbiblical methods must be avoided.

The chapter now focuses on the **Levites**. First, they were given to assist Aaron, v. 6. Not all of them were content with that; Korah had his eye on the priesthood, 16. 8-10, and his rebellion cost him his life. Let us be satisfied with the task that God has given us, and avoid the attitude expressed by the foot saying, 'Because I am not the hand, I am not of the body', 1 Cor. 12. 15.

Next, we notice that the Levites were substitutes for 'all the firstborn' whom God had intended for the task, vv. 12, 40-51. God will see to it that His work is done even although some shirk their responsibilities; Boaz was willing to replace an unwilling kinsman, Ruth 4. 8-10. Because they had lazy nobles, Tekoite labourers repaired 'another piece' of the wall of Jerusalem, Neh. 3. 5, 27. The Samaritan was willing to do what the priest and the Levite avoided, Luke 10. 30-35. The lesson is, if we will not do it, another will; we should see to it that 'no man take thy crown', Rev. 3. 11.

It is also interesting that the Levites were to be numbered from 'a month old and upward', v. 15. Probably the first month would pass to ensure the survival of the child when infant mortality would have been common in the wilderness, but then he was 'numbered'. Obviously there was no possibility of one so young giving help in the work. However, God was looking to the future. There is huge potential connected with youth, and it is sad when that potential is not brought to fruition. Vines 'in blossom' with the promise of fruit can be spoiled by 'little foxes', S. of S. 2. 15. We should aim to realize our full potential.

Finally, we note that the three families of the Levites each had their own specific tasks, to avoid intruding into the responsibilities of the others. Thus it is with us: 'to every man his work', Mark 13. 34. Let us be diligent in the tasks allotted uniquely to us.

April 24th
Numbers 4; Proverbs 1; Mark 14. 1-26
VARIOUS TASKS
Our chapter envisages the tabernacle on the move, with each branch of the Levitical family having different responsibilities for its transportation. Common to the three groups was the length of their service; they functioned from the age of thirty to fifty. The best years of their lives were devoted to God. Are ours? God's wisdom and kindness are seen in Him setting these parameters. A level of maturity was needed, hence the lower age limit; the retirement age recognized that passing years diminish physical powers. The lessons seem obvious and yet they are often ignored. Inexperienced young people should never be pressed into activity beyond their ability. Elderly overseers should be willing to oversee a transition of responsibility to the next generation.

Before the Levites removed the tabernacle, the priests had to cover the vessels and attend to other duties, vv. 5-16. No curious eye would look on these holy vessels. Space allows only brief comment on these matters. The outer covering of the ark was blue, the colour of the heavens, v. 6. It reminds us that when our Lord Jesus moved through this world there was visible evidence that as 'the second man' He was 'the Lord from heaven', 1 Cor. 15. 47.

The sons of Kohath were charged with carrying the vessels of the tabernacle. This was strenuous work, for some of these vessels were heavy, being gold, and others would be awkward to convey. Other branches of the family had wagons to assist in transporting the various parts of the structure; the Kohathites had to bear the vessels 'upon their shoulders', Num. 7. 6-9. Six separate verses use the word 'burden' to describe each aspect of service, whatever group was involved. Are we prepared to share the burden of maintaining testimony in wilderness conditions? When God had directed how the ark should be carried, an innovation proved disastrous, as David found to his cost, 1 Chr. 13. 7-14.

Curtains and cords were the responsibility of the Gershonites, while the sons of Merari cared for the rest, from the tall heavy boards to the little pins. In God's things meticulous care has to be taken, even with what may appear to be small and insignificant.

130

April 25th
Numbers 5; Proverbs 2; Mark 14. 27-52

UNCLEANNESS, UNRIGHTEOUSNESS AND UNFAITHFULNESS

There are three major issues here. Firstly, lepers and others who were ceremonially unclean had to be 'put out of the camp'. No exceptions were allowed: 'every leper'; 'every one'; 'whosoever'; 'male and female'. There were two reasons for such drastic action. (1) Their continued presence would 'defile' the camp, vv. 2-3, because ceremonial uncleanness was contagious, Hag. 2. 13; it would impact on others. (2) God dwelt 'in the midst' of the camp, v. 3, and His presence demanded a standard of purity.

The New Testament equivalent is the fact that certain sins require the offenders to be 'put away' from the assembly. Their continued presence would 'leaven' the whole company, and the holy God who dwells among His people cannot countenance the presence of evil, 1 Cor. 5. 1-13. Such action is severe, but necessary.

The second matter relates to a sin that affects someone else financially. It is a trespass against that person, v. 7, but more seriously, it is 'a trespass against the Lord', v. 6. While our sins can damage others, in reality they are acts of rebellion against God, Gen. 39. 9; Ps. 51. 4. The main thought in this section is the need for reimbursement. Restitution has to be made, Num. 5. 7 RV, with a fifth of the principal added. If the defrauded party had died or was untraceable, his kinsman would benefit. If the kinsman was unavailable, the price would be given to the priest – in fact given 'unto the Lord', v. 8. There was no let-out for the offender. It all emphasizes the need for scrupulous honesty, and if there has been a breakdown in integrity the victim must be fully recompensed. The previous section linked with 1 Corinthians chapter 5; this section lines up with chapter 6; persistent dishonesty puts a man's profession of faith in doubt, vv. 8-11.

The rest of the chapter deals with the relationship of a man with his wife. A man could have doubts about his wife's fidelity, suspicions either groundless or justified, vv. 12-14. An elaborate routine with a miraculous element was put in place to establish whether his jealousy was warranted. In our relationship with the Lord, He is never content with divided affections; He is 'a jealous God', Exod. 20. 5.

April 26th
Numbers 6; **Proverbs 3**; Mark 14. 53-72
MY SON: DON'T FORGET, DON'T DESPISE, DON'T IGNORE
Solomon wrote three of the Old Testament books. In Ecclesiastes he is depicted as a preacher, 1. 1; in the Song of Songs he is seen as a king; in the book of Proverbs he features as a father. Thus, the Proverbs are interspersed with the phrase, 'My son'. That form of address divides our chapter into three sections.

'My son, forget not my law', v. 1. Evidently, Solomon had taken parenting seriously, and had given sound advice that he wanted his family to follow. He was particularly concerned about their relationship with the Lord, and so he restated his instructions: 'Trust in the Lord', v. 5; 'Fear the Lord', v. 7; 'Honour the Lord', v. 9. Trusting in the Lord is in contrast to leaning unto our 'own understanding' which often leads to poor choices in life. Fearing (revering) the Lord will be a powerful incentive to 'depart from evil'. Honouring the Lord will motivate us to be generous, and then to harvest a rich reward, v. 10.

'My son, despise not the chastening of the Lord', v. 11, is an injunction that a later generation had forgotten: 'Ye have forgotten the exhortation', Heb. 12. 5, followed by the quote from Proverbs chapter 3. As Father, God reserves the right to chasten His children. It is evidence of His love for them, Heb. 12. 6. It is proof that they belong to Him, vv. 7-8. It has the objective of promoting holiness and righteousness, vv. 10-11. So we must not treat lightly His chastening, v. 5, or 'faint' under it, v. 5; rather, we should be 'exercised' by it, v. 11, and allow it to produce righteousness.

'My son . . . keep sound wisdom and discretion', v. 21. These features must not be ignored: 'Let not them depart from thine eyes', v. 21. The sporting world frequently highlights the disaster of taking one's eye off the ball. As believers, we must always be focused on wisdom and discretion. These qualities must be preserved, the basic meaning of the word 'keep' in our verse. Subsequent verses show the great benefit of these virtues. They are crucial to your own spiritual health, 'life unto thy soul', v. 22. They are vital to your spiritual attractiveness, 'grace to thy neck'. They are essential for your spiritual safety, enabling you to 'walk . . . safely', and keeping you from stumbling, v. 23.

April 27th
Numbers 7; **Proverbs 4**; Mark 15. 1-23
THE ROAD OF LIFE

Life is like a journey, described by Jacob as 'the days of the years of *my pilgrimage*', Gen. 47. 9. Aspects of the pathway of life feature in today's chapter. Firstly, we need someone to show us the road, and Solomon assumed the responsibility of giving guidance to his family: 'I have led thee in right paths', v. 11. Fathers have a duty to 'rule' their households, 1 Tim. 3. 4, a word that carries the idea of standing before them, leading by example. Just as the Shepherd leads us 'in the paths *of righteousness*', Ps. 23. 3, never guiding us to do anything contrary to His word, so Solomon led in 'paths of uprightness', v. 11 RV; he was a role model of integrity.

Then there is a road to be avoided, 'the path of the wicked', 'the way of evil men', v. 14. The warning is not just to avoid turning down that street, but to keep well away from it, v. 15; it is easier to avoid sin than to recover from it. 'A young man' sauntered down an alley that he should have avoided, and loitered at a corner; it led to him being ensnared and doomed, Prov. 7. 6-27. Dallying in proximity to temptation is disastrous. The blessed man does not stand 'in the way of sinners', Ps. 1. 1; he will steer clear.

The better route in life is 'the path of the just', Prov. 4. 18. 'The shining light' illuminates that path as surely as the light of dawn dispels the gloom of night. Those on that pathway are enlightened by the Holy Spirit and scripture, and with their progress along the road and increasing maturity, that light of dawn develops until there is the blaze of the meridian sun, 'the perfect day'. The light of divine illumination increasingly develops the light of personal holiness in the believer's life. By contrast, the darkness that makes it easy to stumble enshrouds 'the way of the wicked', v. 19.

Route planning is another important factor: 'Ponder the path of thy feet', v. 26. As far as the twists and turns of life are concerned, it is impossible to anticipate all that could transpire. The word of God is not a spotlight that shows us the whole road ahead, but it is 'a lamp unto [our] feet', Ps. 119. 105; it directs us *a step at a time.* Weigh up every step, for to deviate 'to the right hand' or 'to the left', v. 27, would soon take us into evil. Follow the map!

April 28th
Numbers 8; **Proverbs 5. 1 – 6. 19**; Mark 15. 24-47
FIDELITY, FINANCES, FORESIGHT, AND FAILURES
It is remarkable that in the book of Proverbs there is counselling for every aspect of human experience. In the first two sections of today's reading, Solomon adopts the twin roles of marriage guidance counsellor and financial advisor. He then focuses on attitude in the workplace, before turning to give spiritual counsel.

The imagery of chapter 5 is dramatic; in poetic fashion Solomon portrays the disaster of marital infidelity. The danger is occasioned by a seductress, vv. 3-7, a predator like Potiphar's wife, Gen. 39. 7. The disaster involves lasting regret that upsets the mind, and the possibility of diseases that affect the body, v. 11.

The instruction that Solomon gives is as follows; steer clear of such a person, v. 8, just as Joseph fled from the temptress, Gen. 39. 12. Then, pay heed to your spiritual mentors who warn of the perils of illicit liaisons, vv. 12-13. Finally, be fully content with the intimacy of the bond with your own wife; a marriage is the only legitimate context for a sexual relationship, vv. 15-21.

Chapter 6 opens with some financial advice. If, unwisely, you have signed up as a guarantor for 'thy friend', involving his commitment to 'a stranger', v. 1, then do all in your power to extricate yourself from that commitment. If your friend was in real need it would have been better for you to have been a benefactor rather than a guarantor. If his indebtedness was the result of covetousness, why aid and abet him? If the guarantee is called on, any resentment you have could signal the end of the friendship.

The work-shy individual then comes under scrutiny. In the humble ant, v. 6, the natural world provides a role model. Foresight and the work ethic are built into her, so that without constant guidance or pressure from a foreman or line manager, she gets on with her work. Her future depends on it; winter is coming! One should never allow the safety net of benefit payments to encourage complacency, and induce the laziness that makes one a prime candidate for being paid off in days of redundancies.

On a spiritual level, let us be aware of failures that offend God to the extent that He hates them, 6. 16-19. By the Spirit's power let us eradicate these disagreeable characteristics from our lives.

April 29th

Numbers 9. 1 – 10. 10; **Proverbs 6. 20 – 7. 27**; Mark 16

PARENTAL COMMANDMENTS

Chapters 6 and 7 repeat the warnings of chapter 5 regarding the disastrous consequences of immorality. Solomon saw a slide into sexual sin as a danger to which his family was exposed. We will focus on features of these parental commandments.

First, it is wonderful to see that both parents were united in the counsel that they gave, 6. 20. They had no separate agendas; their thinking was at one, unlike Jacob and Rebekah whose diverse preferences created tension in the home, Gen. 25. 28.

Next, a proper attitude to these commandments is encouraged. Figuratively they had to be bound to the heart and tied around the neck, v. 21. It all starts in the heart. The truth of God has to be welcomed into the heart and if implemented it will create a winsomeness that is the spiritual equivalent of the physical adornment of an elaborate necklace.

The benefits of these commandments are then stressed, v. 22. They give guidance for life: 'it shall lead thee'. They afford protection from spiritual danger: 'it shall watch over thee', RV. They provide instruction for each new day: 'when thou awakest, it shall talk with thee'. Like the Saviour, let us have an awakened ear, Isa. 50. 4, starting each day listening to God. His commandments impart enlightenment and issue cautions which if heeded enhance the life, for they are 'the way of life', v. 23. They are also the safeguard against what was a major anxiety for these protective parents: the peril of their family being ensnared, v. 24.

A metaphor is used to stress the value of these commands, and by extension, God's truth; 'the apple of thine eye', 7. 2. The pupil of the eye is so valuable that whenever it is endangered, the eyelid instantly closes. Divine instructions are as precious, so we should bind them on our fingers and write them on our hearts, v. 3. Heart and hand should act together to obey God's command.

Solomon's concern is explained by an incident that he had witnessed, when a naïve young fellow was led astray with disastrous consequences, vv. 6-27. Sin cannot be concealed; not only does God see it, 5. 21, but others observe it, 7. 6. Solomon had no wish for his family to be thus shamed in public.

April 30th
Numbers 10. 11 – 11. 3; **Proverbs 8**; Jude
WISDOM PERSONIFIED
A hectoring flattering evil woman took centre stage in chapter 7, but the scene changes dramatically as we enter chapter 8. A different kind of woman steps forward, someone who speaks the truth and to whom wickedness is an abomination, v. 7; this is wisdom personified, a dignified lady whose advice is more valuable than gold or silver or rubies, vv. 10-11.

Her guidance is universally available, for she calls on men in various locations to heed her, vv. 2-3. The evil woman of the previous chapter is 'loud', 7. 11. Wisdom is as insistent on being heard, for 'she crieth *aloud*', 8. 3 RV. We dare not ignore her, whether we deem ourselves to be among those that are at 'the gates', the ancient seat of administration, v. 3, or rank ourselves among the 'simple' and the 'fools', v. 5. Whatever our status, we need wisdom, and if we are aware of a deficiency, we can 'ask of God', Jas. 1. 5. The man who penned our chapter had longed for wisdom, and God gave him 'a wise and an understanding heart', 1 Kgs. 3. 12. In turn Solomon urges us to crave wisdom earnestly with the assurance from wisdom herself that, 'those that seek me diligently shall find me', v. 17 RV.

Wisdom is necessary as far as our way of thinking is concerned, the overriding attitude being 'the fear of the Lord', 9. 10, which regulates our outlook on so many issues, 8. 13. Wisdom is also crucial as far as our speech is concerned, v. 13b. It is a vital factor as we discharge our responsibilities, vv. 15-16. Let us 'love' wisdom, and in turn reap the benefits of her love for us, v. 17.

For the earthly people of God, material prosperity was linked to their loyalty to God and obedience to His word; hence their need to allow wisdom to 'lead in the way of righteousness', v. 20. Only then would they 'inherit substance' and have full 'treasuries', vv. 18-21 RV. Our blessings are spiritual but enjoying them is dependent on being 'filled with the knowledge of his will in all spiritual *wisdom* and understanding', Col. 1. 9 RV.

The divine wisdom exhibited in the work of creation, vv. 22-31, is available to us. Those who watch expectantly at wisdom's gate will be 'blessed', finding 'life' and 'favour of the Lord', vv. 32-36.

May 1st
Numbers 11. 4-35; Proverbs 9; 1 Peter 1
COMPLAINING
This chapter reveals to us the damage which complaining can do amongst believers. It reveals to us firstly the failure of Israel, then the failure of Moses, and then the failure of Joshua. Unlike secular books, the Bible tells us about the weaknesses in even the best of people: 'man looketh on the outward appearance, but the Lord looketh on the heart', 1 Sam. 16. 7.

We are told at the outset of this chapter: 'And when the people complained, it displeased the Lord: and the Lord heard it', Num. 11. 1. It is a good thing to learn, early on in our Christian life, that the Lord knows not only what we say, but what we think. This fact should encourage us to be careful in our speech and thought. The reading of the scriptures each day, and prayer, has a much needed cleansing effect: 'every word of God is pure: he is a shield unto them that put their trust in him', Prov. 30. 5; Ps. 119. 9.

In verse 5 of our chapter it is instructive to notice what the people remembered about Egypt: 'the fish, which we did eat in Egypt freely; the cucumbers, and the melons, and the leeks, and the onions, and the garlic'. There is no mention of the cruelty of their taskmasters. How easy it is for us to forget what we have been saved from. May we be thankful each day for our salvation! There are many things we can complain about, and, if we continue in it, we can lose the joy of our salvation. We may complain about our elders, or the preachers who come to bring a message from the Lord, indeed any number of things. One way which can help is if we add these things, and more, to our prayer list. A prayer list is something which should be added to and updated regularly, as situations change. I think it is true, that it is more difficult to criticize, or complain about, something or someone for whom you are praying positively.

The Apostle, when writing to the church at Philippi wrote: 'In nothing be anxious; but in everything by prayer and supplication with thanksgiving let your requests be made known unto God. And the peace of God, which passeth all understanding, shall guard your hearts and your thoughts in Christ Jesus', Phil. 4. 6-7 RV.

May 2nd
Numbers 12-13; Proverbs 10; 1 Peter 2
THE OMNIPRESENCE OF GOD
It would appear from the first verse of chapter 12 that Miriam is the instigator of a challenge to Moses, as she is mentioned first and the Hebrew verb is in the feminine gender. This warns us that the best of people can give place to the flesh. We also see, from verse 2, another truth, which should make us ever aware that the Lord knows everything we say: 'And the Lord heard it'. The Lord also states that He speaks to Moses 'mouth to mouth', v. 8, and asks a very telling question of Miriam and Aaron, 'Wherefore then were ye not afraid to speak against my servant Moses?' There is surely a serious lesson here which is still relevant to us today, as the warning is given in Romans chapter 14 verse 13, 'Let us not therefore judge one another any more'.

In chapter 13, we observe that the Lord speaks to Moses directly once again: 'Send thou men, that they may search the land of Canaan', v. 2. It is significant that the Lord mentions each one of the men individually, who have to go and 'search the land'. As with scripture genealogies, each is mentioned individually, and reminds us that we also, as individuals, are accountable to the Lord for the work that we have done in His name, 2 Cor. 5. 10.

After forty days the spies returned. The report they gave started well, 'We came unto the land whither thou sentest us, and surely it floweth with milk and honey; and this is the fruit of it', v. 27. Yet, as can so often happen, there was a 'nevertheless'. They reported that 'the people be strong that dwell in the land, and the cities are walled, and very great: and moreover we saw the children of Anak there'.

How different the response from Caleb, v. 30! Later in the book of Numbers, 32. 11-12, we read the following, 'Surely none of the men that came up out of Egypt, from twenty years old and upward, shall see the land which I swear unto Abraham, Isaac, and unto Jacob; because they have not wholly followed me: Save Caleb the son of Jephunneh the Kenezite, and Joshua the son of Nun; for they have wholly followed the Lord'. May we say with the psalmist, 'Make me to go in the path of thy commandments; for therein do I delight', Ps. 119. 35.

May 3rd
Numbers 14; Proverbs 11; 1 Peter 3
MURMURING
In the previous chapter of the book of Numbers, we read that Caleb 'stilled the people'. The reason he had to still the people was that even after the good report having been given concerning the land, 'we came into the land whither thou sentest us, and surely it floweth with milk and honey; and this is the fruit of it', 13. 27, there was a 'nevertheless'. It is possible in our daily living, in the knowledge of all that the Lord does for us, to have a 'nevertheless'. After hearing the good report, the people murmured about the opposition of the Amalekites, the Hittites, the Jebusites, and the Amorites. There is no mention of the Lord. How easy it is to be taken up with the problems in our lives, and yet never to take them to the Lord!

In our chapter we read, 'And all the children of Israel murmured against Moses and against Aaron', 14. 2. There is a very serious and relevant lesson here. These murmurings made against the chosen servants of the Lord were, in fact, complaints against the Lord Himself. We, in our day, need to be aware of the seriousness of this, at all times. What they said to Moses and Aaron, requires quotation, but perhaps little comment, 'Let us make a captain, and let us return to Egypt'. How easy it was, and indeed it is, to forget what 'Egypt' was like!

It is of great comfort to read what Joshua and Caleb said to all the congregation, v. 8, 'If the Lord delight in us, then he will bring us into this land, and give it us; a land which floweth with milk and honey'. But there is also a warning issued in verse 9: 'Rebel not'. This is an important warning to us about the dangers of a rebellious spirit, because ultimately it is 'against the Lord', and not against his appointed servants, cp. 1 Sam. 8. 7. Notice also that the people are admonished, 'Neither fear ye the people of the land', and the reason is that 'they are bread for us'.

A further precious reason why they are told not to fear is that 'the Lord is with us'. Let us carefully note that murmuring against the Lord is an extremely serious matter, so we should ensure that in our individual and local church circumstances we are not found to be responsible for such conduct, Phil. 4. 8.

May 4th
Numbers 15; Proverbs 12; **1 Peter 4**
LIVING FOR GOD
The Apostle Peter in this chapter gives instruction as to how we can live to please God, in spite of difficult circumstances. He uses expressions such as 'arm yourselves', v. 1. This anticipates a conflict. This conflict can be from false accusation, or by opposition from outside, or it can be from within ourselves, as the Apostle Paul wrote to the believers in Rome, 'But I see another law in my members, warring against the law of my mind, and bringing me into captivity to the law of sin which is in my members', Rom. 7. 23.

It is true that some of the believers had been saved from a life which had been lived in the depths of sinfulness, as mentioned by the Apostle in verse 3 of the chapter: 'lasciviousness, lusts, excess of wine, revellings, banquetings, and abominable idolatries'. When the grace of God becomes evident in the life of the believer, old acquaintances are unable to comprehend it, and their response often demonstrates that. The apostle gives the reason for this reaction in verse 4 of the chapter. He states it is because 'ye run not with them to the same excess of riot'. Unsaved people do not generally understand the marked change in the behaviour of the person they know, but it is an evident testimony to the grace of God. There should also be a noticeable change in the behaviour of someone who has not gone to the same level of excesses, but who has become a 'partaker of the divine nature', 2 Pet. 1. 4.

The writer goes on to encourage and instruct the new believers in a variety of ways. He says in verse 7, 'Watch unto prayer.' It is a precious thing to pray individually and collectively. It is a most valuable thing to have an individual or family prayer list to use at the appropriate times. It is so easy for our minds to wander and for us to forget details of the needs of those for whom we are praying.

The apostle now encourages the believers to 'rejoice' in verse 13. He gives us the reason why we can, and should, rejoice: 'inasmuch as ye are partakers of Christ's sufferings; that when his glory shall be revealed, ye may be glad also with exceeding joy'.

May 5th
Numbers 16. 1- 40; Proverbs 13; 1 Peter 5
REBELLION AGAINST DIVINE AUTHORITY
As we reverently consider this chapter, we are forcibly confronted with the holiness of God. We also have another solemn truth brought before us, that sin against the chosen servants of God is sin against God Himself. In the New Testament we find the main character in this chapter mentioned in Jude verse 11.

Korah was a Levite, and he had a most honourable charge. It was his duty to carry the most holy things of the tabernacle. As with all such duties, there is not only great privilege but great responsibility. Sadly Korah was dissatisfied with the position he had been graciously given, Num. 4. 15, because we read in verse 10 that he sought 'the priesthood also'. As often happens with rebellion against God, there were others who wished to join such rebellion. Three others joined him – Dathan, Abiram, and On. If we are disobedient to the Lord, there are others who may join us in our disobedience. There is never any occasion when disobedience to the will of God results in good. They tried to undo what God had decreed. The judgement of God upon their actions was swift. The Lord said, 'Separate yourselves from among this congregation, that I may consume them in a moment', v. 21.

We are now told of the instructions given to Moses by the Lord. In verse 26 Moses directs the congregation, 'Depart, I pray you, from the tents of these wicked men, and touch nothing of theirs, lest ye be consumed in all their sins'. What is about to take place is from the Lord Himself, v. 28. 'And Moses said, Hereby ye shall know that the Lord hath sent me to do all these works; for I have not done them of my own mind'. Moses then gives the people a sign, v. 29: 'If these men die the common death of all men, or if they be visited after the visitation of all men; then the Lord hath not sent me'. What took place next is testimony to the holiness of God as seen in verse 32: 'And the earth opened her mouth, and swallowed them up, and their houses, and all the men that appertained unto Korah, and all their goods'.

We must respect those whom God has raised up as elders. They are God's stewards, Titus 1. 7. It is a very serious thing therefore to oppose or to seek to undermine their leadership.

May 6th
Numbers 16. 41 – 17. 13; Proverbs 14; **2 Peter 1**
ADD TO YOUR FAITH

The Apostle Peter begins his second letter by describing believers as having 'obtained like precious faith with us'. This faith is precious because, firstly, it is unique. It is the same faith as the apostle's. It is faith in the Lord Jesus Christ. It is the faith that saves us. It is the faith that sanctifies us. It is the faith that keeps us. It is 'obtained through the righteousness of God and our Saviour Jesus Christ', v. 1.

Two words are used in verse 2, 'grace' and 'peace'. These are precious words indeed. You will notice the order in which they are written. There can never be peace with God without first knowing the grace of God. In Romans chapter 5 verse 1 we have the statement, 'Therefore being justified by faith, we have peace with God'. We are also told, 2 Pet. 1. 4, that we have received 'great and precious promises' from the word of God.

When we reach verse 5 we find a different emphasis. From the first verse down to the end of the fourth verse we read that we have received many blessings through the grace of God. We should now note the expression 'and beside this', v. 5. This may be better rendered 'as a result of this'. What the Apostle is now going to teach us, is that because of this work of grace wrought in our lives, we should be different to what we were before. Peter begins by emphasizing that we should give due diligence to what he is going to tell us. He says we must 'add to our faith' He tells us additionally *what* we must add. He says firstly, 'Add virtue', which is moral goodness or clean living. We have then to add 'knowledge' of spiritual truth. Then, follows 'temperance' or self control! Someone who was known for fits of temper should no longer be so characterized. What is required to be added now is 'patience', which is the ability to bear difficult situations and to recognize them to be the will of God. The next three spiritual attributes are, 'godliness', that is, dependence on God for everything, 'brotherly kindness', love for other believers, and 'charity', i.e., including concern for the lost, as well as those who belong to Christ, 1 John 3. 16. Finally, it is important to see that the word 'add' is in the *present* tense: we need to *continue* to 'add' to our faith.

May 7th
Numbers 18; **Proverbs 15**; 2 Peter 2

A SOFT ANSWER TURNS AWAY WRATH

When we are annoyed about something the first thing we do, perhaps, is to answer unkindly. We can regret it immediately, but more often than not the damage has been done. How frequently have we been recipients of such behaviour? We know how much a loose word can hurt us. We may also know how much we have injured somebody else by the same kind of unguarded comment.

The title of today's reading is one which every believer should ponder and make a regular matter for prayer. How many believers have been stumbled by an unguarded comment or a slanderous statement? Verse 4 of the chapter we are considering, is one worth reading regularly: 'a wholesome tongue is a tree of life: but perverseness therein is a breach in the spirit'. In the Epistle of James, much is said about the damage the spoken word can do, and also the benefit which can be achieved by our tongue being controlled by the Spirit of God. We are told that 'the tongue can no man tame', Jas. 3. 8. In Ephesians chapter 6 verse 18 we are encouraged to take practical issues like this to the Lord in prayer, as He is able to free us from such difficulties as the control of our tongue: 'Praying always with all prayer and supplication in the Spirit'. It would be of benefit to us to pray about our speech every day.

Often our first reaction when we feel we have been wronged is to retaliate. The Apostle Peter knew about reacting in this way, yet when he came to write his New Testament letters, led by the Spirit of God he could say, 'For even hereunto were ye called: because Christ also suffered for us, leaving us an example, that ye should follow his steps: who did no sin, neither was guile found in his mouth: who, when he was reviled, reviled not again; when he suffered, he threatened not; but committed himself to him that judgeth righteously', 1 Pet. 2. 21-23. If we experience difficulty in this important area of life we should make it a matter of daily prayer. As we start each day it is of great benefit to take practical things, such as this, to the Lord in prayer. The promise made to Jeremiah, 'call unto me, and I will answer', Jer. 33. 3, can be ours.

May 8th
Numbers 19; **Proverbs 16**; 2 Peter 3

THE PROVIDENCE OF GOD

The beginning of the day can be a time when everything is done in a hurry. It can be a time when we are constantly looking at the clock, trying to remember everything we have to take with us before we leave home. In verse 3 of this chapter we are given instruction as to something we should begin each day by doing. We are instructed to 'commit thy works unto the Lord.' This word 'commit' can be translated 'roll'. When we 'roll' our daily circumstances over on the Lord we will find that He will bring them to a proper completion. With this in mind, we must be aware that if we commit all to Him, we no longer choose what the outcome will be. We can be sure that 'as for God, his way is perfect', Ps. 18. 30.

In verse 7 of this chapter we have a divine principle: 'when a man's ways please the Lord, he maketh even his enemies to be at peace with him'. No amount of scheming or endeavour can make this happen. For example, in Daniel chapter 1 verse 8, we find that 'Daniel purposed in his heart that he would not defile himself with the portion of the king's meat'. He knew that the food he was being offered had already been offered to idols, and he therefore could not eat it. In verse 9 of the same chapter, we read, 'Now God had brought Daniel into favour . . . with the prince of the eunuchs'. There is a principle here that is of vital importance to all of us. It is essential to be courteous to those with whom we are in contact in our daily lives at school, university, our place of employment, or at home, in order that our testimony for God is maintained.

We can sometimes think that we are having our own way with our circumstances, when in fact the Lord is testing us through some unusual means for our discipline and further blessing. We find this in verse 9 of our chapter: 'A man's heart deviseth his way: but the Lord directeth his steps'. We hear all around us of things happening by 'chance'. We have, in the last verse of our chapter a very precious verse, which has to do with the providence of God, 'The lot is cast into the lap; but the whole disposing thereof is of the Lord'. Let us be encouraged today, whatever our circumstances, that 'the steps of a good man are ordered by the Lord; and he delighteth in his way', Ps. 37. 23.

May 9th
Numbers 20; Proverbs 17; James 1
OBEDIENCE
This chapter, as with many others, is an example of what Paul wrote to the Romans, Rom. 15. 4, 'For whatsoever things were written aforetime were written for our learning that we through patience and comfort of the scriptures might have hope'. As we come to the scriptures in our daily readings, it is good to ask the question as to what the Holy Spirit would have us learn for that specific day. The manna had to be gathered daily.

Moses was subject to much provocation, as seen in verse 4, 'Why have ye brought up the congregation of the Lord into this wilderness, that we and our cattle should die there?' As a result of this, 'Moses and Aaron went from the presence of the assembly unto the door of the tabernacle of the congregation, and they fell upon their faces: and the glory of the Lord appeared unto them'. Here is an example of what to do under severe trial. Is prayer our first resort, or do we tend to retaliate? Moses was given specific instruction, 'Take the rod, and gather thou the assembly together, thou, and Aaron thy brother and speak ye unto the rock before their eyes; and it shall give forth his water'. As we continue to verses 10 and 11, we see that Moses altered the message given to him by the Lord. He first of all called the people 'rebels', and, instead of speaking to the rock, he 'smote the rock twice: and the water came out abundantly, and the congregation drank, and their beasts'. Refreshment was enjoyed by the Israelites, but as a direct result of this Moses was not permitted to bring the people into the Promised Land.

Despite Moses' failure, God in His grace took him to the top of Mount Pisgah in Deuteronomy chapter 34 and showed him the land of Canaan from that vantage point. It was also the grace of God that provided a grave for Moses, and buried him there.

There are, of course, lessons to be learned. The lesson that God is holy, righteous, omniscient, omnipotent, and omnipresent. This account also shows us that obedience to Him and His word is of the utmost importance in our walk with Him. 'Behold, to obey is better than sacrifice, and to hearken than the fat of rams', 1 Sam. 15. 22.

May 10th
Numbers 21; Proverbs 18; **James 2**
FAITH WITHOUT WORKS IS DEAD

In this chapter James deals with a number of difficult subjects. At the outset he deals with the showing of preference to certain types of individuals. It is good to notice that once again he refers to his readers as 'my brethren'. This shows us that he has a concern for the welfare of his readers, and that what is written is written for their benefit. The subject taken up in the early part of the chapter is that of showing 'partiality' 'with respect to persons', v. 1. This can be shown in many ways, but seems here to be in respect of the social status of an individual. James states in verse 9, 'If ye have respect to persons ye commit sin'. The choice of David as king of Israel highlights the importance of not being influenced by such prejudice. We read that 'The Lord said to Samuel, For the Lord seeth not as man seeth; for man looketh on the outward appearance, but the Lord looketh on the heart', 1 Sam. 16. 7. The Lord sees motives, which, of course, we cannot see.

At the beginning of verse 14, James asks a question to the readers then, and, indeed, to us now. 'What doth it profit, my brethren, though a man say he hath faith, and have not works? can [such] faith save him?' What this verse is asking for is evidence of a work of God having been done in our lives. Evidences of faith can be seen in many different ways. We have already seen that our attitude to believers rich or poor would be an area where evidence is seen. The great example is given of Abraham in this chapter of his offering up of Isaac, when the question is asked by James, 'Was not Abraham our father justified by works, when he offered Isaac his son upon the altar?', and he continues, 'Seest thou how faith wrought with his works, and by works was faith made perfect?'

We see the fulfilment of Genesis chapter 15 verse 6: 'He believed in the Lord; and he counted it to him for righteousness'. We also see the truth of Romans chapter 15 verse 4, 'For whatsoever things were written aforetime were written for our learning that we through patience and comfort of the scriptures might have hope'.

May 11th
Numbers 22. 1-38; Proverbs 19; **James 3. 1 – 4. 12.**

TONGUE IS A LITTLE MEMBER . . . BOASTS GREAT THINGS

We observe that he again refers to those to whom he is writing as 'brethren'. Although James is about to say some very straight and heart-searching things to his readers, he says it in a way which shows his care and concern for them, as they live their lives for God. Quite frequently it is not so much *what* is said but the manner in which it is said. It also shows us that he is identifying himself with them ('brethren'), and therefore he himself is not exempt from these matters. In this chapter he deals with the important subject of the spoken word and how it can do much good or much harm.

He illustrates what he is teaching with *three examples*. A large animal is controlled by a small 'bit' in its mouth, v. 3; a large ship is directed by a small 'helm', v. 4; and a 'little fire' can start in a very small way, but spread very quickly and cause enormous damage, v. 5. We are given three descriptions of the unguarded tongue: 'a world of iniquity', v. 6; 'it defileth the whole body', v. 6; and 'the tongue no man can tame', v. 8. 'Therewith bless we God, even the Father; and therewith curse we men', v. 9. The *inconsistency* of the tongue is what James is warning every believer about. The writer then tells us, 'My brethren, these things ought not so to be'. Challenging indeed!

Three rhetorical questions are posed: 'Doth a fountain send forth at the same place sweet water and bitter?'; 'Can a fig tree, my brethren bear olive berries' and 'Either a vine figs', vv. 11-12.

The Apostle James then identifies two types of wisdom: 'heavenly wisdom' and 'earthly wisdom'. If we have 'bitter envyings' and 'strife' in our hearts 'this wisdom descendeth not from above' vv. 14-15. We are told this wisdom is 'earthly, sensual, devilish'. The chapter ends by describing 'heavenly wisdom'. The last two verses of the chapter require contemplation: 'But the wisdom that is from above is first pure, then peaceable, gentle and easy to be entreated, full of mercy and good fruits, without partiality, and without hypocrisy. And the fruit of righteousness is sown in peace of them that make peace'. Similarly our Lord declared: 'Wherefore by their fruits ye shall know them', Matt. 7. 20.

May 12th
Num. 22. 39 – 23. 26; **Proverbs 20. 1 – 21. 11**; Jas. 4. 13 – 5. 20

THE FEAR OF THE LORD IS THE BEGINNING OF WISDOM

What heartache, wasted lives, and broken hearts have come about by failure to take notice of the warning in the first verse of this chapter, 'Wine is a mocker, strong drink is raging: and whosoever is deceived thereby is not wise'. This is a timely verse for the present day, as encouragement to indulge in strong drink is being glamorized all around us. Since as far back as Noah, Gen. 9, and Lot, Gen. 19, strong drink has been breaking up families and causing heartache.

In the second verse we are encouraged to have respect to those who have authority over us. It is also good to appreciate that those in authority are accountable to a higher Authority. In the book of Daniel we see how respectful and yet honest he was in his day to rulers. Daniel's mind was settled because he understood the very important truth that 'the most High ruleth in the kingdom of men', Dan. 4. 17. When we are tempted to think that things are becoming out of control this is a good verse to keep in mind. The Apostle Paul wrote to the Romans 'The powers that be are ordained of God', Rom. 13. 1.

In verse 4 of the chapter we are encouraged to be industrious and not lazy. It is a good testimony for God when a believer can be relied on to be industrious, honest, respectful, and reliable. 'The sluggard will not plough by reason of the cold; therefore will he beg in harvest, and have nothing'. In verse 14 we see someone who is trying to obtain something by deceit or trickery. The thought here is that the person is attempting to buy something, but does not want to pay the 'going rate' so he says 'it is naught, it is naught'. After the deal is done to his satisfaction, he then boasts as to how little he paid. This person thought, no doubt, that he had won the day but, 'good understanding giveth favour: but the way of the transgressors is hard', Prov. 13. 15.

Finally, 'Say not thou, I will recompense evil: but wait on the Lord, and he shall save thee', v. 22. Sometimes we may feel we can put something right when we have been wronged. This verse tells us to leave it to the Lord: 'As for God, His way is perfect', Ps. 18. 30.

May 13th
Numbers 23. 27 – 24. 25; **Proverbs 21. 12 – 22. 16;** Luke 1. 1- 25

THE TRIUMPH OF THE RIGHTEOUS

Earlier in the book of Proverbs there is a verse which is perhaps one of the best known in the entire book. It is found in chapter 14 verse 12: 'There is a way which seemeth right unto a man, but the end thereof are the ways of death'. In the word of God we are not told what to all appearances *seemeth* right, we have revealed to us what *is* right. In our daily lives we can be given much advice as to what to do, and when to do it. The most important part of the day for the believer is when we come to the holy scriptures in order to listen to what God has to say to us for the day ahead in His will.

In verse 21 of this chapter we read, 'He that followeth after righteousness and mercy findeth life, righteousness, and honour'. In the days in which we live such a verse stands in stark contrast to what goes on around us. We live in times where it seems that 'righteousness' is the last consideration. Our verse is speaking of a life lived for God, which means living according to the scriptures. It has to do with what we say, 'Whoso keepeth his mouth and his tongue keepeth his soul from troubles', v. 23. A lot can be learned about a person by what they talk about. 'Proud and haughty scorner is his name who dealeth in proud wrath', v. 24.

In chapter 22 verse 3 we read 'A prudent man foreseeth the evil, and hideth himself: but the simple pass on, and are punished'. We need to be constantly aware of the dangers around us. We are told where genuine riches are to be found when we read verse 4: 'By humility and the fear of the Lord are riches, and honour, and life'.

Then we read two verses which are in great contrast one to the other. In verse 8 we read, 'He that soweth iniquity shall reap vanity; and the rod of his anger shall fail'. The word 'vanity' is really 'emptiness'. The verse tells us that iniquity always leads to emptiness. In contrast to that in verse 9 we read, 'He that hath a bountiful eye shall be blessed; for he giveth of his bread to the poor'. There is a striking contrast in the two verses. What we sow is what we reap. 'Cast thy bread upon the waters; for thou shalt find it after many days', Eccles. 11. 1.

May 14th
Numbers 25. 1 – 26. 51; **Proverbs 22. 17 – 23. 11;** Luke 1. 26-56

THE WISDOM OF GOD

The message of verse 17 of this chapter is to 'hear' and, importantly, 'apply' the wisdom we have been reading about. Sometimes in our daily reading it is possible to read the verses allocated, but not to apply them to the circumstances of the day in which we read them. We can see, in verse 19, the specific individual application which is required of us as we read the scriptures. Firstly, that our trust 'may be in the Lord' and, secondly, that the instruction is personal and uniquely individual, 'even to thee'. Further, it is for immediate attention and action, 'this day'. It is quite often easier to apply the word of God to others than to ourselves. We should remember the admonition given in Revelation chapters 2 and 3, 'he that hath an ear, let him hear'.

The question is asked in verses 20 and 21, 'Have not I written to thee excellent things in counsels and knowledge?' The value of the word of God is brought forcefully before us here. The things written are the very oracles of God. Here we have the Lord Himself marking out individually for us the path He would have us take in life. These great truths revealed to us here, are beyond any human wisdom, and by them we can 'know the certainty of the words of truth'. As we study lessons from the book of Proverbs, may we be struck by the teaching therein and through our study may we apply the instruction given to our everyday changing circumstances.

As we move into chapter 23 we find further instruction on godly living. In verse 12 we read, 'Apply thine heart unto instruction'. We can see from this verse that instruction does not come to us without effort on our part. We are directed to 'apply thine heart' unto instruction. To 'apply' means to be serious about it, to continue in it, to spend time on it. The source of instruction is the word of God. Not only the reading of scripture, but the contemplation of it and the application of it! By the use of these terms, we can see that this involves time. The importance we place on the holy scriptures will determine how long we spend with them each day. 'I wait for the Lord, my soul doth wait, and in his word do I hope', Ps. 130. 5.

May 15th

Numbers 26. 52 – 27. 23; Proverbs 23. 12-35; **Luke 1. 57-80**

HE SHALL BE CALLED JOHN

We have in the verses before us the account of the birth of John the Baptist, of whom the Lord could say, 'Among those that are born of women there is not a greater prophet than John the Baptist', Luke 7. 28. John's parents were a godly couple named Zacharias and Elizabeth who had this testimony 'they were both righteous before God, walking in all the commandments and ordinances of the Lord blameless', 1. 6. Yet, we read that 'they had no child', 2. 7. However, it becomes apparent that they had been praying for a child, as we learn in verse 13 that 'the angel said unto him' 'Fear not, Zacharias: for thy prayer is heard; and thy wife Elizabeth shall bear thee a son, and thou shalt call his name John'. Zacharias did not believe the message from the angel and was struck dumb. Although this is a unique situation, we can be encouraged that things we have been praying for, although not yet answered can still, in God's time, be answered.

When the time came to name the child at his circumcision 'they called him Zacharias', as it was common for a male child to be named after their father. We learn in verse 60 that his mother answered and said, 'Not so; but he shall be called John'. At this time Zacharias still could not speak because of his unbelief but he was given somewhere to write and he wrote 'his name is John', whereupon Zacharias' 'mouth was opened immediately, and he spake, and praised God'.

There are many lessons which can be taken from this account of the circumstances of the birth of John the Baptist. High spiritual privilege, such as Zacharias the priest enjoyed, brings great responsibility, and unbelief is all the more serious. Unbelief can hinder our work for God. Until that unbelief, whatever it may be, is confessed to God, there will be no progress spiritually, and we can find ourselves merely going through a routine of things without peace or joy. Another lesson to be learned is that 'with God nothing shall be impossible', v. 37. We may feel at times that there is no way back from a situation we find ourselves in, but taking lessons from this account and many others from the pages of scripture we can be sure that there is.

May 16th

Numbers 28; Proverbs 24; **Luke 2. 1-21**

THE TIMING OF GOD

In Proverbs chapter 21 verse 1 we read, 'The king's heart is in the hand of the Lord, as the rivers of water: he turneth it whithersoever he will'. We also read in Proverbs 16 verse 33, 'The lot is cast into the lap; but the whole disposing thereof is of the Lord'. When we come to Luke chapter 2 we see also the timing and sovereignty of God. When Caesar Augustus put out his decree that all the world should be taxed, he was, unknown to himself, carrying out the eternal plan of God. In verse 3 we are told that 'all went to be taxed, everyone into his own city'. Accordingly, Joseph and Mary went up from Galilee to Bethlehem, vv. 4-5. Also unknown to Caesar Augustus, this was the fulfilment of prophecy from Micah chapter 5 verse 2, 'But thou, Bethlehem Ephrata, though thou be little among the thousands of Judah, yet out of thee shall he come forth unto me that is to be ruler in Israel; whose goings forth have been from everlasting'. We have another lovely, accurate example of the timing of God in verse 6: 'and so it was, that, while they were there, the days were accomplished that she should be delivered'. On a practical note, we can be sure that in our experience we can rely on God's timing in relation to our circumstances. We can be sure that as we ponder these verses and many others that we can, in the detail of our lives, rely on the timing of God.

We may observe the *urgency* and the *faith* of the shepherds as soon as the angels 'were gone away from them into heaven', since they said, 'Let us now go even unto Bethlehem, and see this thing which is come to pass, which the Lord hath made known unto us', v. 15. We can see here their faith shown by what they say. Immediately they heard the announcement of the angel they determine to go and see this thing which is come to pass. They did not say 'if' it has come to pass; there was no doubting the message. Perhaps there is a lesson in that for us today.

When we see the timing of God and His omniscience as seen in His word, and in the circumstances of life, we may confess with Daniel, 'The most High ruleth in the kingdom of men and giveth it to whomsoever he will', Dan. 4. 25.

May 17th

Numbers 29; **Proverbs 25. 1 – 26. 12**; Luke 2. 22-52

SELF-CONTROL

Whoever has no rule over his own spirit is like a city broken down, without walls, Prov. 25. 28. The Hebrew verb 'rule over' has its root in shutting up, retaining, or restraint. A man who cannot control, discipline or restrain himself is very vulnerable, in the same way that a city without walls was open to attack.

Throughout the Bible the virtue of self-control is taught for the people of God. The supreme example is the Lord Jesus who was always in full control of His words, thoughts, and actions. Unlike the Lord Jesus, we have to contend with bodies that require discipline and a sinful nature that responds to temptation. Every believer has this struggle; Paul wrote, 'I discipline my body and bring it into subjection', 1 Cor. 9. 27.

We can see examples from the Old Testament of people who lost control. Moses who was the meekest man in all the earth 'spoke rashly with his lips', Ps. 106. 33, and paid a high price for his loss of self-control. Lot who had been a just man living in the depraved city of Sodom allowed himself to get drunk and, with his defences removed, committed incest and fathered Moab and Ammon. David, with his sins of adultery and murder in relation to Bathsheba, and many other examples demonstrate the absence of that self-control which protects against the temptations and assaults of the devil. The word 'capricious' describes one who acts according to impulse or whim. It's a perfect word for one who lacks self-control.

The ability to restrain the impulses of the flesh and turn away from temptation does not come naturally. The Spirit of God is able to produce fruit in the Christian, which is the evidence of His presence. One aspect of this fruit is self-control. As we yield to His authority and allow Him control in our hearts we will find that we are able to discipline our bodies and minds and are less vulnerable to sin.

'For the grace of God that brings salvation has appeared to all men, teaching us that, denying ungodliness and worldly lusts, we should live soberly, righteously, and godly in the present age', Titus 2. 11-12.

May 18th

Numbers 30-31; Proverbs 26. 13 – 27. 27; **Luke 3**

PLEASING GOD

Your perspective changes as you grow older. I have distinct memories of looking at men with grey hair and thinking that they were old and now I realize that they were in their forties or fifties. When you are a teenager life stretches out in front of you and there appears to be plenty of time for everything, even for pleasing God.

There is not much information given to us in the Bible about the early years of the Lord Jesus. We know what took place when he went with his family to Jerusalem as a twelve-year-old boy. Apart from that insight the Spirit of God has drawn a veil over the years that the Lord Jesus spent in Nazareth working as a carpenter and being part of a family. We have no detail of His interaction with the people of His town or customers of His business. In fact, it is not until He is about thirty years of age that we read more of His life as He moved into public ministry.

Although we know nothing of the Lord in His teens and twenties in Nazareth we do have the verdict of God the Father, v. 22. During these early 'hidden' years the Lord Jesus had lived quietly and had done no miracles. There had been no water turned into wine, sick healed, dead raised, or sermons preached. Disciples had not been called and crowds had not formed to listen and be fed. Yet each day had been observed by heaven and His impeccable, holy, and devoted life had brought pleasure to God the Father.

It is an encouragement to us all that a life without public recognition or acclaim, yet carefully observed by heaven, can bring pleasure to the heart of God. It was daily routine as a teenager and later as a man in His family and business life that had been marked by holiness and righteousness. Likewise, simple devotion, although not impeccable like the Lord Jesus, still brings joy to God today.

Let us determine that wherever we are, and whatever we have to do today, we will live conscious of the gaze of heaven and seek to honour and glorify God in the unseen and routine aspects of our lives. Pleasing God should not be simply a weekend pursuit.

May 19th
Numbers 32; Proverbs 28; Luke 4. 1-15
DISCOURAGEMENT

They stood on the banks of the river Jordan with Canaan before them. Forty years had passed and an older generation had perished in the wilderness since they first arrived on the borders of the Promised Land. Finally, they were on the brink of entering their inheritance and experiencing the fullness of what God had promised them so long ago.

It was at this moment of joy and anticipation that history repeated itself. Having passed through the Red Sea, their fathers had sent spies into the land. Their report had discouraged the people to such an extent that they decided to turn away from the land and so incurred the discipline of God, which caused their wandering for the last forty years. You would think that forty years in the wilderness would ensure that such a blunder would never happen again. You would be wrong.

It seemed a perfectly reasonable request from the children of Reuben and Gad. They had cattle and the land of Gilead, and Jazer was good for cattle. Why bother going over Jordan and fight for land when there was an easier option? Why not stay where they were on good cattle country that was easily available and seemed ideal for their purposes?

Moses had to remind them of the hard-learned lessons of their history. By pursuing their own agenda they would discourage their brethren from crossing the Jordan and entering into the inheritance that God had promised for them. God would visit judgement upon them as He had done to their fathers. They had forgotten that God is displeased when His people are discouraged.

Discouragement can come in many forms. The spies had previously brought a message of fear which had discouraged the people from stepping forward in obedience to the Lord. On this occasion it was the example of some of the people settling for the attraction of an easier option. Let us be careful lest anything other than full commitment to the Lord brings discouragement to others in their walk with the Lord. How sobering it is that our wilful disobedience, fear, or selfishness could discourage other saints and cause them to settle for second best!

May 20th

Numbers 33; **Proverbs 29**; Luke 4. 16-44

ENGAGE BRAIN

'Do you see a man hasty in his words? There is more hope for a fool than for him', Prov. 29. 20.

We should never underestimate the power of words. It is an acknowledgement of their influence for good or evil on a small or grand scale that lies behind the warnings throughout the Bible.

In the New Testament, James says that a person who can control their tongue is able to control the whole body; such is the power and danger of words, 'For we all stumble in many things. If anyone does not stumble in word, he is a perfect man, able also to bridle the whole body', Jas. 3. 2.

There are all sorts of dangers associated with words. We can gossip, tell lies, flatter, deceive, curse and use words to express selfish ambition, envy, and jealousy. We can destroy relationships, cause strife, wound, and break down.

On the other hand words can be a real blessing. We can express our worship and testify for God. We can heal relationships and repent of sin. We can encourage and comfort those in need, and help build up the people of God.

The Lord Jesus was masterly in the use of words. He never spoke inappropriately and always had the right word for the right occasion. There were times when He used many words, and then in different circumstances He said very little.

The Lord Jesus was never hasty in His words. As a result there was never the need for Him to rethink what He had said or apologize for speaking out of turn. His words were thought through and measured.

How often we regret speaking without thinking properly! Perhaps in anger or frustration we speak in haste and have to repent of our words quickly spoken. Sometimes we say the wrong thing or speak in the wrong manner.

It would be good for us to consider the proverb and take a little thought for the consequences of our words, and, in the words of a pointed current saying, 'Engage brain before opening mouth'. Our words, which can be spoken in haste, can cause damage which requires the wisdom of Solomon and the patience of Job to amend.

May 21st

Numbers 34. 1 – 35. 8; Proverbs 30; **Luke 5. 1-16**

NOT SAFE BUT GOOD

C. S. LEWIS wrote the very popular *Chronicles of Narnia* which, among other things, serve as an extended allegory of Christianity. If you are familiar with the books, then you may know that Aslan is a golden lion that represents the Lord Jesus. He gives his own life as a sacrifice but rises from the dead to lead his people in a victorious battle.

In *The Lion, the Witch and the Wardrobe*, Susan, one of the children in the story, has a conversation with talking beavers about Aslan, who tell her that anyone who comes to Aslan without knees knocking is either braver than most, or silly. Lucy, another of the children, then asked the beavers if Aslan were quite safe. 'Safe?' said Mr. Beaver; 'Don't you hear what Mrs. Beaver tells you? Who said anything about safe? 'Course he isn't safe. But he's good. He's the King, I tell you'.

When Peter saw the reality of who Christ was, expressed in the miraculous catch of fish, he was appalled. His response was wholly appropriate as he realized he was in the presence of God and was unworthy to be in close proximity to the Lord.

We can easily become overly familiar with our Lord and speak of Him and to Him as we would of, or to, any other person. However, we would do well to remember that He is not any other person. He is the Lord, and the writer to the Hebrews reminds us that we should 'serve God acceptably with reverence and godly fear. For our God is a consuming fire', Heb. 12. 28-29.

Happily, Peter's experience did not drive him and his associates away from the Lord. When the boat came to shore they didn't run and hide, as Adam and Eve had done in the Garden of Eden. The experience brought them to the point of decision in relation to the Lord, and they gave Him first place in their lives as they left everything to follow Him.

The Lord is not 'safe' but He is good and we should respond as Peter and his friends did on that boat by giving Him first place in our lives. The Lord Jesus spoke in terms of taking up one's cross and following Him; that was not the 'safe' option, but to any who followed it was for their good.

May 22nd
Numbers 35. 9 – 36. 13; Proverbs 31; Luke 5. 17-39
REFUGE
Only one tribe among the children of Israel was not allocated land in the distribution of the Promised Land. The tribe of Levi provided the priests of the Lord and the overseers of the tabernacle and all its rites and furnishings, and as such were not to spend their time working the land.

The Levites were given forty-eight cities throughout the land. Of these cities, six were designated as cities of refuge. The cities were Kedesh, Shechem, Hebron, Bezer, Romath, and Golan, Josh. 20. 7-8.

As part of their sophisticated judicial system, murder was punishable by death. However, the Lord gave them a safeguard against the avenger by providing cities to which the killer could flee for refuge. He was safe from retaliation from a member of the deceased's family until the case could go to trial. If he was judged to have killed unintentionally then he could reside in the city of refuge without fear of attack until the death of the high priest who was in office at the time of the trial, at which point he could return to his property. If he left the city before the death of the high priest the avenger could lawfully kill him.

The Levites were probably chosen to provide these sanctuaries as the most suitable and impartial judges. By their consecration as priests, the Levites were mediators between the Israelites and God. As such, they would have been gifted to calmly mediate between the attacker and the victim's family, ensuring that no further bloodshed would occur.

The cities of refuge are a picture of Christ, in whom sinners find refuge from the destroyer of our souls. Just as the guilty person sought refuge in the cities set up for that purpose, in the same way we flee to Christ for refuge from sin's penalty, Heb. 6. 18. Only Christ provides refuge from the just consequences of our sin and it is to Him alone that we must run. Just as they were open to anyone so Christ provides a refuge to anyone who comes to Him seeking refuge from sin and its punishment. As our Great High Priest He will never relinquish His priesthood through death, hence our safety is assured.

May 23rd
Deuteronomy 1; **Ecclesiastes 1. 1 – 2. 11**; Luke 6. 1-19
VANITY
Every age has its heroes. I am not sure if our age is different from any other but it does seem that nearly all our heroes are wealthy. The media focuses on the lifestyle of the rich and famous and presents to us their triumphs and disasters as we watch with an almost morbid fascination.

Most people who are not rich in terms of money or experience long for the perceived freedom and satisfaction that wealth would bring. If only we didn't have to work to pay the bills! If we could afford to fly in a private jet; drive the most expensive cars and mix with the glamorous people we would be happy and content, except it doesn't seem to work out that way for those who are rich and famous.

Solomon was a man who had it all, and had done it all. He had more wealth than could be imagined and had used his wealth and unrestricted power to experience every pleasure and pursuit that was available at that time. He tried everything to find satisfaction and meaning in his life, but failed. All he could find was emptiness and hopelessness in his pursuit.

We may wonder why people who are famous, successful, and rich have often afflicted themselves with substance abuse, have broken families and seem so sad. They are meant to have it all. They can do what they want. Everything is possible for them.

Solomon discovered that life without God has no hope, satisfaction, or meaning. If ever there was a man on earth who could arrive at such a conclusion it was Solomon. He learned that a proper relationship with God is the key to knowing what life is all about and thus experiencing satisfaction, peace, and joy.

As a Christian I should seek true contentment that only comes through walking with the Lord and enjoying daily communion with Him through His word and prayer. 'Two things I request of You (deprive me not before I die): remove falsehood and lies far from me; give me neither poverty nor riches – feed me with the food allotted to me; lest I be full and deny You, and say, "Who is the Lord?" Or lest I be poor and steal, and profane the name of my God', Prov. 30. 7-9 NKJV.

May 24th
Deuteronomy 2; Ecclesiastes 2. 12 – 3. 15; **Luke 6. 20-49**

WHO WILL YOU FOLLOW?

The kingdom of our Lord Jesus is not like any other kingdom. The laws are different and seem to be an inversion of what would seem natural. As the Lord Jesus taught the multitude they listened with astonishment. No one else would tell them to love their enemies and return hate with love, and violence with kindness. His teaching was very different from any easy 'prosperity gospel' that you come across on television from time to time.

To follow Jesus Christ and live out His teaching was going to be demanding. If you put His teaching into practice it may threaten your wellbeing and put a strain on your resources. However, He did instruct His audience that day that true blessedness was only found in belonging to His kingdom.

The Lord Jesus was the perfect example of all He taught. He had shown kindness to everyone who crossed His path. He fed and healed without partiality and without any expectation of reward. He blessed in every way, weeping with the sorrowing, living with the poor, and in His future suffering would allow men to strike Him without the terrible retaliation which was in His power to visit upon His tormentors.

He finished His sermon with a parable which challenged the people to make a decision. Who would they follow? Where did they want to go? Who did they want to emulate? What kind of fruit did they wish to produce? These are the big questions that we face as we consider the realities that Christ's teaching declares. Who are we following, and where are they taking us? If we have never stopped and considered these issues then it is time that we do so.

We all face a decision when we are confronted with the gospel. The Lord Jesus was clear in His preaching. He informed His audience of the price that they would pay by following Him. He explained the standards of His kingdom and the new lifestyle it would demand. He never hid the opposition or hatred they would experience.

Following Christ will be hard, but the pathway is a blessed one and leads to an eternity with Him in His kingdom.

160

May 25th
Deuteronomy 3; Ecclesiastes 3. 16 – 4. 16; Luke 7. 1-29

IT SEEMS HARSH

As a parent facing a naughty child you can be guilty of at least two errors. On the one hand you can let the problem slide and take the easy way out by overlooking the misdemeanour, or conversely you can over-react and pronounce a punishment that is excessive. We know that the punishment should fit the crime; sometimes we just react badly to a situation.

Moses had failed God in the area where he was strongest. The meekest man in all the earth lost his temper under severe provocation by the children of Israel. He was their leader, shepherd, and guide, yet he lost control – with terrible consequences. Moses had led them for forty years, and now they would leave him behind and cross into the Promised Land. Could there have been any more devastating news for Moses to hear from the Lord?

Was it too harsh? Would the Lord reconsider? Surely there would be some middle ground, some compromise? You can understand Moses asking, 'I pray thee, let me go over, and see the good land that is beyond Jordan, that goodly mountain, and Lebanon', Deut. 3. 25.

The Lord charged Moses with unbelief after he had struck the rock and called the children of Israel rebels. It is a measure of the seriousness of unbelief that the Lord told Moses he would not go into Canaan. It seems harsh: after all it was a spur-of-the-moment thing and he was surely sorry.

Moses was guilty of the same sin that had kept Israel in the wilderness for forty years. 'And to whom sware he that they should not enter into his rest, but to them that believed not? So we see that they could not enter in because of unbelief', Heb. 3. 18-19. The sin that kept them out would keep Moses out as he bore the consequences of his sin.

What a challenge to any child of God! Through the experience of Moses we see the fixed attitude of the Lord towards unbelief and disobedience; we should heed the solemn warning from the writer to the Hebrews, 'Take heed, brethren, lest there be in any of you an evil heart of unbelief, in departing from the living God', Heb. 3. 12.

PROMISES, PROMISES

'When you make a vow to God, do not delay to pay it; for He has no pleasure in fools. Pay what you have vowed – better not to vow than to vow and not pay', Eccles. 5. 4-5 NKJV.

Sometimes it happens when we get carried away with emotion. We are listening to a hymn well sung, get caught up in the moment and make a vow to God. We promise God we will do some great thing for Him; we will give our time or resources for His work, we will evangelize our workmates or neighbours, we will speak to the brother or sister with whom we have had a problem, and as the singing lifts our hearts and emotions we are sincere in our passionate vow.

Time passes and our emotion fades. The wallet remains shut and the vow unfulfilled. It would have been better not to say anything to God.

Often we make promises to God that we do not keep. How often have you sinned and, in the aftermath of guilt and regret, vowed that you would never do it again? But you sin again, and in so doing break your vow to God.

The Bible has many examples of people who made vows and kept them. In the early church some of the Christians sold their land and gave the proceeds to the church. They made a commitment to God and carried it through to a conclusion.

God does deserve and demand our full commitment to Him. He does not require us to make emotive and ill-thought-out vows that we do not fulfil. It would be better for us to make fewer vows and make sure that we fulfil what we have vowed. Ananias and Sapphira did a good thing by selling their land and giving some of the proceeds to the apostles for the benefit of others. However, they said that they were making a commitment to sell their land and give *all* of the proceeds. Their vow was not paid in full, and they received severe judgement for their lie.

Sometimes we get carried away and say too much, even to God. Take a moment when you feel the emotion rise, and consider carefully whatever vow you are about to make. If you make a vow, don't neglect to pay.

May 27th
Deuteronomy 5; Ecclesiastes 7; **Luke 8. 1-21**

SOWING THE SEED

Of all the parables told by the Lord Jesus, the story of the farmer sowing seed into different ground conditions is perhaps one of the best known.

The farmer is unnamed as this story applies to anyone who spreads the word of God. It may be conversation with a family member or friend. It can take place in a factory, office, or shop. Whenever the word of God is communicated to another person the seed is being sown.

The focus of the parable is not so much about the farmer who does the sowing, or even the seed which is sown, but rather the different *conditions of the ground* into which the same seed falls. There is an indiscriminate broadcasting of the seed and inevitably it falls into different soil conditions.

This parable is an encouragement to anyone who speaks, preaches, writes, or in any way communicates the word of God. As sowers, our responsibility is to the seed to make sure it is broadcast far and near. We are not to carefully select the people who hear, and think that we know whose heart is ripe to receive the word. Our selection would be flawed, as the true condition of the heart is known only to God, and usually seen by us over the longer term rather than any instant response to the word.

There is a field all around us with needy souls rubbing shoulders with us every day. The challenge to our hearts today is: are we keeping the seed in our bag, or are we scattering it over the soil? We don't know whether it will land in good soil or not. It may land in soil that has no depth, and produces good results that wither over time. It may produce an instant hostile response, or Satan may pluck it out of the ears of those who hear. None of that is our business, and none of that is within our control.

The farmer sows the seed, and without the sowing of the seed there is no fruit from the soil. Let us determine this day that some of the good seed of the word of God will leave our hand, or mouth, and land in a person's heart for God to do His work. Let the seed go!

May 28th
Deuteronomy 6. 1 – 7. 11; Ecclesiastes 8. 1 – 9. 10; Luke 8. 22-39

THE WORD OF GOD

It is remarkable how you remember some things from your childhood and others are long forgotten. I have a vivid memory of a Bible verse that was framed and hung above the piano in the living room. I have never forgotten that text, and wonder if part of the reason is that it was seen by me every time I entered the living room, which would have been most days of my young life.

It is a good thing to display the word of God in our own homes, and by so doing keep it in front of our eyes and near the forefront of our minds. Another example of this is a text above a dining room table that I saw when visiting some Christian friends. It said, 'Speak not evil one of another, brethren', Jas. 4. 11. It was a timely reminder not to gossip over supper, and must surely have checked any temptation to stray into that type of conversation.

Moses instructed the children of Israel to ensure that the word of God had a prominent place in their lives. They had to teach it to their children, talk about it wherever they were, display it on their homes, and wear it on their person. Scripture was to be at the heart of their lives and communities.

'Out of sight, out of mind', is a phrase that is true of the word of God and the truth of it was reflected in the instruction to display and discuss the scriptures. When you have the scriptures in your pocket, on your phone, above your desk, and before your eyes it is a constant reminder of the truth we have learned and that should govern our lives. It calibrates our conscience and can keep us on track when otherwise our thoughts could be shaped by the ethos of the world that is practiced all around us.

How important it is not just to display the word of God but to chat about it in our everyday lives! We can often talk about other Christians, or discuss the latest controversy, or gossip, but how often do we start a conversation with someone about the scriptures that we have read that morning and talk about what we learned and found helpful? It is wonderful to encourage each other with the little nuggets of truth found in our daily reading.

Why not start a daily reading group and share your thoughts which can be so helpful to others?

May 29th

Deut. 7. 12 – 8. 20; **Ecclesiastes 9. 11 – 10. 20;** Luke 8. 40-56

APPRECIATE WISDOM

A poor wise man saved his small city from a great king who had a large army. He used his wisdom to bring deliverance, yet he was unrewarded with wealth or social esteem. His wisdom was only sought in desperate times. When the crisis was past the poor wise man was soon forgotten. Solomon knew the value of such wisdom, v. 13, and drew important lessons from the parable.

Godly wisdom is greater than strength, v. 16. The exploits of David as he slew Goliath, or the children of Israel as the walls of Jericho fell, or the confrontation between Elijah and the prophets of Baal on Mount Carmel are just a few examples which remind us that wisdom from above is greater than any strength of men. God has often used the seemingly weak to confound the seemingly mighty. 'This is the word of the Lord unto Zerubbabel, saying, Not by might, nor by power, but by my spirit, saith the Lord of hosts', Zech. 4. 6.

Godly wisdom is often rejected, v. 17. Most of us do not want to hear wise words, as they often expose our folly and sin. When someone starts to speak with wisdom, we metaphorically put our fingers in our ears and start singing, 'La la la la la . . .'. It can be as childish as that scenario. As a result we often ignore what wisdom we receive, and do not honour those who speak such wisdom into our lives. We can become like Rehoboam, 2 Chr. 10, who rejected the wisdom of the elders and sought advice from the young men who told him what he wanted to hear. The outcome was the sad division of Israel into the two nations of Israel and Judah, the consequences of which remain to this day.

Godly wisdom can be destroyed by one person, v. 18. As effective as godly wisdom is, a single person – 'one sinner' – can cancel much good. This clause 'one sinner destroys much good' is like our 'one rotten apple ruins the whole barrel'. It only takes one person or one moment to ruin what wisdom has accomplished. We must always be on our guard against such moments and influences that can be so destructive. Let's take care to appreciate the wisdom we receive and honour those who bring wisdom into our lives.

May 30th
Deuteronomy 9. 1 – 10. 11; Ecclesiastes 11-12; **Luke 9. 1-17**
WANTING TO SEE JESUS

Herod was not at peace. He had beheaded John Baptist and now was hearing rumours about the miracles that Jesus and His disciples were performing. Some were saying that it was Elijah who had appeared, and others said one of the old prophets was back among the people.

The rumour that Herod feared most was that John Baptist had risen from the dead. He was perplexed, as no other man he knew was like the man whom he had beheaded. John had made a lasting impression on Herod and it troubled him.

Herod wanted to see Jesus to put his mind at rest. If he saw Jesus and could satisfy himself that John Baptist had not risen from the dead then he would have nothing to fear. He wanted to see Jesus to get some peace of mind.

The crowd wanted to see Jesus to hear His teaching and experience His healing. They would not give Him peace and pursued Him into a desert place. They were curious and wanted to experience what Jesus could provide. They took their sick to be healed and were not disappointed. As the day wore on they got the unexpected bonus of being fed freely through the miracle of the loaves and fish.

Most people wanted to see Jesus for selfish reasons. They wanted something from Him. He was astonishing to listen to and when He performed miracles they were not the tricks of a cheap charlatan. He was impressive in every way. However, when He taught them that following Him would be costly the attraction faded. It was one thing to go and get, it would be another thing to follow and give. The crowd melted away, and at the end of the story are found shouting for Him to be crucified.

It is a test for any person to examine why they want to see Jesus. Is it to get from Him what He can provide for this life? Do we want peace of mind like Herod from the consequences of our sin which troubles us? Those who sought to see Jesus in order to follow Him, even when that involved taking up their crosses, found true blessing. They were prepared to give up their sin and self, and give Him their all. Are we?

May 31st
Deuteronomy 10. 12 – 11. 32; S. of Sol. 1. 1 – 2. 7; Luke 9. 18-36
REQUIREMENTS
Rabbi Simlai counted 613 different commandments in the law that Moses brought to the children of Israel. Scattered throughout the Old Testament scriptures there are verses which summarize the Lord's requirements of His people. Such verses emphasize the overriding principles which the many commandments applied to daily and national life in Israel.

Although the law was given to Moses for the regulation of a theocratic nation, the underlying principles of righteousness are timeless. They represent the character of God and are as unchangeable as He is.

All God's people should fear Him and walk in His ways. We should love and serve Him with all our hearts and souls. Moses told the people that they should keep the commandments and statutes of the Lord for their own good. It was not just the case of bringing pleasure to God through their obedience. The commandments would ensure their national and individual happiness and tranquillity.

Obedience to God's requirements remains the key to contentment in our life. We might think that in an age of grace God has no requirements for us, but that would be far from the truth. We do not have God-given legislation to govern the details of our lives but we do have inspired apostolic doctrine which brings the righteousness of God to bear upon us in our homes, workplaces, and local churches. By continuing in that teaching we will be responding to the Lord's requirements for us, which bear a striking similarity to the overriding principles found in the Old Testament.

How refreshing it must have been for Israel to hear that the yoke of Christ was not a legalistic straightjacket, but rather a means of blessing and rest! True joy and peace can only be found in willing obedience to God's requirements, which find their application to our lives in the apostles' doctrine.

The Lord Jesus told the people who were listening to His preaching, 'Take My yoke upon you and learn from Me, for I am gentle and lowly in heart, and you will find rest for your souls. For My yoke is easy and My burden is light', Matt. 11. 29-30 NKJV.

June 1st
Deuteronomy 12; Song of Solomon 2. 8 – 3. 5; Luke 9. 37-62
MEETING WITH GOD HIMSELF
In Deuteronomy chapter 12 we see three major things brought before Israel. (1) Their gift from God: they would be in *'the land'*, v. 1. (2) Once in the land they were to come to *'the place'*, v. 5. There would be a gathering place that God would choose where they would meet with Him. Of course to come to 'the place' they had first to be in the land. (3) What would make the place God's place is that He would 'cause his name to dwell there', vv. 5, 11. His presence there established God as the sole authority. All other names were to be destroyed and only the Lord's name alone would identify the Lord's gathering centre, vv. 3-5.

There are five truths here that show the purpose for the Lord's place. (1) A place of **coming**: 'Thither [there] thou shalt come', v. 5. They would find that worship and service to meet with God required travel to get there. Is He worth such? (2) A place of **bringing**: 'Thither ye shall bring your burnt offerings, and sacrifices', v. 6. Here the motive was to give to God, not get from God. (3) A place of **eating**: 'There ye shall eat before the Lord your God', v. 7. Eating what He desired would show fellowship with God. (4) A place of **rejoicing**: 'There . . . ye shall rejoice before the Lord your God', vv. 11-12. (5) A place of **obeying**: 'There thou shalt do all that I command thee', v. 14. They did not have permission to add tradition to His commands nor to subtract from them things they did not feel were relevant.

When we come to the New Testament church in 1 Corinthians we find that we have something that is a gift from God. We are not in a promised land but in the promised Son, 'in Christ', 1. 2. We also find that we are to 'come together into one place', which is called, 'in the church', 14. 23, 35. And we find that all other human names are not to be taken as identification, for God has put His name of 'Lord' upon Jesus. So they gathered together 'in the name of the Lord Jesus Christ', ch. 1 and 5. 4. When they came together they were to eat the 'Lord's supper', bring sacrifices of praise, and obey the Lord Jesus' commandments for His church, chs. 11, 14, 16.

Isn't it amazing that the Lord desires to be with His saints?

June 2nd

Deut. 13. 1-14; **Song of Solomon 3. 6 – 5. 1**; Luke 10. 1-24

A LOVE STORY

In a book that speaks of something being 'inlaid with love' we should not be surprised to see 'love' or 'beloved' mentioned over sixty times, 3. 10. In the Song of Solomon we have love *awakened* and love *sought.* In the following chapters there is love *separated*, love *abiding,* and love *secured.* But in today's reading we have love *formalized* (into a legal union), 3. 6-11, and then love *enjoyed*, 4. 1-16; 5. 1.

After a kingly wedding procession, 3. 6-11, we see love intimately enjoyed between the king and his spouse. The object of the king's love is his 'bride' as she is personally called, 'my love' who has ravished his heart. Yes, it's what the bride means to the bridegroom here as he finds his full delight in her.

In the shade of the banner of love in the 'fountain of gardens' one can hear the sound of music from this enchanting Song of Songs. The beautiful flowers of the Lily of the Valleys and the Rose of Sharon adorn the atmosphere. Inhale deeply as the soft south wind awakens the pleasant spices intoxicating the heart. They send their fragrant scents in a wafting aroma that bids one to eat of the pleasant fruits that are sweet to the mouth as romance is experienced in a never-failing and abiding love.

The bridegroom likens his bride to a garden. First, she is a 'garden inclosed' and 'a fountain sealed', 4. 12. No others have access to it. It is exclusively for him. Secondly, she is a watered garden as 'a fountain of gardens', 4. 15. She is nourishing and flourishing. Thirdly, she is a fruitful garden and invites her beloved to 'eat his pleasant fruits', 4. 16. She knows she is for him. Fourthly, she is an open garden – to him alone, 'I have come into my garden' he says, as he responds to her invitation, 5. 1.

Such a love story can take us to at least three levels. (1) The marriage relationship between a man and a woman that God has ordained – where the husband is to love his wife, Eph. 5. 25. (2) God and Israel. With an everlasting love He will restore her to Himself some day, Jer. 31. 3. (3) 'Christ and the church', who loved her and gave Himself for her. He wants us to know His inheritance in *us* – 'the fullness of Him', Eph. 1. 18-23.

June 3rd

Deut. 14. 22 – 15. 23; **Song of Solomon 5. 2 – 6. 9**; Luke 10. 25-42

LOVE SEPARATED – LOVE REVIVED

We now see that love has become separated in practice, 5. 2-8, but once the bride expresses her admiration for her beloved we see them united, vv. 9-16. The bridegroom is then captivated by her, 6. 4-9. To her, he is 'my beloved'; to him, she is 'my love'.

The problem begins when she is sleeping. She hears the knock of her beloved wanting to come in. However, having intimate communion with him seems to be inconvenient for her right then. She would have to go through the trouble of putting on her coat to answer the door, and since she had just bathed, her feet would get dirty again. So she delayed communion with him.

But then her heart sensing his nearness finally stirred and went to open for him – but he was gone. She called, but there was no answer: silence. With a yearning heart she pursued him toward the city. But she only found disrespect and hurt. She was looking in the wrong places but she kept pursuing him.

In love sickness she asked for help in finding him again. They asked her what was so special about him. She then describes the glories and value of 'my beloved' from head to foot concluding, 'he is altogether lovely' – far above others. Then, after hearing these glories, they wanted to seek him too.

The bride finally discovered him in his garden enjoying the sweet fruits. She exults in the reunion, 'I am my beloved's, and my beloved is mine'. The bridegroom is so taken up with her desire in seeking and finding him that he is consumed and delighted with the beauty of the one he calls, 'my love'. He values her continued purity and that she is for him alone.

Could not this take our minds to Christ, 'who loved us and gave himself for us'? We see a church leaving its first love, Rev. 2. 4. Oh we still love Him! But the cares of this life seem to make it weary to do His will and draw near to Him. We see the Lord knocking on the door of His church desiring sweet communion, 3. 20. He desires us to open the door now so that He can come in. He delights in His people's true fellowship. Paul's goal was that the church at Corinth would be a chaste virgin (devoted to Him alone) when they meet their bridegroom, 2 Cor. 11. 2.

June 4th
Deuteronomy 16; Song of Sol. 6. 10 – 8. 14; Luke 11. 1-13

A PLACE OF REMEMBRANCE

Deuteronomy chapter 16 is mainly focused on when Israel would come into their inheritance of the Promised Land. But here the activity is not so much their behaviour in the Land, but their keeping the feasts at the place where God's name is – His house.

The feast of Passover (Unleavened Bread), vv. 1-8; the Feast of Weeks, vv. 9-12; and the Feast of Tabernacles, vv. 13-17, were to mark the three festival seasons. And when they came into the Lord's presence, they were not to come empty, v. 16.

We will now look at the character of the first feast, Passover. It wasn't to be kept whenever or however one chose, but had seven main characteristics to it. (1) Who was it for? 'Unto the Lord', v. 1. It was to be designed for God's delight. (2) Who was to partake of it? Those redeemed by blood, who were brought 'forth out of Egypt', v. 1. No uncircumcised person was to eat of it, Exod. 12. 48. (3) What was to happen? They were simply to 'eat it in the place', showing fellowship, v. 7. (4) Why did they keep it? 'That thou mayest remember', v. 3. It would keep the means of their redemption from Egypt before them as a memorial. (5) Where were they to keep it? 'At the place which the Lord thy God shall choose to place his name', v. 6. It was not to be kept at home but where God's presence was. Sacrificing in remembrance unto the Lord required travel. (6) How was it to be kept? 'Thou shalt eat no leavened bread with it', v. 3. That was something the Lord did not want present at His feast. (7) When was this feast to be kept? 'Observe the month of Abib . . . thou shalt sacrifice the passover at even, at the going down of the sun', vv. 1, 6. Since it was to be a memorial it was to match the original Passover.

For the Christian, the *Lord's* supper has a special character. Believers met on the first day of the week to mark His resurrection from the dead, Acts 20. 7. It was for baptized believers, Acts 2. 41-42; 18. 8. The bread and cup are to be eaten and drunk by all when the church comes together in one place in the Lord Jesus' name. It's in remembrance of Christ, 1 Cor. 11. 17-26. The leaven of malice and wickedness is to be purged out, for 'Christ our Passover is sacrificed for us', 1 Cor. 5. 7.

171

June 5th
Deuteronomy 17. 1 – 18. 8; Obadiah; **Luke 11. 14-36**
TEACHING OPPORTUNITIES

In these verses of Luke 11, the Lord Jesus draws lessons from four situations: the criticism of His enemies, vv. 14-26; the interruption of a woman, vv. 27-28; the people's knowledge of the scriptures, vv. 29-32; and an everyday object, vv. 33-36.

(1) When His enemies accused Him of using satanic power to cast out demons, the Lord taught that a divided house cannot stand. Satan defeating his own army wouldn't make sense. But if they were to acknowledge the logical evidence that Jesus' power was from God, then they must face the fact that the kingdom of God is among them in the person of the King, Jesus the Christ. Here we learn that just being neutral on the person of Jesus Christ is to be against Him, v. 23. Not to help His gospel is to hinder it.

(2) As the Lord preached the kingdom of God, a woman interrupted Him and turned the focus to His blessed mother who bore and nursed Him. The Lord turned this into a positive: Mary was truly blessed among women to have this privilege, but she was only the vessel and not the object, Luke 1. 28. Jesus then taught that one could be more blessed than Mary by hearing the word of God and keeping it. God is pleased when one obeys His word in a world that doesn't – not walking by sight or wisdom, but trusting His word and walking in faith. May we do Mary's one command, 'Whatsoever he [Christ] saith unto you, do it', John 2. 5. As the Bible closes it mentions this blessing again, 'Blessed are they that do his commandments', Rev. 22. 14.

(3) With a great crowd of Jewish people gathered who were still seeking signs from Christ, He turns to their biblical history to teach them. He mentions Solomon their greatest king of national peace and prosperity, and Jonah their most successful prophet who saw a whole city repent. Yet the Lord says, 'a greater than Solomon is here' and, 'a greater than Jonas is here'.

(4) Finally, a lesson from a simple candle. A lit candle is not meant to be covered with something dark but open to provide full light. To have a single eye (not compromising with darkness) for the Lord is to shine brightly for Him, like a burning candle.

June 6th

Deuteronomy 18. 9 – 19. 21; Joel 1; **Luke 11. 37-54**

THE DANGER OF RELIGIOUS LEADERS AND THEOLOGIANS

In this passage the Lord Jesus exposes the religious Pharisees and religious lawyers. He pronounces *'woe'* on the Pharisees, vv. 37-44. Then He pronounces *'woe'* on the lawyers, vv. 45-54. The Lord displayed more passion against religious sin than He did against moral sin. Not that He was in favour of immorality; He wasn't, and would call it evil too, Mark 7. 21-23. Immorality affects one's person, and perhaps others. However, religious sinners in authority could blind a multitude of people to knowing and worshipping God in truth. Such sin misrepresents God.

First, He responds to the Pharisees. In addition to the Old Testament books the Pharisees recognized oral tradition as a standard of belief and life. They put the emphasis and praise on observance of external rites such as ceremonial washings, fastings, prayers, and almsgiving. They were comparatively negligent of genuine holiness but prided themselves on their fancied good works. They sought for distinction by loving the chief seats in the religious gatherings and titles of honour, based on their education and position. They were absorbed with self and not with God. Yet because of their externals they looked holy. It wasn't that some of their rules were wrong, but they became unbalanced as they would 'pass over love and judgment', v. 42.

Then the Lord Jesus turned to the religious lawyers. These lawyers were interpreters and teachers of the Mosaic law. They were learned and were regarded as experts. Whilst it is not wrong to study the scriptures to know God in the revelation of Himself, to play verbal gymnastics with His word in order to match a system of belief and tradition is a very serious sin.

The Lord levied a weighty charge against these theologians. He said, 'Woe unto you, lawyers! for ye have taken away the key of knowledge: ye entered not in yourselves, and them that were entering in ye hindered', v. 52. They not only refused God's way in Christ Jesus, but with the intimidation of their learning and their ability to obscure the true meaning with their wisdom, they took away true knowledge from genuine seekers.

Remember, our Lord said, 'Thy word is truth', John 17. 17.

June 7th
Deuteronomy 20-21; Joel 2; **Luke 12. 1-21**

THE DANGER OF AN UNHEALTHY DIET

In this section of Luke chapter 12 the Lord gives two things of which to beware. We are to beware of leaven, vv. 1-14, and we are to beware of a covetous appetite, vv. 15-21. He is speaking of our spiritual diet and appetite. Leaven is human reasoning rather than God's wisdom that affects our thinking. It can spread, effecting many beliefs and practices. Covetousness affects the desires of the heart and seeks satisfaction and security in things, rather than in God. Both will disappoint you and God.

In the Gospels the Lord speaks of three types of leaven. In verse 1 of our chapter, the Lord Jesus warns of *'the leaven of the Pharisees'* which is hypocrisy. Elsewhere He speaks of *'the leaven of the . . . Sadducees'*, Matt. 16. 6. In both cases He is referring to their teaching. Further, the Lord warns of *'the leaven of Herod'*, Mark 8. 15. The Herodians were taken up with causes like political freedom, lower taxes, and better living. Let's examine these spiritual 'junk foods' more closely.

(1) **Leaven of the Pharisees**
Consisting of formalism, traditionalism, and ritualism.
Hypocrisy: they didn't keep the law faithfully that they professed.
Legalism: addition to what God said.
How they taught: they believed the answer was in religion.

(2) **Leaven of the Sadducees**
Consisting of rationalism, modernism, and progressivism.
Liberty: free from God's way; confidence in human wisdom.
Liberalism: denial of what God literally said; subtraction.
How they thought: they believed the answer was in the intellect.

(3) **Leaven of Herod**
Consisting of secularism, sensualism, and materialism.
Worldly: pursues the physical and discounts the spiritual.
Humanism: rejection of what God said.
How they sought: they believed the answer was in politics.

The Epistles speak of 'the leaven of malice and wickedness' as well as the leaven of adding to the terms of the gospel, 1 Cor. 5. 8; Gal. 5. 9. May we be content to have a diet of the sincere milk of the word and strong meat (deeper truths), 1 Pet. 2. 2; Heb. 5. 14.

June 8th

Deuteronomy 22. 1 – 23. 8; **Joel 3**; Luke 12. 22-40

A WAR THAT BRINGS PEACE

The context of Joel 3 is the 'day of the Lord', judgement. In this chapter, the Lord has a message for the Gentile nations. It is to *'Prepare war'*. He calls for their armament, not their disarmament: *'Beat your plowshares into swords'*. They will be in a world coalition to attack Jerusalem, the city where God has put His name. But they will then find themselves in a battle against the Lord Himself as He returns in power to claim His kingdom.

Why is God doing this?

God's judgement is being poured out on the world's armies because of their hatred of *'my heritage Israel'*. And that they have *'parted my land'*, v. 2. The nations' hatred against Israel is really rebellion against God and His right to choose. When for 'peace' purposes they divide and partition the land of Israel they are really disagreeing with God, and they touch *'my people'* and *'my heritage'* and *'my land'*, claims the Lord, v. 2.

How does God do this?

He says, 'I will also gather all nations, and will bring them down into the valley of Jehoshaphat', v. 2. The Lord will use their hatred of Israel to cause them to unite and assemble all their armies in one place. In Revelation chapter 16 that one place is called Armageddon. God lets demons seduce the nations to think they can actually annihilate Jerusalem. Thus, He will 'gather them to the battle of that great day of God Almighty', Rev. 16. 14. Their opponent will turn out to be, not Israel, but the Lord Jesus Christ: 'in righteousness he doth judge and make war', Rev. 19. 11.

The nations' armies are quickly defeated by the Lord Jesus in Israel. Now the opposition to God and Israel are gone. Then, 'the Lord will be the hope of his people, and the strength of the children of Israel', Joel 3. 16. And the remnant of Israel will return to their land and be saved politically and spiritually, vv. 1, 17. Then 'Judah shall dwell for ever, and Jerusalem from generation to generation', v. 20. Peace on earth after God's war!

It is wonderful that the church is assured concerning 'the day of the Lord' that 'God hath not appointed us to wrath, but to obtain salvation by our Lord Jesus Christ', 1 Thess. 5. 2, 9.

June 9th
Deuteronomy 23. 9 – 24. 22; **Jonah 1-2**; Luke 12. 41-59

SALVATION IS OF THE LORD

In Jonah chapters 1 and 2 we have four themes concerning Jonah. We have a *Disobedient* Prophet, 1. 1-3; a *Disciplined* Prophet, 1. 4-17; a *Distressed* Prophet, 2. 1-6; and a *Delivered* Prophet, 2. 7-10.

As a disobedient prophet, Jonah, because of prejudice, made a deliberate choice to run 'from the presence of the Lord', 1. 3. First of all, that is impossible – God is omnipresent. Secondly, to be where God does not want you can be very lonely. Jonah had the money, and found a ship going in the opposite direction to God's call. The circumstances worked out. But circumstances are not the final proof of God's will; only His word is.

As a disciplined prophet, his voyage was interrupted when 'the Lord sent a great wind into the sea' and he was in a storm, v. 4. Eventually he was thrown into the raging sea. But the Lord had prepared a great fish to swallow him up. And there Jonah would be in the belly of the fish three days and three nights. God was not out to destroy His servant, but to correct him.

As a distressed prophet in such dire circumstances Jonah 'prayed unto the Lord', 2. 1. With seaweed wrapped around his head and becoming seasick by taking a dark and twisting 'roller coaster' ride day and night, his self-will was broken. There in that darkness he turned toward God in His holy temple – and was heard, for whom the Lord loves, He chastens, Heb. 12. 6.

As a delivered prophet, he would find himself vomited out by the fish onto dry land again. This was after he realized that his only hope was the Lord. He cried out, 'Salvation is of the Lord', 2. 9. He then, in the gratitude of his salvation, obeyed God.

The message to us from Jonah is not so much what the prophet preached, for he only preached one sentence to Nineveh. But it is Jonah's *life* that is prophetic. The Lord Jesus when on earth taught that the prophet Jonah depicted (not preached) the death and resurrection of Christ, Matt. 12. 39-40. For as Jonah was three days and nights in the fish's belly so Christ would be three days and nights in the earth and then rise again. And this is the sign today that salvation is in the Lord Jesus Christ.

June 10th
Deuteronomy 25. 1 – 26. 15; Jonah 3-4; Luke 13. 1-21
FOLLOW THE BASKET
We will consider the first eleven verses of Deuteronomy chapter 26. The subject is *'worship'*, v. 10. To understand worship here we want to follow the movements of the *'basket'*, v. 2.

(1) What is in the basket? 'The first of all the fruit of the earth . . . in a basket', v. 2. God's portion is first. The basket is not to be presented to the Lord empty.

(2) How did it get into the basket? 'And shalt put it in a basket', v. 2. The worshipper had to gather the fruit and personally place it in the basket, or it would not get there. The full basket would come from you, not someone else.

(3) Who is to bring the basket? 'When thou art come in unto the land which the Lord thy God giveth thee for an inheritance, . . . take of the first of all the fruit of the earth, . . . and shalt put it in a basket', vv. 1-2. One had to be in the land first, the gift God gave them, to be able to bring the fruits of it. Today, only those who are in Christ, the inheritance gift that God has given the believer, can truly worship the Lord, Eph. 1. 1-12.

(4) Where did one bring the basket? 'Put it in a basket, and shalt go unto the place which the Lord thy God shall choose to place his name there', v. 2. They would have to travel to get the basket to God's house. Worship would require travel, sacrifice.

(5) Who did they give the basket to? 'The priest shall take the basket out of thine hand, and set it down before the altar', v. 4. It had to pass through a priest to the altar of sacrifice. Our worship must come through the forgiveness of the blood of Jesus Christ our Lord and His high priestly intercession for us to God.

(6) In what attitude did one bring the basket? 'Say before the Lord thy God, a Syrian ready to perish . . .', vv. 4-10. There was a confession of ruin, a profession of redemption, and a recognition of having a great gift from the Lord. Ephesians teaches our sin, our redemption, and our gift inheritance in Christ.

(7) What did this cause one to do with the basket? 'And thou shalt set it [basket] before the Lord thy God, and worship before the Lord thy God: and thou shalt rejoice . . .', vv. 10-11. They worshipped and rejoiced in the Lord for His goodness and gift.

177

June 11th
Deuteronomy 26. 16 – 27. 26; Amos 1-2; **Luke 13. 22-35**

DISAPPOINTMENT AND DESTRUCTION

These verses in Luke divide into two sections. The first has a question for the Lord. The second has a piece of news for the Lord. He addresses both of them.

In verses 22 to 30 the Lord answers the question, 'Are there few that be saved?' His answer is basically Yes and No. In verses 24 to 28 He teaches that one is to give serious diligence to enter in at the narrow gate. For the gate is not wide enough for all religious beliefs and philosophies. Many will be surprised as they knock at the door. They will hear the dreadful words, 'I know you not'. They will then claim that they ate in His presence (perhaps a reference to religious feasts) and He taught in their streets (perhaps a reference to them listening to His word read in religious gatherings) – so of course He knows them. But they will hear the chilling words from the Lord, 'Depart from me', for even with their religious practices they were far away from God.

There will be heart-breaking disappointment. They will cry in agony as they see themselves ushered away from the kingdom. So in that sense there will be few saved for many who think they are saved, are not. However, from the four corners of the earth people will come and sit down in the kingdom, v. 29. In that sense compared to the Jews he was talking to, there will be many saved. Indeed the gospel of grace by the blood of Christ has saved those from 'every kindred, and tongue, and people and nation', Rev. 5. 9. Then those that were last (Gentiles) in the eyes of Israel shall be first, v. 30. What grace!

In verses 31 to 35 the Lord responds to the warning given to Him, 'Depart hence: for Herod will kill thee'. The Lord sent a message back to Herod 'the fox' that seemed coded, 'The third day I shall be perfected', v 32. In light of His rejection by Israel, the Lord Jesus then weeps over Jerusalem, the city of God. He weeps and says, 'Your house is left unto you desolate'. The reason is: 'how often would I . . . and ye would not', v. 34. The Lord does not force Himself on anyone, but desires their will. They will suffer their choice. But Jerusalem's destruction is not final; He's coming back, v. 35!

178

June 12th
Deuteronomy 28. 1-37; Amos 3-4; Luke 14. 1-24
BLESSINGS AND CURSINGS
In Deuteronomy 28 we have two major sections. First, verses 1 to 14 promise blessings to Israel in the Land: 'All these **blessings** shall come on thee', v. 2. Second, verses 15 onwards promised cursing: 'All these **curses** shall come upon thee'. There are three major truths in correctly understanding this passage.

(1) This is part of the old covenant (legal promises) given to Israel for their land, 29. 1. This is law.

(2) It promises both blessing and cursing. The promises are physical concerning their earthly welfare. They concern their health, wealth and national safety. The promises did not have to do with salvation, heaven or hell.

(3) The covenant terms of the promises worked on an 'if-then' formula. 'If thou shalt hearken . . . to do all his commandments . . . all these blessings shall come on thee', vv. 1-2. Only if they did the law, would God bestow the blessings. However, if they did not obey the law, then God would equally dispense 'the curses of the covenant', 28. 15; 29. 21. 'If thou wilt not hearken . . . to do all his commandments . . . that all these curses shall come upon thee'. The old covenant comprised physical promises that were *performance based* and included cursing.

Believers in the Lord Jesus are not under law, and are now connected with the new covenant, 1 Cor. 11. 25. There are three major differences between the old and new covenants.

(1) The new promises spiritual blessings, not physical ones. The blessing involves sins forgiven, no cursing of judgement, acceptance with God, the indwelling Spirit of God (law in heart) and eternal life. Yes, He 'hath blessed us with all spiritual blessing in heavenly places in Christ', Eph. 1. 3.

(2) The new does not operate on an 'if-then' formula. It operates by grace alone on an 'I will . . . and therefore' principle. God makes promises in Christ that He will do, and therefore they are certain. 'Their sins . . . will I remember no more', Heb. 10. 17.

(3) The new never promises cursing – not even one. It is salvation in Christ Jesus from the curse of the law, Gal. 3. 13. It only promises blessing, Gal. 3. 14. Yes, gospel means '*good news*'!

June 13th
Deuteronomy 28. 38-68; **Amos 5-6**; Luke 14. 25 – 15. 10
GOD IS FAITHFUL
Here in Amos chapters 5 and 6, though hundreds of years later, we have the Lord keeping His word in applying the covenant curses He threatened, Deuteronomy 28-29. To not judge Israel for her continued disobedience to the law would not be justice on God's part, but would make Him a liar and unrighteous.

Chapter 5. The situation is, 'Israel is fallen; she no more shall rise', v. 2. The reason is: 'For I know your manifold transgressions and your mighty sins', v. 12. Yet if they would redirect their passions and 'hate the evil and love the good' there was still time to repent before their Creator. They didn't.

The chapter closes, vv. 18-27, with a warning about desiring the 'day of the Lord'. To Israel, that would be viewed as a positive thing with deserved judgement and justice visited on the sinful Gentile nations. Though that is true, judgement will fall on Israel too, for their sin cannot be covered by religious activity.

In spite of their outward piety – worshipping God by bringing sacrifices and singing beautiful melodies unto the Lord – judgement will come upon them. For God is holy and righteous. The Lord directs to take away the songs from His ears. While their worship songs might be popular, they nauseated the Lord with their hypocrisy. The Lord Jesus taught something similar about useless worship when He was on earth, Matt. 15. 7-9.

Chapter 6. Amos faithfully, like his God, delivered this negative message to Israel and Zion. Later in the book he would be criticized and rejected by the leadership and asked not to preach such a message at 'the king's chapel', 7. 13. But he remained faithful to God and man. Amos preached in chapter 6 that two things were deceiving them concerning God's promised judgement. They were deceived by their perceived strength and their blessings of materialism. They were rejoicing when they should have been repenting. They were 'at ease in Zion', vv. 1, 4-6, 12-13.

Now the Lord's justice has been fully satisfied in the death of His Son on our behalf, Rom. 3. 24-26. Now His new covenant promises to the believer are to never remember our sins, and never to leave us. 'He is faithful that promised', Heb. 10. 23.

June 14th
Deuteronomy 29; Amos 7-8; **Luke 15. 11 – 32**

THE FATHER'S HEART

In Luke 15 we have the well-known parable of the prodigal (wanton) son. This chapter started with a criticism against Jesus, 'This man receiveth sinners, and eateth with them', v. 1. All three parables in this chapter show that this charge was true. There are three characters in this last story: a rebellious son, a caring father and a self-righteous older brother. 'The lost is found' is the plot.

A Sinful Son. To the Jewish mind he would picture the Gentile pagan sinners. Those lost with no knowledge of God and His law. Living their lives 'in the lusts of our flesh, fulfilling the desires of the flesh and of the mind; and were by nature the children of wrath, even as others', Eph. 2. 3. Or perhaps even depicting a depraved despised Jew, like a tax collector.

A Forgiving Father. When the broken son returns with the stench of the pigs still on him, his yearning father runs to meet him, and embraces him in tender compassion. Upon hearing the son's broken words, 'I have sinned', the father robes him to hide his shame, gives him a ring to show his acceptance, and gives him shoes to be able to walk. The father then has a great feast made for the penitent son to nourish him. And because the lost was now found, merriment was in order.

This would point us to why the Father sent His Son into the world. 'This is a faithful saying, and worthy of all acceptation, that Christ Jesus came into the world to save sinners', 1 Tim. 1. 15. The gospel of God now clothes us in righteousness, accepts us in the Beloved, gives us power to walk, and invites us to partake at the Lord's table.

A Bitter Brother. Here we have someone who is performance-based. He measures acceptance only by the worth of his works. And while he lived much better than his younger brother he could not enter into the joy and grace of forgiveness and restoration. He was angry and exclusive. The father reminded him of his continued daily privileges, but there is a time to cry and a time to laugh. When the dead come alive, it's a time for joy. Later, the publican would discover the Lord's heart, and be justified when he said, 'God be merciful to me a sinner', Luke 18. 13.

June 15th
Deuteronomy 30. 1 – 31. 13; Amos 9; Luke 16
A PANORAMIC PREVIEW OF THE PLAN FOR ISRAEL

In Deuteronomy 30 verses 1 to 9, we have a seven-point outline of Israel's history and future.

(1) **Removal.** Because of the 'curses of the covenant' Israel would be removed from their Land of Promise: 'the nations, whither the Lord thy God hath driven thee', v. 1. Many Jews are still among those nations today.

(2) **Repentance.** 'And thou shalt return unto the Lord thy God, and shalt obey', v. 2. The chastening of the Lord will eventually cause Israel to fully repent towards Him.

(3) **Rescue.** 'Then the Lord thy God will turn thy captivity . . . and gather thee from all the nations', v. 3. This deliverance has already partially happened in history and there is more to come.

(4) **Regathering.** 'Will the Lord thy God gather thee from thence . . . and the Lord thy God will bring thee into the land', vv. 4-5. History and the present day show the first stages of this.

(5) **Regeneration.** 'And the Lord thy God will circumcise thine heart . . . to love the Lord thy God with all thine heart . . . that thou mayest live', v. 6. Notice the *spiritual* salvation of Israel comes after their physical return. They return in unbelief in Christ Jesus and are then reborn by the Spirit. Ezekiel chapter 37 teaches the same.

(6) **Retribution.** 'The Lord thy God will put all these curses upon thine enemies', v. 7. This is the great day of His wrath that comes upon the world after Israel's tribulation. This is also taught in Zechariah chapter 14 and Revelation chapters 16-19. Yes, 'all Israel shall be saved' spiritually and politically by Jesus Christ, Rom. 11.

(7) **Rejoicing.** When Israel's heart finally turns to the Lord Jesus Christ there will much rejoicing in heaven and earth. 'The Lord will again rejoice over thee [Israel] for good', vv. 8-9. Yes, peace on earth and goodwill to men!

Chapter 30 closes not with the future, but with a call for the present. Moses set before them 'life and death'. He invited them to 'choose life' by loving and obeying the Lord, vv. 19-20. He shows his replacement Joshua ('Jehovah is salvation') who would bring them into their inheritance, 31. 7. What the law (Moses) could not do, Jesus (prefigured by Joshua) would do, Rom. 8. 3.

182

June 16th
Deuteronomy 31. 14 – 32. 14; **Hosea 1**; Luke 17. 1-19

MAN SOWS, AND GOD SOWS TOO

Although Hosea is reckoned among the twelve so-called 'Minor Prophets', his ministry was one of the longest of any prophet of the Lord, some sixty years or so. In that time he saw the collapse and dispersal of the northern kingdom of Israel at the hands of the Assyrian empire, and warned the southern kingdom of Judah that they were also heading for divine judgement.

Uniquely, Hosea had to begin his ministry by practically demonstrating the unfaithfulness of Israel to her God. He was instructed to marry a woman whose character was flawed, and who would prove unfaithful to him after bearing his three children. Ultimately, in chapter 3, Hosea would have to go to the slave-market where his unfaithful wife had finished up as a result of the brutality of her loveless companions, and purchase her back to himself. The real-life account of Hosea and Gomer displayed the current condition and future path of the nation of Israel in relation to her 'husband' Jehovah. In sowing the seeds of spiritual unfaithfulness in her persistent worship of Baal, Israel would reap misery, shame, and judgement. There is an abiding principle stated in Galatians chapter 6 verse 7: 'Be not deceived; God is not mocked: for whatsoever a man soweth, that shall he also reap'.

But if Israel was sowing the seeds of her own destruction, the God who loved her was sowing the seeds of national repentance and restoration. The first of Hosea's children was called Jezreel, 'God sows'. The reason why God told Hosea to give his son that name lay in the deeds of Jehu, whose dynasty God was going to bring to an abrupt end. Some seventy years before, Jehu had been instructed, through Elisha, to destroy the house of Ahab and Jezebel. He did so at Jezreel, and God commended him for it, 2 Kgs. 10. 30. However, Jehu also killed Ahaziah the king of Judah and forty-two of the king's relatives. God had not sanctioned this violence towards the house of David, so after the promised four generations Jehu's dynasty must end – at Jezreel, Hos. 1. 5. But divine judgement on His people ever has restoration in view, and verses 10 and 11 speak of Israel's future glory. When will that be? In 'the day of Jezreel', v. 11. What God sows He also reaps, in abundance!

June 17th
Deuteronomy 32. 15-52; Hosea 2-3; Luke 17. 20 – 18. 14
YOUR HEARTS . . . YOUR CHILDREN . . . YOUR LIFE
On the selfsame day that Moses left the encampment of Israel to ascend Mount Nebo and die, he rehearsed in the ears of the people the wonderful song recorded in chapter 32. He reminded them of God's power and faithfulness. He recalled their failure and rebellion. The history of Israel since their deliverance from Egypt was one of disobedience as a response to divine blessing, and repentance as a response to divine judgement. Their future as a nation was going to be the same.

Knowing that external discipline, even from God, never brought lasting correction, Moses exhorted the people, 'Set your hearts unto all the words which I testify among you this day', v. 46. Here is an important lesson for us today. A consistent godly life is not the outcome of simply knowing the word of God, but allowing it to touch the *heart*. David's response to the divine call 'Seek ye my face' was 'my heart said unto thee, Thy face, Lord, will I seek', Ps. 27. 8. The godly scribe Ezra 'prepared his heart to seek the law of the Lord, and to do it', Ezra 7. 10.

'Ye shall command your children', Moses continued. Another important lesson comes to us from this commandment. Great emphasis is given to a good secular education for our children, and there is certainly nothing admirable about ignorance. But is even more emphasis being placed upon the spiritual education of our young ones? Surely our chief aim is to see our children grounded in the word and ways of God so that, in His gracious will, they might be saved in early years, and go on to live fruitful lives for His glory?

'It is not a vain thing for you, because it is your life', said Moses. To set our hearts to the word of God, teach it to our children and live it out for the glory of God should, for every believer, be 'your life'. It used to be a popular cliché, usually said with a curl of the lip, 'Get a life!' What better life could there be than the daily enjoyment of eternal life through Jesus Christ our Lord? 'And this is life eternal, that they might know thee the only true God, and Jesus Christ, whom thou hast sent', John 17. 3. The path to divine blessing has always been through obedience to God's will.

June 18th
Deuteronomy 33; Hosea 4. 1 – 6. 3; **Luke 18. 15-43**

THE RICH YOUNG RULER

The importance of the encounter between the rich young ruler and the Lord Jesus is clear from its inclusion in the records of Matthew, Mark, and Luke. The story is generally well known, at least superficially, but we do well to observe the details. For example, only Matthew tells us (twice) that the man was *young*, Matt. 19. 20, 22; only Mark records that he *kneeled* to the Lord, Mark 10. 17, and that Jesus loved him, v. 21; only Luke tells us that the man was a *ruler*. All three writers record the young ruler's sorrow and his riches.

These details help us picture the scene. Luke's description of the man as a ruler, without further qualification, implies that he was a member of the Sanhedrin, the Jews' ruling religious body. If we took note only of Luke's Gospel, we would perhaps picture a middle-aged or old man, a stern Pharisee in his long robes. But Matthew says that he was young, so that modifies the picture. As a ruler, the man must be at least thirty years of age, but as a *young* ruler he was probably only a little more than that.

So had we been present, we would have seen two men of about the same age, the one in all the fine garments of a very wealthy and important ruler, the other in the humble clothes of a man who possessed nothing, Jesus of Nazareth. With amazement we would observe the detail provided by Mark; the ruler ran to Him and kneeled to Him! This ruler was not one of those Pharisees who paid lip-service to the Lord but despised Him in their heart. This ruler was sincere, genuine in his acknowledgement that the Lord's evident goodness proclaimed His deity. But he lacked one thing. Only one? Yes, only one. He either already possessed, or had the means to possess, all that this world could give – he lacked nothing materially. His great need was to surrender all to the lordship of the Man with whom he spoke, and he decided he couldn't do that. He went away desperately sorrowful.

Is that the end of the story? Perhaps, but consider this. Might that young ruler have been Saul, born in Tarsus but trained in Jerusalem? The man who, once saved, learned to count all things as refuse; who said, 'The Son of God . . . loved me', Gal. 2. 20?

June 19th
Deuteronomy 34; Hosea 6. 4 – 7. 16; **Luke 19. 1-28**
'WE WILL NOT HAVE THIS MAN TO REIGN OVER US'
The Parable of the Pounds concerns the different attitudes of the people of Israel to Christ in the days of His absence from earth. Today the Lord Jesus is that 'certain nobleman' who has gone 'into a far country to receive for himself a kingdom, and to return', Luke 19. 12. The attitude of His servants is seen in the context of the tribulation period that will follow the rapture of the church. There will be a remnant of the nation of Israel who will be faithful to the Lord, others who will only acknowledge Him in a nominal way, and others still who will actively reject Him. It is these enemies of Christ who say, 'We will not have this (man) to reign over us'. At the conclusion of the parable the Lord Jesus said, 'But those mine enemies, which would not that I should reign over them, bring hither, and slay them before me', v. 27. The awfulness and absolute futility of opposing the Lord could not be made more plain! And yet . . . is it possible that the one reading this page, or a member of the family listening as it is being read, is refusing in their heart to acknowledge Jesus Christ as Lord?

The refusal to bow the knee to the Lord Jesus is not only the attitude of His enemies from within the nation of Israel. David wrote, 'Why do the heathen rage, and the people imagine a vain thing? The kings of the earth set themselves, and the rulers take counsel together, against the Lord, and against his anointed, saying, Let us break their bands asunder, and cast away their cords from us', Ps. 2. 1-3. The response of God to this rebellious insolence is to laugh! Listen to the declaration of the living God; 'Yet have I set my king upon my holy hill of Zion', v. 6.

The world of men decided to give the Son of God a cross, but God has determined that He shall have a throne. All who challenge God's appointment will share the fate of those described in this parable as 'those mine enemies', Luke 19. 27. Perhaps somebody hearing this page being read would be horrified to be described as an enemy of the Lord Jesus. But if you refuse to bow the knee, repent of your sins and trust Him for salvation, you are really saying, 'I will not have this man to reign over me'. If you will not bow to Him willingly, you will be made to do so one day!

186

June 20th
Joshua 1; Hosea 8-9; Luke 19. 29-48

POSSESSING THE LAND

At last, wilderness days had come to an end! The bitter cost of rebellion and disobedience had been paid and the nation of Israel stood on the verge of their God-given inheritance. Within three days they were to go in and possess the land which the Lord their God had given them. Moses had died and been replaced by Joshua, and a whole new chapter of Israel's history was beginning. All was well . . . or was it?

All was certainly not well with the tribes of Reuben, Gad and Manasseh! Joshua said to them, 'Remember . . . your wives, your little ones, and your cattle, shall remain in the land which Moses gave you on this side Jordan', Josh. 1. 13-14. The whole sorry story comes out in Numbers chapter 32, and we learn that the men of Reuben and Gad had a very great multitude of cattle and the land of Gilead had excellent pasture for them. Their request to Moses was 'let this land be given unto thy servants for a possession, and bring us not over Jordan', Num. 32. 5. They refused to go in and possess the land that God had for them because they set their material prosperity before their God-given inheritance! It is in Numbers chapter 32 that we first read of the half tribe of Manasseh – a division caused by men who walked by sight rather than by faith. The consequences were very sad. The men of Reuben, Gad, and half the tribe of Manasseh agreed to help the other tribes subdue Canaan, but they were fighting for a possession that neither they nor their children would enjoy. Indeed, they had to leave their wives, children, and cattle in fenced cities because of the inhabitants of the land, Num. 32. 17. The men endangered their families in pursuit of material wealth!

Once the Israelites crossed Jordan and entered the land, the manna ceased. What would now sustain the families that had been left on the other side of the Jordan? Oh what tragedy ensues when the people of God refuse to go in and possess the land that God has given them! How true are the lines penned by JOHN SAMMIS, 'Trust and obey, for there's no other way to be happy in Jesus, but to trust and obey'. Remember God's promise, 'I will not fail thee, nor forsake thee', Josh. 1. 5.

187

June 21st

Joshua 2; **Hosea 10. 1 – 11. 11**; Luke 20. 1-19

FRUITFULNESS FOR GOD

The physical act that brought sin into the world was the taking of fruit that belonged to God. Any and all of the other fruit in the Garden of Eden was there for the enjoyment of Adam and Eve but, notwithstanding the wonderful goodness of God, they stole what belonged to Him. Thus, from the beginning of time, man's sin has selfishly deprived God of fruit.

In scripture the nation of Israel is often likened to a vine, and Isaiah's description of God's earthly people is very lovely: 'My wellbeloved (Jehovah) hath a vineyard in a very fruitful hill: and he fenced it, and gathered out the stones thereof, and planted it with the choicest vine . . . and he looked that it should bring forth grapes, and it brought forth wild grapes', Isa. 5. 1-2. Out of the grieved heart of their God came the question, 'What could have been done more to my vineyard, that I have not done in it? wherefore, when I looked that it should bring forth grapes, brought it forth wild grapes?' Isa. 5. 4. The respective ministries of Isaiah and Hosea overlapped by about thirty years, and Hosea identifies the reason for the problem recorded by Isaiah. As the goodness of God abounded, so did the nation's self-reliance and idolatry. Outwardly things looked fine and prosperous, but God was being systematically robbed of the fruit that was rightfully His. The problem in Eden was also the problem in Israel, and potentially the problem is in your heart and mine, too.

The Lord Jesus spoke of Himself as the True Vine, and His fruitful life was immensely precious to God. Today God is not seeking fruit from the nation of Israel but from those who are saved by His grace. To every believer comes the word of the Lord Jesus, 'As the branch cannot bear fruit of itself, except it abide in the vine; no more can ye, except ye abide in me . . . for without me ye can do nothing', John 15. 4-5. Are we failing God in the same way as did our first parents and His people Israel? Are we receiving all His goodness but, rather than using it to produce fruit for His pleasure, are we using it only for our own selfish ends? Think on this particular truth today: 'Herein is my Father glorified, that ye bear much fruit; so shall ye be my disciples', v. 8.

June 22nd
Joshua 3; Hosea 11. 12 – 14. 9; Luke 20. 20 – 21. 4
JORDAN WAS DRIVEN BACK
The title for today's meditation is a quotation from Psalm 114 verse 3. The writer is extolling the greatness of God and, in particular, the awesomeness of His presence: 'Tremble, thou earth, at the presence of the Lord, at the presence of the God of Jacob', Ps. 114. 7. On the day that Israel crossed Jordan and entered into Canaan, their promised inheritance, the presence of the Lord was key to all the mighty works that He wrought. Joshua had told the people, 'Tomorrow the Lord will do wonders among you', Josh. 3. 5. Not only would the full torrent of Jordan in flood be miraculously dried up, but the inhabitants of Canaan would be terrified by the disappearance of the natural barrier they were sure would prevent Israel from entering the Land.

'What ailed thee . . . thou Jordan, that thou wast driven back?', Ps. 114. 5. It was the presence of the very God that had first brought His people 'out of Egypt, the house of Jacob from a people of strange language', v. 1. God's purpose in bringing Israel *out* of Egyptian bondage was that He might bring them *in* to the rest and enjoyment of the land of Canaan. As Moses and the people of Israel stood on the wilderness side of the Red Sea they sang, 'Who is like unto thee, O Lord, among the gods? Who is like thee, glorious in holiness, fearful in praises, doing wonders?' Exod. 15. 11. The God who parted the waters to deliver His people from Egypt was the same God who would now part the waters of Jordan to bring them into Canaan.

The miracles that began and ended Israel's wilderness experience both picture the death, burial, and resurrection of our Lord Jesus. However, when the Hebrews crossed the Red Sea they were very much aware of the presence of the waters. They were heaped up on either side, so much so that the people were seen as being 'baptized unto Moses in the cloud and in the sea', 1 Cor. 10. 2. The picture is of the believer's death with Christ as taught in Romans chapter 6. When Israel crossed the Jordan, however, the waters were nowhere to be seen. Believers are pictured here as risen with Christ, in all the value of His death, and able to enter in to all their inheritance as a present possession.

June 23rd

Joshua 4. 1 – 5. 12; **Isaiah 1**; Luke 21. 5-38

REALITY, NOT MERE RITUAL

There is something of a courtroom scene in the opening verses of Isaiah's prophecy. God has a case against His people, Israel, and He calls the heavens and the earth to witness the righteous way in which He had dealt, and would deal in the future, with the nation. Isaiah speaks of future judgement as though it were already present, and he paints a word picture of the awful human and national conditions that would soon be very real.

Greed, disobedience, selfishness, and rebellion had turned the hearts of the people away from their God and all His righteous ways and yet, almost incredibly, they were still going through the ritualistic motions of their religion. Externally they were devout Jews, but internally they were 'rulers of Sodom . . . people of Gomorrah', Isa. 1. 10. Terrible judgements were going to fall on them for this behaviour, and repentance would be produced – but not for long! When He moved amongst the people of Israel, the Lord Jesus had to reprimand the rulers, 'Woe unto you, scribes and Pharisees, hypocrites! for ye are like unto whited sepulchres, which indeed appear beautiful outward, but are within full of dead men's bones, and of all uncleanness. Even so ye also outwardly appear righteous unto men, but within ye are full of hypocrisy and iniquity', Matt. 23. 27-28.

How easy it is for us to allow outrage to well up against the repeatedly rebellious children of Israel, and yet not truly examine ourselves to see if the same attitude lies within our own hearts! We rightly take such care to dot all the 'I's and cross all the 'T's when we gather together. Pious prayers, carefully correct doctrinal ministry, dress, and deportment to say that we realize we are in the presence of God. But inwardly? What lies behind this besetting sin? Is it not that we (as did the children of Israel) lose sight of the majesty, terrible holiness, and omniscience of God? Do we truly think that we deceive Him as to our real condition?

'Come now, and let us reason together, saith the Lord', Isa. 1. 18. We often use this verse in the gospel, but it is addressed to God's disobedient people. He demands from us honesty, humility, and repentance. In gracious response, He promises to richly bless.

June 24th
Joshua 5. 13 – 6. 27; Isaiah 2; **Luke 22. 1-30**
THE PASSOVER FULFILLED
The main purpose of the annual Feast of Passover was to be a memorial to the great occasion in Israel's history when God brought them out of Egyptian bondage. In that respect it looked back to one momentous night, the events of which are recorded in Exodus chapter 12. But Passover can also be seen as *a process* that began on that unique night and which has still to be fulfilled. Immediately the question might be asked as to whether the Passover was fulfilled in the sacrificial death of the Lord Jesus at Calvary. Did not Paul write to the Corinthians, 'For even Christ our Passover is sacrificed for us', 1 Cor. 5. 7? Yes indeed, the Passover and its link to the Feast of Unleavened Bread is used as an illustration by Paul, and the principle of substitutionary sacrifice undoubtedly finds its fulfilment in the death of the Lord Jesus. But the Passover does not stand in isolation – it marked a new beginning for Israel. Their calendar changed, their relationship with their God changed, and their relationship with Egypt changed. What a glorious picture of the believer's new life in Christ!

Momentous as Passover was for Israel, the morning light still saw them as slaves in Egypt. Pharaoh was still their master. The miraculous crossing of the Red Sea, a picture of the believer's death with Christ, ended their Egyptian bondage but saw them now a people in the wilderness. After forty years they would cross the Jordan and enter Canaan, but disobedience would deny them the rest that should have been theirs. God's stated purpose for Israel after delivering them from Egypt was, 'Ye shall be unto me a kingdom of priests, and a holy nation', Exod. 19. 6, but that has not yet been fulfilled. It will happen in the future though, when the nation repents and is restored at the end of the tribulation period to enter into their millennial rest. It was to this joyful time that the Lord Jesus looked forward in the Upper Room. He anticipated, in wonderful grace, the time when He would sit and eat bread, and drink wine, in fellowship with the very nation that was about to crucify Him. What joy there will be for the Lord, and for Israel in the fullness of their redemption, when the Passover is 'fulfilled in the kingdom of God', Luke 22. 16!

June 25th
Joshua 7; Isaiah 3-4; Luke 22. 31-53
I SAW . . . THEN I COVETED . . . AND TOOK

The conquest of Canaan by the nation of Israel provides many clear illustrations of New Testament truth for the believer today. The crossing of Jordan, the events at Gilgal, and the victory over Jericho all have vital lessons for our admonition. So too does the defeat that Israel suffered at Ai. Understandably our attention is drawn particularly to the sin of Achan in Joshua chapter 7, but there are also indications that complacency had set in. There is no record that Joshua had a word from the Lord about going up to take Ai, and there is no reference to prayer being made before the men went up to fight – the attack was based solely on the report and suggestion of the spies.

Complacent leadership of God's people will soon result in departure from God's word. Was this not how sin came into the world? Adam was warned by God that there could be a threat to the fair order of Eden: 'And the Lord God took the man, and put him into the garden of Eden to dress it and to keep it', Gen. 2. 15. The word 'keep' in that verse means 'to be on one's guard'. When the subtle attack came, complacency on Adam's part meant 'the woman saw . . . desired . . . took of the fruit thereof', 3. 6.

Achan's sin followed the same pattern as that of Eve, and just as Adam's sin (for he, as head of the woman, was to blame) affected the whole of the human race, so did the sin of Achan affect the whole camp of Israel. Applying the illustration of Joshua chapter 7 to our daily lives as believers, we must remember that spiritual victory requires dependence upon God and obedience to His word. Strong spiritual leadership will help to prevent a lax atmosphere in which others become relaxed about sin in the camp. Achan could not have carried off the forbidden booty and buried it in his tent without others being aware. The bulk of the garment and the weight of the gold meant his sin could not be hidden. Was that why his family died with him? What a tragedy! How important it is to remember that 'every man is tempted, when he is drawn away of his own lust, and enticed. Then when lust hath conceived, it bringeth forth sin: and sin, when it is finished, bringeth forth death', Jas. 1. 14-15.

June 26th
Joshua 8; **Isaiah 5**; Luke 22. 54 – 23. 12
TWENTY-FIRST CENTURY LIFE – IN ISAIAH!
One of the reasons why the experiences of the nation of Israel are recorded in scripture is to provide warning lessons for the people of God today: 'Now all these things happened unto them for ensamples: and they are written for our admonition, upon whom the ends of the world are come.' 1 Cor. 10. 11. These lessons are for us personally as believers in the Lord Jesus, and collectively as local companies of Christians. But they also warn us nationally as to the definite outcome of sinful godless living. Such is the warning in Isaiah chapter 5, regardless of the particular nations to which we belong.

Isaiah pronounces six woes upon Israel because of their godless, materialistic lifestyle. In 1957, British Prime Minister Harold Macmillan told the nation 'most of our people have never had it so good', and the relentless pursuit of pleasure and material gain has taken the nation ever further away from God. The same six woes pronounced upon Israel in the 8th century BC could well be pronounced upon the UK and most other nations today.

Notwithstanding the principle of the Year of Jubilee that ensured a redistribution of wealth every fifty years, Israel had a housing problem. Property magnates made ordinary people live in cramped conditions so that they could live in glorious seclusion, Isa. 5. 8. The consumption of alcohol had become an all-day affair, v. 11, and feasting accompanied by raucous music and excessive drinking resulted in harm to people and their property, v. 12. The third woe was upon those who lamented the passing of the days when God was honoured in the nation, but they would neither humble themselves nor repent. They were bound by sin 'as it were with a cart rope', v. 18. Divine order had been overthrown so that evil was declared to be good, and good things evil, v. 20. How accurately that describes much of our present legislation today! The final two woes sum up the arrogance, godlessness, and corruption of the commercial world.

The nation of Israel brought down terrible divine judgement on their own heads for their wickedness and refusal to repent. Will God eventually deal any differently with nations today?

June 27th
Joshua 9; Isaiah 6; **Luke 23. 13-46**
LORD, REMEMBER ME
Of the Gospel writers, only Luke records the dealings of the Lord Jesus with the repentant malefactor. Concerning those crucified with Him, John simply records, 'Where they crucified him, and two other with him, on either side one, and Jesus in the midst', John 19. 18. Mark adds a further detail, 'And with him they crucify two thieves; the one on his right hand, and the other on his left. And the scripture was fulfilled, which saith, And he was numbered with the transgressors', Mark 15. 27-28. Matthew tells us, 'Then were there two thieves crucified with him, one on the right hand, and another on the left', before recounting the mockery and jeers of those that passed by, and the chief priests. He then adds, 'The thieves also, which were crucified with him, cast the same in his teeth', Matt. 27. 38, 44.

The repentance of the dying thief was truly remarkable. Salvation is through faith in the Lord Jesus, and the faith of this man cannot be doubted. He was looking at a man hanging on a cross, suffering judicial execution at the hands of the Romans. It was very evident that His fellow Jews hated Him, the chief priests being at the forefront of His mockers. Was the thief able to read the superscription that was written above the man on the centre cross? In three languages it said, 'THIS IS THE KING OF THE JEWS', Luke 23. 38. The eyes of the thief, dimmed by pain, saw a man dying in weakness and shame. Faith saw the King of the Jews, a man who would one day come into His rightful kingdom. The thief believed in the person of the Lord Jesus and he clearly believed in His resurrection too. How else would He come into that kingdom? Ah, but faith embraced even more. The thief believed not only that the Lord Jesus would be raised and come into His kingdom, but that He would have a place in that kingdom for a person like him! Reason saw a rejected and crucified man; faith saw the blessed Saviour of sinners! The salvation that day of a wretched dying thief proves that neither baptism, good works, nor even a public confession of faith is necessary for sins to be forgiven (although it happened in this instance, cp. Rom. 10. 9). It is by grace alone, through faith alone, in Christ alone.

June 28th
Joshua 10; Isaiah 7. 1 – 8. 4; Luke 23. 47 – 24. 12
AND THE SUN STOOD STILL
In this age of so-called 'enlightenment', fuelled by man's huge ability to exploit technology, things that are truly miraculous are treated with scorn. Everything has to be exposed to the test of man's reasoning, and if no credible scientific evidence can be found to explain a miracle the event itself and all who are associated with it are ridiculed. One can only imagine the derision that would greet a reading of Joshua chapter 10 in the presence of scientific 'experts' on a radio or television programme today. 'The sun . . . stand still?' The laughter of the studio audience would reach the rafters! 'Why', the panel of 'experts' would say, 'Those simple folk who fought with Joshua didn't even know that the earth orbits the sun, not the other way round'.

Some believers, stung by the arrogant ridicule of such men, seek to retaliate by taking on the scientific community in debate. They come up with arguments based on scientific assumptions and go into battle against the scoffers. That was precisely what happened some years ago when it was widely reported that NASA scientists were doing some calculations to determine the positions of the sun and other heavenly bodies. In the course of these calculations, the computers seized up. The scientists found that the computers had reported a day was missing, and they were unable to solve the problem. Then, the story goes, a scientist who was a Christian said that the Bible speaks of a missing day. He took out his Bible and read, 'So the sun stood still, and the moon stopped, till the people had revenge upon their enemies. Is this not written in the Book of Jasher? So the sun stood still in the midst of heaven, and did not hasten to go down for about a whole day', Josh. 10. 13. Many Christians were delighted: science proves the Bible is true! The problem was, the account was not true. That computer lock-up never happened. The whole thing was a modern twist on a story that originated in the nineteenth century.

It might be tempting to try and take on the scornful scientific world, but every miracle in the Bible is, by definition, inexplicable by man's reasoning. God can do anything that is consistent with His character, and the Bible is His inerrant word. Believe it!

195

June 29th

Joshua 11-12; **Isaiah 8. 5 – 9. 7**; Luke 24. 13-35

FOR UNTO US A CHILD IS BORN

If ever there was a magnificent jewel embedded in the Old Testament scriptures, surely it has to be Isaiah 9 verse 6, 'For unto us a child is born' – the beginning of Christ's humanity; 'unto us a son is given' – His pre-existence and deity; 'and the government shall be upon his shoulder' – His universal reign in a day to come. His glorious name will have further titles of honour associated with it: 'Wonderful' – not an adjective but a noun, meaning that in Christ all that is marvellous will be embodied; 'Counsellor' – the Fount of all wisdom, discretion and judgement; 'the Mighty God' – the fullness of divine power in omnipotence and omniscience will be displayed in Christ glorified; 'the Father of Eternity', in other words, all that there is in time or eternity is wholly dependent on Him; 'The Prince of Peace' – the One who bears all these titles is still wholly in submission to His Father, hence He is the Prince, not the King, of Peace. What a delightful description there is in this verse of our glorious Lord!

We wonder what Isaiah himself understood of the things that he wrote by the inspiration of the Holy Spirit. In his first epistle, Peter wrote, 'Of which salvation the prophets have enquired and searched diligently, who prophesied of the grace that should come unto you: searching what, or what manner of time the Spirit of Christ which was in them did signify, when it testified beforehand the sufferings of Christ, and the glory that should follow', 1 Pet. 1. 10-11. We can imagine these godly prophets striving to understand what they were writing, knowing that there was a substance to their work that was eluding them. How could Isaiah have understood that as his pen moved from writing 'For unto us a child is born, unto us a son is given' to 'and the government shall be upon his shoulder', it was spanning a period of time of over two thousand years? He did not know that he was writing not of one advent of the Messiah, but two! Christ's first advent would be about suffering. His second would be all about glory. The church age was in mystery, that is, it was already there in the purpose of God but the time had not yet come to reveal it.

June 30th
Joshua 13; Isaiah 9. 8 – 10. 4; **Luke 24. 36-53**
THE ASCENSION OF THE LORD JESUS
Two defining features of the church age are that there is a man, the Lord Jesus, resident in heaven, and a divine Person, the Holy Spirit, resident on earth. Without the first of those great truths, the second could not have taken place. On the occasion of the Feast of Tabernacles, the last of the seven annual Feasts of Jehovah and a picture of Israel's millennial blessing, the Lord Jesus spoke of the Holy Spirit 'which they that believe on him should receive: for the Holy Ghost was not yet given; because that Jesus was not yet glorified', John 7. 39. The primary sense of that verse has to do with Israel's national restoration and blessing, the result of their repentance when they see the Lord Jesus appearing in power and great glory to effect their deliverance at the end of the tribulation period. When their rejected Messiah is acknowledged by Israel and glorified amongst them, the long-promised outpouring of the Holy Spirit upon them will take place.

That which is still future for Israel has its counterpart in the church age. The descent of the Holy Spirit as recorded in Acts chapter 2 was dependent on Jesus being glorified. In His Upper Room ministry the Lord told His disciples, 'I will pray the Father, and he shall give you another Comforter, that he may abide with you for ever', John 14. 16. Again He said, 'It is expedient for you that I go away: for I if go not away, the Comforter will not come unto you; but if I depart, I will send him unto you', 16. 7. Hence the coming of the Holy Spirit demanded the ascension and glorification of the Lord Jesus.

Peter, preaching to the men of Israel after the Holy Spirit had descended, spoke of 'Jesus of Nazareth, a man approved by God . . . This Jesus hath God raised up, whereof we are all witnesses. Therefore being by the right hand of God exalted, and having received of the Father the promise of the Holy Ghost, he hath shed forth this, which ye now see and hear', Acts 2. 22, 32-33. With Jesus glorified, the Holy Spirit could come down. How precious are these things to the believer's heart! The presence of our Saviour in heaven is the guarantee that we will also be there. The presence of the indwelling Holy Spirit seals us against that day.

July 1st
Joshua 14-15; Isaiah 10. 5-34; **1 Thessalonians 1. 1 – 2. 12**

EARLY DAYS

The 'church of the Thessalonians' was planted by Paul and the divine record of that event is in Acts chapter 17. The first messages preached in the local synagogue over three Sabbath days highlighted the sufferings of Christ and His glorious resurrection. The result was that 'some' Jews, a 'multitude' of Greeks, and 'not a few' important women believed. These formed the nucleus of the new church. Satan moved quickly to disrupt and discourage, but was frustrated. Nevertheless, Paul and Silas, after an uproar, had to flee the city leaving the new Christians to fend for themselves. A little time later, Paul who constantly worried about them, wrote this Epistle to encourage them and to clarify some of the teaching, both doctrinal and practical, he had hastily imparted to them.

This first section of the Epistle includes Paul's reflections on the early days of the work and emphasizes the integrity of the preachers, while at the same time calling on the personal, first-hand experience of the believers as witnesses to these things.

It the opening chapter it is striking that many things are described in three ways. Verse 1 speaks of three authors and three positions of the church. Verse 3 is well known and reminds us of 1) the work of faith; 2) the labour of love; and, 3) the patience of hope. As you read the passage, mark all the other 'threes' you can find. There are quite a few of them.

It is wonderful that the gospel 'came' to them as so many others had not, and have not yet, heard it. It came in three ways: in power, in the Holy Spirit, and in much assurance. The believers became living examples of the power of the gospel as they did three things; turned to God from idols, served the living and true God, and waited for His Son from heaven. In chapter 2 Paul speaks of his recent sufferings in Philippi and his boldness in Thessalonica as he preached with clarity, power and selflessness. His devotion to them was such that he described himself as being their nursing-mother. They responded, grew and developed spiritually and effectively carried on the work themselves in Paul's absence. The challenge for us is to testify boldly, live honourably and trust in God's almighty power. Let's decide to do that today!

July 2nd
Joshua 16-17; Isaiah 11-12; **1 Thessalonians 2. 13 – 3. 13**

HEARTFELT THANKS

There is no doubt that Paul was fearful when he had to leave Thessalonica. After all, he had been in the city for only a short time, and the new converts were facing persecution on all fronts. At the end of chapter 2 Paul sympathizes with their predicament but encourages them by pointing out that they were not alone in such trials. Now, he was anxious to return to offer personal support and to ensure they were not only enduring but progressing in faith and in love. He had a very deep care for these people and was convinced that Satan was actively hindering his return.

So, unable himself to visit, he sent Timothy whose mission was to assess the situation, encourage the saints, and report back to Paul as soon as possible. While Timothy was away, Paul grew increasingly anxious, fretting about what might, or might not, be happening and fearing the worst. It had come to the situation that Paul himself was enduring affliction and distress, 3. 7. He needed information; without it, his own faith in God was suffering.

Eventually, Timothy returned bearing good, even great news! There was no cause for worry – the Thessalonians continued in the faith, increased in love, and had good remembrance of the fellowship of those early days. Indeed, they even had questions of doctrine and practice to be answered and, furthermore, they really did want Paul to come back to them every bit as much as he desired to see them. All was well in Thessalonica, yet Paul had convinced himself otherwise and had sunk into despair. There was no need – God was in control. So what a huge relief! Paul was delighted with the news and re-invigorated in his service. He gave God the glory and with heartfelt thanks said, 'What thanks can we render to God again for you?', 3. 9.

Such feelings of anxiety and fear are still the lot of many of God's people today. In a world where persecution against Christians is increasing, for some such fears are perfectly justified. Then there are anxieties in connection with family, health, and the assembly – cares which arise on a daily basis. But sometimes we worry needlessly. Indeed, can worry ever be justified? We need to learn how to leave the situation with the Lord in faith.

July 3rd
Joshua 18-19; Isaiah 13; **1 Thessalonians 4**

HE IS COMING

In this fourth chapter of the First Epistle to the Thessalonians some very important truths are dealt with by the Apostle Paul. Verses 1 to 8 describe the purity of life that *faith* demands, while verses 9 to 12 remind us of the ongoing opportunities provided by *love.* Then verses 13 to 18 encourage and excite us by describing the *hope* that is set before us. These three, *faith, hope,* and *love* are the themes of the Epistle as set out in chapter 1 verse 3 and chapter 3 verse 13.

The believers who wait for the 'Son from heaven' to return will order their walk so as to please God. They will keep themselves pure by avoiding immorality of all kinds. Similarly, they will practise brotherly love to all the saints. This latter is something which only God Himself can teach, and He does so thoroughly so that none may be lacking in it. If we do not love the brethren then it seems that even the best Teacher can do nothing with us!

Best of all, we as believers have the blessed privilege of looking forward to the rapture when we will be snatched away from this wicked world without dying. In the darkest days of Christian experience this is a light that cannot be dimmed nor extinguished. It is indeed true that even as Christ promised in John chapter 14 verse 3, He will return and receive us unto Himself so that we may be ever with Him. This third section of the chapter provides many details of that coming again. Just as God brought Jesus Christ out from among the dead in glorious resurrection power, so too will He bring dead and buried believers from their graves. This coming is imminent and when it happens the dead in Christ will rise first, followed in divinely arranged order by those who are 'alive and remain'. What a glorious prospect!

It will be the Lord Himself who comes, with a shout and with the trumpet of God, and all living and dead saints will rise together to meet Him in the air. Wonderful words and phrases such as 'caught up', 'together', 'to meet him' are employed to make this awesome experience a personal one too. As we await this event with growing anticipation may we show our enthusiasm for His return by purifying ourselves even as He is pure; and also by loving our fellow-believers. 'Even so, come, Lord Jesus', Rev. 22. 20.

July 4th
Joshua 20-21; Isaiah 14; **1 Thessalonians 5**
WATCH AND BE SOBER
In the concluding chapter of this wonderful Epistle the author looks forward to the day of the Lord and teaches that this day is a day of judgement as distinct from the day of the rapture in chapter 4. We are children of the day, not of the night – we are in light and not in darkness. Therefore, to demonstrate this, we are exhorted not to sleep nor to be drunken but to 'put on the breastplate of faith and love; and for a helmet, the hope of salvation', v. 8. This verse reminds us yet again of the Epistle's themes of *faith, love,* and *hope,* as mentioned in our previous meditations. It is also emphasized in verse 10 that whatever our situation at the rapture (dead or alive), the death of Christ and His glorious resurrection have achieved our salvation and eternal security.

Paul's closing remarks in the Epistle are very practical, challenging, yet encouraging. Paul asks that recognition, obedience and respect be shown to elders in their endeavours to guard and to feed the flock of God. But he emphasizes that service is not limited to elders, as shown in verse 14, when he says, 'Now we exhort *you*, brethren', so indicating that all assembly members have responsibilities in ongoing service. Let us look at some of these quite detailed instructions.

Verses 14 and 15 teach that all assembly members should be willing to warn, support and comfort their fellows and in so doing show utmost patience, avoiding retaliation, and ever following good inside and outside the assembly. It is also stated that each should personally, 'Rejoice evermore. Pray without ceasing. In every thing give thanks', vv. 16-18. These truly Christian characteristics are described as 'being the will of God in Christ Jesus concerning you', v. 18. How good to know God's will for us so clearly! Then other instructions are given regarding spiritual matters, 'Quench not the spirit. Despise not prophesyings. Prove all things', vv. 19-21.

For any who feel that such things are beyond them, the Epistle closes with the wonderful assurance, 'Faithful is he that calleth you, who also will do it', v. 24. As ever, we can rely on the Lord to see us through not only our trials but also our responsibilities.

July 5th
Joshua 22; Isaiah 15-16; 2 Thessalonians 1
A SERIOUS MISUNDERSTANDING
The war was over, the land had been captured and subdued, and now, after seven years, it was time for the soldiers to go home to their families. For some this meant leaving the 'Lord's Land', crossing over Jordan to where they had settled on the east side of the river. This was not where God had planned for them to be, but both Moses and Joshua had given their blessing for the two and a half tribes to live there, conditional only on loyalty in time of war.

The returning troops now realized they were separated from their brethren, far from Shiloh, and not following the Lord's plan for their lives. So, they decided to build an altar, a rather special one – large and impressive. The nine and a half tribes settled west of the River Jordan were perhaps already disappointed in their brethren and maybe were growing somewhat suspicious. When they heard that an altar had been built without their knowledge or approval, it seemed that their worst fears had been realized. It was clear to them that a rival altar and place of sacrifice and burnt offerings had been set up. They did not like that and so they prepared for war – against their own fellow-countrymen! Shiloh, and all it stood for, must be protected at all cost – even civil war!

Fortunately, before the troops crossed over Jordan to attack the usurpers, they decided to send a delegation to investigate, led by Phineas. Both sides attended the talks with a view to finding a settlement; and they did! It transpired that the two and a half tribes had never intended their altar to be for sacrifice and burnt offerings, though it certainly looked like that. Their plan was that it should be a memorial, a witness, to show that, though separate, they were still part of the nation of Israel and worshipped the same God. Phineas and the delegation accepted this assurance in good faith and rejoiced in resolving the issue and avoiding the serious damage to which it might have led through division.

This story would teach us that whenever rumours and differences go around it is good to select reliable persons to check them out. Given goodwill and transparency on both sides almost any situation can be resolved. If left they will cause division and promote disputes; irrecoverable damage is done to the Lord's people.

July 6th
Joshua 23; Isaiah 17-18; 2 Thessalonians 2
THE LORD YOUR GOD

Quite a number of years had passed since the events of chapter 22, maybe as many as twenty-five. During that time the people had been at rest, enjoying peace and security, but now a big change was coming in that Joshua, their unchallenged leader for so many years, soon would die. Knowing this himself, Joshua summoned the leaders to speak to them, to prepare them for their upcoming responsibilities – the first of his two farewell speeches, though some say it is two accounts of the one speech.

Many men in the Bible, in both Testaments, spoke famous last words and here we have the last and important words of Joshua. The main thrust of his speech is the *faithfulness of God* to His people. He is Lord of all the earth, 3. 11, and yet He is also 'the Lord your God', nationally and individually. This description is used thirteen times in chapter 23 and the word 'Lord' is additionally used four times. Described earlier in this book by Moses as the Lord who does wonders, Joshua now describes Him as 'the Lord your God is he that hath fought for you'. Not just once, but time and again as the people prevailed over their enemies it was the Lord who guaranteed their victory. He is faithful.

In his dramatic speech, Joshua shares three exhortations with the leadership that they must achieve going forward. Firstly, in verse 6, he says, 'Be ye therefore very courageous to keep and to do all that is written in the book of the law of Moses'. An understanding of, and a commitment to, the word of the Lord produces men and women who act courageously and, though fearful, such will continue to stand bravely for the truth. Secondly, in verse 8, Joshua demands that they continue to 'cleave' unto the Lord their God. They are to become detached from the nations around and firmly attached to the Lord. This will give them power and enable, as need be, one man to chase a thousand, v. 10. Thirdly, in verse 11, they are to 'take good heed . . . that ye love the Lord your God'. Their personal affection for God and a recognition of all He has done for them will bring them into the enjoyment of all the good things the Lord God had promised. So, too, if we take on board these exhortations, we will be blessed in similar fashion.

July 7th
Joshua 24; Isaiah 19-20; 2 Thessalonians 3
CHOOSE YE THIS DAY WHOM YE WILL SERVE

As mentioned in our previous meditation, some take the view that chapter 24 records the same event as chapter 23, but from a different perspective. Others believe that Joshua made two farewell speeches, one primarily to the leadership of the nation and the other directly to the people. Chapter 24 brings us to Shechem, located at the foot of two famous mountains – Gerizim and Ebal. Incidentally, this is close to Jacob's well where, later, our Lord called for a decision from the woman of Samaria.

In his speech, Joshua, now well over 100 years old, goes through the history of the nation of Israel and shows the part that God had played in its development. In fact, God Himself says, 'I took', 'I multiplied', 'I gave', 'I sent', 'I brought', and many other things He personally did for them, right through to verse 13, 'I have given you a land for which you did not labour, and cities which ye built not . . . [and of] vineyards and oliveyards which ye planted not do ye eat'. It was abundantly clear that without their God they were nothing and nobody. So, how strange that some were considering worshipping the gods of the Amorites while others hankered after the gods of Egypt who not only had done nothing for them but actually could not do anything for anybody!

Joshua felt compelled to call for final decisions to be made. 'If it seem evil unto you to serve the Lord' then follow the hopeless and helpless gods of your enemies. Make your decision now! And while you are doing so know this, 'As for me and my house, we will serve the Lord'. Joshua felt his responsibility to deliver his message and to press for decisions to be made there and then.

Perhaps someone reading this meditation is unsaved? The message is that here and now you must decide for Christ. Or are there believers who need to make a decision to serve the Lord wholeheartedly? Well, do it now! Joshua's message was heard and his appeal heeded. The people dedicated themselves to the service of the Lord their God and turned away from other gods. Joshua lived for another year, and for years after he died the people kept their promise and were blessed by God. Will you do the same? Commitment to God's service will always bring blessings.

July 8th

Judges 1. 1 – 2. 5; Isaiah 21. 1 – 22. 14; **1 Corinthians 1**

PREACH THE GOSPEL, THE CROSS, CHRIST CRUCIFIED

The city of Corinth was situated on trade routes which crossed Greece. This meant that many visitors passed through and they had to be catered for in a variety of ways. Thus Corinth became infamous for immorality and loose living of all kinds. In the midst of this wickedness a Christian assembly was founded, but it soon took on something of the character of the city. In or around AD 55 Paul writes to correct certain erroneous doctrines and practices that had arisen. This Epistle contains many weighty matters such as the need for love, the Lord's supper, the Lord's table, the table of demons, the resurrection, etc. Without the teaching of 1 Corinthians believers today would be very much poorer spiritually.

In chapter 1 Paul shows that all the blessings that Christians enjoy, both then and now, are built upon the foundation of the gospel. He speaks of (1) the preaching of *the gospel*, v. 17; (2) the preaching of *the cross*, v. 18; and, (3) the preaching of *Christ crucified,* v. 23. These references show us that without the message of the gospel it is impossible to come into the benefits of a personal and productive relationship with God.

Paul reminds his readers that *the preaching of the gospel* was his primary concern; Christ had sent him to do that. In preaching it he did so simply, not with wisdom of words, so that the message might be effective in presenting Christ and keeping the preacher 'under the radar', as it were. Even now the prime objective of every believer is to preach the gospel to whosoever, avoiding divisions, pride and other things that would reduce its power.

The message consists of *the preaching of the cross* which is considered foolishness by those who believe themselves to be wise – but even the foolishness of God is wiser than the wisdom of men. It pleases God through the preaching of the cross to save them that believe.

If the preaching of the cross is considered by men to be foolishness then salvation through *the preaching of Christ crucified* is a complete nonsense. Yet, through this gospel message Christ is known as the Saviour of the world. It is the basis of every blessing. Let us agree with Paul: 'Woe is me if I preach not the gospel'.

July 9th
Judges 2. 6 – 3. 4; **Isaiah 22. 15 – 23. 18**; 1 Corinthians 2
A NAIL IN A SURE PLACE
Spiritual conditions in Jerusalem, the city of David, were not good and an attitude of 'let us eat and drink, for tomorrow we die', v. 13, was pervasive. The failings of the people should have been seen as an opportunity to repent. God instructed Isaiah to go to 'this treasurer, even unto Shebna' to tell him that judgement was imminent and that he would be removed from his position of responsibility. God planned to replace him with 'my servant Eliakim', whose name means 'God will raise up'.

God's determination to secure this is emphasized with a seven-fold repetition of the words 'I will' in verses 19 to 23: 'I will drive thee (Shebna) away'; I will call him (Eliakim); clothe him; strengthen him; commit government to him; lay upon his shoulder the key of the house of David; fasten him as a nail in a sure place. While these promises concerned Eliakim they also prophesied of a greater One to come, our blessed Lord Jesus Christ.

The nail that is spoken of is not just an ordinary nail driven into a wall, but was a substantial curved metal peg set into the wall of a house while it was being built. It was therefore very strong indeed and could not be pulled out without destroying the wall, and causing damage to the house as well.

Verse 21 speaks of his *garments*, his *girdle,* and his *government*, while verse 24 tells of his *glory* and that of his father's house. Following the failure of the people to keep the law and other aspects of the old economy, God sent His Son. He was God incarnate and He lived, died, and rose again; such was the perfection of His achievements that God exalted Him to the highest place in heaven. Truly, He is a nail fastened in a sure place and we can hang on Him all our needs, concerns, hopes for the future, and our eternal security. Also hanging on Him are the glories God has bestowed on Him as well as those eternal glories which were His from before the foundation of the world. Indeed, 'He shall bear the glory, and shall sit and rule upon his throne', Zech. 6. 13.

It is good to know that He is the One upon whom we can trust and rest for salvation, and for preservation in our daily lives. He shall not fail, and we are secure in Him. Praise the Lord!

July 10th
Judges 3. 5-31; Isaiah 24; 1 Corinthians 3
THE FAT MAN
The Lord raised up various judges to lead His people during the years recorded in these chapters of the book of Judges. These were exceptional men and women of character and leadership who came to the rescue of the nation. The first was Othniel, vv. 5-11, and the second, the subject of our meditation today, was Ehud. The experiences of the nation in this period were cyclical in that they would fall into sin, then be disciplined by God, followed by repentance, deliverance and blessing, followed by sin . . . and so on. At this particular time they were under the yoke of Eglon, king of Moab, as a direct result of their 'evil in the sight of the Lord', v. 12, following Othniel's death.

Moab had co-operated with Ammon and Amalek to achieve military dominance; together they held Israel in bondage and insisted on the payment of annual tribute and oppressive taxes. Scripture describes Eglon as being 'a very fat man' – suggestive of natural prosperity, extravagance, and selfish indulgence. He had, for example, built in his palace grounds a 'summer parlour, which he had for himself alone'. All this would suggest that Israel was in bondage to 'the flesh'. Similar problems affect the Lord's people today – we all have 'fat men' in our lives. To escape spiritual lethargy the 'fat men' must be identified, challenged, and destroyed.

Ehud decided the time had come to stand against the oppressor and he devised a plan to free his people. It meant destroying the fat man rather than feeding him. How he did this is graphically described, vv. 15-30. He fashioned a dagger, sharp on both edges. He concealed it under his clothing. Being left-handed he strapped it to his right thigh, thus avoiding detection by the palace guards. Having delivered the tribute, he left the palace but shortly returned with what he said was a secret message. As the two were alone he drew the dagger, smote Eglon, and disembowelled him. Eglon died and Ehud escaped. Under his leadership Israel enjoyed eighty years of peace.

Is there a 'fat man' controlling my spiritual life? If so, I need to take decisive action to restore my relationship with God, and thereby continue to enjoy the benefits of salvation and peace.

July 11th
Judges 4; Isaiah 25; 1 Corinthians 4
THE GODLY WOMAN
In this chapter we are introduced to a woman called Deborah. She is the only woman among the judges raised up by God during these years of Israel's history. The other leading character in the chapter is Barak. These two worked together for their God and for their people. Following the death of Ehud and the deliverance of Shamgar, the nation yet again fell into sin. This brought them, in God's permissive will, into bondage to Jabin, king of Canaan and his military commander Sisera. Together, they 'mightily oppressed' the people of God for twenty desperate years. Interestingly, we do not read of a cry to God for deliverance. Neither was there a man to lead; thus Deborah was judge at that time.

Let us think about Deborah. She was a woman who had a relationship with God; she was in touch with Him; she was a prophetess; she was a godly woman, a 'mother in Israel'. She was married to Lapidus, and we assume that in domestic things she was subject to him. She was able to balance these responsibilities and did not allow one to conflict with another. She 'dwelt under the palm tree between Ramah and Bethel', suggestive of peace, refreshment and safety. She did not travel around the country as did Samuel and other leaders, but people came to her place for judgement in connection with the difficult issues they faced.

It seems the Lord had told her that she must deliver Israel out of the hand of Jabin, but, as a woman, she knew the front line was not her place. It would be the right thing to find a man to take the battle to the enemy. She finds Barak, who declared himself willing to serve, provided he had her continuing support. He did so, and with great distinction, against vastly superior forces. She needed Barak, and Barak needed her. Together they made a great team.

Godly women are often able to identify young men who can be used by God in spiritual matters and to encourage them with good words and prayerful support. Thus 'mothers in Israel' are a huge benefit to the people of God. Without Deborah's encouragement Barak would never have become the man who is commended in Hebrews chapter 11 for his faith in God. Our sisters have a vitally important role to play. Sister, be 'a mother in Israel'!

July 12th
Judges 5; Isaiah 26; 1 Corinthians 5
THE SONG OF DEBORAH AND BARAK
This chapter brings to us the well-known song composed by Deborah and sung together with Barak after God had given them victory over the Canaanites. As one would anticipate, Deborah gives praise to the God of Israel for the decisive victory. She delights that the leaders were up to the challenge, and that many people voluntarily made themselves available for the fight against what must have seemed overwhelming odds. She speaks of some of the great victories of the past and how that at times God had used supernatural means for the deliverance of His people. She then reviews not only those who had fought in the battle but also some who determined not to involve themselves, nor to risk defeat. It has been suggested that the judgement of Deborah perhaps mirrors in some ways the coming judgement seat of Christ.

There were a number of tribes in Israel who decided against fighting. They had better things to do! These folk did not see that it was their God who was asking them to help Him. I am sure that from time to time they had asked for God's help but when He asks for theirs . . . forget it! Verse 23 states, 'They came not to the help of the Lord'. We must remember that when God calls us to battle if we do not respond positively then at the judgement seat of Christ we will suffer loss and be ashamed.

Deborah then thinks of the work of Jael and her aggressive attack on Sisera who was the sole person to escape the battle alive. As Deborah had described herself as 'a mother in Israel' so now she speaks of Jael as 'blessed above women'. The song then mentions yet another woman, the mother of Sisera, and describes her lament for her son who had so ferociously been slain by Jael.

As a result of this comprehensive victory in which Barak was helped by the two quite different women, the children of Israel prevailed against their enemies and prospered. They enjoyed a restful and blessed situation of peace for forty years.

Whatever we do for the Lord is seen, and will be reviewed and rewarded in a coming day. We should remember that just as we need the Lord in our lives, so too He will call us to help Him. We must respond positively to this honour.

July 13th
Judges 6; Isaiah 27; 1 Corinthians 6
GIDEON
Chapter 6 of Judges, together with chapters 7 and 8, is all about Gideon, one of the best-known judges or 'saviours' of Israel. We imagine him, at the start of the story, to be a somewhat shy and retiring person who had deep inner feelings about the sad state of the nation and the waywardness of his people individually.

The Israelites had been living in constant fear of the Midianites for seven years. Their strategy of oppression was to allow the local farmers to prepare the soil, sow the seed, and nurture it. Then, when the crops were ready for harvesting they would come in like locusts and destroy the harvest. This went on year after year and became absolutely unbearable. It was grinding the people down and they became impoverished. It seems that during all these years none had called upon God for His help, but eventually they did so. God, in response, sent to them an unnamed prophet to tell them it was all happening because of their disobedience, sin, and departure, but, nevertheless, He would help them yet again in delivering them from Midianite persecution.

Our God is a God of mercy and He devised a plan to rescue His people from the hand of the Midianites. He chose not to execute the plan Himself, as He could well have done, but to use the little-known Gideon to bring deliverance to the people. Thus, the Angel of the Lord comes upon Gideon as he is secretly threshing corn, not out in the open, but in a wine press facility, lest he be discovered by the Midianites and relieved of his fine produce yet again. The Angel addresses him as 'a mighty man of valour', no doubt not a reference to the Gideon that then was, but to the man that God would turn him into, should he heed God's call. The instruction was clear, 'Go in this thy might, and thou shalt save Israel'. Gideon brings an offering and sees it consumed by fire. This galvanizes him into action and that very night he pulls down the altar of Baal, so risking his own life being taken in retribution. However, with God's help he emerges unscathed and ready to do further exploits, though he needs continuing re-assurance from God, which is graciously given to him. May we too, conscious of personal weakness, be persuaded to stand for God and His truth.

July 14th

Judges 7; Isaiah 28; 1 Corinthians 7

MORE ABOUT GIDEON

In the fleece tests, God had provided Gideon with vital re-assurance of His presence with him, which was what he needed in order to secure victory against the marauding Midianites. Gideon managed to assemble a force of 32,000 men who had volunteered to fight against enemy hordes; verse 12 describes them as 'like grasshoppers for multitude'. God was concerned that if Gideon used all his men and won the battle Israel would say that their own military prowess had carried the day. So, God told Gideon he should make an offer to his troops that if any of them were fearful they could return home, no questions asked. I think Gideon must have been shocked when 22,000 took up the offer and headed back home leaving him with only 10,000. But for God this number was still too great, and He therefore directed Gideon to test the others by drinking water from a nearby river. Those who lapped like a dog, virtually putting their faces into the water, should be sent home while those who cupped water in their hands and drank should stay to fight. One would have thought it might result in a 50/50 split; but no, only 300 cupped their hands to drink. The other 9,700 were dismissed!

To reassure Gideon, God sent him and his personal servant, Phurah, into the Midianite camp under cover of darkness, and as they secretly listened to a discussion between soldiers inside one of the tents, they were absolutely convinced that God would defeat the Midianites with just the 300 men. The enemy were apparently already resigned to defeat by Gideon and his God.

Gideon returned to his men and gave them instructions. Armed only with trumpets, pitchers, and lamps, they headed down to the valley to face the enemy. As they broke the pitchers, and blew the trumpets, the lamps shone out in the darkness and the men shouted in unison, 'The sword of the Lord, and of Gideon'. They routed the enemy who slew each other as they ran. Victory was secured by dependence on God, in obedience to His word. We too may have to face persistent foes, or occasional crises in our lives. If faithful, then we also will overcome, remembering that His 'strength is made perfect in weakness', 2 Cor. 12. 9.

July 15th
Judges 8; **Isaiah 29**; 1 Corinthians 8
JUDGEMENT AND RESTORATION

This chapter teaches us, amongst other things, that the world often seems to be a topsy-turvy experience for the people of God. Sometimes sin comes in and turns what should be an opportunity for blessing into times of sorrow, and, on occasions when God intervenes, judgement may well result in blessing, vv. 16-17.

Isaiah is explaining that the Lord's people at this time were spiritually drunken or asleep, vv. 9-10. In such conditions the word of God through the prophets meant little or nothing to them. The words were like a sealed book which was seldom opened. On occasions when it was opened it seemed the people could neither understand it, nor even read it. All pressed on with no help from the greatest spiritual resource – the word of God. Religious activity of course continued, but is exposed by God as not being in any way heartfelt but following the precepts and traditions of men, 'This people draw near me with their mouth . . . but have removed their heart far from me', v. 13.

As a result, things would be turned 'upside down' by the actions of the people, yet God in grace announces that in 'a very little while' He would turn things upside down Himself. As a result of divine action, the wasted forest of Lebanon would be turned into a fruitful garden, the deaf would be able to hear His word, and the blind be able to see the light provided by the word, instead of their obscurity and darkness. The meek would increase joy in the Lord, and the poor 'shall rejoice in the Holy One of Israel', vv. 17-19. Enemies, scorners, faultfinders, and other critics would be dealt with by God and rendered impotent.

Further outcomes of this grace, based upon a return to the Book, ensure that blessings will ensue. Weakness will be turned into strength, children will again bring joy to their fathers, those who once did not appreciate spiritual things are brought to a place of understanding, and those who murmured against God and His word will now read and understand doctrine, and experience the joy of practising it in daily life. While this great change is undoubtedly millennial in character, the same blessings can be enjoyed today by a return to the word of God, through His grace.

July 16th
Judges 9. 1 – 10. 5; **Isaiah 30**; 1 Corinthians 9. 1-23
IN QUIETNESS . . . SHALL BE YOUR STRENGTH
The Lord refers to His people as 'rebellious children', v. 1. The background is that they were in danger from the Assyrians and could do little to save themselves. But, rather than turn to God who had helped them so many times before, they decide to look to Egypt for help. They had not asked counsel from God – rather they had ignored Him, and, turning their back upon Him, seek refuge in the shadow of the Pharaoh's wings, and choose to rely upon his strength, v. 2. God, through Isaiah, tells them in advance that this approach is doomed to failure. Rather than mobilize against the Assyrians, Egypt will sit still and achieve nothing. All this in spite of the high price levied by Egypt for protection, v. 6!

It would be important that when all this was over, Judah should understand that Isaiah had, indeed, warned them in advance as to the outcome. God instructed him to write his prophecy in a book so that it would be a matter of record exactly what had been said, including the words, 'This is a rebellious people, lying children, children that will not hear the word of the Lord', v. 9. They had turned their back on the things of the Lord, did not want to be reminded of God or His word, but did have an ear for the 'smooth things' of carnality and deceit. Of course, inevitably, judgement follows explosively, swiftly, and overwhelmingly. All this when they had refused salvation, peace, and quietness!

Once the people understand the error of their ways, God waits for a period in order to ascertain whether or not there is appropriate repentance for their folly, before coming to them in grace. Verse 18 states, 'Therefore will the Lord wait, that he may be gracious unto you . . . blessed are all they that wait for him'.

At this time of restoration the word of God will again be appreciated and teachers will minister it with clarity and power. There will be divine guidance for the repentant, as they hear a voice behind them saying, 'This is the way, walk ye in it'. Consequently there will be songs to sing – as songs in the night – piping, and gladness of heart. Inevitably, there will be times when we too might trust in the flesh, but provided we repent, and return, the Lord will cause His glorious voice to be heard in our restoration.

July 17th

Judges 10. 6 – 11. 28; **Isaiah 31**; 1 Corinthians 9. 24 – 10. 13

ARE YOU 'LOOKING UP' OR 'GOING DOWN'?

The language of a believer who is looking upwards in times of need is, 'The Lord is on my side; I will not fear: what can man do unto me?', Ps. 118. 6. If the people of Judah had exercised this same confidence in the face of the growing threat from Assyria they would have avoided a great deal of unnecessary humiliation and suffering. Instead, they took their eyes off 'the Holy One of Israel' and went 'down to Egypt for help', v. 1. They erroneously believed that the best prospect for deliverance from the enemy was to be found in Egypt's impressive array of horses, chariots, and horsemen, v. 1. They failed to remember that the Lord had already delivered them from the bondage of Egypt and totally destroyed these outward evidences of its strength in the Red Sea, Exod. 14. 28. Indeed, it did not register with them that 'the Egyptians are men, and not God; and their horses flesh, and not spirit', v. 3. It was therefore folly of the highest order that they became dependent on such a feeble and unreliable nation, when they could have turned to the Lord. Their failure to do so meant that both Judah and Egypt would 'fail together', v. 3. Unlike the Egyptians, the Lord is always faithful to His word, v. 2. He promised to carry out His purposes for Jerusalem, vv. 4-5, and also deal in judgement with the Assyrians, vv. 8-9, cp. 37. 33-38. These promises, of course, stretched beyond the immediate circumstances to a future day, Mic. 5. 4-6.

Abram was the first person recorded in the Bible to take this fateful journey down to Egypt in a time of famine and he too reaped the bitter consequences of his action, Gen. 12. 10-20. Sadly, many believers have followed the same pathway. Egypt is a picture of the world, and those who have looked to the world for help in times of need have always come away disappointed and scarred spiritually. The word of God is clear: 'Love not the world, neither the things that are in the world', 1 John 2. 15. Let us keep looking upwards and resist the temptation to turn to the world for support as we 'fight the good fight of faith, 1 Tim. 6. 12. We can 'come boldly unto the throne of grace, that we may obtain mercy, and find grace to help in time of need', Heb. 4. 16.

July 18th

Judges 11. 29 – 12. 15; Isaiah 32; **1 Corinthians 10. 14 – 11. 1**

FLEE FROM IDOLATRY

At first glance it might appear strange to discover Paul telling his readers to 'flee from idolatry', 10. 14. More often than not we associate idolatry with Old Testament times. It was, indeed, a tragedy that the children of Israel who had been redeemed out of Egypt by the blood of the lamb should so easily forsake the Lord and turn to idolatry. However, it is an even greater tragedy when those who have been 'redeemed . . . with the precious blood of Christ', 1 Pet. 1. 18-19, choose to go in the same direction. Sadly, idolatry is still present among the Lord's people today. It might display itself in different forms from that of the days of the kings of Israel, but it is just as damaging to their spiritual well-being and remains totally abhorrent to the Lord. His frequent judgement of the children of Israel for their worship of idols and the words of Paul to the believers at Corinth stand as a timeless warning to believers of all generations to be on their guard against allowing idolatry to infiltrate their individual and collective lives. The Lord demands our complete loyalty; therefore, the moment we give our allegiance to another, we are guilty of the sin of idolatry. WILLIAM COWPER'S words are appropriate:

The dearest idol I have known,
Whate'er that idol be,
Help me to tear it from Thy throne,
And worship only Thee.

Paul makes it absolutely clear why we should flee from idolatry. The idol is, of course, nothing, but it can be used by Satan to lead us into sin. Idolatry is, therefore, demonic and must be shunned. It is unthinkable that a believer should desire fellowship with demons, 10. 19-20. God's word to Israel still stands true: 'Thou shalt have no other gods before me', Exod. 20. 3. It is important to remember that we have a responsibility towards each other in this matter. We have freedom in Christ: 'all things are lawful to me', v. 23; however, some activities that I feel free to be involved in may cause a 'weak' believer to stumble, vv. 23-33. Therefore, I need to hold things in balance and recognize that 'all things are not expedient', v. 23.

July 19th
Judges 13; Isaiah 33; 1 Corinthians 11. 2-34
AMAZING GRACE!

Paul wrote, 'But where sin abounded, grace did much more abound', Rom. 5. 20. The truth of this statement was fully displayed during the time of the judges. The children of Israel continually did evil in the Lord's sight; therefore, if they had been left to themselves, they would never have risen out of the ashes.

The Lord does not need the dramatic backdrops of men against which to work the wonders of His grace. A childless couple and a small town in the territory of Dan, one of the less prominent tribes, provided the unlikely setting for the promise of a deliverer at this time, v. 2. It reminds us that Christ, the perfect Saviour, came out of Bethlehem Ephratah that was 'little among the thousands of Judah', Mic. 5. 2.

The darkness was lifted for the children of Israel when the Angel of the Lord appeared (a pre-incarnation appearance of Christ) with a stirring message of grace for Manoah's wife: 'But thou shalt conceive, and bear a son', v. 3. We can rejoice that an even greater darkness was lifted for all mankind with the angel Gabriel's gracious message to Mary: 'And, behold, thou shalt conceive in thy womb, and bring forth a son, and shalt call his name JESUS', Luke 1. 31. Unlike Samson, who would only 'begin to deliver Israel', v. 5, He *completed* the work that he came to do. He is indeed 'the author and finisher of our faith', Heb. 12. 2.

Manoah and his wife proved to be fit vessels to receive the Lord's gracious plan of deliverance. Total trust in what the Angel said would come to pass, was mingled with their desire to know more, vv. 8, 11-12, 17. The Lord dealt gently with them and they grew in their understanding of Him. It led them to worship Him, vv. 19-20, and to appreciate that the purpose of His grace was to bring salvation, not death, vv. 22-23. The influence of a godly home on children should never be underestimated, vv. 4, 7.

The Lord was true to His word, and the point came when the deliverer arrived, v. 24. Let us praise the Lord today for the time when 'the grace of God that bringeth salvation . . . appeared to all men', Titus 2. 11. As a result of this, we can join Paul and say, 'By the grace of God, I am what I am', 1 Cor. 15. 10.

216

July 20th
Judges 14-15; Isaiah 34; **1 Corinthians 12**
DO NOT BE IGNORANT – BE INFORMED

Let us begin today's meditation by going back to the thrilling days of the early church. Thousands were saved in Jerusalem; many were saved in Samaria; and Gentiles were saved in Antioch, where a multicultural assembly was established. Five unlikely people were saved: an Ethiopian eunuch, Saul of Tarsus, Cornelius, Lydia, and the Philippian jailer. They were, indeed, thrilling times. People were saved from a variety of backgrounds and they met together in various localities. There was no élite group – all believers came into the good of what happened once for all on the day of Pentecost. We can stand alongside them and say, 'For in one Spirit were we all baptized into one body', v. 13 RV. However, the challenges were immense. How could this wide variety of believers function as local assemblies, in different locations? The complete scriptures were not in existence; therefore, they had no final ground of authority as we have today. Thankfully, God had the answer! Each believer was given a gift by the Holy Spirit.

There should be no rivalry, jealousy, or competition between believers in the exercise of their gifts in the local assembly. Paul employs the illustration of the human body to clear up any confusion we might have about gifts, vv. 12-26. The body has many members and each member is important, which reminds us that we do not all possess the same gifts; therefore, we must never belittle or covet the gifts of others. The fact that each member of our body has a function to perform teaches us that each member of the body of Christ should exercise their particular gift. Each member of our body has its place and needs the other members if it is to function effectively. Similarly, God gifts each believer, but there is no room for pride or for acting independently of others. The importance of our individual bodily members does not rest on appearance: therefore, we should never regard others as weak and insignificant. God has designed our bodies so that all members receive equality of honour, which encourages us to use our spiritual gifts to promote unity rather than division and to resist praising certain believers at the expense of others. Gifts should never be used to compete with others, but to 'feel' for each other.

July 21st
Judges 16; Isaiah 35; 1 Corinthians 13
THE LAST JOURNEY
One of the saddest statements in the Old Testament is to be found in the final stage of Samson's life: 'He wist not that the Lord was departed from him', v. 20. This chapter tracks the journeys that he took in reaching this lowest point of his life, i.e., the journeys of lust, vv. 1-3, love, vv. 4-20, and loss, v. 21. Today's meditation will focus on his last journey, vv. 22-31.

The sad scene in the prison house might lead us to the conclusion that the Lord's purposes had been thwarted. Certainly, it led the Philistines to believe that they, and their god, had gained the victory, vv. 23-24. However, they failed to see that a work of grace and recovery was taking place in the darkness of this depressing place that would mean the purposes of God would be fulfilled. It is encouraging to know that the chastening of the Lord is never intended to be an end in itself. He is always looking for recovery. Clearly, although unable to see what was going on around him, Samson began to recover his devotion to the Lord: 'Howbeit the hair of his head began to grow again after he was shaven', v. 22. It was from this point that he began the last stage of his journey.

The sight of Israel's deliverer being led by a 'lad that held him by the hand', v. 26, filled the Philistines with a false sense of security. They had restricted his movements but they could not control the stirrings in his heart. His prayer was that of a penitent man, who voluntarily chose death as the means of removing his shame and restoring the Lord's honour, v. 28. If it had been purely for personal vengeance, the Lord would not have answered, v. 30. The magnitude of his victory is captured in a simple statement: 'So the dead which he slew at his death were more than they which he slew in his life', v. 30. It speaks of the grace of God that allowed His restored servant to fulfil the promise that he would 'begin to deliver Israel', 13. 5.

The words of C. A. COATES bring home the challenge to our hearts: 'He had to learn that his own death was the secret of power ... When I come to accept my death, the great secret of the power of God works in me, and I become an efficient instrument for the use of God'.

July 22nd
Judges 17-18; **Isaiah 36. 1 – 37. 7**; 1 Corinthians 14
WINNING THE BATTLE

The Old Testament historian gave Hezekiah, king of Judah, the highest of commendations: 'And he did that which was right in the sight of the Lord, according to all that David his father did', 2 Kgs. 18. 3. Today's reading teaches us important lessons for victorious living as we engage in spiritual warfare, Eph. 6. 12.

First, we learn that the pathway of faith and obedience does not shield us from the trials and pressures of life. Paul writes, 'Yea, and all that will live godly in Christ Jesus shall suffer persecution', 2 Tim. 3. 12. The Lord does not promise to save us *from* persecutions, but assures us that He will deliver us *out of* them, 2 Tim. 3. 11. Hezekiah proved this as he faced the Assyrians.

Second, we discover that yesterday's victories do not guarantee success today. We must pray for fresh strength each day as we engage in 'the good fight of faith', 1 Tim. 6. 12. Hezekiah had once been given the ability to stand against the king of Assyria, 2 Kgs. 18. 7; however, this same enemy returned and he needed the Lord's help to face him again, Isa. 36. 1-2.

Third, Hezekiah's experience teaches us that our enemies will use a variety of tactics to intimidate us; therefore, we need to be watchful and steadfast at all times. Sennacherib, through Rabshakeh (his cupbearer), did all he could to undermine Hezekiah's confidence, even to the point of boasting that the Lord was with him in his attack on Jerusalem, vv. 4-10. It is impossible to reason with such men, vv. 11-13.

Fourth, we learn the value of silence in the face of intimidation and false promises. Rabshakeh encouraged the people not to trust in Hezekiah's assurances, but to respond to Sennacherib's attractive offer of a life of luxury, vv. 14-17. He must have been surprised by the wall of silence that greeted his proposals. Silence is often the best form of attack in such situations, v. 21.

Fifth, the believer's first recourse in times of testing ought to be to turn to the Lord and His word. Hezekiah's immediate response to events was a desire to hear the word of the Lord through Isaiah, 37. 1-2. He was reassured by the comforting message he received that the Lord was in control, vv. 6-7.

July 23rd

Judges 19; **Isaiah 37. 8-38**; 1 Corinthians 15. 1-34

EFFECTIVE PRAYER

Clearly, the king of Assyria was disturbed by the rumour of an impending attack by the king of Ethiopia, v. 9. It led him to renew pressure on Hezekiah and Jerusalem. He needed control of Judah to secure his position. He employed the same tactic as he had used in the past, i.e., he boasted about the achievements of the kings of Assyria in order to intimidate him and thereby secure his surrender, vv. 10-13. He failed to realize that he was no match for a praying king and a prophet with the word of the Lord.

Although Hezekiah's prayer was short, it testifies to the truth expressed by James, 'The effectual [effective] fervent prayer of a righteous man availeth much', Jas. 5. 16. It is a powerful reminder to us today of the importance of prayer in our spiritual warfare, Eph. 6. 12. Our prayer life would be greatly enhanced by considering its features. First, he had a vision of the Lord's greatness. The terminology used revealed the depth of his appreciation of the Lord, v. 16. He referred to Him as both 'the Lord' (Jehovah – the self-existent, eternal, and covenant-keeping God) and also 'God' (Elohim – the supreme God). He appreciated that He was present in the midst of His people, cp. Exod. 25. 21-22, the one supreme God among all the kingdoms of earth and the Creator of the universe. We would do well to give more thought to the language we use when addressing the Lord in prayer. Second, Hezekiah revealed that his prime concern was for the glory of God, vv. 17, 20. Our prayers would be more effective if they were underpinned by the desire to see the honour of His name upheld above everything else. Third, his consideration of the greatness and glory of the Lord enabled him to get the enemies into perspective, vv. 18-19. They were formidable but they had succeeded in destroying only the gods of others that were not gods at all. They had never faced the living God of Israel. Fourth, within the context of these great truths he confidently made his specific request for salvation, v. 20. If our requests are *specific* we will come to appreciate the power of prayer as God answers them.

Hezekiah's prayer was effective. It was not only heard, v. 20, but also the Lord answered in a remarkable way, vv. 33-38.

July 24th
Judges 20; **Isaiah 38-39**; 1 Corinthians 15. 35-58

THE POWER OF PRAYER

Isaiah's message concerning Hezekiah's terminal illness comes as a surprise within the context of the positive things that the historian has already placed on record about his godly reign. His prayer portrays his struggle to accept the Lord's will for him, 38. 10-20. The Lord is sovereign in His dealings with each believer. Living a God-fearing life does not guarantee freedom from trials, 2 Tim 3. 10-11. We will never fully understand in this life the way in which the Lord leads us, but we can rest assured that it will always be for His glory and for our good.

The response. True to character, Hezekiah 'turned his face toward the wall, and prayed unto the Lord', 38. 2. He probably did this to shut out distractions, so that he could engage in earnest prayer to the Lord. At first sight his prayer might appear to be arrogant; however, in the light of all that is known of his godly character, it is much more likely that the driving motive for it was his desire to remain on the scene to look after the welfare of Judah in the face of Assyrian aggression. He had confidence in the Lord to answer his prayer and to change the seemingly inevitable course of events. He inspires us to believe in the power of prayer.

The reply. It is encouraging to know that God hears and answers our prayers. The answer came swiftly and embraced the desire of Hezekiah's heart, 38. 4-6. The Lord added fifteen years to his life, v. 5. He is an unchanging God, but this does not conflict with the fact that He is compassionate, gracious, and merciful when men turn to Him in genuine repentance. God changes His response to men, when they change their attitude towards Him.

The recovery. It is unlikely that the fig poultice was a natural means used by the Lord to bring about Hezekiah's recovery. It is more likely that it was a sign or symbol of the cure the Lord would bring about through His word.

The request. Hezekiah's request for a sign is understandable, considering the fact that he did not possess the complete scriptures or the indwelling of the Holy Spirit, 38. 22. However, we should not seek to emulate his actions as far as this is concerned. We must learn to trust the Lord and take Him at His word.

July 25th
Judges 21; **Isaiah 40**; 1 Corinthians 16
VOICES OF COMFORT
Many voices are heard today that seek to lead us from the pathway of divine truth. In contrast, a meditation upon the voices heard in the first part of today's reading will comfort us and draw us nearer to the heart of God.

First, God's voice is heard with a call to the returning Jewish exiles to speak words of comfort to each other, vv. 1-2. The message they were given spoke of warfare (sufferings, trials) accomplished and iniquity pardoned (the disciplinary punishment of sin endured). In spite of their past failures God was once again able to call them 'my people'. Such thoughts point us towards Calvary, where the debt of our sin was met in full by the sacrifice of Christ and God's justice was satisfied. Well might we say, 'Who is a God like unto thee, that pardoneth iniquity?' Mic. 7. 18.

Second, we hear John the Baptist's voice preparing the way for the coming of Christ, vv. 3-5. As the forerunner it was fitting that he should be described as a 'voice'. He reminds us that Christ 'must increase, but I must decrease', John 3. 30. He called the people to be spiritually ready for His coming. Are we in the right spiritual condition for Christ's return for us? John ended with the hope that 'the glory of the Lord shall be revealed, and all flesh shall see it together', v. 5. This was partially fulfilled at Christ's first advent but it will be completely fulfilled when He returns to reign, Rev. 1. 7. Are we longing for this appearing, Col. 3. 4?

Third, God's voice is heard speaking either to John the Baptist or Isaiah, v. 6. The message they are instructed to give is clear, i.e., man is transient, but the word of God abides forever, 1 Pet. 1. 23-25; therefore, His promises are totally sure. Let us reaffirm today our total confidence in the reliability of the inspired word.

Fourth, the inhabitants of Jerusalem are encouraged: 'Lift up thy voice with strength', v. 9. Their voice will be heard in a coming day when they announce to the cities of Judah the coming of the Messiah to reign. They will speak of Him as the mighty God but also as the tender Shepherd, who will feed, gather, carry, and gently lead His flock, vv. 10-11. These characteristics ought to be seen today in all those who care for 'the flock of God', 1 Pet. 5. 2-4.

Ruth 1; Isaiah 41; 2 Corinthians 1

NO LONGER STRANGERS

G. MATHESON writes, 'Often have I been tempted to express surprise that the strong age of the judges should have produced a spirit so silent. Silent indeed she (Ruth) is, and gentle beyond measure; but I do not think that this is incompatible with extreme decision of character'. The life-changing decision she made in today's reading was truly remarkable. It took her from being one of the 'wives of the women of Moab', v. 4, and led her to become the wife of Boaz, 4. 13. The Moabites came from the fleshly union of Lot with one of his two daughters, Gen. 19. 36-37. The law stated that they must 'not enter into the congregation of the Lord . . . for ever', Deut. 23. 3. It was divine mercy and grace that took Ruth, a stranger, and brought her into contact with Naomi, Bethlehem, and Boaz. She pictures the spiritual journey taken by all Gentile believers: 'aliens . . . strangers . . . no hope, and without God in the world . . . far off . . . made nigh by the blood of Christ . . . no more strangers and foreigners, but fellow citizens with the saints, and of the household of God', Eph. 2. 12-13, 19. We should never forget the distance the grace of God has brought us.

Initially, it would have appeared as if there was little difference between Ruth and Orpah; however, the latter soon revealed that her heart was still in Moab, vv. 12-15. In direct contrast Ruth made one of the great biblical statements of faith that revealed her gentle spirit and strength of character. She expressed her deep affection for Naomi: 'Intreat me not to leave thee . . . for whither thou goest, I will go; and where thou lodgest, I will lodge', v. 16. She witnessed to true repentance of heart by pledging her allegiance to Naomi's people and God: 'Thy people shall be my people, and thy God my God', v. 16. She 'turned to God from idols to serve the living and true God', 1 Thess. 1. 9. Furthermore, she even identified herself with Naomi's death and burial: 'Where thou diest, will I die, and there will I be buried', v. 17. Do we display the same commitment and devotion to Christ? We are not only linked with His death and burial, but also with His resurrection, Rom. 6. 3-4. Our lives ought to be lived in constant communion with Him and His people.

July 27th
Ruth 2; Isaiah 42; **2 Corinthians 2**
SPIRITUAL LEADERSHIP

Where there are people there will always be problems – even in local churches. The believers at Corinth could witness to the truth of this; indeed, the sin of one man had disturbed the unity and order of the local assembly there, vv. 5-9. Paul had attempted to resolve the problem by visiting the believers. The majority appear to have agreed with his views as to how the matter should be resolved, but they had failed to take action to put matters right. There was, no doubt, a minority who supported the offender in his wrongdoing. The way in which Paul dealt with the issue is an example as to how spiritual leaders should deal with problems that arise in local assemblies.

First, he does not take the obvious pathway, i.e., to visit them again. He had the discernment to see that this would not have been the right course of action at this time. We need to pray for the elders in our local assemblies that they may be given wisdom to discern the correct action to take in difficult circumstances. The obvious answer is not always the right one.

Second, Paul was entirely open in his dealing with the Corinthians. He made it clear to them what he was doing and why. Problems can arise among us when we are not open and honest with each other. Paul realized that there was a need for mutual dependence upon each other if the problem were to be resolved, v. 2. Problems will never be solved if a leader seeks to act independently of everyone else.

Third, Paul was driven by a desire for restoration, i.e., restoration for the offender, v. 7, and for the relationship between himself and the believers in Corinth, v. 3. The true Christian leader will never pursue a personal agenda or evidence a vindictive spirit when dealing with issues that are potentially divisive.

Fourth, Paul had no desire to lord it over the believers. This letter was stained with his tears, v. 4. Clearly, the problem had touched his heart; therefore, he appeals to them from the heart.

Let us pray that our spiritual leaders might be strengthened and given the wisdom to make right decisions when challenging situations arise.

July 28th

Ruth 3-4; Isaiah 43. 1 – 44. 5; **2 Corinthians 3. 1 – 4. 6**

YE ARE OUR EPISTLE

In the absence of a written letter of commendation, what would you be able to point to that testified to the fact that you were a true believer and a faithful servant of the Lord? Letters of commendation to those who do not know us are scriptural and necessary for believers in all generations. Sadly, many elders in local churches today believe that they are outdated and unnecessary. On the other hand, we ought to be able to point to more than a written letter to testify to our service for the Lord.

Paul was opposed by those who poured scorn on what they deemed to be his lack of credentials for serving the Lord in Corinth, 2. 17; 3. 1. Nevertheless, he was able to point to what he had achieved in the city that went beyond any credentials that his opponents could produce, i.e., sinners who had been changed inwardly by the Spirit of the living God, 3. 3. If anyone wanted evidence that Paul was involved in a true work for the Lord, they had only to look at the fruit of his labours for confirmation that went beyond what any letter could produce. Paul declares to the Corinthian believers, 'Ye are our epistle written in our hearts, known and read of all men', 3. 2. Similarly, he says to the Thessalonian believers, 'Ye are our witnesses, and God also, how holily and justly and unblameably we behaved ourselves among you that believe . . . For ye are our glory and joy', 1 Thess. 2. 10, 20. Paul was quick to avoid taking the credit for the outcome of his service. He attributed all the glory to God and to Christ, 2 Cor. 3. 3-6. Let us make it our aim to ensure that our testimonies are not only 'paper exercises', but are evidenced by genuine fruit for our labours to the glory of God. How many people can we look at and claim, in deep humility, that we have been instrumental in leading them to Christ?

We will, of course, only be able to stand alongside Paul at the judgement seat of Christ, with a clear conscience and surrounded by 'our epistles', if we have preached the same gospel that he did: 'For we preach not ourselves, but Christ Jesus the Lord; and ourselves your servants for Jesus' sake', 4. 5. It is only 'the glorious gospel of Christ', v. 4, that can give light to darkened hearts.

July 29th
1 Samuel 1; Isaiah 44. 6-23; 2 Corinthians 4. 7 – 5. 10

A MEEK AND QUIET SPIRIT

Within any home there is the potential for division, but in some it may be greater than in others. Such was the case in this home in Ramah. Hannah had a burden and a vision that no one else shared. Her husband Elkanah loved her, but did not appreciate her deep spiritual exercise. Even Eli, the high priest, misjudged her, v. 13. Peninnah, her adversary, took delight in provoking her, vv. 6-7. The question might well be asked, 'How can this family be saved from being torn apart?' The answer is found in Hannah. She has been an inspiration to many wives as to the key role they can play in promoting unity within the home.

Her name means 'gracious', a characteristic that she displayed in all her movements. She possessed 'a meek and quiet spirit, which is in the sight of God of great price', 1 Pet. 3. 4. 'The Lord had shut up her womb', v. 5, but she showed no resentment. Neither did she criticize or humiliate her husband, even though he showed a lack of insight into the reason for her grief by suggesting that he was better to her than ten sons, v. 8. Remarkably, she was not vindictive towards Peninnah, thereby teaching us the value of silence in the face of provocation.

Instead of creating discord, Hannah turned to God in prayer and found 'grace to help in time of need', Heb. 4. 16. Her prayer was personal, v. 13, persistent, v. 12, and passionate, vv. 15-16. She is the first one in scripture to refer to God as 'Lord of hosts', v. 11, a title that speaks of Him as sovereign of the armies of heaven and earth. She believed that He had the power to bring fruit out of her barrenness. Indeed, she recognized that He needed a man child in Israel more than she did, v. 11. It is no surprise therefore that her prayer was productive. She was able to point to Samuel and say, 'For this child I prayed', v. 27.

Her actions following Samuel's birth displayed the high regard that she had for the home. She was prepared to make personal sacrifices until he was weaned, v. 22. She appreciated how vital his early years were and the importance of her role during them. Let us seek to promote harmony in our homes by cultivating the same meek and quiet spirit seen in Hannah.

July 30th
1 Samuel 2; Isaiah 44. 24 – 45. 25; 2 Corinthians 5. 11 – 6. 10
THE SELFLESS LIFE
Selflessness was the hallmark of Hannah's life. In contrast, the corrupt priests of the day selfishly and unashamedly robbed God and His people, vv. 12-17. She had already fulfilled her vow and given back to God the son He had given to her, 1. 28. Far from causing her grief and regret, this selfless act of sacrifice led her to worship the Lord, 2. 1-10. Her prayer looked forward to the time when the Lord's enemies will be vanquished and Christ reigns, v. 10. Her prime concern was not for her own vindication but for God's honour to be upheld, both then and also in the future.

The selfless believer desires to see spiritual growth in fellow believers, and Hannah was no exception. She could so easily have felt that her responsibility was over, once she had weaned Samuel and left him with Eli in Shiloh; however, nothing could have been further from the truth. She expected him to grow physically: 'moreover his mother made him a little coat, and brought it to him from year to year, when she came up with her husband to offer the yearly sacrifice', v. 19. She kept a motherly eye upon him and would have noticed immediately if he had failed to develop physically. There is no doubt that such a godly woman would also have been equally observant as to his spiritual development.

Samuel did not disappoint Hannah. He displayed the same selfless spirit that was seen in her. Even though he was a child, his service was first and foremost 'unto the Lord', v. 11, and 'before the Lord', v. 18. There was no desire to honour and enrich himself at the expense of others. It is no surprise therefore to discover that he 'grew before [in full view of] the Lord', v. 21, and 'grew on and was in favour both with the Lord and also with men', v. 26. He was not content to stand still in his spiritual life in spite of the declension surrounding him.

This remarkable mother and son challenge us to be concerned about our own spiritual development and also that of others. Paul exercised the care of a nursing mother for the new converts in the church at Thessalonica, 1 Thess. 2. 7. Peter's closing desire for his readers was that they would 'grow in grace and in the knowledge of our Lord and Saviour Jesus Christ', 2 Pet. 3. 18.

227

July 31st
1 Samuel 3; Isaiah 46; **2 Corinthians 6. 11 – 7. 16**

BE SEPARATE

There is a clear Old Testament command that was given to the children of Israel: 'Thou shalt not plow with an ox and an ass together', Deut. 22. 10. The two creatures were not compatible; indeed, the ox was a clean animal and the ass was unclean. They would make a difference to an unploughed field if they were yoked together, but it would be the wrong kind of difference! Some of the children of Israel might have seen the sense of the command and yet been tempted to ask the question, 'But what if . . .?', i.e., 'But what if a particular ass was obedient, accommodating, gentle, and the two creatures got on well together? Would it not then be acceptable for them to be yoked together?' There might also have been occasions when there were no other oxen available; therefore the only other option available was not to plough. However, God's word does not allow for any exceptions to the rule – the command still stands, 'Thou shalt not'. The Lord was teaching His people the important truth of separation.

There is an equally clear New Testament command to believers: 'Be ye not unequally yoked together with unbelievers', 2 Cor. 6. 14. Before we can even ask, 'But what if . . . ?', Paul challenges us with five key words: fellowship, communion, concord (harmony), part (share), and agreement, which emphasize the incompatibility of believers and unbelievers, vv. 14-16. He also presents us with five features linked with believers: righteousness, light, Christ, belief, temple of God. They stand in direct contrast to five features linked to unbelievers: lawlessness, darkness, Belial, infidel, and idols, vv. 14-16. Clearly, believers and unbelievers are two different 'creatures', 5. 17. It is little wonder that Paul goes on to say, 'Wherefore come out from among them, and be ye separate, saith the Lord, and touch not the unclean thing', 6. 17.

Let us pray that God will give us the needed grace, courage, and strength to be separate in an increasingly immoral society. Another has written: 'To be separate is to be different: to live among people, yet to be distinct from them; to get close to them, without being identified with them in aims, habits, partnerships or fellowships'.

August 1st
1 Samuel 4-5; Isaiah 47; 2 Corinthians 8
THE ARK OF GOD IS CAPTURED
War had broken out between Israel and the Philistines. In the first encounter Israel's army was routed. The elders of the people asked the right question: why had the Lord defeated them? They should have known the answer. God had allowed defeat because of disobedience, Lev. 26. 14, 17. Instead of enquiring of the Lord, they came up with the idea of bringing the ark of the covenant from the sanctuary to the battlefield. This was *superstition,* almost idolatry. They were using the ark as a talisman. They seemed to think that the *symbol* of God's presence among His people guaranteed His actual presence. The ark had been at the head of Israel's armies in great days of victory, Num. 10. 35, Josh. 3. 13-17, 6. 12-14. However, it was never the ark which had carried the day. It was the Lord of hosts. The elders were trying to manipulate God. They thought that He would not permit His people to suffer defeat if the ark was among them. We must never substitute religious externality for spiritual reality. God will never permit us to use Him for our purposes.

The army of Israel shouted for joy when the ark came into their camp. At first the Philistines trembled because, as idolaters, they thought that the gods of Israel had come to fight against them. They banished their fear and fought courageously. The Israelites melted away in total defeat. Their losses were staggering. Hophni and Phinehas, the wicked sons of Eli, were among the slain. Thus God's death sentence against these false shepherds was executed, 1 Sam. 2. 34. We dare not trifle with the living God. Worse still, the ark fell into the hands of the Philistines.

The account ends with two more deaths. Eli, shocked by the news of Israel's defeat, the death of his sons, and especially the capture of the ark, falls and breaks his neck. The wife of Phinehas dies in childbirth. She names her son, Ichabod, meaning 'the glory has departed', because the ark had been taken. Actually, the ark had been captured because God's glorious presence had already departed. How tragic for that ever to happen. May we always cherish the gracious, abiding presence of the Lord. May 'Ichabod' never be written over any of our churches.

August 2nd
1 Samuel 6-7; Isaiah 48; 2 Corinthians 9

THE MINISTRY OF SAMUEL

We are given no record of Samuel's service for a period of over twenty years. Now he reappears in three scenes.

We meet Samuel in the *revival at Mizpah*. Israel began to lament after the Lord, seeking a renewed sense of His presence and grieving over their sins. Yet hearts can be moved without being changed. Repentance involves more than emotion. In his preaching, Samuel appealed for a wholehearted return to the Lord. The people must give Him their sole allegiance. He demands exclusive loyalty. In radical repentance, Israel must completely renounce the Canaanite male and female fertility deities they found so alluring. The people obeyed God's word. They put away their cherished idols to serve the Lord alone. Samuel gathered the penitent nation at Mizpah. They confessed their sin in word and action.

Then we meet him in the *victory at Ebenezer*. The Philistines marched against Israel as soon as they heard of the assembly at Mizpah. Satan resists every spiritual advance. In complete contrast to their attitude in their last battle with the Philistines, Israel cast themselves on the Lord's mercy, trusting in Him, not in the ark. They called for Samuel's intercession. He offered a lamb to secure their acceptance with God, and cried out for them to the Lord. The Lord heard. He routed Israel's foes with a thunder storm; Samuel won the battle on his knees. His burnt offering reminds us of Christ's sacrifice and his intercession pictures the all prevailing advocacy of the Saviour. To commemorate the triumph of the Lord, Samuel erected a memorial, Ebenezer, the stone of help. The message of Ebenezer is, 'Thus far the Lord has helped us'. We can draw from our past experiences with God the assurance that He will guide and guard us until we reach heaven.

Finally, we observe Samuel on *circuit in Benjamin's territory*. Tirelessly, he goes round in his work as a judge, leading the people of God and encouraging them in their relationship with Him. This was a routine ministry without the glamour of Mizpah or Ebenezer, but it was needed to consolidate the revival and deliverance. Often, our ministry more resembles Samuel's circuit than his days of high drama. Do we carry it out faithfully, as he did?

August 3rd
1 Samuel 8. 1 – 9. 14; **Isaiah 49**; 2 Corinthians 10
THE SECOND SERVANT SONG

Here we have the incredible privilege of listening to a conversation between the Lord and *His Servant*, clearly an individual. We know Him to be the Lord Jesus.

The dialogue begins with the Servant calling on remote lands and distant peoples to heed Him. His will be a worldwide ministry. He declares that He was called to His unique role before His birth. His service involves the prophetic proclamation of God's powerful, piercing word. The Lord will conceal Him from public view in preparation for that public ministry.

The Lord replies by identifying the Servant as the embodiment of the true Israel, and promising that He would be supremely glorified by the Servant's ministry, John 13. 31; 17. 4.

The Servant responds by lamenting that He had laboured to the point of weariness yet all His toil had not achieved the desired result. However, the Lord Jesus did not succumb to discouragement, Isa. 42. 4. He committed the issues of His service to God. How encouraging that we have a High Priest who fully understands our disappointments at apparent lack of success in God's service! He feels with us and for us, because on earth He felt like us, Heb. 4. 15. We are challenged not to grow weary in doing good and not to lose heart, Gal. 6. 9.

God emphatically assures the Servant that His appointed ministry of restoring Israel will be fulfilled. Indeed that restoration is too small a task for the Servant. Rather He will be a light to the nations. He himself will be the salvation the whole world needs.

The Lord then declares the humiliation the Servant will endure, followed by His supreme exaltation. The Lord Jesus was demeaned and despised by the world, the object of popular repugnance. He submitted Himself to the authority of Gentile governors, John 19. 11. However, the day will dawn when He will receive the homage of all the rulers of the earth.

The Servant will lead Israel in a new and greater exodus. He will liberate the restored nation, and regather them from the furthest corners of the earth. No wonder the song concludes with an appeal for heaven and earth to join in joyful celebration!

231

August 4th

1 Samuel 9. 15 – 10. 27; **Isaiah 50. 1 – 51. 8**; 2 Corinthians 11

THE THIRD SERVANT SONG

In this song the Lord Jesus, speaking as the Servant of the Lord, discloses the inner attitudes and motivations of His life.

The Servant was **teachable.** He was the perfect disciple, learning from His Father. Thus, He was equipped to be the teacher of others, sustaining the weary with the words the Father gave Him, John 8. 28. Each morning He had an appointment with His Father to hear His voice and enjoy His fellowship. Do we? All disciples need to have their ears filled with God's word so that their tongues can be filled with words of encouragement for others.

The Servant was **submissive.** He was devoted to carrying out the will of God whatever the cost. He was prepared to be flogged as the worst of criminals. He was willing to suffer the degradation of men pulling out his beard and to be spat upon, the ultimate of contempt and insult. The Gospels record the fulfilment of these prophetic words, John 19. 1; Matt. 26. 67; 27. 30. What physical and psychological abuse was heaped on our Saviour!

The Servant was **resolute**. Knowing all that would befall Him in Jerusalem, the Lord Jesus set His face like flint to go there to endure all the sufferings which awaited Him, Luke 9. 51. He did so confident of complete vindication by His Father. That took place in His resurrection, ascension, and exaltation, Acts 2. 32-33; Rom. 1. 4; 1 Tim. 2. 14. The language of the law court is used to describe the vindication of Christ. Every charge against Him was totally dismissed in heaven's supreme tribunal. His accusers are compared to a worn out garment falling to pieces and destroyed by moths, Isa. 50. 9. In Romans chapter 8 verses 33-34 the language of this song is triumphantly used by Paul to celebrate the justification of Christ's people. *His* vindication is *our* vindication.

The song ends by drawing the sharpest possible contrast between the followers of the Servant and those who reject Him. Those who obey His voice are exhorted to trust in the Lord, relying entirely on Him however dark their experience. We can depend on God in the most difficult circumstances of life. Those who are the Servant's foes, relying solely on their own resources, face a sorrowful, hopeless future. Is our faith in Christ, or ourselves?

232

August 5th
1 Samuel 11-12; Isaiah 51. 9-23; 2 Corinthians 12. 1-13

SAMUEL'S FAREWELL ADDRESS

A bloodless revolution had taken place. Israel's form of government had totally changed. The people had come to Samuel and requested a monarchy in place of leadership by judges appointed and equipped by God. God instructed Samuel to agree, even though the people's desire involved a rejection of His kingship. Samuel anointed Saul as the first king. Saul then gained a victory over the Ammonites. Samuel gathered the people at Gilgal to confirm Saul's kingship, and witness his stepping down as the last judge. In doing so, he addressed the people.

Samuel began by emphasizing his lifelong consistency and complete incorruptibility. He challenged the assembly to agree that he had never used his office to enrich himself, had never taken a bribe nor oppressed any of the people. The facts compelled them to do so. Christians, especially Christian leaders, must be people of *honesty* and *integrity*.

Samuel went on to remind Israel of God's faithfulness in delivering them throughout their history by leaders whom He raised up in times of danger when they cried to Him. Yet, faced with the Ammonite threat, they had not relied on the Lord, their King, but had sought a human king. They and their king would be blessed if they obeyed the Lord. If they rebelled, His hand would be against them. Samuel demonstrated how severe that judgement would be by praying for God to send thunder and rain. The Lord did so, displaying His almighty control of the weather. It was late May, when rain was never seen. The people were brought to penitence, confessing that their request for a king had added to their sins.

Samuel appealed to them, despite their wickedness, to serve the Lord with all their heart. They were God's people by His sovereign grace alone. He would never ultimately abandon them, nor would Samuel; he was going to keep on *interceding* for them. To fail to do so would be sin. Do we intercede for others? Not only so but he would go on *instructing* and *counselling* the people. How selfless he was. His final appeal rings out to us, as to his hearers: 'Fear the Lord and serve Him in truth with all your heart; for consider what great things He has done for you'.

August 6th
1 Samuel 13; Isaiah 52. 1-12; 2 Corinthians 12. 14 – 13. 14

SAUL'S DISOBEDIENCE

Samuel did not give up his prophetic ministry when he stepped down as a judge. He continued to be in touch with God. He was Israel's intercessor and instructor. How different things would have been if Saul had relied on Samuel and followed the mind of God. That was what Saul could not bring himself to do. Our chapter shows how very quickly he disobeyed God's word.

The Philistines remained a major threat to Israel. They monopolized all iron implements. Even the Israelites' farm tools were sharpened for them by the Philistines at a heavy price. The aim was to keep Israel disarmed. Only Saul and Jonathan, in the whole of their army, possessed a sword or a spear. Yet Jonathan bravely struck at Philistine oppression, attacking one of their garrisons. That provoked a full-scale invasion. Saul gathered a defensive force at Gilgal.

The inference we draw from verse 8 is that Samuel had told Saul to remain at Gilgal for seven days to wait his arrival, cp. 1 Sam. 10. 4, 8. Just before the seven days had ended, with no sign of Samuel, Saul rashly took matters into his own hands and offered a burnt offering. Just then the prophet appeared. Saul greeted him nonchalantly, as if nothing was amiss. He certainly did not expect Samuel's challenging question: 'What have you done?' His proffered excuses were lame. The root of the matter was that in disregarding Samuel's word Saul had disobeyed the word of the Lord. He had acted foolishly. He was blameworthy. Samuel pronounced a solemn sentence. Saul's line would not continue. No dynasty would bear his name. Disobedience to the commandments of God is a matter of the *utmost gravity.*

Saul thought he could reign with only a token recognition of the Lord and His word. Samuel told him that he would be replaced by 'a man after God's own heart'. David's faults were many, but he had a heart for God, desiring to let His word be the rule of his life and of the nation. Saul could not get it into his mind that he ought to rule for God. David could not have got it out of his mind if he had tried. Is God a reality to us? Do we seek to know His will? Do we *obey* it?

August 7th
1 Samuel 14; **Isaiah 52. 13 – 53. 12**; Romans 1. 1-17

THE FOURTH SERVANT SONG

This wonderful poem is one of the key passages in the Bible. Over 700 years in advance, Isaiah vividly predicts the sufferings and glory of Christ. The song reads as if it had been composed in the shadow of the cross. Such exact fulfilment confirms that the Bible is the inspired word of God. The song stirs us to worship the Saviour, reflecting on all we owe Him.

The first stanza, 52. 13-15, foretells the Servant's complete exaltation. He will receive universal dominion. Yet, in astonished horror, men had seen Him so savagely disfigured that He was unrecognisable as human. From the lowest depths, He has been raised to the highest heights.

The second stanza, 53. 1-3, portrays the Servant growing up in obscurity before God's delighted, approving eye. In contrast, men saw nothing in Him to attract them. He lacked all outward majesty. People shunned and scorned the Lord Jesus, regarding Him as nothing. Yet He keenly felt humanity's sorrows.

The third stanza, vv. 4-6, recounts the Servant bearing the load of human suffering in His miraculous healings, Matt. 8. 16-17. Yet men viewed Jesus on the cross as suffering for His own sins. How utterly mistaken! Totally guiltless, He suffered for others. He took our place and bore our doom, pierced and crushed that our sins might be forgiven. Penal substitution is the heart of the gospel.

The fourth stanza, vv. 7-9, emphasizes the meek, unresisting attitude of Jesus as He stood before His judges. In silent dignity, He did not utter a word of reproach. From His mock trials, He was hustled to His unjust execution, history's worst miscarriage of justice. But not for Jesus the intended common grave of criminals; God ensured that He received the use of Joseph of Arimathea's new tomb.

The final stanza, vv. 10-12, declares that the sinless Servant's intense sufferings, bearing others' sins, were God's sovereign purpose for Him. Raised from the dead, He shall be fully satisfied with the final results of all His toil, a spiritual seed, justified by His sacrifice and His total supremacy by right of conquest. The Servant is the strongest of the strong!

August 8th
1 Samuel 15; Isaiah 54; **Romans 1. 18-32**

THE GENTILE WORLD CONDEMNED

Paul has just rejoiced in the saving power of the gospel and the righteous standing God confers on all who believe. Now he tells why the gospel must be proclaimed. To grasp how good the *good news* really is we first need to hear the bad news of our guilt!

Our reading asserts the awful reality of *God's wrath*, an essential dimension in the Bible's revelation of the living God. There is nothing capricious or disproportionate in God's wrath. Nor is it an expression of personal pique. Rather it is the total revulsion of a God who is utterly righteous against all that contradicts His holiness. God does not react with indifference to man's defiance and disobedience. He is resolved to act against it. Our culture has a deep seated animosity to the whole idea of the wrath of God. Liberal theology dismisses it as sub-Christian. We must resolutely yet sensitively proclaim it in our generation. Thank God it was fully satisfied by the death of Christ!

Although the full display of His wrath awaits a future day, Rom. 2. 5, God has already revealed it in His dealings with the Gentile nations by acting against their sins. Their primary sin was ungodliness, a denial of God's claim to worship, leading to unrighteousness, a denial of His claim to obedience. High ethical standards do not long survive the rejection of the true God.

The Gentile nations stand without excuse before God. He gave them a witness to His greatness and glory in the created order of earth, sky, and sea. The visible works of creation silently revealed the invisible attributes of the Creator. Yet men suppressed the truth God had disclosed to them. They failed to thank or glorify Him. Worse still, in utter foolishness which they thought was intellectual sophistication, they substituted idols for the living God. Our contemporaries do the same. Pleasure, wealth and success are today's gods in post-Christian western society.

God reacted to the root sin of idolatry by completely abandoning nations to their sinful desires. Same sex relationships flourished along with moral breakdown in every sphere of life, the tragic results of a rejection of the Creator. What a warning to our contemporaries! They need the gospel. What a challenge to us!

August 9th
1 Samuel 16; **Isaiah 55. 1 – 56. 8;** Romans 2

AN OLD TESTAMENT EVANGELIST

Isaiah is often called 'the Fifth Evangelist', because his prophecy is full of messianic predictions fulfilled in the Lord Jesus. In chapter 55, he preaches a gospel message, making a personal appeal to each of his hearers.

He begins with a *gracious invitation.* Like a water vendor in Jerusalem, he cries 'Ho' to attract attention. It is living water which he offers. His promise is *spiritual fulfilment.* Isaiah calls on his hearers to come to the Lord, the only source of satisfaction who can assuage the deepest human thirst. He will abundantly supply refreshment, joy, and nourishment from the rich resources of His grace. Yet the call is to 'buy' the offered water, wine, and milk – addressed to those who have no money! There is a purchase and a price, but it is not theirs to pay. The Servant of the Lord has paid the price. Ours is the freeness of His provision. Have we heard and responded to His call to come to Him for life eternal?

Those who accept the prophet's invitation are promised the unconditional blessings of God's covenant with David, fulfilled in the risen Christ. One day He will reign over restored Israel. Indeed, His will be a world-wide kingdom.

Isaiah continues with an *urgent exhortation.* He reminds hearers who are wicked that they must call on God for mercy, while the day of opportunity lasts. They are called to repent, forsaking sinful deeds and thoughts. They are encouraged to come to the Lord who will have compassion on them. His heart will surge with love towards them, and He will abundantly pardon. What a promise! God bridges the mighty gulf between us in our sin and His majestic holiness. He does so by His powerful word which produces repentance just as rain produces the harvest.

The chapter ends with a vision of a *transformed environment.* The curse imposed in Eden will be removed. The thorns and briars are gone, replaced by evergreens. Repentant Israel will experience joy and peace from the Lord. Creation will join in their rejoicing. Paradise will be restored. Those coming wonderful days will reveal God's *name,* what sort of God He really is, to all the earth.

August 10th
1 Samuel 17. 1-31; Isaiah 56. 9 – 57. 21; **Romans 3**

JUSTIFICATION BY FAITH

This chapter is written in golden letters. It answers one of the most searching questions, how can sinful people be just before God? It provides the clearest statement of the gospel anywhere in the Bible. It is a crucial passage.

The bad news comes before the good news. Every individual, whatever their background, stands guilty before God, the righteous Judge of all the earth. Justification is absolutely necessary.

What does justification mean? It is a term taken from the courts of law. It is the opposite of condemnation. It is the verdict of acquittal – 'not guilty'. It is not moral transformation but *judicial declaration*. God justifies the ungodly, Rom. 4. 5, without making them godly first. God Himself is the One who justifies, 8. 33. He provides a saving righteousness.

The source of justification is God's grace. No human merit is involved. No one deserves justification. No one can achieve it. It is a gift freely bestowed by God on the believing sinner.

How can God do this and remain utterly righteous? Because 'Christ died for the ungodly', 5. 6. The basis of justification is the work of the Lord Jesus on the cross, described in three ways in our reading. Paul refers to the *blood* of Christ, His violent death as a sacrifice under God's judgement. He tells us that the Lord Jesus accomplished *redemption*, liberation from the guilt of sin by the payment of a ransom. The death of Christ was also a *propitiation*. It altogether satisfied the righteous claims of God's throne and removed His wrath, His holy anger against sin, from all who trust the Saviour. Indeed because of Calvary the justification of a believing sinner actually displays the righteous character of God as much as His grace.

How do we experience the tremendous blessing of justification? We receive it by means of faith alone, trusting in the crucified and now living Saviour. Faith has been described as 'Forsaking All I Trust Him'. It is like the empty hands of the beggar stretched out to receive the rich man's gold.

We need to preach this gospel to ourselves every day. Let us rejoice that we are justified freely by God's grace alone.

August 11th
1 Samuel 17. 32 – 18. 5; Isaiah 58; **Romans 4. 1-22**
ABRAHAM'S FAITH AND MINE

Paul has laid out the theology of justification with crystal clarity. Now he works through a case study to demonstrate it. How is any one put in the right with God? The answer is in Genesis chapter 15 verse 6. Abraham believed God and it was counted unto him for righteousness. He is the classic example of justification by faith, a truth to which the entire Old Testament witnesses, 3. 21.

Paul uses the metaphor of crediting an account. An account can be credited by what we have worked for. On the other hand, it can be credited by a gift. Righteousness was not credited to Abraham by works in which he could boast. It never is. It is a gift of grace, not the payment of a debt. Justification is not by works.

Nor is it by any religious rite. Paul shows from Genesis that Abraham was put in the right with God fourteen years before his circumcision, not after it. His circumcision was the outward sign of his inward faith. Abraham is the spiritual father of all believers, Jew and Gentile alike.

Nor is it by keeping the law. Abraham was granted the wonderful promise from God that he would be the heir of the world through his seed in whom all the nations would be blessed, Gen. 22. 18. He received it by faith, not through the law. If it is those who adhere to the law who inherit the promise, then faith is null and the promise is void. God's saving promise entirely depends on Him, not on us. It is granted by grace and relied on by faith. The law's true purpose is to condemn, not to save.

Justification is *by faith alone.* Faith is the only way to receive salvation consistent with it being bestowed by God's unmerited favour. The promise which God made to Abraham of children as numerous as the stars was humanly impossible. Abraham believed it because He *believed* the God who made it – the God of resurrection and creation. He relied on what God had told him in hope, against all human grounds of hope, that it would come to pass. He knew a miracle had to happen before he and Sarah could have a child, yet he did not waver in faith. Rather he glorified God, fully persuaded that the all-powerful One *could* keep His word of promise, and the wholly faithful One *would* keep it.

August 12th

1 Samuel 18. 6 – 19. 7; Isaiah 59; **Romans 4. 23 – 5. 11**

SO GREAT SALVATION

God's salvation is comprehensive. The *past is settled.* The guilt of our sins has gone. Christ bore them on the cross. His sacrifice was accepted because He was raised from the dead. By raising Him, the Father vindicated Him, and guaranteed our justification. Now we have peace with God, a new harmonious relationship. The Lord Jesus grants us entry into *the present blessings* of His grace. We rejoice in confident expectation of the *future glory* which God will bestow.

Surprisingly, Paul says we also rejoice in *tribulations.* For many Christians worldwide this means persecution. For all of us it takes in all the hard knocks of life. We rejoice because of the effects of trouble in our experience. It produces endurance. Endurance then produces tested character, as we are refined like precious metal. This strengthens our hope. Christian hope is sure and certain. It will never fail us because God has poured out His love to us in our hearts by His Spirit, granted to us when we trusted the Saviour. He has already flooded our lives with a real sense of His deep affection for us. Present grace secures future glory.

Paul now meditates on God's love. All human love finds its cause in the person who is loved. This is true even of the Christian's love to Christ. God's love is *causeless.* God loved us while we were spiritually strengthless, ungodly, sinners, and His enemies. We were certainly not righteous or good. Despite all that we were, God demonstrated His love to us. His love is *active*: 'Inscribed upon the cross we see in shining letters God is love', THOMAS KELLY. Christ's death is the supreme proof of God's love for undeserving sinners. God gave heaven's best for earth's worst. The love of God is *victorious.* By Christ's blood it removes the barrier of sin. It justifies and reconciles us. How much more will God deliver us from His wrath, and bring us safely home to heaven. Christ's risen life now secures present and future salvation.

Through Christ, we rejoice in God Himself. He is the ultimate source of true delight. God's goal in creation and redemption is that we might enjoy Him for ever, finding in Him our deepest satisfaction. Do we rejoice in the God of our salvation?

August 13th
1 Samuel 19. 8 – 20. 42; Isaiah 60; **Romans 5. 12-21**

ADAM AND CHRIST

This passage explains why salvation is accomplished by union with Christ. In the western world great emphasis is placed on the individual, largely due to Christian influence. However the Bible also teaches solidarity. That principle still operates. For example, all citizens of the United States are affected by the American Revolution. A signature on a treaty by a statesman binds the nation he represents. Solidarity is supremely displayed in Adam and Christ. Their acts affect all under their headship. Everyone is united to either of them. Puritan THOMAS GOODWIN expressed this quaintly but powerfully: 'In God's sight there are only two men, Adam and Christ, and all other men hang from their belts'.

In verses 12-14, Adam and Christ are **introduced**. Adam really lived. The Fall actually took place. Adam prefigured Christ by contrast. By introducing sin into the world, he introduced death, the penalty of sin. He represented us all. When he sinned we all sinned. Death became a universal experience. God's sentence on Adam applied to all of humankind.

In verses 15-17, Adam and Christ are **contrasted**. Christ is much more powerful to save than Adam was to ruin. God's grace abounds. Adam's one transgression led to judgement. The free gift of God resulted in justification from innumerable transgressions. Adam's offence led to the reign of death. Those who by personal faith receive God's abundant grace and His gift of a saving relationship will reign in life through the One Man, Jesus Christ, for all eternity.

In verses 18-21, Adam and Christ are **compared**. One trespass, a deviation from God's command, by one man, Adam, led to judgement and condemnation for all men. Equally, one act of righteousness, His saving death, by One man, Christ, led to all who are in Him receiving justification and eternal life. Adam's one act of disobedience constituted all who are in him sinners. Christ's one climactic act of obedience in laying down His life on the cross constituted all who are in Him righteous. Sin abounded but grace much more abounded. It is reigning through Jesus Christ, our Lord. He has recovered all that Adam lost.

August 14th

1 Samuel 21-22; Isaiah 61; **Romans 6. 1-14**

FREE FROM SIN'S POWER

In salvation Christ delivers both from sin's guilt and its power: 'He breaks the power of cancelled sin', CHARLES WESLEY. The Lord Jesus declared that everyone who commits sin is a slave of sin but if the Son makes us free we shall be free indeed, John 8. 34, 36. In our passage sin is personified as the most brutal of masters. The Lord Jesus is the supreme Emancipator, far greater than Wilberforce, Lincoln, or Livingstone.

The passage begins with the question of *cheap grace*. Does unmerited salvation mean that we can go on living under sin's unchallenged sway, so that grace abounds? Paul vehemently rejects the very suggestion.

He explains logically why he reacted so emotionally. The Christian has *died* to sin. That is his *identity in Christ*. It is not that we cannot respond to sin's allurements. Rather, judicially we died with Christ to its claims upon us.

Water baptism is the *dramatic picture* of death and resurrection with Christ. In New Testament times every Christian was baptized on confession of faith. The new convert emerged from the baptismal water to live a radically new life.

When the Lord Jesus died, all His people died *in Him*. When He rose we all rose *in Him*. This union with Christ became ours by faith at conversion. All that we were in Adam was crucified along with Him. Thus we are liberated from sin's slavery. The risen Lord Jesus can never die again, He lives forever. By His death He cleared all sin's obligations once for all.

How does this teaching make a daily difference? Paul gives us the first imperatives in Romans. We need to realize who we are in Christ. No longer sin's slaves, we are Christ's freed men. We may not feel free, yet by God's grace we are. We are called to resist sin's attempts to assert its broken mastery. We should present ourselves to God to be His willing servants, with the members of our bodies to be used for His glory. In the service of Christ there is perfect freedom.

Today let us enjoy the tremendous promise: sin shall no longer be our master.

August 15th

1 Samuel 23-24; Isaiah 62. 1 – 63. 14; **Romans 6. 15 – 7. 6**

NOT UNDER LAW BUT UNDER GRACE

Paul declares that the Christian is not under law but under grace. Does that encourage sin? With deep emotion, Paul vehemently repudiates such a suggestion.

Every Christian has been emancipated from the oppressive bondage of sin. Using the illustration of the slave market, our liberation has been accomplished by transfer to a *new master.* Our new master is God. We either belong to Him or to sin. Being a slave of God is the truest freedom.

Our new slavery requires *obedience*. Obedience to God leads to practical righteousness. It involves submission to His word. The Christian message is pictured as a mould into which we have been poured. Each aspect of our lives should bear the imprint of its challenging demands. We should be shaped day by day by the gospel which we accepted from the heart at our conversion. Once we were moulded by the capital 'I'. That mould has been broken, replaced by the cross of Christ.

Paul recognizes our continuing moral weakness. Thus, he exhorts us to present the members of our bodies as slaves of righteousness to produce practical holiness, no longer as slaves of uncleanness producing lawlessness. The old life produced deeds of which we are now ashamed and led ultimately to death. The new life, set free from sin and devoted to God, will produce holiness and eternal life. Sin's slavery pays the wages of death. God grants us the free gift of eternal life in union with Christ, our Lord.

The Christian is also freed from the whole system of *the law*. Paul uses the illustration of marriage. Death dissolves that relationship, and permits a new one to be formed by remarriage. Christ's death and resurrection free us from the law and bring us into living union with Him. Only He can produce fruit for God in our lives. The law could not restrain sinful desires. It stimulated them, producing fruit which led to death. Christ has introduced a new age replacing the old. His people no longer serve Him according to the mere letter of a written code but by the empowering of His life giving and indwelling Spirit. We should thank God today for the tremendous privileges of being under grace.

August 16th
1 Samuel 25; Isaiah 63. 15 – 64. 12; **Romans 7. 7-25**

THE WRETCHED MAN

Our passage raises one of the most perplexing questions of the New Testament. Who precisely is the 'wretched man'? Equally gifted Bible expositors offer different answers.

Is the passage Paul's spiritual autobiography? Taking that view, verses 7-14 refer to his pre-conversion experience as a devout Jew seeking to keep God's commandments. The tenth commandment, forbidding coveting, was radical. It challenged Paul's inner attitude. Its very demand provoked such resentment that it stirred up the desires it prohibited. This revealed the strength and depth of sin in Paul's heart. He was not only a sinner because he sinned; he sinned because he was a *sinner.* Thus the commandment displayed the exceeding sinfulness of sin.

The debate primarily relates to verses 15-25. The autobiographical approach reads them as referring to Paul's experience when he wrote them and as applying to all spiritually mature Christians. They describe an intense conflict leading to frustration. Aspirations for holiness are rarely fully attained.

Those who disagree point out that to read verses 15-25 with their emphasis on the continuing role of the law and the absence of any reference to the Holy Spirit as Paul's current experience seems to contradict verses 1-6.

Thus, some excellent scholars suggest that in verses 15-25 Paul is still speaking as someone seeking to keep the law without the aid of the indwelling Spirit or is using himself as a *personification* of Israel under the law.

Whatever our conclusion, we can learn three practical lessons on sanctification. Firstly, *the flesh,* the sinful self-centred nature, remains in every Christian. It cannot be removed or reformed. Sin no longer reigns over us, but it remains in us. Secondly, the law can never sanctify any more than it can justify. How much less can a man-made list of rules and restrictions improve the quality of our Christian living! Living by a rule book only produces smugness or frustration. Only the Holy Spirit can produce authentic holiness. Thirdly, *full deliverance* from the presence and influence of sin will be attained at life's end or the Saviour's return.

August 17th
1 Samuel 26- 27; Isaiah 65; Romans 8. 1-17

VALIANT FOR THE LORD'S ANOINTED

The first three kings of Israel set a pattern followed by all of the remaining kings. Saul was a man who never followed the Lord, except when it suited his own purpose to do so. David was a man who wholly followed the Lord. Although there were exceptions in his life, he was never happy or settled in disobedience, and always found his way back to the Lord. Solomon was a man who partially followed the Lord. Sometimes he was obedient, and at other times disobedient. All of the kings that followed were like one or other of these three. We should desire to be like David, but sadly characteristics of Saul and Solomon often creep into our lives.

In 1 Samuel chapters 26 and 27, David shines as one wholly following the Lord. In difficult circumstances he demonstrated the kind of man he was. In such circumstances our true spiritual condition is seen. David could have acted in vengeance against Saul's unjust treatment. But David knew, despite Saul's ungodly behaviour, that Saul was still 'the Lord's anointed'. David understood the importance of this, and could see that the Lord's authority was more important that his personal circumstances. By thus yielding to the Lord, David honoured the Lord and left the rest with Him.

Likewise, we are sometimes faced with apparent injustices in life's circumstances. Things may not always seem fair at all times. But taking matters into our own hands when it would undermine the Lord will only make matters worse. David leaves us the best example by making the Lord's honour his priority and leaving the personal cost to God.

And God did honour David in due time. David was vindicated in the end. And Saul too faced the results of his own poor choices.

When tempted to act hastily without the will of God, remember David who under great pressure would not act against the Lord's anointed king. In due course God will deliver and put things right. 'Dearly beloved, avenge not yourselves, but rather give place unto wrath: for it is written, Vengeance is mine; I will repay, saith the Lord', Rom. 12. 19.

August 18th

1 Samuel 28-29; **Isaiah 66;** Romans 8. 18-39

NEW HEAVENS AND THE NEW EARTH

The general condition of God's people was deplorable in Isaiah's day. The favoured nation who had known God's unfailing purpose and protection responded in idolatry and religious corruption. Their tragic disobedience grieved the God who loved them so.

And yet in the midst of such departure there were those responsive to the prophet's word. The Lord knew that there were those 'poor and of a contrite spirit, and trembleth at my word', Isa. 66. 2. The 'poor' means those of a humble heart. There were those who acknowledged the grace and greatness of the Lord and made every effort to live obediently to Him.

The New Testament reminds believers of this age that we too can be guilty of idolatry, Col. 3. 5. Our modern day idols can also capture our affections. In more subtle and less obvious ways we can grieve our Lord, too. May we reject the proud spirit of the natural man, and ever be of the 'poor' or humble spirit of the spiritual man.

But while God's people may fail, the Lord never does. God would deal with a rebellious nation, but this would not prevent His purposes unfolding. Without doubt there will be a new heaven and a new earth. The present state of things will not continue. Darkness may seem great, but God will not be defeated. He has always had His own purpose and plan throughout human history, and it will end in glorious triumph.

Peter reminds us, 'We, according to his promise, look for new heavens and a new earth, wherein dwelleth righteousness.' 2 Pet. 3. 13. The challenge is to live for righteousness *now*, in defiance of an unrighteous world system and its philosophy. To live this way honours the Lord, and is an exercise of faith in His promise. Such living that rejects popular thinking is saying that God's truth will eventually prevail. We thus confess allegiance to Him in the face of a world that rejects Him. Regular reading of scripture and fellowship with God's people strengthens us to live this way.

'Blessed are the poor in spirit: for theirs is the kingdom of heaven', Matt. 5. 3.

August 19th
1 Samuel 30-31; Micah 1-2; Romans 9. 1-29

ENCOURAGEMENT

Do you ever feel discouraged? If so, you are not alone. Discouragement touches everybody from time to time. In today's reading we learn of David's discouragement. Here was a man in touch with God and yet he was not exempt from discouraging circumstances.

David's discouragement was particularly acute because he was, humanly speaking, alone. The people in their despair looked for someone to blame and David was the easy target. David was facing his own grief. He too faced the pain of these circumstances, yet somehow he was the object of the people's frustration.

But was David alone? No. He was *never* alone. The Lord had not abandoned him. Despite the depth of sorrow and grief, the Lord was still there. He was David's only hope, and to the Lord he went. There was no human encourager, so David encouraged himself in the Lord.

What a tremendous encouragement this should be to us. We are never alone, and the Lord is always there for us. Yet, life's experiences demonstrate that it does not always feel like that. Sometimes our circumstances can make us think the Lord does not care, nor hears our prayers. But this is simply not true. The nature of faith is such that it needs to be tested, otherwise it remains incomplete and weak. We *need* the 'spiritual workout' of trial – so much so that James exhorts us to rejoice when we are brought into such trial, Jas. 1. 2. The effect on our faith and growth completes and matures us.

David went to the Lord. He called for the priest and the ephod. These represented to David the presence of the Lord. He made inquiry, as James exhorts us in trial, 'If any of you lack wisdom, let him ask of God, that giveth to all men liberally, and upbraideth not; and it shall be given him.' Jas. 1. 5. David did just that and sought the Lord's wisdom. And the Lord did answer and delivered David in a mighty way.

Admittedly, the Lord's answers do not always come instantly. Often we are called to wait. But such waiting is not unproductive. God is never wrong in His timing. Be encouraged today.

August 20th

2 Samuel 1; Micah 3. 1 – 4. 8; **Romans 9. 30 – 10. 21**

SAVED

Salvation – what a beautiful word! But it is vital to be a possessor of it. Romans chapter 10 is one of the great salvation chapters of the Bible. It begins with Paul's desire that his beloved nation Israel might be saved. He then proceeds to explain the obstacle that stands between them and their salvation – an obstacle that hinders anyone from knowing God's salvation. Israel were ignorant of God's righteousness, 'and going about to establish their own righteousness, have not submitted themselves unto the righteousness of God', Rom. 10. 3.

Their ignorance can only be described as wilful. If any people should have known the righteousness of God it would have been Israel. Abraham, the founder of the nation, stands as the father of not just Israel, but all men and women who would thereafter believe God and be declared righteous.

But in the absence of knowledge of truth, Israel attempted a poor substitute, 'going about to establish their own righteousness', v. 3. This has always been man's way. It is a proud spirit of independence from God that believes in the merit of human effort. Man either deludes himself into thinking he is good enough for God, ignoring the gravity of the guilt of his sin, or acknowledging his inability presumes there is no hope for sinners. No amount of self-effort will ever save anyone.

Paul states that the real problem is a refusal to yield to God's way of salvation. They 'have not submitted themselves unto the righteousness of God', v. 3. How utterly foolish this is! The self-will of man refuses to yield to God. The proud and unyielding spirit will guarantee eternal perdition.

No wonder this broke the Apostle's heart, when God's way of salvation is open to all. Its invitation tells us that salvation is a gift, to be received by faith without claiming credit of our own making. To abandon ourselves to Christ is the only way to step into the blessing and security of salvation: 'If thou shalt confess with thy mouth the Lord Jesus, and shalt believe in thine heart that God hath raised him from the dead, thou shalt be saved', Rom. 10. 9. Are *you* saved?

August 21st

2 Samuel 2; **Micah 4. 9 – 5. 15**; Romans 11. 1-12

BUT THOU, BETHLEHEM

Bible prophecy is a stunning proof that the Bible is divine revelation. The prophet Micah wrote around 710 BC. Yet, with pinpoint accuracy, he boldly declares that the birth of Christ would be in Bethlehem Ephratah.

The Bible is the only book in the world that has this miraculous element of prophecy. It is a mistake to think that Christianity is one among many religions. It stands unique, and, as well as other things, prophecy proves that. No other religious book in the entire world can make this claim. The only rational explanation for the existence of Bible prophecy is that it is supernatural *revelation.* Only God could speak through a man at one point in history about an event to occur centuries later, an event over which the prophet had no control or influence, and see that event actually happen. If this were the only example, one might be able to make a case for coincidence. But there are in excess of three hundred fulfilled prophecies concerning Christ.

However, it is the Person of the prophecy that is of supreme importance. It was in the humble village of Bethlehem, 'little among the thousands of Judah', where Christ was born, 5. 2. This alerts us to His humility and gentleness as He entered humanity. For He was as the prophet stated, One 'Whose goings forth have been from of old, from everlasting', v. 2. This is language describing His eternal being. It was the eternal Son of God that was born in Bethlehem. God has entered human history through the mystery of the incarnation.

Man's philosophies and religions attempt to make man a god. But it is the gospel that tells us that the eternal God has become a man. This astounding movement by God is central to the salvation He provides. It was this perfect Man, our Lord Jesus Christ, who could be my substitute and bear the punishment for my sin, conquer death by resurrection, and guarantee an eternally secure salvation. Further, His human experience was intended that He might sympathize with us in our human experiences. Although apart from sin, His pathway was not apart from sorrow. In becoming a man He sympathizes with us.

August 22nd
2 Samuel 3; Micah 6; **Romans 11. 13-36**

MERCY UPON ALL

Romans 11 is evidence that God has not forgotten His people Israel. He will take them up again and fulfil all His promises to them. The notion that the church is the new Israel and that Israel no longer features in divine purpose is not supported by this chapter, nor any other in scripture; 'God hath not cast away His people which He foreknew.' v. 2.

However, they have been set aside because of their unbelief. And God has turned His purposes to the Gentile nations. The gospel goes to the whole world in its offer of a full and free salvation. Paul warns these Gentile believers lest they should assume a position of superiority over Israel; he warns Gentile believers against being 'wise in [their] own conceits', v. 25.

Spiritual pride is always a serious danger. It breeds contempt and produces a disregard for God and His word. This was Israel's downfall, even though she had been the recipient of God's goodness. He redeemed her from Egypt, provided for her in the wilderness, gave her kings, and fought her battles in a hostile environment. Yet, in spite of all that she became proud, arrogant and presumptuous of her place before God. She became independent from God.

Christians are likewise warned by Paul against presuming upon the privileges of place in God's purpose and becoming full of self-conceit. This was the downfall of Satan, Ezek. 28. 17.

Paul's prescription for prevention of this kind of condition is to remind us of the *mercy* of God towards us. God showed mercy to Israel and He has shown mercy to the nations. We were all in unbelief, and He has shown mercy to all.

Never let us lose sight of what the Lord has done for us. Our salvation did not come about based on our own worth and merit. Our security and standing in Christ is not because of what we have done or are in ourselves. It rests solely on His mercy towards us in providing His Son.

The Christian should be a worshipper, acknowledging that, 'For of him, and through him, and to him, are all things: to whom be glory for ever. Amen', v. 36.

August 23rd
2 Samuel 4-5; Micah 7; **Romans 12**
CONFORMED OR TRANSFORMED?

Romans chapter 12 begins with one of Paul's many 'therefores'. 'I beseech you therefore . . .', v. 1. His exhortations often begin this way pointing us back to something that has been said previously. In this instance we could go back to the preceding eleven chapters of the Epistle as he has expounded the majesty of the gospel. The gospel of the grace of God is sufficient ground for Paul to make His appeal to us. In light of what we are asked to do, captured in that word 'sacrifice', the only sufficient basis for us to yield is what God has done for us in the gospel. A life yielded to Christ is the only intelligent thing that a believer can do.

But we notice two more important words: 'conformed' and 'transformed'. They have two different meanings and are just the right words to use. To be conformed is to be changed into the shape of something else in the sense of that something else being the model or standard. It means to change what we are to something we are not. In this logic Paul warns the believer to not be conformed or changed into the shape of the world. We are not of the world, and to compromise to be like it is a contradiction of what we are in Christ and an insult to the grace of God.

On the contrary we are to be transformed. This, too, is just the right word. It means to change, but to change into what we really now are. The word is used in the Gospels in respect of the Lord's transfiguration. He was transformed from visible human view to the reality of His glory. The word is also used by Paul in 2 Corinthians chapter 3 verse 18 where Paul speaks about the believer being changed from glory to glory, that is, one degree of glory to another. As believers we are to be transformed to what we really are intrinsically.

This transformation comes through a renewed or renovated mind. Such a mind is one that does not take direction from a godless worldly system around us, but takes direction from the word of God. The fact you are reading this book shows you are pursuing that transformation in your own life. A transformed life is an offering of worship to God.

August 24th
2 Samuel 6; Nahum 1; Romans 13
GOD'S WORK IN GOD'S WAY
David was unrestrained in his joy before the Lord. The return of the ark of God to Jerusalem thrilled David's heart as he saw the presence of the glory of God returned to the centre of His people. A spiritually minded believer is always interested when the Lord is given His rightful place of supreme honour. How we too should rejoice when the Lord is given His rightful place among us.

David's heart was in touch with the Lord. When he made mistakes in spiritual things he could not rest. He must be obedient to his Lord. This too is characteristic of the spiritually minded believer. It is not that he or she never makes a mistake, but is quick to change whenever error is discovered.

David was enthusiastic about bringing the ark of God back to His people. But he went about it the wrong way. It was transported on a cart. This was not the Lord's specified way of moving the ark. The chapter tells of the awful consequences of doing a good thing in a wrong way. We cannot think that Uzzah's action was a well-intentioned practical act. The Lord's response shows that Uzzah was presumptuous without regard to the holiness and glory of God, and thought he could simply put human help in the place of God. His swift death shows the nature of his actions. This warns us that we dare not introduce man made ideas into God's way of doing things, regardless of how sensible they may seem to us. When scripture speaks, we follow. We must be vigilant in case self subtly attempts to insert itself in what belongs to the Lord.

We learn from the companion chapter, 1 Chronicles chapter 15, that David learned God's way of transporting the ark. It was to be carried by the priests. In obedience, David brings the ark of God to Jerusalem. Verse 12 tells us that he did it with gladness. We do well to copy David's joy for the glory of the Lord.

But, sadly, David's wife Michal resented David's enthusiasm for God. She shows herself to be a true child of Saul, and was never interested in God's way. The spiritual will always be subjected to criticism by the unspiritual. Such attacks can only be ignored and even pitied. Michal lived a barren and unfruitful life. Likewise, the fleshly attitude will never yield spiritual fruit and joy.

252

August 25th
2 Samuel 7; Nahum 2-3; Romans 14. 1-18
THE GOD TO BE WORSHIPPED

David was always ready to be a worker for God. Such commitment and enthusiasm for spiritual things is to be admired, and copied in our lives. As Paul later wrote, 'We are labourers together with God', 1 Cor. 3. 9. But not every desire to do something *for* God is *of* God. Mere enthusiasm for service can deceive us. In David's case, even Nathan the prophet was swept up and initially confused whether David's fervour was from the Lord. Happily Nathan quickly corrected course when he understood the Lord's will in this matter.

The Lord was not looking for David to work; He was looking for David to *worship*. And in this David readily responded. We have to ask ourselves the question, 'Are we *worshippers* of God?' It can be easy for us to be busy, even in Christian service, and yet lose sight of being worshipper. This is not to diminish the vital importance of service. But it is to remind ourselves that worship should never suffer because of service.

David truly was a man of worship. 2 Samuel 7 verse 18 tells us David 'sat before the Lord'. Here was a man who knew how to cease from activity and think about the Lord. His worship was full of God and empty of self. David worshipped God for His greatness and what He had done for His people. David's well-intentioned desire to work was quickly set aside that he might worship.

One of the reasons that David was a worshipper was that he listened to God's word. He heard a tremendous promise and prophecy from God. He learned of the Lord's promise to establish his house and kingdom and throne forever. And further, David would see it!

But David did not see it in his lifetime. But he will see it in the resurrection. This prophecy, v. 14, cited by the writer to the Hebrews in chapter 1 verse 5, shows that this promise will be fulfilled in our Lord Jesus Christ. He will be the sovereign of David's throne and will rule forever.

We have every confidence today by resting on the fact that God's purposes will prevail and that He will be vindicated. Nothing can stand in His way. As Christians we should be worshippers.

2 Samuel 8-9; Habakkuk 1; **Romans 14. 19 – 15. 13**

OTHERS

As Paul brings the masterpiece of Romans to a conclusion, he takes up the practical matters of Christian living, both in connection with the world in which we live, and in the fellowship of believers.

Divine revelation comes to us in the context of real people, and over centuries through history. This demonstrates that it is truth, and not man's ideas. When we come to practical Christian living it is often explained in the context of the times in which it was written. This could have been an insurmountable barrier that would have made much of Paul's exhortation unintelligible to us. We live in a different time and culture. The practices of Paul's day are entirely different from ours. But the Holy Spirit moved the Apostle to not only give us their immediate circumstances, but the timeless principles that would apply to any time or culture.

As the early church grew, both Jews and Gentiles were brought together. They brought their own personal histories and experiences. In Christian experience, we meet things that in themselves are neither good nor bad, but can be offensive to some, because of their association with evil things in our thinking or experience. There were things among the Romans that some believers found morally offensive, and yet had no such effect on others. Such differences threaten to bring division and upset among God's people. How can such differences be resolved? In this, Paul supplies principles to follow.

In chapter 14 verse 19 he gives us a guiding truth that should govern all of us, 'Let us therefore follow after the things which make for peace, and things wherewith one may edify another'. This is the test I must apply to everything I allow in my life. Even things that to me are harmless are to be rejected, if they do not meet this test.

However, it is a dangerous thing for me to impose on others a prohibition on things which I find offensive. That is legalism. Likewise, I should refrain from engaging in things others find offensive. This, of course, applies only to those things that scripture does not specifically prohibit.

August 27th
2 Samuel 10-11; **Habakkuk 2**; Romans 15. 14-33

THE JUST SHALL LIVE BY FAITH

The prophecy of Habakkuk is mostly about the schooling of the prophet himself. As we listen in on the Lord's message to Habakkuk we take it to heart as He is speaking to us as well.

Habakkuk was deeply troubled on two accounts. Firstly, he was distressed at the deplorable spiritual condition of his people. It is likely that Habakkuk lived amidst the conditions described at the end of 2 Kings chapter 23, just before the carrying away to Babylon. His nation had sunk very low.

But, secondly, the Lord had showed Habakkuk how the evil Chaldeans were going to come and have a cruel victory over the people of God. While Judah was not walking with God, the Chaldeans were much worse. How God could allow such a thing was the source of Habakkuk's distress.

This is not a problem unique to Habakkuk's day, and it has sometimes driven the faithful to despair. Why does evil appear to prosper? Our chapter begins with Habakkuk's response: 'I will stand upon my watch, and set me upon the tower, and will watch to see what he will say unto me', v. 1. Watch and wait.

Watching and waiting is not easy, but it is necessary in the life of faith. It was during this watching and waiting that Habakkuk learned something of how God works. He learned, for example, that God's promises *will* be realized, and are not to be assessed based on present conditions. Even though it may seem, humanly speaking, impossible for God to hear and answer, He will. 'Though it tarry, wait for it; because it will surely come, it will not tarry', v. 3. God will care for His erring people. He will use the enemy to discipline them, but He will never abandon them. Circumstances said one thing, but God said another.

It is this principle that Habakkuk teaches men and women of faith everywhere. The statement 'the just shall live by faith' is echoed three times in the New Testament with a different emphasis each time, Rom. 1. 17, Gal. 3. 11, Heb. 10. 38. Faith in God, not circumstances or reason, is the principle of the Christian life. This proves difficult at times but it never fails, because the Lord never fails.

August 28th
2 Samuel 12; **Habakkuk 3**; Romans 16
FAITH TRIED AND TRIUMPHANT
Habakkuk's faith was tried. Circumstances seemed so contradictory to God's promises. But Habakkuk knew enough to watch and wait. Chapter 3 opens with Habakkuk in prayer. Here is a lesson to learn. Always turn to the Lord in prayer no matter how difficult or distressing circumstances seem. We notice that as Habakkuk prayed his faith seemed to grow stronger. The despair of previous chapters melts away, and the prophet goes from strength to strength as he rehearses in the Lord's presence the truth he knew about Him. It was not the circumstances that changed, but Habakkuk did. It has been said that 'prayer changes things' and it does. It often does change the circumstances. But it changes *us* too. That may be prayer's chief value.

Habakkuk's prayer was for revival and mercy. He shows his spiritual depth in this. Habakkuk sought not merely relief from the impending invasion: he knew his people needed more than that. He sought spiritual restoration; it was spiritual prosperity the prophet sought. He longed for his people to be walking again with God. Do we identify with Habakkuk's prayer?

But he prayed for *mercy* as well. He knew God's wrath had its limits, but His mercy is greater. When we turn from a wrong path and turn back to the Lord, He delights to show mercy. He does not always exact the consequences of our actions. His disciplines are extended to produce spiritual fruit in our lives and He knows how to measure it in mercy.

Habakkuk finds great relief in looking to the character of God and His goodness. He turns away from the circumstances and confidently affirms that even if the worst should come he will rejoice in the Lord. Here is faith at its finest. It is one thing to rejoice when all goes well, but quite another to rejoice in the midst of difficulty. It is one thing to claim His peace when the seas of life are calm. It is a higher level of faith to rest with Him in the midst of the storm.

When trial of faith occurs, we do well to follow Habakkuk's example: 'Yet I will rejoice in the Lord, I will joy in the God of my salvation.' v. 18.

256

August 29th
2 Samuel 13; Zephaniah 1; **Galatians 1**

ANOTHER GOSPEL?

A counterfeit exists only because there is a genuine item. This is true of money and art. And it is true of the gospel. Even during the Apostle's lifetime counterfeit 'gospels' emerged. We can be grateful for the method by which the gospel came to the world, such that the imitation and the genuine can be easily identified.

It alarmed Paul that the Galatians were 'so soon' taken in by false teachers who corrupted the gospel, v. 6. The occasion of the Galatians' grievous error has provided the church with a timeless warning lest it should happen to us as well.

The point of error introduced by false teachers was to add the lethal ingredient of works to the gospel of grace. They could not accept the free and unmerited nature of God's salvation. They insisted on corrupting it, and thereby robbing hearers of its saving power, by adding to the work of Christ as the basis of salvation. We can never be saved by adding anything of our own merit or work to salvation. It is total acceptance of Christ – who He is and what He has done at Calvary – that brings us into the benefit of salvation.

Paul would not allow any compromise in a matter so vital. He pronounced the strongest censure against the false teacher, 'Let him be accursed', vv. 8-9. This is strong language. It needs to be, and not only in Paul's day, but in ours as well. Respectability, academic or intellectual credentials, or popularity of preachers carry no weight if the message of the gospel has been tampered with.

Further, Paul goes so far as to the say that if even he or an angel were to bring a message different from what had already been laid down, such a messenger likewise is to be accursed. How easily people can be deceived by orators or miraculous revelations so-called! The truth of the message is not governed by the eloquence of the messenger, but rather the *content* of the message.

Paul's preaching of the gospel came by 'the revelation of Jesus Christ'. This was the Apostle's authority. This gospel that is already recorded for us is the standard. Happily we have it in the written word to give us the foundation of our faith.

August 30th
2 Samuel 14; Zephaniah 2; **Galatians 2**

DEAD, YET ALIVE

The false teachers of Galatia insisted on law-keeping. On the surface it may have had some appeal to keep God's law. After all the law was holy, who could argue against such an idea? The problem was that self-righteous merit accompanied such an attempt to keep the law. It is in this context that Paul destroys the case for self-righteousness. 'I have been crucified with Christ', v. 20 ESV.

What a statement! Paul shows what happens when a person puts their faith in Christ for salvation. It is, among other things, the condemnation of self, and a sentence of death. Any attempt to portray the Christian life as one of trying our best and receiving credit for success is exposed as contradictory to what actually happens in salvation. We are identified with Christ in His taking our place and suffering what our flesh deserved.

But Paul goes on to say, 'Nevertheless I live', v. 20. The death of the self does not mean the annihilation of the person. As Christ rose from the dead, so we have already risen with Him to a new kind of life. We did not realize that this took place when we trusted Christ. But that is precisely what happened. We are now constituted entirely different from before conversion. Our perception of it in experience does not affect *the fact* of such a transformation. We live now according to a new life operating within us.

Paul goes on to describe this life. He says, 'But Christ liveth in me', v. 20. Think about this for a moment. Christ lives in you. This hardly seems possible, but it is true. The Christian life is a lifelong learning experience. The solution to many of our difficulties requires us to recognize the corruption of the flesh, and allow the reality and control of Christ through His Holy Spirit in our lives. This is not a one-time experience worked out in an instant, but day by day we learn more of the power of Christ living in us.

Paul further tells us, 'The life which I now live in the flesh I live by faith in the Son of God, who loved me, and gave himself for me', v. 20. Faith is an act of dependence. We live by faith in Him in seeing this life lived out. He loves us. He gave Himself for us. He is our resource and strength. Trust Him fully, and don't despair.

August 31st
2 Samuel 15; **Zephaniah 3**; Galatians 3. 1-14

HOPE FOR THE FAITHFUL

We are told that Zephaniah means 'hidden by Jehovah'. He was God's prophet hidden from view until his ministry was needed. God always has His servants available, often waiting in the shadows away from public view.

Zephaniah's ministry was during the faithful reign of Josiah. But despite Josiah's courageous and thorough purging of the land from evil practices, and his zeal in restoring obedience to God, it seems that the hearts of the people were not turned back to God. Judgement was still on the horizon, although kept back until after Josiah's death. He was the last good king of Judah before the Babylonian captivity.

Zephaniah speaks to the faithful remnant, assuring them of the certainty of God's coming judgement against evil. The burden of these faithful ones was not only their grief over the departure of their own people from God, but also their despair over the enemy's contempt for their nation. Zephaniah assures them that God would deal with both.

The certainty of God's judgement could not be denied. In the midst of man's rebellion it seems that he can sin with impunity. Sin, violence, perversity, and injustice seem to go on unabated. 'Where is God?' godly people wonder.

It is in these conditions that Zephaniah encourages God's people to remain faithful. God has not forgotten them; the day of the Lord will come. God and His faithful people will be vindicated. As we look out on a world that largely rejects God, and holds Him and His people in contempt, we must remember the end is not yet. Our duty is to be loyal amidst faithlessness. We wait God's time. Happily our calling is to preach the gospel, teach the word of God, and encourage and build one another up.

Zephaniah's prophecy is largely a solemn message of God's judgement, but it turns in this chapter to a message of certain hope and joy. The prophet assures God's people that there will be singing and joy in a future day. The reproach that was a burden will be taken away, v. 18. God's beloved nation has not been forgotten. We will see God fulfil His every promise.

September 1st
2 Samuel 16-17; Jeremiah 1; Galatians 3. 15-29

FOUR INTERESTING CHARACTERS

The two sections of 2 Samuel 16 deal with events as they occur in respect to the two camps that have arisen in Israel. Firstly, we have the scene of David's journey into exile. Secondly, and seemingly alongside that, we have the actions of the usurper, Absalom, as he takes up his position in Jerusalem.

The Journey into hiding, vv. 1-14

There are two main characters in these verses: **Ziba** and **Shimei**. Ziba is the opportunist; Shimei is the antagonist of simmering resentment. Ziba comes prepared, v. 1; displays a degree of thoughtfulness and care, v. 2; and is selective in his comments, picking out the most vulnerable and needy to maximize the impact of his seeming generosity. Ziba is a deceptive and dangerous man! How important to avoid making decisions based upon evidence that one has been unable to verify. Shimei is a bitter man. He has remained silent and subject for many years, but now, in the moment of David's weakness and rejection, he seizes his chance to mock and curse. With loyal subjects such as Abishai it would have been easy to resolve this situation, but David judges that his plight has been brought about as a direct result of divine judgement against him. David chooses rather to cast himself upon the mercy of God, v. 12. What a lesson for us!

The Jerusalem Council, vv. 15-23

In chapter 15 verse 37 we are told 'Absalom came into Jerusalem'. The narrator now considers Absalom's actions as he arrives there, but the man central to this section is **Ahithophel**. Ahithophel's advice fulfilled the earlier prophecy of Nathan in chapter 12 verses 11 and 12. It is not that Ahithophel was a spiritual man but that God is in control, and the counsel of the ungodly can be used to bring about God's purposes, albeit unwittingly as far as Ahithophel was concerned. What of **Hushai**? Was he justified in his deception? The end does **not** always justify the means, yet we see the righteous judgement of God in respect to Absalom, for Hushai adopts the same tactics that Absalom had used to steal the hearts of the men of Israel, 15. 6. Beware of half-truths!

September 2nd
2 Samuel 18. 1 – 19. 8; Jeremiah 2. 1 – 3. 5; Galatians 4. 1-20
THE END OF ABSALOM'S REBELLION
The balance of the verses provide an interesting background to the chapter as a whole: five verses deal with the preparation for the battle; eleven verses detail the battle itself; seventeen verses outline the carrying of the message of Absalom's death to David.

The Conflict, vv. 1-8
It is important to note here that, although Absalom had assumed the throne, David is still called, 'the king', vv. 2, 4 (twice), 5. Whatever men may decide, and seemingly enact, God's chosen is still regarded as the rightful ruler of His people. Later, we shall see that God was in the success of His anointed king. However, in respect of Absalom's rebellion, there is another lesson. David allowed his natural affection to cloud his judgement. To spare Absalom would be to retain the cause of rebellion, and provide a potential focus for a repeat. How careful we have to be to ensure that the ties of nature do not cloud our spiritual judgement!

The Capture of Absalom, vv. 9-18
There is a certain irony in these verses. It was the animal that Absalom had selected, befitting his aspiration for the kingdom, that was involved in his demise. 'Pride goeth before destruction, and an haughty spirit before a fall', Prov. 16. 18. The loss of Absalom's mule signified his loss of the kingdom. The sadness of the end of Absalom is indicated by his tomb – a pit and a heap of stones. Is it not significant that Absalom had reared up a pillar of stones for himself as a memorial to his supposed triumph? In reality, the pile of stones that formed his grave was his memorial. Some have suggested that they were also an indication of an appropriate end for a disobedient son, Deut. 21. 18-21.

The Communication with David, vv. 19-33
As the news of Absalom's death reaches David, he is deeply moved. In the phrase 'would God I had died for thee', we see recognition that this was part of the divine judgement for David's sin with Bathsheba – judgement that had seemingly fallen upon David's family rather than upon him personally. However, we need to remember that Absalom's death was also the result of his own folly. Sin has far-reaching consequences!

September 3rd
2 Samuel 19. 9-43; Jeremiah 3. 6 – 4. 2; Galatians 4. 21 – 5. 9
MEETINGS WITH THE KING

These verses of 2 Samuel 19 can be divided by the meetings that took place with David. There are the meetings with Shimei, Mephibosheth, and Barzillai, before the men of Israel come to complain about the men of Judah.

As David approached the Jordan, the first meeting was with **Shimei**, the man who had cursed him and thrown stones, 16. 5-6. Shimei's decision to meet with David was to seek David's favour as an attempt at self-preservation. He 'fell down before the king', v. 18. Abishai, the man who had offered to resolve the Shimei issue before, proffers his 'help' again. Shimei was guilty, but was Abishai or David right? David's wish was to stop the bloodshed, and to restore peace to the people of God. In my view, Abishai's action, had it been adopted, would have perpetuated the strife within David's kingdom. Mercy prevailed, although justice was later meted out against Shimei by Solomon, 1 Kgs. 2. 46. In any times of strife, do we seek to restore peace?

Mephibosheth had been badly treated and gravely slandered by his opportunist servant, Ziba. David greets him with a degree of suspicion, but the truth is revealed, not necessarily in Mephibosheth's words but in his demeanour. He appeared as one that mourned the departure of David. However, in Mephibosheth we see a man for whom the presence of the king is worth more than all the property and produce that he had formerly enjoyed! What value do we put upon the fellowship of Christ?

Barzillai is remarkable – what consistency! See the end of chapter 17. Here he returns to conduct David over the Jordan. He was 'a very aged man', and 'a very great man', v. 32. In deteriorating health, and eighty years old, he was prepared to support the king, and conduct him on his way back to Jerusalem. Here is a man who ends his life as he had led it – in faithfulness to the king. Here, too, is a man who used the wealth with which he had been blessed, and used it faithfully in the service of the king. What an example for those in their twilight years! Perhaps we are feeling the weakness that comes with old age. Let us learn from the pattern of this man's life, and remain faithful in our testimony.

September 4th
2 Samuel 20; Jeremiah 4. 3-31; Galatians 5. 10-26
THE SWORD OF JOAB
Following on from chapter 19, and building upon the discord at the end of that chapter, Sheba, a Benjamite, takes the opportunity to increase his power and influence. Seeing the friction between the ten tribes and the two, he seizes the moment to assume leadership. Initially, it would appear he had a following: 'every man of Israel . . . followed Sheba', v. 2. However, as the men of David pursue after him, his followers disappear, and he seems somewhat isolated when he takes refuge in the city of Abel, vv. 14-15.

David had appointed Amasa as captain of the host, 19. 13. In this capacity, David now calls upon Amasa to lead the pursuit of Sheba, and to silence the dissident. Whatever the reason for Amasa's delay in gathering the men of Judah, David loses patience and commands Abishai to pursue. Although Abishai is a man that does not delay in fulfilling the king's business, the troops that he took with him were 'Joab's men', v. 7.

The meeting with Amasa at the great stone which is in Gibeon is decisive. Joab's approach to Amasa, his cousin, was one of deception. He spoke words of kind greeting, v. 9, but his actions belie his intentions. He demonstrates that his right hand is empty, yet in Joab's left hand was the sword that would kill Amasa. The matter-of-fact way in which the killing is described in verse 10 gives us a picture of this ruthless man, Joab.

The thoroughness of Joab's killing is clear – it took but one blow before Amasa was dead. Joab took no time or trouble to bury the body. It would seem as if he left it there as a testimony of the fate of those who cross him. It was one of his men that removed the body from its public place, and covered it from the inquisitive gaze of the troops. Joab is a ruthless man who, though loyal to David, is unwilling to submit to David's rule. In all this we are reminded of the words of Nathan, 'the sword shall never depart from thine house', 12. 10. Both Amasa and Joab were related to David and each other. Yet, although Joab seems untouchable, as we come to 1 Kings chapter 2 we find that the man who lived by the sword, died by the sword. God is not mocked and whatsoever a man sows he reaps!

September 5th
2 Samuel 21; Jeremiah 5; Galatians 6
GIBEONITES AND PHILISTINES
The chronological account of the history of David ends with chapter 20. There now follows a section of four chapters which mention additional facts and historical events concerning David; the precise sequence of these events is difficult to determine and some may well be summative.

The Blight of the Gibeonites, vv. 1-11
This event may have taken place early in David's reign because it relates to the error of King Saul. When the children of Israel entered the Promise Land, the Gibeonites were responsible for a deception that led Joshua to 'make peace with them . . . to let them live', Josh. 9. 15. Saul had broken this agreement by seeking to eradicate the Gibeonites. This seeming 'zeal to the children of Israel and Judah', v. 2, brought divine judgement upon the nation in the form of three years of famine. Clearly, God upholds covenants, even if His people choose to reject or break them! The principle here is that sin must be atoned for. Saul's sin, which had national implications because of his position as king, must be dealt with, and death and bloodshed is the way in which it can be done. The lessons are profound: (1) In contrast to Saul, David does not allow misplaced zeal to break a covenant; (2) David does not shirk his responsibilities in choosing those who would be given to the Gibeonites; (3) The impact of Saul's sin is widespread, with particular effects upon his family; (4) The wrongs of God's people do not go unpunished, because the honour of His name is at stake, cp. vv. 6, 9. Oh to be faithful in the tough times of life!

The Battle with the Philistines, vv. 15-22
God had said, 'By the hand of my servant David I will save my people Israel out of the hand of the Philistines', 3. 18. These verses demonstrate that God keeps His word, and honours His promises. But we should note those mentioned and honoured as a consequence of their loyalty to, and support for, King David. They are Abishai, Sibbechai, Elhanan, and Jonathan. All prove their loyalty in the most difficult of circumstances. Though fighting against mighty warriors they were not deterred. The believer's foes are equally implacable, but the victory is ours in Christ, 1 Cor. 15. 57!

September 6th

2 Samuel 22; **Jeremiah 6**; Ephesians 1. 1-14

THE REFINER OF HIS PEOPLE

It is difficult to read the prophecy of Jeremiah and not be consumed with the gloom of impending judgement in one form or another. This chapter is no different. Here the invader from the north will bring 'great destruction', v. 1. Jerusalem will be besieged. Like a shepherd, the invader will come with his flocks and will feed upon the land, stripping it of its assets until little is left, v. 3. Ultimately, Jerusalem will fall, v. 9. The last stronghold gone, the enemy will gather up the remnant and take them into captivity. The prospect is bleak, for none will be spared, vv. 11-12.

The reason for this war and bloodshed is clear. The ear of the people is 'uncircumcised', v. 10. God has sent warning after warning but all to no avail. He says, 'I set watchmen over you . . . but they said, We will not hearken', v. 17. Indeed, Jeremiah laments his position and the failure of his task, knowing that he will be caught up in the ensuing conflagration.

Was this fearful judgement appropriate and just? It is not only that the people have failed to heed the numerous warnings, but that they have continued in their sin. The scope of the problem is given: 'from the least of them even unto the greatest . . . and from the prophet even unto the priest', v. 13. The specification of the problem is 'covetousness', v. 13; false dealing, v. 13; lies, v. 14; no shame, v. 15; and disobedience, to the point of rebellion, v. 16. Whilst these serious issues afflict the heart of the people, what good can be accomplished by incense, burnt offerings, or sacrifices, v. 20?

What purpose would be served by the judgement? Though the process was ineffective, yet the purpose was simple – to refine! Jeremiah was 'made . . . a tester of metals among my people, that you may know and test their ways, v. 27 ESV. Sadly, the outcome of the judgement was only 'reprobate silver', v. 30.

The practical import of these verses is significant. We see the nature of sin, how offensive it is to God, what a barrier it is to worship and service, and how God will use the circumstances of life to refine His people, and remove the dross. We might also pause to consider the burden of a faithful servant, Jeremiah!

September 7th
2 Samuel 23; **Jeremiah 7**; Ephesians 1. 15 – 2. 10

THE TEMPLE OF THE LORD

This chapter is the first of a series dealing with the temple and God's message concerning it, and the place that it occupied in the thinking of God's people.

The people placed great confidence in the presence of the temple as a guarantee that they would be safe in Jerusalem. God would not allow the city to be overthrown because the temple was there. The message to Jeremiah takes up their boast in 'the Lord's house', v. 2, 'this house which is called by my name', vv. 10, 11, 14, and addresses it.

Sadly, as the opening verses unfold, the heart of the people was as far away as possible. Their manner of life took nothing by way of moral standard from the temple in which they boasted. They did not live in the light of the Lord's presence, and their allegiance to any form of piety was a complete sham, vv. 9-10. Such hypocrisy had not gone unnoticed, 'I have seen it, saith the Lord', v. 11.

As is so often the case, Israel had failed to learn the lessons of history. God reminds them of that place to which the young Samuel was brought, 'the house of the Lord in Shiloh', 1 Sam. 1. 24. What of it now? Was it preserved from judgement and destruction? The psalmist's survey of Israel's history gives the answer: 'God . . . was wroth . . . so that he forsook the tabernacle of Shiloh, the tent which he placed among men', Ps. 78. 59-60. The presence of God amongst His people in the past is no guarantee of His presence in the future. There are conditions that need to be met for God's fellowship and blessing to be experienced. As they would not submit to correction, they faced a judgement that would bring the land into desolation.

Old Testament scripture is the history of Israel. That history should serve as a warning to God's people in every generation, Rom. 15. 4. We may boast in the truth of Matthew chapter 18 verse 20 but, without the corresponding manner of life, it will be as empty as Israel's confidence in the temple in Jeremiah's day. Do we need to amend our ways in the light of God's presence in order that we might experience His blessing once more?

266

September 8th

2 Samuel 24; **Jeremiah 8**; Ephesians 2. 11-22

PEACE, PEACE; WHEN THERE IS NO PEACE

The phrase that forms the title of our meditation today is taken from verse 11 of this chapter and is a repeat of chapter 6 verse 14. In that repetition, we have an indication of the false security which the people felt. There is a reminder of the words of Paul in 1 Thessalonians chapter 5, 'when they shall say, Peace and safety; then sudden destruction cometh', v. 3. Jeremiah's concern was that even the animal kingdom seemed to know more of the impending judgement than God's people, v. 7. Yet, in contrast to reality, they boasted in their wisdom, confident that 'the law of the Lord is with us', v. 8, blind to the fact that, like Stephen's comments to a later generation, they had 'received the law . . . [but had] not kept it', Acts 7. 53.

At the end of this chapter we have a further glimpse of the heart of Jeremiah. Although he had an unrelenting message of judgement, he was not a hard man. We see him deep in sorrow with little in his message to offer comfort. He entered into the plight of his people already taken into captivity, dwelling 'in a far country', v. 19. It is almost as if he can hear their voices and their cries as he appreciated the fact that 'the harvest . . . [was] past, the summer . . . ended' but they had not been saved, v. 20. The prospect was that others would be taken captive as the desolation of the land and the people was brought to completion. Thus, says Jeremiah, 'For the hurt of the daughter of my people I am hurt. I am mourning; Astonishment has taken hold of me', v. 21 NKJV. The physician was there. The restorative balm was there. But the recovery was not seen because of the people's obstinacy!

Jeremiah was a large-hearted prophet. Although he suffered at the hands of those to whom he ministered, and his message was one of righteous judgement because of the people's disobedience and rebellion, yet, he still wept over Judah, identifying with them as 'my people', v. 21. The judgement which he predicted, and the people deserved, he witnessed as it was brought to pass in fulfilment of his words. In the days in which we live, do we have a heart for the people of God? As we view the folly of professing Christians, does it cause us to weep, 9. 1?

September 9th
1 Kings 1; **Jeremiah 9**; Ephesians 3
THEIR FATHERS TAUGHT THEM
The chapter is a sad tale of sin. Jeremiah surveys his people and comes to the conclusion that it would be better to separate himself from them, v. 2. Such is their perilous state!

We have seen in previous chapters that the nation did not see the nature of the problem. They were blind to their awful moral and spiritual condition. Yet, a simple survey of this chapter will show how desperate it was: 'adulterers', v. 2; liars, vv. 3, 5; supplanters and slanderers, v. 4; deceivers, vv. 5-6, 8; disobedient, v. 13; idolators, v. 14; and vain persons, v. 23. Sadly, as we see decisions being taken in various church organizations, we wonder at the moral and spiritual state into which some are heading, and their blindness to its consequences. The ability to relegate biblical truth in pursuit of social acceptability is frightening. Over it all might be written what the Lord states in this chapter, 'They have forsaken my law . . . and have not obeyed my voice . . . but have walked after the imagination of their own heart', vv. 13-14.

The phrase in verse 14 that forms the title of our meditation is particularly distressing. It stands as a warning to every parent, and every Christian leader. What example are we leaving for the generation that will follow us?

As Luke wrote his account of the activities of the early church he reminded his reader, Theophilus, of the example left by the Lord: 'all that Jesus began both to do and teach', Acts. 1. 1. In that simple statement we find guidance for those who confess Christ as Saviour. It is the way that we *live* our lives, what we *do*, that will give weight to what we later *teach*, what we *say*. Equally, as in the perfect example of the Lord, there should be a harmony between walk and witness. We cannot expect people to do what we say if we do not live it ourselves! Although, unlike the Lord, we will never display these traits to perfection, we can strive to end our life with joy. We don't strive in our own strength, vainly trying to keep the law. We have the indwelling presence of the Spirit of God and, as Paul reminded the Galatian believers, 'If we live in the Spirit, let us also walk in the Spirit', Gal. 5. 25. May we be encouraged to leave a bright testimony for those that follow!

September 10th
1 Kings 2; Jeremiah 10; **Ephesians 4. 1-16**

MAINTAINING UNITY

This chapter commences the practical section of the Epistle and, from the second word of the first verse, it can be seen that practical truth is built upon right doctrine.

The Conduct of one's life, vv. 1-3

The plea of the Apostle is based upon that which he has taught, chapters 1-3, and that which he is living as the prisoner of the Lord. First, our steps along the Christian pathway are to be in keeping with our confession of faith, v. 1. That means we are to be characterized by lowliness and meekness, longsuffering and forbearance, v. 2. The reason for such effort is given in the verse following, that the unity of the Spirit might be kept! Thus, the custom or habit of our lives should be to guard what is already ours.

The Character of Unity, vv. 4-7

The significant word throughout this section is obviously the word 'one'. The **one body** is a living organism, a spiritual entity constructed and maintained by God. The **one Spirit** is fundamental to the one body, as it is the Spirit of God who unites each believer to the one body and indwells them. It is **'one hope'**, because it is the same for Jew and Gentile alike. It is **'one Lord'**, as the Lordship of Christ is of fundamental importance in dispelling disputes, party spirit and personal ambition. The **'one faith'** refers to the time of our salvation – when we came to know the Lord. Equally, **'one baptism'** flows out of that statement. In verse 6 we have reference to **'one God and Father of all'**. In the maintenance of unity, the responsibility applies to all of us, v. 7. May the Lord grant us to realize that we are not able to exist independently, and that we cannot dispense with the service of any believer, for each one has a task to fulfil!

The Conquest of Calvary, vv. 8-10.

Think upon the Lord's victory at Calvary. It is a victory acknowledged: Christ is 'ascended up on high', v. 8. Death could not hold Him! It is a victory honoured, 'far above all heavens', v. 10, a place of unrivalled glory. It is a victory that is extensive, for it is purposed that He will 'fill all things', v. 10. In our desire to maintain unity, let us look up to the One on the throne!

September 11th
1 Kings 3; Jeremiah 11; **Ephesians 4. 17-32**

CHARACTERISTICS OF NEW LIFE

From verses 25 to 32, there are two strands of truth. There are seven negatives, detailing what should be absent from the life of the believer as a consequence of new birth, and developed alongside these seven negatives there is a list of five positives.

Firstly, we should have made a clean and definite break with falsehood in every form, whether verbal or by action, v. 25. Secondly, we should always set a timely limit upon our righteous anger, v. 26. Thirdly, and following from the previous point, we should give no scope or opportunity to the devil to do his slanderous work, v. 27. Fourthly, we should no longer steal, v. 28. There are areas of laxity in modern society where things that are wrong in God's eyes are tolerated, or overlooked. Do not lower standards! Fifthly, no corrupt communication is to proceed out of our mouths, v. 29. Nothing that is rotten, dubious, or unfitting should pass our lips. Sixthly, we are not to grieve the Holy Spirit of God by the course of our lives, v. 30. Remembering that He is holy and indwells all believers, we should be sensitive to His presence. Finally, we are to put away all bitterness, wrath, anger, clamour, and evil speaking, v. 31. These facets of human nature are to be swept away, and the root of malice with them.

Then, there is a list of positives. Firstly, we are to 'speak every man truth with his neighbour', v. 25. This truthfulness should be a habit of life, because we are united to Christ in a bond of Christian fellowship. Secondly, our righteous anger is to be controlled by the mind, and not the emotions, v. 26. Thirdly, we are to be engaged in honest toil as opposed to stealing, v. 28. As stealing would occupy the hands for evil we should use our hands for good. Fourthly, our conversation should be to edification, capable of ministering grace to the hearers, v. 29. This takes us beyond keeping our speech pure. Finally, we are to be kind, tenderhearted, and forgiving, v. 32. Rather than the hardened and embittered heart that characterizes the unbeliever, we are to be gracious, touched with the feelings of fellow believers.

The standard is high, for the Christian life is immensely challenging! May we seek the Spirit's help, moment by moment!

September 12th
1 Kings 4-5; Jeremiah 12; **Ephesians 5. 1-21**

WALKING

The predominant thought in these verses is the believer's walk. In verse 2 we are told to 'walk in love'; in verse 8 we are told to 'walk as children of light'; and in verse 15 we are to 'walk circumspectly'. The conduct of our lives is of paramount importance!

Walking in Love, vv. 1-7

The overriding objective is given us in the opening verse of the section, 'Be ye therefore followers of God', v. 1. Those who have been made 'children beloved' (YLT) should seek to imitate the one who has saved them. What this means in reality is explained in greater detail in the verses that follow: love should be the sphere of our activity, v. 2; liberation from the former evil practices and lusts should have taken place, vv. 3-5; and learning the truth of God should be our desire, vv. 6-7.

Walking in the Light, vv. 8-14

Rather than partnership with the world there should be a partition between us and our former lives. In our unconverted days we were in moral and spiritual darkness, but now we are not merely in the light but we *are* 'light in the Lord', v. 8. The active illuminating power of the Lord is in us, and it should radiate from us as a consequence of our union with Him. We should conduct our lives as 'those whose souls have been penetrated and gripped by the truth of God', ALBERT LECKIE.

Walking in Line, vv. 15-21

We should seek to walk to the divine standard, where each step is important and precision is essential. We should not be blinded to spiritual facts and consequences but those who apply their knowledge of the scriptures to form the best plan for our lives. Every moment is a precious moment to live for the Lord, v. 16. We should buy up every opportunity for ourselves, 'culling your times of good out of a land where there are few such flowers', HENRY ALFORD.

Do we have a desire to be a useful servant of the Lord? If we are prepared to come out from the midst of those who are spiritually dead, and allow the warmth of the divine presence to transform our spiritual outlook and life, then we could be!

September 13th

1 Kings 6; Jeremiah 13; **Ephesians 5. 22 – 6. 9**

CHRISTIAN RELATIONSHIPS

Within this section of verses, Paul covers the whole range of Christian relationships. In chapter 5, he deals with husband and wife. In chapter 6, he follows that with parents and children, and servants and masters. As with the first section of this chapter, the overriding objective is given in the opening verse, 'Submitting yourselves one to another in the fear of God', v. 21. This leads to the thought that wives are to be obedient to their husbands, children to their parents, and servants to their masters.

Submission is a military term applied to a soldier who accepts the command of another, and lines himself up with his fellow soldiers. There is an acceptance of order and discipline that characterizes the lifestyle assumed. Hence, FRANCIS FOULKES says, 'there must be a willingness in the Christian fellowship to serve any, to learn from any, and to be corrected by any'. The world speaks of its rights; the scriptures speak of our duties.

The response of the wife to her husband is one of voluntary subjection, v. 22. The tense here signifies that this attitude is to characterize her life in her relationship to her husband. Even though the wife may be the equal of her husband intellectually, or professionally, she accepts this position 'as unto the Lord'.

The responsibility of the husband is to love his wife, v. 25. The measure of love required of the husband is the love that was displayed by the Lord for His church. This is a self-sacrificing love. He 'gave Himself for it'. His desire was that He might 'sanctify and cleanse it', v. 26, and that He might 'present it to Himself', v. 27. Thinking of the sacrifice of the love of Christ and the scope of the work of Christ Paul says, 'so ought men to love their wives', v. 28. Here is a moral obligation of continuing significance.

In a world where governments have changed the definition of marriage, and have done so much to destroy the biblical concept of the family, these are vital truths. To apply them will demand a manner of life that is diametrically opposed to the thinking and practice of the world. It will draw criticism, even condemnation of those around us. 'Therefore be imitators of God, as beloved children', v. 1 ESV.

September 14th
1 Kings 7; Jeremiah 14; **Ephesians 6. 10-24**

PREPARATION FOR THE BATTLE

In verses 10-18, Paul instructs us on the need for preparation for the battle that is characteristic of the Christian pathway.

The Adversary and his allies, vv. 10-12

There is no room for complacency. We cannot fight the battle alone. We need to be 'strong in the Lord', v. 10, and we need to don 'the whole armour of God', v. 11. We depend upon the resources of God as we face the enemy! But it is wonderful to know from this book that we have divine power toward us, 1. 19; divine power in us, 3. 16; and divine power for us, here. The purpose of this much needed power is that 'ye may be able to stand', v. 11. The idea is of one who is asked to hold out in a critical position on the battlefield. As ALBERT LECKIE wrote, we are asked to 'stand before the attack, v. 11, stand during the attack, v. 13, and be still standing after the attack, v. 13'. The nature of the battle is personal, individual, hand-to-hand combat, v. 12.

The Armour and its aim, vv. 13-18

Without such armour, the whole armour of God, we cannot hope to stand in the heat of battle against such foes. The armour is in a number of pieces which we have to make a conscious effort to take and put on. As HANDLEY MOULE states, we should take 'as from the hands of another'. Each piece of armour is to be put on prayerfully, and each situation which demands that armour must also be approached with prayer. Verse 18 lays great stress upon 'all'. ADAM THROPAY wrote, 'Although prayer is not part of the armour, the armour cannot be used without it'.

The Apostle's needs, vv. 19-24

For the first time, Paul mentions his own needs, as well as sending his own benediction. We have seen little of his personal circumstances. Here, he reminds them that he too needs prayer, as one in the forefront of the spiritual battle. He seeks prayer that he might be given boldness to speak, the words to use, and the opportunity to speak them, v. 19. In the capital of the then known world, this divine help was essential.

The vital importance of the prayer life of the believer shines out of this passage. It is a challenge to all of us!

273

September 15th
1 Kings 8. 1-30; **Jeremiah 15**; Philippians 1. 1-20
'THY WORDS WERE FOUND, AND I DID EAT THEM'
The sad proclamation of judgement that is found within this chapter is traced back to 'Manasseh the son of Hezekiah king of Judah' and 'for that which he did in Jerusalem', v. 4. The nation's forsaking of God was so extensive that even the presence and intercessory activity of Moses and Samuel would not have been enough to stave off the inevitable, v. 1. What a tragedy! The judgement that was to be visited upon Judah involved violent death, famine, captivity, and the scattering of the nation 'into all kingdoms of the earth', v. 4.

What of Jeremiah? Jeremiah's feelings are evident. He says, 'Woe is me, my mother'. He had not followed the practices of those that were now bringing judgement upon the nation, but he was caught up in the consequences of their folly. He pleads with God. He had not 'sat . . . in the assembly of the mockers', v. 17. Indeed, his faithfulness to God had brought him loneliness and rejection. He had been persecuted, and rebuked, v. 15. Yet, along with others, God says to him, 'I will make thee to pass . . . into a land which thou knowest not', v. 14. Can we appreciate the sadness of Jeremiah's plight? What is the answer?

The title of our meditation today supplies the answer: 'Thy word was unto me the joy and rejoicing of mine heart', v. 16. This was Jeremiah's resource, and that of all the faithful in the day of apostasy. It was in that word of God that Jeremiah would find the promise 'If thou return, then will I bring thee again, and thou shalt stand before me', v. 19.

WILLIAM KELLY sums up the practical import of this chapter: 'The word of God is always to be the distinguishing mark, and the anchor of hope for the believer in God'. In Malachi's day, 'they that feared the Lord . . . thought on his name', Mal. 3. 16. As Paul took his leave of the Ephesian elders at Miletus, he commended them to God, and 'to the word of his grace, which is able to build you up', Acts 20. 32. As Peter anticipated his death, his concern for the people of God was 'that ye may be able after my decease to have these things in remembrance', 2 Pet. 1. 15. In the good times, or the bad, what value do we put upon the word of God?

September 16th
1 Kings 8. 31-66; **Jeremiah 16**; Philippians 1. 21 – 2. 11

HOPELESS, YET THERE IS HOPE

The low spiritual condition of Israel in Jeremiah's time is demonstrated by the sobering instructions that the Lord gives to this weeping prophet, Jer. 9. 1. He was commanded not to marry or have children because of the imminent judgement that was about to fall on the land. Israel's idolatry, self-will, and neglect of God's word stored up for them tremendous wrath, 16. 10-13. The extreme circumstances surrounding the imminent Babylonian captivity made normal activities such as starting a family impossible. Similarly, conditions facing the first century Corinthian saints caused Paul to advocate singleness as a preferable state of being, 1 Cor. 7. 26. Other regular activities like funerals, burials, and weddings would be abandoned due to the catastrophic devastation caused by the invasion, Jer. 16. 4-9.

Amidst the gloom, the beautiful light of God's grace shines forth to offer hope and comfort to Israel. Despite their failure, the Almighty will not forget His promises. When they might reasonably expect divine abandonment and utter annihilation, the Lord assures them that His discipline would not be permanent. Instead of referring back to the time when He rescued them from Egyptian slavery, people would remember their – as yet future – deliverance from Babylon's clutches. In His words, 'Therefore behold, the days come, saith the Lord, that it shall no more be said, The Lord liveth, that brought up the children of Israel out of the land of Egypt; but, The Lord liveth, that brought up the children of Israel from the land of the north, and from all the lands whither he had driven them: and I will bring them again into their land that I gave unto their fathers', vv. 14-15.

Not only will Israel's future restoration to the land benefit them, it will also bring about a mass conversion to the Lord among the Gentiles, vv. 19-21. Romans chapter 11 verses 11-32 describe this tandem work of grace among Jews and Gentiles that brings salvation and sets the stage for Christ's millennial reign. The Lord's grace knows no limits. He works even when all seems lost. Sometimes when things appear to be at their worst, He is actually preparing us for unparalleled blessing.

275

September 17th
1 Kings 9; Jeremiah 17; **Philippians 2. 12-30**
SALVATION LIVED OUT

God's salvation is designed to operate in real life. It is not a theoretical belief system that is best suited for university philosophy faculties. The gospel produces a lifestyle that is more than equally suited to this world's everyday challenges. But what does the gospel life look like when it is lived out? Paul, Timothy, and Epaphroditus are put forward as examples for us to copy.

Eternal life flows from Christ's selfless sacrifice; therefore, it is not surprising that His gift of salvation produces behaviour in believers that resembles His unselfish attitude, Phil. 2. 5. Before his conversion, Paul – formerly called Saul – was an arrogant, self-righteously religious zealot, 3. 5-6, who committed himself to the destruction of Christians and their doctrine, Acts 26. 9-11. However, as a Christian Paul became a completely different man. Now he was prepared to sacrificially offer himself as a drink offering on the 'living sacrifice', Rom. 12. 1, of the Philippian saints' faith, Phil. 2. 17. His service toward God's people was a measured pouring out of his own life in order that their lives would burn more brightly for their mutual Lord.

Timothy shared his mentor's unselfish zeal, by sincerely caring for the Philippians' condition, v. 20. Paul knew that he could send this young man to them without fearing the result, for his emissary would behave in a Christ-like fashion toward this cherished assembly, vv. 20-21. Of course cynics might dispute the widespread nature of such Christian altruism: 'Surely this is restricted to a few super-Christians – people like Paul and his inner circle'. But the Apostle cites another example of the gospel life in action from one of their own: Epaphroditus, vv. 25-30.

Originally sent out as Philippi's messenger, Epaphroditus served God rigorously thereby imperilling his health, v. 30. Yet even in his illness, this godly man was thinking only of how the news of his malady would trouble the minds of his fellow Philippian saints, v. 26. Like their Lord, the needs of others dominated the thoughts of these three devoted servants. Living out the implanted eternal life that one receives at conversion, v. 12, ought to lead one to self-denying service for the blessing of others.

September 18th
1 Kings 10; Jeremiah 18; Philippians 3. 1 – 4. 1

THE WISE KING WHO ANSWERS QUESTIONING HEARTS

Life poses many difficult, even seemingly insoluble, problems. People seek answers in philosophy, religion, and science. While these disciplines may provide facts on some earthly matters, they cannot speak to the deepest issues of life. The purpose for this universe must be learned from its Creator. Thankfully, He has revealed Himself in the person of His Son, the Lord Jesus. The One 'in whom are hidden all the treasures of wisdom and knowledge', Col. 2. 3, can give the answers that we seek.

In the early days of his reign, Solomon was a fitting picture of the all-wise King of kings and Lord of lords. Foreign dignitaries like the Queen of Sheba travelled to consult this glorious and brilliant monarch; as the Bible says, 'she spoke with him about all that was in her heart', 1 Kgs. 10. 2 NKJV. In a matter-of-fact tone, it continues, 'So Solomon answered all her questions; there was nothing so difficult for the king that he could not explain it to her', v. 3. His knowledge was comprehensive and exhaustive. She sought wisdom and was not disappointed. Even more so, those who seek wisdom of Christ are conclusively answered by His word, see Jas. 1. 5.

The finery of Solomon's house, food, servants, and entryway to the temple thoroughly impressed the visiting queen, who breathlessly exclaimed: 'The half was not told me: thy wisdom and prosperity exceedeth the fame which I heard', v. 7. In this age, one might similarly be impressed with Christ's house, the church, which He is building out of 'living stones', 1 Pet. 2. 5. As regards food, the Lord describes Himself in these terms: 'I am the living bread which came down from heaven: if any man eat of this bread, he shall live forever: and the bread that I will give is my flesh, which I will give for the life of the world', John 6. 51. His servants are drawn from every human class, Col. 3. 11, and are empowered by the Holy Spirit to endure awful conditions while spreading God's message to the ends of the earth. Christ is the way to God, and the Spirit whom He sends enables worship, John 4. 23-24, and builds His people into 'a holy temple', Eph. 2. 21-22. How good it is that the kingdom of God is built on wisdom!

September 19th
1 Kings 11; Jeremiah 19-20; Philippians 4. 2-23
THE TRAGEDY OF A SPIRITUALLY WAYWARD HEART

Though he began his reign with tremendous advantages such as unprecedented wisdom, 1 Kgs. 4. 29-30, Solomon later greatly erred in defying the scriptural teaching against kings multiplying wives, Deut. 17. 17. His disobedience to this instruction led to serious problems in his kingdom. Polygamy was a serious error, but his mistake was compounded by the idolatrous convictions of his brides. This is precisely why the Lord told the Israelites not to intermarry with the Gentile nations surrounding their land, 1 Kgs. 11. 2. One ignores the Bible's warnings at one's peril; just as they predicted, 'his wives turned away his heart', v. 3. Many of these unions were probably associated with peace treaties; therefore they were supposed to ensure Israel's safety. Instead these marriages led to the disruption of Solomon's peace as God disciplined him for his partial embrace of idolatry. Disobedience cannot bring security, and always leads to trouble, Gal. 1. 6-7.

Mixing elements of the worship of the true God with idols, technically known as syncretism, is a recurring problem in the scriptures as well as in modern times. This sin is a matter of disloyalty to the Creator, as the Bible demonstrates: ' When Solomon was old . . . his wives turned his heart after other gods; and his heart was not loyal to the Lord his God, as was the heart of his father David', 1 Kgs. 11. 4 NKJV. His father was a man after God's own heart, Acts 13. 22, but the son permitted his own heart to stray after powerless vanities. Furthermore, adoring idols like Ashtoreth, Molech, and Chemosh, 1 Kgs. 11. 5-8, entailed gross moral perversion and, sometimes, child sacrifice. Although there is no record of him performing this last activity, he identified with false religions that devalued life and debased their adherents.

Taking warning from this tragedy, we need to heed the Bible's exhortation: 'Keep thy heart with all diligence; for out of it are the issues of life', Prov. 4. 23. Friendships with the lost must be carefully managed, so that they do not become unequal yokes, 2 Cor. 6. 14-17. Marriage with an unbeliever must never be contemplated by children of God. Above all, loyalty to the Lord must displace anything else in this world.

1 Kings 12; **Jeremiah 21-22**; Colossians 1. 1-20

THE LORD'S SIGNET

Jeconiah, also called 'Jehoiachin' or 'Coniah', was one of Judah's last kings. His three-month reign was characterized by wickedness, 2 Chr. 36. 9. Though his names meant 'Jehovah establishes' and 'Jehovah is firm/enduring' respectively, his regime quickly toppled. God showed Himself to be firm in judgement by banishing this evil monarch to Babylonian captivity. Truly, the Lord exalts and puts down governmental authorities according to His will, Dan. 4. 31; Rom. 13. 1-7. His displeasure was evidenced by His words: 'As I live, saith the Lord, though Coniah the son of Jehoiakim king of Judah were the signet upon my right hand, yet would I pluck thee thence', Jer. 22. 24. The signet ring conveyed authority and was used like a signature on royal documents. An important object like this would be cherished, not carelessly discarded, but the Almighty values His holiness more than protecting a sinning king.

False prophets always arise to dispute the reality of coming divine judgment, Deut. 13. 1-5; 2 Pet. 3. 3-9. On cue, Hananiah the son of Azur prophesied that Jeconiah would be restored to his throne within two years, Jer. 28. 1-4. Attractive as that message would have seemed to the masses, it was hopelessly optimistic and plainly wrong. This pseudo-spokesman was oblivious to the imminent danger facing the nation and him. Worse still he was contradicting the earlier legitimate prophecies of the Lord's true servants – men like Jeremiah, 25. 11. Hananiah learned the reality of divine wrath first-hand, and paid for his deceit with his life, 28. 17.

Although God removed Coniah, His signet, He was not finished with Israel. Man may fail, but the sovereign Lord never does. After the exile, He promised to make Zerubbabel – another descendent of David, but not through the cursed Coniah – 'as a signet; for I have chosen thee, saith the Lord of Hosts', Hag. 2. 23. Of course this man was merely a governor, not a king. But his great Descendent would take on flesh through the Davidic line, Matt. 1. 12. The Son of God is the seal of authority that determines the destinies of Israel and this world.

September 21st
1 Kings 13. 1-32; **Jeremiah 23**; Colossians 1. 21 – 2. 7
GOOD SHEPHERD . . . BRANCH OF RIGHTEOUSNESS

Israel's leaders were meant to represent God to the people. Yet the kings and priests in Jeremiah's day repeatedly acted as negligent shepherds. Rather than feeding and protecting the people, they fleeced them for their own ends. These 'sheep' were about to be scattered by the Babylonian captivity that was brought on by the negligent shepherds' disobedience. Since they failed to 'visit' the people in their need, v. 2, the Lord uses the same Hebrew word to say that He would 'visit' the shepherds with correction. Nevertheless, within this judgement oracle the Lord offers a hopeful look at the future centring on the Messiah, who is described as 'the Branch', v. 5. He will gather, not scatter; He will defend, not desert. Through Him, their future would lead to vindication and blessing, instead of desolation and discipline.

'The Branch' – also translated 'shoot' or 'sprout' – was a growth that would become a tree; Isaiah and Zechariah both use the same symbol to speak of the Messiah's future reign. As R. K. HARRISON explains in his commentary: 'The shoot is that which sprouts from the roots of a fallen tree. New life will thus spring forth from the fallen dynasty'. Despite the failure of Israel's last four kings – not to mention the false prophets and corrupt priests – God is going to raise up a righteous King who is associated with spiritual prosperity, justice, and righteousness, v. 5. Unlike any human predecessor, He will eventually bring evil to an end. Through the Branch's rule during the millennial kingdom, every enemy of God will be subdued beneath His feet, 1 Cor. 15. 24-28. As Isaiah chapter 53 verse 10 says, 'the pleasure of the Lord shall prosper in his hand'.

Since bad governance is common in this fallen world, we rejoice to know that a perfectly righteous regime will one day prevail. Christ is the good shepherd who demonstrated His care for the sheep by sacrificially dying for them, John 10. 11. As the Chief Shepherd He feeds His people in this dispensation with spiritual food from His word, Acts 20. 28. The Branch's kingdom will grow: 'Of the increase of his government and peace there shall be no end', Isa. 9. 7, and God will reign supreme in justice and glory.

September 22nd
1 Kings 13. 33 – 14. 31; **Jeremiah 24-25**; Colossians 2. 8 – 3. 4

MERCY TEMPERS DISCIPLINE

After centuries of warning the Israelites God finally brought severe judgement on the nation. Already there had been one deportation, and more extensive ones were to come. Those who were left in the land might have clung to the possibility that they would be spared further discipline. But the Lord's parable of the good and bad figs settled the matter: those taken away to Babylon would survive, and those who remained in Israel or Egypt would be destroyed, Jer. 24. 4-10. The former would repent and be restored to the Lord, for in every age He has a remnant preserved by grace, Rom. 11. 5. That He preserved *any* of the Jews given their endemic sin was a clear example of His great mercy. Even in judgement the holy God always maintains His grace, mercy, and love. He is both righteous and merciful at the same time.

The Lord's mercy is further displayed in that the captivity was for a carefully defined period of time. They would be exiled, but it was only for seventy years, and a remnant would eventually return to Israel, Ezra 1. 1-4, a harbinger of a future more extensive restoration, Zech. 2. 10-13. He would preserve them on foreign soil for seven decades, and He would not cease working in their midst during that exile. Ezekiel and Daniel would speak for God among them.

Sometimes divine mercy and justice operate simultaneously. This is seen in the Lord's judgement against Babylon and the other Gentile nations, Jer. 25. 12-17. He employed them to discipline His people and then in turn judged them for their own wickedness, Hab. 1. 6 – 2. 4; Zech. 1. 20-21. The removal of Israel's enemies was an indirect instance of mercy towards His people. It paved the way for their return to the land.

His character has not changed: He remains righteous and merciful. The church often needs correction, but God does not desert her to its foes. 'For whom the Lord loveth, he chasteneth; and scourgeth every son whom he receiveth', Heb. 12. 6. As a loving Father, He faithfully works in His people's lives to perfect holiness in them. His mercies are still new every morning, Lam. 3. 23, and He will continue with us to the end of the age, Matt. 28. 20.

September 23rd
1 Kings 15. 1-32; Jeremiah 26; Colossians 3. 5 – 4. 1

THE IMPORTANCE OF FINISHING WELL

Abijam's relatively brief reign was a testimony to his own infidelity towards the Lord. Even though he was wicked, God showed kindness to Israel in memory of His beloved servant David by setting up his son after him. As the Bible says: '. . . for David's sake did the Lord his God give him a lamp in Jerusalem, to set up his son after him, and to establish Jerusalem: because David did that which was right in the eyes of the Lord, and turned not aside from any thing that he commanded him all the days of his life, save only in the matter of Uriah the Hittite', 1 Kgs. 15. 4-5. From a spiritual point of view Asa's regime began well. He removed male prostitutes and the idols that his predecessors adored from the land, v. 12. He even deposed his grandmother from royal rank, v. 13 NKJV, due to her creation of an obscene image for the worship of the fertility goddess Asherah, thus showing that his reforms were impartial. Likewise, he destroyed her fetish. Although he did not remove the high places in the land, his life's trajectory was to please the Lord, v. 14.

Sadly, Asa did not continue wholeheartedly seeking God's will. Later in life he became complacent, and began following his own thinking contrary to scripture's exhortation to 'trust in the Lord with all thine heart; and lean not unto thine own understanding', Prov. 3. 5. Threatened by an invasion from Baasha and the Northern Kingdom, he relied on his own method of deliverance: he used the silver and gold from the temple to hire Syrian mercenaries, vv. 18-19. In the short term, he removed the threat by defrauding the Lord of some of His things. But in the long term, this was the beginning of his backsliding.

Like Asa, modern believers can take the route of independence from God. But like him, they will also suffer dire consequences if they do so. Asa was diseased in his feet; his walk was wrong both physically and spiritually, v. 23. In spite of this discipline, he continued to seek his own solutions: he consulted doctors rather than sorting out his relationship with God, 2 Chr. 16. 13. Whenever Christians rely on themselves instead of the Lord, they rob Him of glory. Let us finish well by obeying Him!

September 24th
1 Kings 15. 33 – 16. 34; Jeremiah 27-28; **Colossians 4. 2-18**

GOD'S WORK IS A TEAM ENDEAVOUR

Paul was an immensely gifted man. He was an apostle, evangelist, teacher, essayist, shepherd, and missionary strategist. The Holy Spirit used his intellectual brilliance, spiritual understanding, and practical wisdom to accomplish unmatched speaking, writing, and church planting tasks. Nonetheless, he was not a loner. He cultivated deep Christian friendships and co-laboured with younger and older saints – both single people and married couples – from a variety of countries. Perhaps his inclusive attitude is most clearly indicated by his constant request for prayer support from the saints, Col. 4. 2-3. This demonstrates that his confidence lay not in himself and his gifts, but in the power of God, exercised in fellowship with His people.

Some of Paul's choice fellow servants are mentioned in Colossians chapter 4. Tychicus is described as 'a beloved brother, and a faithful minister and fellow-servant in the Lord', v. 7. These lovely terms highlight his membership in the family of God, John 1. 12, as well as his diligent labour and service in the gospel. Onesimus, the runaway slave turned profitable servant of God, Philem. 10-11, is also listed as 'a faithful and beloved brother', Col. 4. 9, and was tasked with updating the Colossians on the Apostle's activities. Aristarchus, the Macedonian of Thessalonica, shared in Paul's imprisonment for the Lord, v. 10. Mark had once been a 'weak link' in missionary service, Acts 15. 38, but now he is mentioned favourably indicating that he had matured in the things of God. Later Paul even requested his presence, saying that he was 'profitable to me for the ministry', 2 Tim. 4. 11. The missionary band was composed of Jews like Jesus Justus and Gentiles such as Epaphras. Stalwarts like Luke the doctor served alongside future turncoats like Demas, Col. 4. 14; compare 2 Tim. 4. 10.

Obviously God's work involves people of all types. The body of Christ is a unified, spiritually organic entity that operates by many individuals contributing to the good of the whole. Those who stay and those who go are called to pray for each other. Even notable servants like Paul need co-workers and those who support him materially and by intercession before God's throne.

283

September 25th
1 Kings 17; Jeremiah 29; **Philemon**
PROFIT AND LOSS
Philemon was the sort of Christian who always seems in short supply: a faithful brother whom one may trust to do the right thing even when it costs him something. Paul had great confidence in him, saying: 'We have great joy and consolation in thy love, because the bowels of the saints are refreshed by thee, brother', Philem. 7. Instead of 'pulling rank' as an apostle, v. 8, he asked this refreshing brother to do something in keeping with his proven character. During his incarceration, Paul met Philemon's fugitive slave, Onesimus. This runaway fled his earthly master, yet ran straight into the arms of a heavenly master. The imprisoned missionary led him to Christ, v. 10, and he became 'a new creature', 2 Cor. 5. 17.

Playing on the meaning of Onesimus' name, Paul acknowledges that he was formerly 'unprofitable' ('useless' ESV) to his master, but then affirmed that he was now 'profitable' ('useful' ESV) to both Philemon and the Apostle – and by extension, to the Lord for His work, Philem. 11-13. To Philemon, Onesimus was now returning as an honest servant, as opposed to a pilfering or lazy one; verse 18 may hint at past thievery. What is more, Paul already perceived his potential usefulness in the Lord's work, v. 13, and wanted to foster that service. Indeed, Colossians chapter 4 verse 9 indicates that he was subsequently helpful in the work in the Lycus River valley (a region of modern Turkey).

To his credit, Philemon worked out profit using a spiritual calculator. Paul was confident that he would forgive Onesimus' former transgressions, and it seems logical that he would emancipate him – or at least grant him liberty to serve the Lord. He lost his servant for a time, but gained a brother in Christ for eternity, Philem. 15-16. He was not motivated by legal demands or financial considerations. He acted in accordance with the Lord's will for the profitability of the church. Monetarily, he might have lost out by forgiving Onesimus, but his gain would be manifest at the judgement seat of Christ. Like Paul, he looked at people from an eternal perspective, 1 Thess. 2. 19-20. Likewise, we need to influence others with the future kingdom in mind.

September 26th
1 Kings 18; Jeremiah 30; Hebrews 1

SHOWDOWN ON MOUNT CARMEL

The reign of Ahab and his wicked queen Jezebel was a time of unprecedented evil in Israel. Their primary mission was to turn the hearts of their citizens from Jehovah to the Phoenician fertility god Baal and his wife Ashtoreth. In keeping with previous warnings to the nation, Deut. 11. 16-17, the true God withheld rain from them, which brought on a severe famine. The point man for the announcement of this discipline was the bold prophet Elijah, 1 Kgs. 17. But the conflict between Jehovah and the idols came to a head at Mount Carmel, where the prophet arranged a memorable demonstration of the supremacy of the living God.

The 450 prophets of Baal appeared as representatives of the false gods. Only Elijah stood up for the true worship of Jehovah. When he threw down the challenge to the bystanders, 'How long will you go limping between two opinions?' 1 Kgs. 18. 21 ESV, but their apathy was marked by their silence. Syncretistic fence sitting gives no spiritual power and enfeebles one from making good moral decisions. If one does not stand for the Lord they will fall for anything. This phenomenon is well described by 2 Timothy chapter 4 verse 4: 'and they shall turn away their ears from the truth, and shall be turned unto fables'. Turning away from God's truth inevitably leads to error.

A brilliant empirical test was arranged: each 'deity' was invited to prove his divinity by consuming a prepared offering with supernaturally generated fire, 1 Kgs. 18. 24. Despite the false prophets' dramatic, ecstatic and passionate efforts, the Bible tersely records: '. . . But *there was* no voice; no one answered, no one paid attention', v. 29 NKJV. Zeal to the point of bloodshed, v. 28, is still unable to make dead gods live! Elijah's approach was strikingly different from his adversaries. He simply prayed, claiming God's promises, and received fire from heaven that incinerated the soaked sacrifice and altar. The people responded: 'The Lord, He is God!', v. 39, NKJV. Centuries later the Almighty again 'answered by fire' when His judgement fell on the Lamb of God, instead of sinners. The true God is the One who has manifested His righteousness, love and grace at the cross of Calvary.

September 27th

1 Kings 19; Jeremiah 31; **Hebrews 2**

FULFILLING MAN'S TRUE PURPOSE

Modern thinking badly skews man's value and purpose in the universe. People fluctuate between extremes, on the one hand affirming that man is the product of mindless forces working on matter randomly over aeons of time, or that he is the measure of all things and is able to solve his own problems on the other. Either he is here by accident and has no value; or he is of ultimate value as the highest animal, possessing godlike intelligence. Both scenarios banish God from their plans. But the Lord rightly balances things: man has value, but it is not ultimate value.

'What is man that thou art mindful of him?' Heb. 2. 6, asked David. That an infinitely wise and omniscient God would have anything to do with lowly mankind is extraordinary. He created them in His image, Gen. 1. 26, and gave His son as a propitiatory sacrifice for their sins. It is this that gives them their worth – not any capabilities or doings of their own. God has appointed humans, not the mighty and glorious angels, to rule over the earth in the coming age, Heb. 2. 5. With its tumult and natural 'groaning', Rom. 8. 20-22, the present world is far different from its future millennial state. How can it get there from its current condition? The Almighty will accomplish it through His appointed man.

Christ took human, not angelic, form at the incarnation, Heb. 2. 14-16, because as the last Adam He will perform what the first Adam failed to do. Adam never brought the world to achieve its full potential; instead he led it into the fall, Gen. 3. By contrast, the Lord Jesus died to redeem the world and to reconcile it to the Father, Col. 1. 20-21. He will one day rid the universe of sin's effects until every enemy is vanquished and God is 'all in all', 1 Cor. 15. 20-28. Mankind – not just Jesus but also the many sons that He is bringing to glory – will live and reign with the Almighty for eternity, Heb. 2. 10. Humans will achieve great heights of glory, but the supreme place of honour will belong to the creator and redeemer of the universe. Thus, people have immense value: they are purchased by Christ's blood; nevertheless, the greatest value belongs to God the saviour, who shares the riches of His grace with us.

September 28th

1 Kings 20; **Jeremiah 32. 1-25**; Hebrews 3

SPIRITUAL ENCOURAGEMENT FROM A REAL ESTATE DEAL

Speaking truth to power is frequently dangerous. Like Paul, Jeremiah was imprisoned for proclaiming God's truth, Jer. 32. 2-3. The last king of Judah, Zedekiah responded to the prophet's message of Jerusalem's inevitable fall to the Babylonians by locking him up. But he could not alter the certainty of the message: they were heading into seventy years of captivity. Both the king and the people saw him as a treasonous purveyor of defeatist thinking. Yet along with these tidings of impending wrath, there is also a harbinger of coming blessing. The physical sign of an enacted real estate purchase provided lasting testimony that God would restore His people to the land, vv. 14-15.

Jeremiah's cousin Hanamel approached him with a proposal that humanly speaking appeared to be awkwardly timed. The city was under siege and would fall to the Babylonians within about a year, so it seemed an inauspicious time to buy property. Even the prophet wondered concerning the wisdom of such a momentous purchase in light of Jerusalem's imminent capitulation, vv. 22-25. The Lord assured him that it was a sound deal, because the land would be reoccupied by God's people after their time of chastisement was ended, v. 36-44.

This faithful prophet was investing in Israel's future because he believed in God's promises. The divine reassurance was couched in bright terms: 'Just as I have brought all this great calamity on this people, so I will bring on them all the good that I have promised them', v. 42 NKJV. In the present age, Christ promises to build His church, Matt. 16. 18. At times it looks like evil is winning, and one needs faith to take this statement literally. The Lord never lies, and thus the church's future is assured. Accordingly, believers ought to invest in what God is building. Our time, talents, spiritual gifts, money – even our bodies, Rom. 12. 1 – should be devoted to His eternal work. He is building a spiritual temple that will one day play a prominent role in the universe, 2 Tim. 2. 12; Eph. 2. 19-22. Others may think that this is a waste, but like Jeremiah, modern saints properly invest for eternity by committing themselves wholly to Christ and to his church.

September 29th
1 Kings 21; Jeremiah 32. 26-44; **Hebrews 4. 1-13**

TRUE REST

Ancient Israel's experience in the wilderness has serious lessons for modern professing believers. That privileged generation saw the Lord bring Egypt, the greatest superpower of the day, to its knees. They observed unprecedented miracles such as the ten plagues and the parting of the Red Sea. Furthermore, they were supernaturally fed by the divinely provided manna and drank water from the rock while sojourning in the desert. Their clothes and shoes were providentially preserved and fierce enemies were defeated by them. In short they had overwhelming evidence of God's existence and kindness, yet they rejected His inheritance and Him, Num. 14. 20-25. R. P. AMOS once described them as 'believers who did not believe'. Sadly, their type is by no means extinct in the contemporary church.

Although Israel in the wilderness missed out on the Promised Land, true spiritual rest is still offered to those who will seek it in Christ, Heb. 4. 9-10. Clinging to self-righteous works or ceremonies rather than the doctrine of salvation by faith in Christ alone is a sure way to miss the Almighty's gracious offer. Still others miss it by making spurious professions of faith in the Lord – perhaps out of a purely emotional response – instead of considering the gravity of their sin and seeking salvation in Christ, John 14. 6. Likewise, some people desire heaven but have no interest in knowing God. All of these are recipes for false professions of faith. If such people do not repent and rest in Christ and His work, they will eventually be lost; in this life they are also in danger of apostasy, Heb. 6. 4-8.

How wonderful it is to rest in Christ who gives us acceptance with God, Eph. 1. 6! As H. GRATTAN GUINNESS' hymn 'Crowned with thorns upon the tree' expresses it:

'Rest in pardon and relief
From the load of guilt and grief
Rest in Thy redeeming blood
Rest in perfect peace with God'.

Nothing can be added to His incomparable person and work. His redemptive work saves us from this world with its vanities to a life of joy, peace, and glory that extends beyond this scene. We now join Him in spiritual warfare, Eph. 6. 10-20; yet He has already won the victory.

September 30th
1 Kings 22; Jeremiah 33; Hebrews 4. 14 – 5. 10
SCATTERED SHEEP AND FAITHFUL KINGS
Geopolitical interests make strange bedfellows. On the face of it the kings of Israel and Judah were extremely different men. While Jehoshaphat was loyal to Jehovah in the south, Ahab was the patron of the Baal cult in the northern kingdom. Sadly, the former king in a lapse of judgement allied himself with the latter monarch through the marriage of his son to Ahab's daughter, 2 Chron. 18. 1. This entanglement led to the wicked king inviting his godly counterpart to join him in a military campaign against their mutual enemy Syria.

To his credit, Jehoshaphat wanted divine guidance before going to battle. Dutifully, Ahab kept on his staff four hundred 'yes men' masquerading as prophets. These false seers were unanimous in their positive message, assuring the two kings that they would cover themselves in martial glory on the battlefield. Jehoshaphat detected a false note in these colourful predictions and asked if there was a prophet of the Lord available for consultation. The true prophet was in prison for no other crime than faithfully preaching God's word, 1 Kings 22. 8-9, 14. He was as good as his name, for Micaiah means 'Who is like the Lord'. He courageously spoke for the true deity and assured Ahab that divine wrath had determined his demise in battle. He foretold this by relating the vision of seeing scattered Israel 'as sheep that have no shepherd', v. 17.

As a murdering idolater Ahab deserved the death that he experienced. Centuries later the greatest Shepherd-King was struck and His sheep were temporarily scattered, Matt. 26. 31, as He laid down His life as a sacrifice for their sins, John 10. 11-16. The Lord Jesus accurately prophesied His own death, resurrection, and ascension, John 13-17. After rising again three days later He gathered His sheep and has been adding to His flock ever since. Much more than triumphing over an earthly army, Christ vanquished the fallen principalities and powers, laying sin and death low in their defeat, Col. 2. 15; Heb. 2. 14-15; 1 Cor. 15. 20-28, 53-57. He now shares His victory with His redeemed ones, inviting whoever will come to share in His spoils, Isa. 53. 12; Rev. 22. 17.

October 1st
2 Kings 1; Jeremiah 34; **Hebrews 5. 11 – 6. 20**
THE NEED TO GROW UP!

Our passages today share a somewhat common theme: God will always challenge His people's failures, and whilst showing us the way to recovery, He clearly demonstrates that there is an end to His patience with us. This is a spiritual consequence we don't often care to reflect upon for very long.

In Hebrews chapter 5 it is the necessity for us to grow up spiritually that is touched upon as an essential for God. The writer here is exasperated with his readers in their inability to let go of the past and come into the full liberty of God's all-transforming work done in them through Christ at their conversion.

Nothing much has changed over the centuries, for in our day also we mourn the sad loss of many who started out so well, and are now turned back into the world, some even despising the profession they once made.

Spiritual growth or development is clearly dependent upon two things; one is our attitude, for the writer accuses them of being lethargic and inactive, unwilling to learn. Secondly growth is also dependent upon a hunger for the truth of God's word, the ultimate food for spiritual health.

Had the initial thrill and vitality that had come with conversion slowed to a smouldering shutdown, and was it now beyond being rekindled? This is a spiritual condition of 'death-like sleepwalking' in which all is dependent upon a powerless form of doing things out of no other desire than to keep every activity just ticking over. We may well have reached this stage in many of our local churches today, so beware and be warned.

The Lord is not satisfied with this state of things. It may mean that we have to start over again and be re-taught truths from the beginning. The first principles of the revelation of God in our New Testament will have to be rediscovered and impact upon us once more. Are we not in such a state that we have remained 'powerless infants' with few attaining full growth?

The appeal here is to leave the elementary and progress towards maturity, no longer unskilful, but rather fully mature.

Have you felt any growing pains recently?

October 2nd
2 Kings 2; Jeremiah 35; Hebrews 7
COUNTING THE COST?
There must have been many times in our lives when we have realized that we needed to count the cost of what we were doing, in terms of 'Is this really worth what it demands of me in time, energy, and commitment?'

Each of our passages today involves that question of the value of that which was gained in the light of what was to be paid for it. Elisha of seeing Elijah taken; the Rechabites of their 'covenant of abstinence'; and in Hebrews chapter 7, the arrival for the people of God of 'another' priesthood and an 'eternal High Priest'. There were costs associated with each, but was the price required worth paying?

Elisha could never be accused of lacking either the commitment or the undeviating spirit that made him tenaciously cling to his master and finally reap the reward he sought. It involved him in an arduous journey through several centres of spirituality, each powerfully reminiscent of the presence of God and each punctuated with the declaration that he was about to lose his spiritual 'father'. Only on the other side of Jordan can he at last ask for the terms and substance of the blessing he sought. Jordan speaks to us of death and separation: we really can now feel he has paid the required price to come into his longed-for blessing. There is a marked suspense of anticipation about all this leading us to ask, 'Could he even now still miss out despite of all that he had done?'

Keeping his gaze fixed upon his master, Elisha takes in this momentous and victorious 'home calling', the sudden lifting away and ascending of Elijah, carried up in a whirlwind into heaven!

With this vision filling his mind he catches the falling mantle, and he can return to the spiritual battlefield expecting the fulfilment of the promises he had secured for his own ministry.

We too have an ascended Master, returned now to the eternal throne and glory. All power resides with Him, the gifts and blessings abounding are all ours. Have we the commitment and vision that will take us on into His battlefield today and win?

Remember, 'We shall reap if we faint not!'

October 3rd

2 Kings 3; **Jeremiah 36;** Hebrews 8

ARE YOU LISTENING?

It's the same old story that is sadly repeated again and again, as God records the history of His past dealings with men. He spoke to them, but they did not listen to Him!

Today's passages are a sharp reminder of the fact that the Lord always wants to communicate His mind to us and particularly in desperate times. Very often He does this only to save us from our own delusions and to draw us back to dependency upon Himself and His promises.

He is not constantly barking at our heels or snapping at our feet, but all too often He is pleading with us just to stop and listen to what He has to say. There was a day when our conference meetings were deeply concerned with hearing God's word for the day from His servants. Servants came burdened to such meetings and prayer was made beforehand asking, 'Is there a word from the Lord?' Such occasions were impressed with a sense of 'meeting with the Lord' and hushed, reverent hearts waited for Him to speak.

The spiritual depravity of Jehoiakim's heart is all too plain to see. Abandoning any remnants of the fear of God and His word as his godly father had so totally done, he wilfully rejects the clear requirements of the Lord conveyed by Jeremiah and disdainfully 'burns the scroll in the fire'.

This act of impiety is well beyond refusing to hear the spoken word of God. It was the written word, read publicly that he refuses to hear and then seeks to destroy. The onus of choice is always ours. Even when it is a word from the Lord that demands return and repentance, we can still choose.

Jehoiakim shows how dark his heart is and how blind his eyes as he sets out to silence the messengers and destroy the message.

The word and work of God will always prevail whatever men seek to do to thwart it. Today we are privileged to have more copies of the scriptures in circulation than ever before, but the enemy will still woo us into refusing or confusing the message. With more opinions today than ever, is it not even more needful to humbly seek out God's word for us again?

October 4th
2 Kings 4; Jeremiah 37; Hebrews 9. 1-14
SYMBOL OR REALITY OF POWER – WHICH DO WE WANT?

The quick resort to the outward symbols of a faith rather than committing to the demands of true discipleship are before us in our scripture reading today.

In the passage we find two women in desperate straits and needing 'the man of God' to be there for them. Our generation also cries out for men and women of God 'to be there for us'. Lonely, despairing and often at their wits' end, many believers are depressed and downhearted. Who is there to respond when they call? Where is the ready servant of God when there is urgent demand for one?

In such instances we can offer either symbolic help or real help that is derived from spiritual power with God. Only the latter will suffice to make any real difference to the need!

Elisha is not lacking when the need is made known and the creditor looms large at the door demanding the widow's two sons. Elisha requires the widow to supply a large number of empty vessels. Her faith will be measured in the number she will supply, but remember that the power that will fill them is limitless. It is only when the empty vessels cease to be available that the supply of oil fails, v. 6! God is always far greater than the need.

Gladly we see the debt is paid off and the future secured because God had a man sufficient for the moment. Are we of such availability?

When later the Shunammite's son lies dead, Elisha sends Gehazi in silence and holding all the outward symbols of power, dignity, and office. Why you ask? It is in this that we truly learn that God's power does not belong to any of these! Gehazi will do what Elisha bids *but* the child still lies unawakened! Learn from this dear saint, that we too can have 'a form of godliness but lacking the power thereof', 2 Tim. 3. 5. There is no point in mere symbolic power.

So 'reality' is the need of the day and must be our choice. We need to know that knowing God and acting in line with Him is to have His sufficiency meet the need of the moment. May this mark us every day from today!

October 5th
2 Kings 5; Jeremiah 38; **Hebrews 9. 15-28**
THE HAND OF OUR GOD

How blessed it is to read these passages and see the hand of God working to deliver, bless, and bring fulfilment despite the opposition and blindness of men! It always has been this way and remains so for our day. He *will* bless us.

It must have been so easy for these Hebrew believers to go back to 'the elementary teaching,' and not to 'press on', Heb. 6. 1. All the spiritual things that they used to do were so literal and material. Now they were being linked with what would be seen as a minority view and ostracized for being nonconformists, heretical and extreme. How tempting to go back to the easier road of conformity to the social norm! We too are being subjected to a similar temptation as nominal Christianity espouses the worldly view of things.

But what riches were theirs to be had in Christ! As we read the passage we note the shortcomings of the instituted rituals of Judaism. Israel's much boasted sanctuary was an earthly one and not the original as is ours now. Their cleansing was also ritualistic and shadow-like, limited and necessarily repeated, but not ours. Christ's one sacrifice once offered and so complete in its efficacy that it has 'put away sin' forever. We now have a High Priest permanently in the presence of God and when He comes out a second time it will not be for dealing with sin, but to take His redeemed into the immediate presence of His Father.

The 'old' may have looked solid and secure but its fulfilment in Christ meant it was now 'obsolete and growing old, and ready to disappear', Heb. 8. 13 NASB. Now the hand of God had brought in the fulfilment of all the foreshadowing, and adjustments needed to be made. The immature and insufficient are to be abandoned whilst the true are to be embraced. Is it still so hard for us to sense the richness and privilege we have in this day of grace? Worshippers 'in spirit and in truth', we draw near with immediate access and approach the eternal throne. A holy priesthood, we offer spiritual sacrifices pleasing to God. Happily outside of the paraphernalia of organized religion with all its limitations, let us hold tenaciously to our freedoms in Christ.

October 6th
2 Kings 6. 1-23; **Jeremiah 39-40**; Hebrews 10. 1-18

SWINGS AND ROUNDABOUTS

When one thinks about the saying, 'life is all swings and roundabouts' it highlights how life is indeed like them. The roundabout whirls you around, disorientates you, and not knowing where you are, you cling more tightly to it. The swing takes you up to some dizzy height, then drops you down to the lowest point, and then whizzes you up again.

Similarly, life has dizzy moments and sometimes these operate to the extreme discomfort of the people of God, and we long for some light in the darkness and a return to normality.

The loss of the borrowed axe head in the middle of all the turmoil of making new homes was little enough, but it kept Elisha busy. Then the sudden appearance of Syria's army surrounding Dothan and with no seeming way of escape was a real threat and one that could bring no end of sorrow.

But it is the plight of Zedekiah, the king of Judah, with all the residents of Jerusalem that touched my heart today. The long drawn out and pathetic decline of Judah is about to come to its well-foretold consummation. Jeremiah and other faithful servants had long predicted this ending. Pleading for repentance, return, and reform was all too sadly of none effect. Refusing all the pleas to surrender and to look to the Lord for His merciful hand in it all, Zedekiah executes an escape plan of his own, and ends up with his family being slaughtered along with his ruling nobles. His own eyes gouged out, in chains, and utterly humiliated, he goes into exile and prison until the day of his death, Jer. 52. 11.

Despite this awesome desolation that surrounded him, are we not pleased to find that Jeremiah is preserved by God? He witnessed the ransacking of the city, the plunder and burning of the temple, and the exile of so many of the people. The swing of events must have seemed to him at its lowest and bitterest with little hope of ever rising again. He chose to stay put and suffer with the remnant of the people. A brave step indeed, and soon touched with regathering under the leadership of Gedaliah. Amazingly, he sees a resettling of the land! With God's 'swings and roundabouts', there is always hope for the future.

October 7th
2 Kings 6. 24 – 7. 20; Jeremiah 41. 1 – 42. 6; Hebrews 10. 19-39
BACKWARDS OR FORWARDS?

Life can be very confusing at times and we say, 'I do not know whether I am going backwards or coming forwards'. We also add, 'Things can't get any worse!' or 'There's always a silver lining'. These are ways in which we address our perplexing situations, but they offer little help to make a difference. It is more a stiff upper lip mentality than anything else.

Our readings today have all of these kind of situations in them and circumstances that seem unresolvable. Some of them are also gruesome reading and the thought crosses the mind as to why God has provided the record of such things in His word. But as always with God there are those touches that thrill the heart and lift the spirit.

As we read the events of 2 Kings 6, we hear the heart-rending plea of one of two women, 'Help, my lord, O king'. We learn of their extreme resort to cannibalism and we realize that we really do have a rock-bottom human crisis. Even a distraught king has little response save the despairing question, 'Why should I wait for the Lord any longer?'

His kneejerk reaction was to assault the servant of the Lord and to reject his relayed promise of God that the situation would all be resolved in the morning. This is a common mind-set that many can arrive at when tragedy strikes. Despair envelops hope if you fail to say with Paul in such situations, 'For I believe God', Acts 27. 25. The royal officer upon whose hand the king rested would have been well advised to have believed it that day but he chose doubt and unbelief instead.

The four leprous men however are a rebuke to all who just sit around and moan about their lot! At least they weighed the options available and took the one they felt best, and found beyond their belief that the Lord had gone before them in it all. A day of gloomy despair was turned into a day of good news, 2 Kings 7. 9! May the Lord help us to give Him room to move in our lives, and to trust Him. That which He has purposed for us can only be good, Rom. 8. 28. Not all of the mouths in Samaria ate the food available that day! Make sure you don't miss out!

October 8th
2 Kings 8; Jeremiah 42. 7 – 43. 13; **Hebrews 11. 1-16**
'BY FAITH' . . . NO OTHER WAY

Today's readings set out classic situations in which faith triumphs, and that in the most disastrous of situations. When men trust God with all their hearts they cannot fail. The Shulamite heeds the prophetic warning, leaves all she has, and returns seven years later to have it returned to her once again. That's trusting God! Jeremiah faithfully seeks the face of the Lord and knows that the answer received ten days later is not what they want to hear. Does he sweeten it up or pronounce a lesser sentence for disobedience? He does not in any way. The reason is because he is a man of faith. What God says he will believe!

Regarded as the 'Honour roll of faith', Hebrews chapter 11 stands out in scripture as a monument to faith as seen in the lives of many Old Testament worthies, and also some we would not expect to have been listed. It identifies moments that pinpoint their utter dependence upon the promises of God and their determination to trust Him even when events failed to translate into their immediate fulfilment or deliverance. Our writer declares that 'by faith they . . . gained approval', Heb. 11. 2 NASB. There is nothing more honouring to God than putting our faith in Him.

So, in a day when there is an all-out attempt by Satan to convince men that creation is an 'evolution' of things already existing, we still maintain that 'the worlds were framed by the spoken word of God and 'the things that are seen were not made of things which are visible', v. 3 NASB.

From creation onwards we note that through believing God men found justification, a translation out of this world, a deliverance from a universal destruction, and a journey of hope which led to that which will never pass away.

Likewise we are called in our day to 'walk by faith'. We learn here that it is not all miracles and the miraculous, but often a matter of isolation and ridicule, waiting and waiting and yet not receiving. What we do know is that the end is as sure as God is, and that of such as ourselves 'He is not ashamed to be called their God'. 'It is the way the Master went, should not the servant tread it still?' HORATIUS BONAR.

October 9th
2 Kings 9; Jeremiah 44; **Hebrews 11. 17-40**
EPITAPHS AND THINGS

'*Young or old, death awaits us all, and the epitaph-writer knows it*'. I'm not too sure where this quotation comes from, but it sums up my thoughts provoked by our readings today. Should the Lord not have returned and we pass through the gate of death into His glory then among those we leave behind there will be someone who will put together *our* epitaph. We all leave one, whether it gets published or put on a gravestone, and it is well that we know this now and think it over.

God ensured that Jezebel would *not* have an epitaph for 'the carcase of Jezebel shall be as dung upon the face of the field . . . so that they shall *not* say, "This is Jezebel"'. The woman had so destroyed faith and testimony that not a single relic of her would remain to perpetuate her memory, 2 Kgs. 9. 37.

Jeremiah had the same message for the Jewish refugees that had sought sanctuary in Egypt and turned to the idols of that land repudiating everything they had ever known of the Lord, the living God. Nothing would remain to mark their treachery and denials; they would disappear from memory, Jer. 44. 26, 27.

How different when we read of the 'so great a crowd of witnesses' in Hebrews chapter 11. Why, the writer says, he has not the time or space to be able to catalogue them and their deeds for us. Just the few are mentioned to give us a taste of the rewards of faith and a life lived for the glory of God. He is a rewarder of them that diligently seek Him!

Firstly, we are confronted with five individuals and one couple who all passed on the torch of the revealed will of God to the next generation. In each of their cases the faith could have perished with them, but instead they did what was needed to keep the light shining for the future. Have we failed this rising generation in this, or are they deeply aware of the truth of God – having got it from us?

In Moses we see faith passed on to the Nation: 'By faith *they* passed through the Red Sea', and so on through the generations the torch was held aloft. Paul concludes his life saying, 'I have kept the faith'. The Lord help us to say the same.

October 10th
2 Kings 10; Jeremiah 45-47; **Hebrews 12. 1-17**
WHEN BEATINGS ARE BENEFICIAL!
In the readings from 2 Kings and Jeremiah we have very vivid records of the judicial and retributive dealings of God. A Jehu becomes the sword of the Lord to bring about the fulfilment of the prophetical declarations of Elijah upon the house of Ahab. Baruch is reminded of God's word against Judah, so recently fulfilled before his eyes. Then Jeremiah pronounces the frightful retributions awaiting the surrounding nations. They are declared as rumbles of thunder before an oncoming storm.

But my thoughts today go to Hebrews and the writer's careful reminder that the ungodly are not necessarily always the object of the divine hands in disciplinary afflictions. Never are His saints the subjects of His wrath, for the matter of our sins was forever dealt with at the cross and will never be raised again! But as regards His sons, God takes the work of parenting us very seriously. I sense the writer here feels the groans and perhaps hears the complaints of these suffering saints. He now explains the necessity and nature of such afflictions, and will exhort them to endurance, 12. 3.

These things are a matter of course in the race that we now run. Be prepared to strip down, and leave off anything that encumbers, he tells them. Keep your eyes looking to our Forerunner Jesus, he exhorts them. The requirement is to follow the trail He has marked out for them with determination of spirit.

We shall never be called upon to pass through the fire as He did, nor have to confront the darkest of opposition He faced in His walk to the cross. He despised such suffering, and accepted it as the price to be paid.

For us the common everyday trials and challenges of life are to be seen as the all wise disciplining of our Father. He wants to mould us into 'family' likeness. As with our natural children who make an awful din when we take up measures to change their behaviour, we too can take this discipline very negatively. Sometimes we are even brought to the point of throwing everything away to dodge the pain. Yet our Father will never exceed that which is needful, and we will even learn to thank Him, vv. 16-17.

October 11th
2 Kings 11-12; Jeremiah 48; Hebrews 12. 18 – 13. 6
'BRINGING IN THE KING'

Isn't it strange how things work out in the end? We have the blessing of 'hindsight' on issues and sense how things could have turned out so differently than they did. With the hand of God there is a sense of certainty that we need to build into our daily Christian outlook on everything. The Lord has not left us to be tossed around as by tide and wind, Eph. 4. 14. We are no longer children but sons of the living God and need to walk in the light as such, 5. 8.

These thoughts came to me as I read of the condemnation of Moab today, for in the final verse we are assured, '*Yet* will I bring again the captivity (restore the fortunes) of Moab . . . saith the Lord', Jer. 48. 47. And He has brought us to Mount Zion and removed Mount Sinai for ever, Heb. 12. 22, 28! We must never forget that His purposes for good in our lives will always outweigh any traumas we are called to pass through on the way.

There could not have been a darker day than when Athaliah moved to 'destroy all the royal seed', 2 Kgs. 11. 1. It was out of the late king's own household that the Lord had a ready deliverer. The young prince and heir to the throne, Joash, was rescued and hidden for a future day. When we are taken off guard, we find the Lord has gone before nonetheless and provided for a brighter day. He will right the wrongs and bring in His resolutions. He always has His faithful remnants for the saddest occasions and even an Elijah can get it very wrong. The forlorn cry of 'I only am left' is never true when God is in the arena.

Isn't it significant to find that the man who brings in the king is named Jehoiada, which means 'Jehovah knows'? It took six years, but the day came when he 'brought forth the king's son', v. 12. On a wider screen in the purposes of God in world history, we need to let it be known that the King is coming, and God will bring Christ back again to where He was once despised and rejected. He is, after all, 'King of kings and Lord of lords.' The new king went on to re-establish the temple as the place of worship, financed by the freewill offerings of God's people and what a day that was! What a reversal of what might have been!

October 12th
2 Kings 13. 1 – 14. 22; Jeremiah 49; Hebrews 13. 7-25
FAMOUS LAST WORDS

A great deal of importance is often put on the last words spoken by a person before they pass away. You can never be sure that they really were their last words but Queen Elizabeth I is reputed to have said, 'So much to do and so little time to do it in'. When we come to the dying Elisha we know by the man's spiritual calibre that his last words are going to be very significant.

The prophet Elisha was regarded as the protecting and preserving shield to the nation, and Joash the king of Israel hearing that he was sick hastens to visit him with this in mind. He is not too surprised, I would imagine, to be asked to shoot the 'Lord's arrow of victory' over the current enemy. Perhaps he was *surprised* to be told to take all the remaining arrows and use his own judgement as to how many times he struck them on the ground. He had faith to strike three times but no more, and so limits future victories to three and leaves the enemy to recover to challenge Israel yet again.

True faith in the promises of God will be *persistent* faith. This is what the writer to the Hebrews is aiming at as he concludes his letter, 'last words' yet again. He argues for a firm and unwavering faith on account of our having faithful forebears, 13. 7; an unchanging Saviour, v. 8; a service and a sanctuary constantly accessible to us, vv. 10-16; a faithful Shepherd to guide and an equipping that will see us home to glory, vv. 20-21. These are powerful 'last words' are they not? Surely now we can walk confidently outside the acceptance of men and make our distinct mark in our generation also?

So Elisha dies and is buried, yet astoundingly still has a ministry for the nation. It is this miraculous resurrection of the man whose dead body touches his bones that becomes a torch that will shine for them into the future. Power from God has not gone with the going of the man of God.

So with faith in the promises of God we 'press on', 'run the race', and 'looking away unto Jesus' we hear Him say, 'I will never leave you nor will I ever forsake you.' He is the same, yesterday, today and forever! Go forward today in His strength!

October 13th
2 Kings 14. 23 – 15. 31; Jeremiah 50. 1-20; **Titus 1. 1 – 2. 8**

LASTING LEADERSHIP

The passage from 2 Kings makes for sad reading. Some of these kings may have reigned for a good number of years but their legacy was often negative and destructive. The assassination of one led to the assassination of the next. An appalling record of the godless plundering of their spiritual inheritance led only to an inevitable exile and the visitation of God in judgement.

We can now appreciate Paul's concern for the local churches in Crete in the matter of leadership which pressed him into leaving Titus there to guide the local Christians into the recognition of spiritual leaders. The same burden was responsible for him putting Timothy into Ephesus. Why this earnest requirement and cautioned encouragement to these two quality young men to see to this singular task? I suggest that there were all too many unsuitable men pressing for the office who would, if recognized, abuse the leadership for their own gains.

No local assembly of God's people can rise above the quality of their leaders. Many have been frustrated by an often enfeebled eldership that have merely 'caretakered' their flocks and not spiritually empowered them to have vision and growth generated by their leadership. The opportunity for carnality to step in and operate a Pharisaic regime is all too evident here.

Spiritual leadership is always recognized by the quality and character of the godly example set in day-by-day practical living in Christian virtues. The outward credentials, so often held up as a checklist of qualification, do not actually qualify if not clearly supported by a calling of God, recognized by the church, and worked out in a shepherding lifestyle.

Mark again the counsel of Paul to the Ephesian elders: 'Pay careful attention to yourselves and to all the flock . . . care for the church of God . . . fierce wolves will come in among you, not sparing the flock; and from among your own selves will arise men speaking twisted things, to draw away the disciples after them. Therefore be alert, Acts 20. 28-31 ESV. So let us encourage the godly leader, and challenge the carnal one constructively. Do not lie down and suffer: the cost is too great.

October 14th
2 Kings 15. 32 – 16. 20; **Jeremiah 50. 21-46**; Titus 2. 9 – 3. 15
HE HOLDS US IN HIS HANDS
God has always dealt with nations and their rulers despite not being recognized or acknowledged by them. The domination of the earth by world powers has always been subject to His will and purpose. It would seem also that from passages in Daniel's prophecy there are spiritual powers, good and evil, in the heavenly realms, which are engaged in the conflicts that have affected the course of world history.

The seemingly inevitable surges of massed armies and the rise and fall of kingdoms have been, from the participants' viewpoint, an undefinable tangle of fortunes. Yet we know from scripture that all the events and their outcomes are known and related to the overall determination of God Himself. This is a great comfort to us when caught up in them, as we are.

Babylon has always played a central part in these purposes of God for mankind and always as a tool of Satan to oppose God or entrap men. Beginning with a city called Babel with its 'clenched fist' approach to the rule of God we see how it nurtures everything that is 'man-centred' and contrary to divine revelation and purpose. This has been the case right from the outset of man's expansion across the earth to occupy it.

From these passages in Jeremiah's prophecy we note Babylon's rise as a world power and as an instrument of God's judgement upon other nations, as it established its dominions under Nebuchadnezzar's leadership. Here also we note that these things bring Babylon itself under judgement and the time had come for its own destruction and fall. The purposes of God were fulfilled and now wrath was awakened for the divine repayment on account of His Jerusalem and His temple.

So Babylon fades into oblivion and becomes the habitation of wild animals, however, please don't think it is finished. In our New Testament it rises once more as a religious and commercial power to which all the world looks as the Man of Sin uses it as his tool to bring the nations under his control. This last throw of the dice in Satan's plan to take over the world fails, as God Himself steps in once more, Rev. 17, 18. Watch this space!

October 15th
2 Kings 17; Jeremiah 51. 1-24; **1 Timothy 1**
ULTIMATELY YOU HAVE TO LEAVE IT TO THE LORD!
There are things and situations that we just have to commit entirely to the hand of the Lord Himself to resolve. To have to lay a thing down and step back comes hard to us, but this is the wisest thing to do in certain situations. Hoshea rebelled against the Assyrian overlord and turned to Egypt, a fickle friend at any time and one which proved to be no saviour! His greatest problem was the spiritual state of his people and having turned away from the Lord despite all the warnings, his doom is sealed, including the resultant exile. Satan is swift to fill the gap, and the Samaritan nation is formed that 'served the Lord *and* their own gods'. Confusion and contradiction reigned as a result 'to this day'.

Jeremiah is now given to see that God had intentions for the recovery of His people and their return to the Land. Helpless to help themselves, only He could bring it about. Despite it being yet in the future for them then, He gives them hope for their day in His declared revenge on Babylon. This later word served Daniel well in his day, and in a day yet to afflict them it will be a source of immense comfort to a desperate remnant. 'But I will repay Babylon for all the evil done to Israel', He declares. No one touches 'the apple of God's eye' and gets away with it.

In the first chapter of 1 Timothy we are presented immediately with the fact that Paul had sensed the dangers of the false teachers in Ephesus and had decided that it was time to send in the troops. Timothy becomes a commissioned servant directed to counter their errors and to set things in order.

He insists that Timothy's service has to be carried out *in God's way and not how he might want.* The objects to be achieved are specified and so is the method, 'love out of a pure heart and a good conscience in sincere faith'. No battle-axe bludgeoning, but an irresistible movement of grace. Here we note how the overwhelming love of God, with its grand objective of sending Christ into the world 'to save sinners', is the sole driving force of the job to be done. It is His way.

Thus we 'fight the good fight' but even then, there were those who would resist and be set apart for divine discipline.

October 16th
2 Kings 18; Jeremiah 51. 25-64; **1 Timothy 2**
'BEHOLD YOU SCOFFERS AND MARVEL, AND PERISH'

Hezekiah's secret strength was that he 'trusted in the Lord God of Israel'. Upon that basis he stepped away from following those that had preceded him as king and became uniquely a devoted servant of God. Destroying all the idolatrous evidences of the past, he reverted to the pathway of doing that which pleases God according to His commands. Clinging to the Lord, he confided fully in Him and became a pillar of vital strength for his people. The times were fearsome and abounding with perils. Truly the earth was about to shake beneath their feet as the Assyrian oppressor rose and bullied his way into their lives.

Despite the early peace deal, Sennacherib cannot resist returning to destroy Hezekiah. Typical of godless men, his word was not his bond. With the northern kingdom humiliated and removed, Sennacherib sweeps down to take Judah in similar manner. The approach is one of open contempt for Hezekiah and his faith in God. Taunting the officials and the general population the envoys of Assyria suggest that their king is deluded and untrustworthy, a simpleton deceived by an ill-placed faith in a God that is weak and powerless. How much lower can you get than this? The strategy is to destroy the people's morale, undermining their trust in Hezekiah and their God.

Satan knows how to destroy faith's foundations, so Paul reminds Timothy of the pillars that need to be in place to defend the people of God in the anti-Christian world we live in. These are firstly, prayer, and to follow that a clear and simple gospel of the grace of God, available for all men. Added to this must be the strength of godly male leadership and a female ministry that displays a God-fearing character so absent in the godlessness of the society around. *We* are the only 'Bible' some will ever read.

As we then seek this pathway, just as Hezekiah did in his day, so we will have to endure the scoffing of the ungodly. Satan's attack today is aimed at undermining a simple faith and commitment to the word of God. The world needs to see Christ in us, the hope of glory. To this world we say again as was said before, 'Behold you scoffers and marvel, and perish', Acts 13. 41 NASB.

October 17th
2 Kings 19; Jeremiah 52; 1 Timothy 3
HOW THE CAGE WAS OPENED

History records Sennacherib king of Assyria's proud boast: 'Hezekiah ... I shut up like a caged bird within ... Jerusalem'. How, at a time of military and widespread political intrigue, he had restricted Judah's king is told in 2 Kings chapter 18. Arrogantly, Sennacherib thought he held the key to that cage.

Hezekiah's resources were considerable, even in a day of trouble, rebuke, and blasphemy, 19. 3. Sennacherib had not taken into account that Hezekiah could call the notable prophet Isaiah, vv. 3, 6-7; 20-34; and had access to God Himself, before whom he spread the threatening letter from Rabshakeh, Sennacherib's envoy, vv. 8-10. Most importantly, God had forces against which Sennacherib had no answer. Hezekiah's God had delayed Assyrian action against Judah by involving Sennacherib in conflict with Libnah. He may not have recognized that a blast from God caused that delay, vv. 7-8. But a far more devastating blow would strike Assyria, when, in one night, 185,000 soldiers were slain. God was not *delaying*; now He was *defending* Jerusalem, v. 34. Before the first Assyrian arrow was fired, before a burnished shield flashed in the sunshine, before a bank was formed to allow access over the city walls, v. 32, an angel destroyed the huge Assyrian army in one night, providing a striking parallel with the night of Passover in Egypt almost eight centuries earlier. Faced with such carnage, Sennacherib returned home. No one was dispatched to Nineveh to recover the key to release Hezekiah from his 'cage'!

Would Sennacherib bring down evil again to the gate of Israel, as Micah described his intervention, Mic. 1. 12? Sennacherib's spokesman had mocked God's ability to defend Jerusalem, classifying Him as ineffective as the gods of Samaria and other city states that Sennacherib had destroyed, 18. 34; 19. 12-13. The God who passed through the land of Egypt had executed judgement against the gods of Egypt, Exod. 12. 12. That same God dealt with Sennacherib. In the temple of Nisroch his god, two of his sons assassinated their father, as Isaiah had prophesied, v. 7. His own god in his own temple could not save Sennacherib! Hezekiah's God is on our side, Rom. 8. 31.

October 18th
2 Kings 20. 1 – 21. 18; **Lamentations 1**; 1 Timothy 4

THE DISTRESS OF THE WIDOWED PRINCESS

Lamentations! The very name prepares the reader for an account of a very sad scene. Immediately, the writer highlights the experience of one who is called a 'princess', v. 1, who is lamenting her change of circumstances. The princes who once attended her have fled like frightened deer, trying to escape the armed band in pursuit, v. 6. She finds herself friendless, v. 2; restless, v. 3; childless, v. 5; defenceless, v. 6; and helpless, v. 7. She no longer has admirers, charmed by her beauty, v. 6; or impressed by her gowns, vv. 8-9. She no longer has a husband, and has lost the numerous lovers she had attracted, v. 1.

But who is this princess? And why is she deserted by her attendants? The opening sentence identifies the princess as the city of Jerusalem. The year is 587 BC and after an eighteen-month siege, the city has fallen to Nebuchadnezzar's Babylonian armies. One month after the wall was breached, when the order was given to systematically burn the city, the invaders set about Jerusalem's destruction, beginning by torching the royal palace and the houses of the residents of that proud city, Jer. 39. 8. The destruction was not completed until one month after the city fell; then the temple of the Lord itself was set alight and the city walls razed to the ground, 52. 12-14. No wonder the city felt like a widowed woman, deserted by her friends and lovers.

Before these calamities befell the 'princess', Jeremiah had warned the city, and the nation of Israel as a whole, of its sins. The loss of all they held dear was the price the nation paid for its many sins against God Himself. The 'princess' is moved to acknowledge that fire from on high had been sent and it had burned into her bones, v. 13. The Lord had delivered her into the hands of the foreign armies, v. 14; He had trodden down the princess under the feet of the Babylonians, v. 15. Wrung from her lips comes the confession: 'The Lord is righteous, for I have rebelled', to which she adds: 'Behold my sorrow', v. 18. Four hundred years before the princess confessed her sin, Solomon wrote: 'The way of transgressors is hard', Prov. 13. 15; and it still is today. Would that men were aware that all sin is against God Himself!

307

October 19th
2 Kings 21. 19 – 22. 20; Lamentations 2; **1 Timothy 5**

OPEN BEFOREHAND

At 1 Timothy 5. 24, TYNDALE'S telling phrase 'open beforehand' was adopted by the translators of the KJV and other versions. It must have startled the first readers into asking themselves what features of their daily living delivered a verdict that onlookers – saved and unsaved – could read, whether good or bad, features that were evident. In the chapter we meet examples of good and bad practices, from which there are lessons to be learned.

Among those good 'open' examples, there are widows, who know the support of their own adult children or nephews. Those supporting those ageing widows are showing piety in their own family circle, v. 4. Not only does God commend this as 'good and acceptable', but so would the ungodly observers. In a world with no welfare state, such piety would be praiseworthy. Conversely, to neglect need in one's own family would be seen by others as a denial of the faith; their callous indifference would be worse than many an unbeliever would show.

But Paul's examples are not restricted to those with the means to support financially close relatives in need. Even a destitute widow – a 'widow indeed', v. 3 – can show piety that is evident to others. Her evident trust in God to meet her needs, and her supplications and prayers night and day, not all restricted to her own needs, would be noted by all who had contact with her, v. 5. Paul provides a catalogue of good works that even a destitute widow could perform until old age would inhibit her. He includes bringing up her own children in the nurture and admonition of the Lord, Eph. 6. 4. If a spiritual woman has manifested her good works in 'washing the saints' feet', as the Lord Himself did in the Upper Room on that night in which He was betrayed, such God-glorifying behaviour cannot be hid. At the judgement seat of Christ, she will have her reward; that, says Paul, is 'open beforehand'. Again, he notes the practices of those who do *not* adorn the doctrine they have been taught, vv. 6, 11-13.

Before the chapter closes, Paul also notes men, who lead among the saints, whose good works are open beforehand, vv. 17-18, men whose faith we should follow, Heb. 13. 7.

308

October 20th
2 Kings 23; Lamentations 3; 1 Timothy 6
WHEN A LITTLE CHILD LED
When, after two disastrous kings – Manasseh and Amon – and after his father's assassination and the violent death of his father's assailants, a young boy of eight years of age was crowned, did the thoughtful wonder that Josiah had 'come to the kingdom for such a time as this?' Esther 4. 14. Yet in the early years of his reign, Josiah was greatly used to reform an idolatrous, morally corrupt nation, 2 Kgs. 23. 4-15. From the age of sixteen it was clear that he repudiated all that his father and grandfather represented, and that he would do that which was right in the eyes of the Lord. The climax of his reformation came in the eighteenth year of his reign, when he was twenty-six years of age.

The discovery of the Book of the Law of the Lord was a momentous event that led to more than the destruction of idols from Geba in the north to Beersheba in the south. The discovery of the Book drew many of the priests back to the worship of God in Jerusalem, despite some resistance, v. 8. Josiah also dealt with the divisive altar that Jeroboam the son of Nebat had set up at Bethel, v. 15. His actions condemned men like Jeroboam but also honoured the man of God, who three hundred and fifty years before had prophesied that the actions of Josiah would destroy the wicked works of Jeroboam, vv. 17-18; 1 Kgs. 13. 32. He also honoured Moses, as a response to whose ministry Josiah commanded that the Passover be kept in Jerusalem in the eighteenth year of his reign, 2 Kgs. 23. 23. Not since the days of the judges like Samuel had such a Passover been kept. The king and his princes gave liberally, 2 Chr. 35. 7ff. and the people received a portion.

2 Kings chapter 23 verse 25 observes that no king of Israel or Judah, past or future, so served the Lord with all his heart and his soul and with all his might. Yet, good king Josiah was cut off in battle at the relatively young age of forty. The words of Huldah the prophetess were then fulfilled: God dealt with Judah for their gross sins, as the Book of the Law had warned, but Josiah himself was cut off 'in peace' before the period of retribution commenced, 22. 14-20.

October 21st
2 Kings 24; **Lamentations 4-5**; 2 Timothy 1
PRECIOUS STONES, PRECIOUS SONS AND THE LOST SHADOW
The utter destruction of the temple Solomon built was heart-breaking to Jeremiah, 4. 1. Well he knew that every one of those stones had been individually prepared off-site so that not a sound of hammer, axe, or other tools would be heard as the house of God was being constructed, 1 Kgs. 6. 7. Now those precious stones were scattered and broken in deliberate acts of vandalism by the Babylonian army. He must have realized that he would never see another temple replace the one he had known from his youth,

In the eyes of a priest like Jeremiah and those who feared God, the sons of Zion – probably the Aaronic priests – were as precious as the gold that adorned the temple, 4. 2. In the eyes of the conquering generals, they were no more valuable than the earthenware to be found in the humblest of homes. One blow and they were ruined. Sadly, for a long time before Babylon invaded, the false prophets and the priests had given scant attention to the holiness of God's house. They had slain innocent blood like that of Urijah, Jer. 26. 20-23, and were known for their defiling ways, vv. 14-15, and not surprisingly, they were abhorred by the people.

For over four hundred years, the nation had been under the shadow of kings of David's lineage. Among those kings were good men who loved the Lord, men like Hezekiah and Josiah, men who were the nation's 'very life breath', v. 20. Even surrounded by heathen nations, they had felt secure. Now, since Josiah's death, four weak, vacillating kings – Jehoahaz, Jehoiakim, Jehoiachin, and Zedekiah – had afforded them no shelter. Those kings had each been acknowledged as the Lord's anointed, v. 20, but not one of the four rose to the standard the Lord's people expected.

There did dawn a day for Israel when Messiah, of the seed of David, was among them. Their leaders failed to encourage the people to sit under His shadow with great delight, S. of S. 2. 3. The same kind of priests who slew Urijah joined hands with the Romans to slay the Lord's anointed at Calvary. Not many years later in AD 70, the Romans destroyed the temple that replaced the one the destruction of which Jeremiah lamented. Nonetheless, Jew and Gentile can still sit under Christ's shadow with great delight.

October 22nd
2 Kings 25; Ezekiel 1; **2 Timothy 2**
ONE MAN AND HIS MANY PARTS
WILLIAM SHAKESPEARE observed that, between their entrances and their exits, all men fill several roles. Centuries before SHAKESPEARE'S brief summary of the seven ages of man, Paul had written to Timothy. In one chapter of that letter, we meet seven parts Paul's son in the faith might fill, v. 1: a good soldier, vv. 2-3; an athlete in competitive sport, v. 5; a farmer, v. 6; reputedly 'an evil doer', v. 9; a workman, v. 15; 'a vessel unto honour', v. 21; a servant of the Lord, v. 24. From these metaphors, Paul will draw many lessons for the younger man Timothy to learn.

Before Paul outlines the roles, he acknowledges that, without added strength, Timothy could not meet the requirements of any role, so he exhorts: 'Be strong in the grace that is in Christ Jesus', the source of inwardly-strengthening grace. Every soldier in every age has needed to endure hardness, for war is no leisure pursuit; it is a life-or-death campaign against various enemies, v. 3. He also needs strength for his level of engagement in active service; indeed so demanding is active service that the good soldier has to put aside entanglement with the affairs of life. The good soldier is always endeavouring to please the general who has chosen him to be a soldier.

In the sports arena, there are encouragements that are not promised to the good soldier. In his preparation for competition, the athlete knows he must strive, if he is to win a crown, v. 5. He will train wholeheartedly, and he must compete legally within the laws of the sport; otherwise he will suffer the shame of disqualification.

The farmer cannot ignore the time constraints of agriculture, as the Preacher of Ecclesiastes notes: 'a time to plant and a time to pluck up that which is planted', Eccles. 3. 2. He must be conscientious. But he does not lack encouragement to be conscientious: the reward for his work is fruit, and the peculiar privilege of being the first to partake of that fruit, v. 6.

The guidance offered to Timothy applies throughout the Christian life. The principles have been set out by Paul that we each might be acclaimed 'a good and faithful servant', Matt. 25. 21.

October 23rd
1 Chronicles 1; Ezekiel 2. 1 – 3. 15; 2 Timothy 3
MADE OF ONE BLOOD
The hardest chapter to write is the first chapter of a book. In a few pages the author has to engage the reader. By providing selective insights into the origins of the community of nations, the author of Chronicles seeks to engage his readers in a book that begins at the beginning of human history, confirming the accuracy of Paul's comment that '[God] hath made of one blood all nations', Acts 17. 26. The Chronicler traces the division into nations of the human race, initially by language and then by geography, v. 19. He also notes that nations would be internally stratified, as kings and dukes begin to appear initially in Edom, the descendants of Esau.

One individual in the chapter – Nimrod of the lineage of Ham – is highlighted as one who 'began to be mighty', v. 10. Neither he nor the kings and dukes of Edom brought pleasure to God. But among those 'made of one blood' in the chapter are three names that are going to matter in the Book – Abraham, Isaac and Israel, v. 34. Only twice in 1 Chronicles is Isaac's son called Jacob, but several times he is called Israel. He had been a supplanter until God dealt with him and called him Israel, 'one who had power as a prince with God', Gen. 32. 28. He was of the one blood, a child of Adam, once a supplanter, but time after time this book acknowledges him as a prince. In the evening of his life, his greatness is emphasized. He blessed Pharaoh, then the most powerful man among the nations. This prince was seen to be greater than even Pharaoh, for the less is blessed of the greater, Heb. 7. 7.

The world that honoured Nimrod failed to see Jacob's greatness. The name David is dominant in 1 and 2 Chronicles, from chapter 3 onwards. Unlike old Jacob, David is honoured in the Chronicler's narrative as a youth of about nineteen years of age. Goliath disdained David, the one who would later be described as a man after God's own heart, Acts 13. 22, who would slay tens of thousands in the battles of the Lord, 1 Sam. 18. 8, as even his Philistine enemies knew, 29. 5. The world that honoured Nimrod still underestimates Christians who will one day reign with Christ, 1 Cor. 6. 3; 2 Tim. 2. 12.

October 24th
1 Chronicles 2; **Ezekiel 3. 16 – 4. 17**; 2 Timothy 4
BY VOICE AND VISUAL AIDS
Ezekiel was not the only servant of God who was a watchman to his nation, warning against impending judgement on both individuals and the nations of Israel and Judah. Normally, a watchman was charged with the security of a city, but Ezekiel is to speak to *individuals* both wicked and righteous, 4. 19-21. Having been warned by the prophet, that person was responsible to God for how he treated the warning. Where no warning was given, the watchman carried responsibility for the stroke of judgement that cut off the sinner, 3. 18, 20.

Mercifully, Ezekiel is commanded to provide visual aids to ensure that the nation was aware of its plight. God had a message to be delivered to both the ear and the eye. The first visual aid was a clay tablet on which was portrayed an easily recognized drawing of Jerusalem's shape. Using that sketch Ezekiel was to portray the siege of Jerusalem and the siege works the besieging army would build against the city's fortification, 4. 2. More ominously, a metal pan was to be used to illustrate that there would come a time when in despair men will attempt to solicit God's help, but in vain, 4. 3. More memorably, Ezekiel would lie on his left side, facing north for three hundred and ninety days, then for forty days on his right side. The prophet is not left to draw a lesson from the numbers; he is told that the larger number indicated the iniquity of the northern kingdom in years, not days; and the smaller number the iniquity of the southern kingdom of Judah, 4. 5. 6.

The third visual aid was to reinforce the awfulness of siege conditions. There would be shortage of all essentials: food would be consumed by weight, water by volume; normal fuel supplies would dry up and animal excrement would be the only substitute, 4. 9-15. God was breaking the staff of bread in Jerusalem, v. 16. The nation was to learn that the way of transgressors is hard, Prov. 13. 15. But not only transgressors, for godly men like Ezekiel were to suffer too. Even those who from their youth had observed the dietary code set out in the Books of Moses would face difficulties they had never encountered before. Even the watchman raised up by God would suffer.

313

October 25th

1 Chronicles 3. 1 – 4. 23; Ezekiel 5-6; **John 1. 1-18**

A METAPHOR OF SUCCOUR AND SECURITY

The introductory section of John's Gospel, 1. 1-18, often called the Prologue, contains interesting metaphors. We read of the Word, vv. 1, 14; light, vv. 4, 5, 7, 8, 9; birth, v. 13; the tabernacle ('dwell', v. 14, means 'to pitch a tent or tabernacle'), and the bosom, v. 18. Of those five metaphors, none conveys so clearly warmth and affection as the noun 'bosom'. The word 'bosom' was used in the Hebrew Bible of a father carrying a young child, Num. 11. 12; of the close relationship of a husband and wife, Deut. 13. 6; and of friends reclining together as they shared a meal, John 13. 23. Here the metaphor relates to God the Father and His only-begotten Son, Jesus Christ, 1. 18. It is a metaphor bereft of all the tensions and disappointments human relationships sometimes experience.

John the writer of the Gospel guards carefully that relationship between Father and Son. His introductory statement emphatically declares that 'no man has seen God at any time', v. 18, making it clear that no man could speak of 'the bosom of the Father' without divine revelation. The relationship between the Father and the only-begotten Son is described by the present participle of the verb 'to be'; it is a timeless relationship without beginning and without end.

John reveals that the only-begotten Son is the One who is charged with declaring what man cannot see. He has come into the world and so men like John 'beheld his glory' and found in Him 'grace and truth', vv. 14, 16-17. John is not suggesting that grace, truth, and glory are the only aspects revealed by the Son, but he is insisting that only the Son is qualified to reveal the Father. Through the apostles, the Son has revealed in the New Testament much about the Father.

In the teaching of the Lord Jesus, the only-begotten Son, there is a statement that suggests one additional feature of 'the bosom of the Father' that encourages every Christian's heart: 'The Father himself loveth you', 16. 27. He limits the meaning of the pronoun 'you' as those 'who have loved me, and have believed that I came from God'. We have the joy of experiencing the love that marks 'the bosom of the Father'.

October 26th
1 Chronicles 4. 24 – 5. 26; Ezekiel 7; John 1. 19-51
THE DECLINE OF JACOB'S FIRSTBORN

Reuben was a bitter disappointment to his father Jacob. There were, at times, glimpses of hidden strength, for example when he intervened to save Joseph, Gen. 37. 22. Although brought up in a God-fearing home, he later stooped to despicable behaviour that dishonoured his father, as well as himself, 49. 4. Despite the disgrace, Jacob still acknowledged Reuben as his firstborn, whilst noting that the one in whom 'excellency of dignity' should be found, was 'unstable as water', 49. 3-4.

Sadly, instability seemed to run in the Reúbenite lineage. Twenty years after Israel left Egypt, Korah the Levite supported by three men of Reuben's tribe rose up in rebellion against Moses and Aaron, Num. 16. 3. The root cause was envy, as the anonymous writer of Psalm 106 records to the rebels' shame, v. 16. They perished for their sin in a most uncommon death, when the earth opened and swallowed them, Num. 16. 29-33.

When Israel entered the land that flowed with milk and honey, Reuben, Gad, and half the tribe of Manasseh were reluctant to take a lot with the other tribes across the Jordan, preferring to remain on the east side, where there was excellent pasture for their livestock, Num. 32. 1-33. The chosen location enabled them to prosper in times of peace. Prudence dictated that the tribes should invest time and effort in developing a battle-ready army, which certainly by King Saul's reign was respected after their defeat of the Hagarities, but they proved no match for the Assyrian invasion under Tilgath-pilneser, 1 Chr. 5. 10, 26.

Exposure to raiding or invading forces was only one danger the Reubenites experienced. The location of the tribal lands did not make for easy travel to the feasts of Jehovah. All males were to be present in Jerusalem three times a year, Exod. 23. 17; Deut. 16. 16. Lapses in this discipline may have led to the reinstatement of the very idolatry the Reubenites had earlier removed, 1 Chr. 5. 25-26, and the subsequent judgement of God when the Assyrians transported them from Transjordan which they had occupied. Enslaved to idolatry and to a foreign power, Jacob's firstborn had forfeited the 'excellence of dignity' that had been his.

315

October 27th
1 Chronicles 6; **Ezekiel 8-9**; John 2. 1-22

THE STATE OF THE NATION

The President of USA gives an annual State-of-the-Union address in which he offers an analysis of the prevalent conditions as he sees them. In Britain the Prime Minister delivers similar analyses. To Ezekiel, then living in Tel-abib on the Chebar canal in Babylonia, 3. 15, God provided a state-of-the-nation report in respect of Ezekiel's nation, a report informed by a number of visits to view the sins of Jerusalem. His nation did not realize that this was also an end-of-term report to a nation that refused to repent, as sinful Nineveh had done three centuries years earlier.

The exiled elders of Judah were assembled before Ezekiel in his own home. We are not given the reason for their audience with the prophet. While they were before him, there appeared to Ezekiel a Man, whose appearance comprised fire and brightness and amber, emphasizing that He was a divine Person about to judge according to the holy standards of God. The divine Visitor lifted him up by a lock of his hair, suspending him between heaven and earth, 8. 2-3. He was then transported in spirit to see the state of his nation's capital city and the temple that had such a central role in the nation's standing before God.

He saw evidence that his nation was no better than the Canaanites, for they also worshipped Asherah, v. 5; or the Egyptians, for they also worshipped creeping things, v. 6. No better than the Phoenicians, for they worshipped the same Tammuz, v. 14; or the Babylonians, for they worshipped the sun-god, v. 16; and no better than the Persians, whom some link with the-branch-at-the nose action, v. 17. These sins were being committed, not by the ignorant, but by the ancients of Israel, v. 11; by women, weeping in their adoration of Tammuz (or Adonis), v. 14. Present too was Jaazaniah, whose godly father read the scriptures to Josiah and whose two brothers followed in their father's footsteps, v. 11, 2 Kgs. 22. 18; 2 Chr. 34. 14-15; Jer. 36. 10; 39. 14. Josiah's son was an idolater!

How *troubling* to the prophet to be confronted with the wickedness of his own nation! How *consoling* to learn that God would preserve others troubled by the state of their nation, 9. 1-11.

October 28th
1 Chronicles 7; Ezekiel 10; **John 2. 23 – 3. 21**
WHEN THE TEACHER MET A TEACHER

Nicodemus' approach to the Lord Jesus was respectful as he addressed Him as 'Rabbi', adding that the miracles He performed were evidence not only that the Man he was addressing had come from God but that God was with Him. Nicodemus acknowledged that the Man from Galilee was 'a teacher', v. 2. As the dialogue continued, the Lord addressed the inquirer as '*the* teacher of Israel', v. 10 YLT. Face to face during that Passover feast day, 2. 23, were One termed '*a* teacher' and one termed '*the* teacher'. How strange to all who now sing: 'None teacheth, Lord, like Thee'!

Jerusalem would be thronging with pilgrims at Passover, but even at night this teacher of Israel could find Christ. The narrow streets would be less congested, but more of an issue than congestion may have been *confidentiality*: he had questions to ask of this new Teacher, and may have preferred to do so without the ever-intruding crowds.

Unlike the teachers Nicodemus had known, this Teacher opened their discussion with an unfamiliar approach. He did not begin to quote Moses and the prophets, or to say, 'We know', as Nicodemus himself had, 3. 2; 7. 27; 8. 52; 9. 24, 29. This Teacher declared His unquestionable authority: 'I say unto thee', words that were preceded by 'Verily, verily', vv. 3, 5. Those adverbs introduced an unexpected testimony of unqualified veracity.

Nicodemus heard truth expounded that day that, despite his much learning he had never understood. Two metaphors were highlighted – one about new birth that he should have understood, Ezek. 36. 25-27; the other of the serpent of brass being lifted up from the earth that would find its fulfilment at Calvary, v. 14; Num. 21. 9. As a good teacher should do, Nicodemus asked intelligent questions: 'How can a man be born again? ... How can these things be?' John 3. 4, 9.

The brief appearances of Nicodemus in John's Gospel make evident the outcome of *the* teacher meeting *a* Teacher: Nicodemus was born again as a result of that meeting with Christ, 7. 50; 19. 39. Nicodemus, Israel's illustrious teacher, met the Teacher who knew what was in man, and how to meet man's needs, 2. 25.

October 29th
1 Chronicles 8-9; Ezekiel 11; John 3. 22-36
RESETTLING AND RESUMING

Prominent in the first nine chapters of 1 Chronicles are three tribes: Benjamin, Judah and Levi. The reason for the Chronicler's emphasis is their links with royalty and the worship of God. Saul, Israel's first king, came from the tribe of Benjamin, so chapter 8 is dedicated to the genealogy of Saul and the generations that followed. Similarly, great emphasis is placed on the lineage of Judah in chapters 2, 3 and 4, from which King David arose. But also important in the Chronicler's judgement is the tribe of Levi, for both priests and Levites were charged with a mediatorial role between the people and their God.

The genealogies that comprise the first nine chapters would be important in determining not only who might occupy the throne of Israel, but also who would ensure that the holiness of the tabernacle was not breached in any way. The chapter opens with a reminder of the deportation of Judah to Babylon – a reminder of the consequences of rebellion at all levels against God.

The Chronicler does not pause to reflect on the causes of the long sad exile in Babylon, but immediately relates the return, noting that the first to resettle in their properties were the common people, the priests, the Levites, and the Nethinims who supported the Levites in their work for the Lord. The focus of those who returned was Jerusalem and their aspirations to see the house of God functioning in the corporate life of the nation. Among the remnant, who resettled in Jerusalem and its environs were able priests, v. 13. Two hundred and twelve gatekeepers (or porters) were available for various duties, including guard duty by night. The Levites were charged with preparing flour, oil, wine, incense, and spices, as in the days of Israel's first high priest Aaron.

From those little steps, the nation found its feet, not initially under King Saul, but once David ascended the throne and put down his enemies. It had been his desire to build a temple to replace the Tabernacle, a task that was undertaken by Solomon, his son. In both the tabernacle and the temple that followed there was a need for priests, Levites, Nethinims and true worshippers to resume honouring God.

October 30th
1 Chronicles 10-11; **Ezekiel 12**; John 4. 1-30

THE TIME IS SHORT

In every generation there are those who reassure themselves that 'all things continue as they were from the beginning', as Peter observed, 2 Pet. 3. 4. Peter added that such false optimism belongs only to those who are 'willingly ignorant'! He pointed to Noah's Flood as evidence that God has already intervened to judge ungodly men. In Ezekiel's day, judgement was near, yet foolish prophets had been able to persuade the general populace that the vision that Ezekiel had received was about 'the times that are afar off', 12. 27. Those, who offered such empty assurances, were 'scoffers, walking after their own lusts', 2 Pet. 3. 3.

The gravity of the scoffers' rejection of Ezekiel's message was compounded by their dismissal of the lessons Ezekiel had been required to act out in the sight of the inhabitants of Jerusalem. First Ezekiel was to pack a bag during the day, as if ready to leave the city. At evening, he was to dig through the wall of his house, emerging from the hole with his face covered, so that he would not be recognized, and carrying his travel bag, Ezek. 12. 3-7. Curiosity would be aroused, and in the morning Ezekiel was to explain his actions. What his actions were portraying related to the actions that 'the prince' Zedekiah would repeat in an attempt to escape from the besieged city. (Jehoiachin was still king, although in captivity in Babylon, 2 Kgs. 24. 12; Ezek. 17. 12.) 2 Kings chapter 25 verses 1 to 7 record the fulfilment of Ezekiel's prophecy in Zedekiah's attempted flight from the doomed city. All the men of war followed the prince's example.

The times are afar off, the scoffers still declare. The world at large does not believe that God will ever intervene in the affairs of this world. Even many, who accept that there is a God, would say in their hearts: 'The Lord will not do good, neither will he do evil', Zeph. 1. 12. Yet Peter reminded his readers that 'the holy prophets and . . . the apostles of the Lord and Saviour' taught that one day the Lord will act to judge this world, 2 Pet. 3. 2ff. To Christians in Corinth, Paul appealed: 'Brethren, the time is short . . . attend upon the Lord without distraction', 1 Cor. 7. 29, 35. We should not say: 'the times that are afar off', Ezek. 12. 27.

October 31st
1 Chronicles 12; Ezekiel 13; **John 4. 31-54**

A SECOND BENEFIT

When Paul planned to visit Corinth, his intention had been to bring further blessing into many lives. When the Lord Jesus 'came again into Cana of Galilee, where he made the water wine', 4. 46, it was to bring blessing to that far-from-prestigious part of Galilee. Cana of Galilee was five miles north-east of Nazareth on the road to Tiberias. He had come to Cana the first time, because He had been called to a wedding. On this second occasion, an unnamed nobleman was drawn to Cana, not by invitation but in desperation because his son was at the point of death. A twenty-mile journey to Cana mattered little if his son's life were spared.

The nobleman was not a member of the royal family, but was employed in the court of Herod Antipas. However, he well knew that Herod could not save the boy. The nobleman addressed as Lord the Man of Galilee, beseeching Him to come down to Capernaum, where the dying boy lay. To our knowledge, the troubled father had never seen anyone, young or old, miraculously healed. Nor had Herod! He may have heard much of the Lord's miracles at Jerusalem at the recent feast, 2. 23; 4. 45. He may have heard of the Lord's touch banishing disease, or of demons departing at the word of Christ from those they had possessed. But had this earnest father heard that the Lord could heal at a distance without ever having visited the home, or the 'patient' having been brought to Him? John comments that the Lord 'needed not that any should testify of man, for he knew what was in man', 2. 25. He knew what was in *this* man. He knew the nobleman's faith was strong. The Lord's command to the man, who had come as a distraught father, was unambiguous: 'Go thy way; thy son liveth', 4. 50. The man believed, and turned to go home. But his new-found faith was not sorely tried, for on his journey home he met his servants bearing the good news: 'Yesterday at the seventh hour the fever left him', the very time at which the Lord had assured him that his son would live, v. 52.

The Lord's second visit to Cana was indeed a second benefit. His disciples and others would realize that the Lord could bless in times of great joy and times of great distress. What a blessing!

November 1st
1 Chronicles 13-14; Ezekiel 14-15; John 5. 1-23
HIS PRESENCE

They should have known. One hundred years previously, after He smote them for looking into the ark, they had lamented, 'Who is able to stand before this holy Lord God?' 1 Sam. 6. 20. Now David desired to retrieve that same ark from where they had left it so many years before, for he said, 'We inquired not at it in the days of Saul', 13. 3. How sad then that such a good desire was spoilt again, not by a misplaced look this time, but by a misplaced *touch* as Uzzah 'put forth his hand to hold the ark', v. 9.

The ark with its mercy seat had been the very place where God had dwelt, in the holy of holies. Such was the holiness of that place that only one man could enter into the divine presence, having carefully discharged the rituals of the Day of Atonement and with his hands full of incense from the golden altar. How privileged then are we that today God's presence can be enjoyed by all believers without exception. We are told that collectively we are 'the temple of God, and the Spirit of God dwelleth in you', 1 Cor. 3. 16, and individually that 'your body is the temple of the Holy Spirit which is in you', 6. 19.

Privilege comes with responsibility, and the Corinthians were warned that 'if any man defile the temple of God, him shall God destroy; for the temple of God is holy, which temple ye are', 3. 17. Just as in defiled Corinth, we do well today to remember the Apostle's exhortation that 'ye are bought with a price: therefore glorify God in your body, and in your spirit, which are God's', 6. 20. If we are enjoying His presence it will be obvious to a visitor, so that 'falling down on his face he will worship God, and report that God is in you of a truth', 14. 25. Is this the case?

> Search me, O God,
> And know my heart today;
> Try me, O Saviour,
> Know my thoughts, I pray.
> See if there be
> Some wicked way in me;
> Cleanse me from every sin
> And set me free.   JAMES ORR

November 2nd
1 Chronicles 15; **Ezekiel 16. 1-34**; John 5. 24-47

FORGETFULNESS

Jerusalem was renowned for beauty, and clothed with silks and jewels and 'a beautiful crown', v. 12. 'It was perfect', v. 14; the divine record is unequivocal, 'thou wast exceeding beautiful', v. 13. Yet it wasn't always so, for at her birth the prophet Ezekiel likens her in parable to an abandoned child; we read that 'none eye pitied thee', and 'thou wast cast out in the open field', v. 5.

What caused the change? The personal pronoun tells the story for, says the Lord to Israel, 'When I saw thee . . . I said unto thee *live* . . . I washed thee . . . I clothed thee . . . I shod thee . . . until we read, 'It was perfect through my comeliness, which I had put upon thee, saith the Lord God', v. 14. How marvellous the change when grace intervenes! It was all due to Him!

Paul reminds the Ephesian Christians that once they too were dead, defiled, and disobedient, 'the children of wrath', 2. 3, 'but God' intervened, v. 4, imparting life and transforming their lives into 'masterpieces' of divine grace, v. 10! How rich indeed is His mercy, and how great is His love! It was all His work!

How sad, then, that in our reading, Ezekiel goes on to describe how Jerusalem squandered her blessings, exchanging them for the pleasures of Egypt, 16. 26, so that instead of prosperity she is 'diminished', v. 27. What went so wrong? We read, 'Because thou hast not remembered the days of thy youth', v. 43. Yet grace is never exhausted: a day of recovery is promised and in that day it is stated, 'then thou shalt remember', v. 61.

We are commanded 'to set [our] affection on things above, not on things on the earth', Col. 3. 2. Despite God's rich blessings the church at Ephesus would later leave 'her first love' and is commanded to 'repent and do the first works', Rev. 2. 5.

Let us never forget what grace has done for us, or that it is ever God's initiative! Recovery is always possible!

> Lest I forget Gethsemane,
> Lest I forget Thine agony,
> Lest I forget Thy love for me,
> Lead me to Calvary.
>
> JENNIE HUSSEY

November 3rd

1 Chronicles 16; Ezekiel 16. 35-63; John 6. 1-21

SPIRITUAL SACRIFICES

It must have been a tremendous moment when, after so many years, the ark was restored to Jerusalem and the burnt offering was presented. We read that they offered 'burnt offerings unto the Lord ... continually morning and evening', v. 40. As David reflects on the Lord's gracious provision for His people, he offers a psalm of repeated thanks to 'the God of our salvation', acknowledging that the very purpose of God in delivering them was 'that we may give thanks to thy holy name', v. 35.

If this was true of His earthly people, how much more of us who are 'blessed with all spiritual blessing in heavenly places in Christ'? Eph. 1. 3. Peter tells us that we are 'built up a spiritual house, an holy priesthood, to offer up spiritual sacrifices, acceptable to God by Jesus Christ', 1 Pet. 2. 5. The New Testament abounds with instruction as to these spiritual sacrifices. God is looking for his portion from us: 'Let us offer the sacrifice of praise to God continually, that is, the fruit of our lips, giving thanks to his name', Heb. 13. 15. The next verse directs us 'to do good and to communicate forget not: for with such sacrifices God is well pleased', v. 16. Note that God expects us to 'to do good' to others and that when this is done out of an appreciation for Him, He invests even our practical good works with all the dignity of priestly service! Elsewhere Paul speaks of himself as being 'offered upon the sacrifice and service of your faith', Phil. 2. 17. But as well as being prepared to die for Him, we must be prepared to live for Him! So, in the light of the unfolding of the glorious doctrines of the gospel throughout his letter to them, Paul beseeches the Romans 'to present your bodies a living sacrifice, holy, acceptable to God, which is your reasonable service'. You see, living like Him can be just as difficult as dying for Him!

Their burnt offerings continually ascended to Him uninterrupted, morning and evening. Do ours?

> All! For it is His own,
> He gave the tiny store;
> All! For it must be His alone;
> All! For I have no more.   F. R. HAVERGAL

323

November 4th
1 Chronicles 17-18; Ezekiel 17; John 6. 22-40

THE PROMISES OF GOD

A heartfelt desire to do something for God is noble indeed! Yet however commendable David's desire, in the Lord's plan it was not to be. Instead of what *David* could do for Him, the Lord reveals what *He* would do for David! Instead of David building Him a house, we read, 'The Lord will build thee a house'!

We are told that this house will involve a seed, a kingdom, and a throne, vv. 11, 12. Sonship also would be conferred, for whilst David is called 'my servant', v. 4, the promise to Solomon is, 'I will be his father, and he shall be my son', v. 13. The terms of the promise are clear. It is *eternal*, 'I will establish his throne forever', v. 12, and 'I will settle him . . . in my kingdom for ever: and his throne shall be established for evermore', v. 14. It is *unconditional*, for 'my covenant will I not break', Ps. 89. 34. Glorious assurances indeed! Under grace we too enjoy the dignity of sonship, Rom. 8. 15. And how blessed our assurance that nothing 'shall separate us from the love of Christ', Rom. 8. 35.

David's response to such a display of blessing is notable. As for himself, he declares, 'Who am I, O Lord God, and what is mine house?' v. 16. At the same time his appreciation of God increases and we read, 'O Lord, there is none like thee, neither is there any God beside thee, according to all that we have heard with our ears', v. 20. In remarkable submission David then dedicates his life to prepare what another would use to build the Lord a house.

But God's promises were not just for David, or for Solomon, but for 'great David's greater Son'. God's plan is always ultimately for His glory!

> Oh to trust Him then more fully,
> Just to simply move
> In the conscious calm enjoyment
> Of the Father's love;
> Knowing that life's chequered pathway
> Leadeth to His rest;
> Satisfied the way He taketh
> Must be always blest.

> J. FULLER

324

1 Chronicles 19-20; Ezekiel 18-19; **John 6. 41 – 7. 11**

FICKLENESS AND FAITH

The question couldn't be avoided. The Jews had already 'sought to slay Him', John 5. 16; 7. 1. Now we read that 'from that time many of His disciples went back, and walked no more with Him', 6. 66. Imagine the scene as He turns to them and asks, 'Will ye also go away?' v. 67. Sadly, He knew the answer, 'for Jesus knew from the beginning . . . who should betray Him', v. 64.

Yet in the midst of such fickleness, conviction as to who He was gave certainty to Peter's faith: 'We believe and are sure that Thou art that Christ, the Son of the living God', vv. 68-69! Is it not so with us? Our assurance also rests on the certainty of divine persons and promise! The Saviour tells us, 'This is the Father's will . . . that of all which He hath given me I should lose nothing', v. 39. And of His own will He says, 'I came down from heaven, not to do mine own will, but the will of Him that sent me', v. 38. We are not surprised then that, on the night of His betrayal, He was able to say, 'Those that thou gavest me I have kept, and none of them is lost', John 17. 12. You see, we belong to Him! The Saviour prayed 'not for the world, but for them which thou hast given me; for they are thine. And all mine are thine, and thine are mine; and I am glorified in them', v. 10. Because of this the Shepherd assures us, 'I give unto them eternal life; and they shall never perish, neither shall any man pluck them out of my hand . . . no man is able to pluck them out of my Father's hand. I and my Father are one', 10. 28-30. The apostle reminds us, 'After that ye believed, ye were sealed with that Holy Spirit of promise, which is the earnest of our inheritance until the redemption of the purchased possession, unto the praise of His glory', Eph. 1. 13-14.

In a day to come the remnant of Israel will enjoy that same promise: 'Yea they may forget, yet will not I forget thee. Behold I have graven thee upon the palms of my hand', Isa. 49. 15-16.

> My name from the palms of His hands
> Eternity will not erase;
> Impressed on His heart, it remains
> In marks of indelible grace.
>
> AUGUSTUS TOPLADY

November 6th
1 Chronicles 21; Ezekiel 20. 1-44; John 7. 12-30
SELFLESSNESS
A love for God's people is surely the noblest of traits. But in numbering the people David incurred God's displeasure. Though quick to admit his own foolishness, Israel still suffered the pestilence as a consequence, and seventy thousand perished. Folly indeed! But as the angel's hand is lifted to smite Jerusalem, David cried, 'I it is that have sinned . . . but as for these sheep, what have they done? Let thine hand, I pray thee, O Lord my God, be on me . . . but not on thy people', v. 17.

Hundreds of years earlier, on the day Moses descended the mount, three thousand died as a result of Israel's apostasy in the matter of the golden calf, yet Moses cried, 'Yet now, if thou wilt forgive their sin- : and if not, blot me I pray thee, out of thy book, which thou hast written', Exod. 32. 32. A thousand years later, in the day of Israel's blindness, Paul exclaims, 'I could wish that I myself were accursed from Christ for my brethren', Rom. 9. 3.

Nothing can compare, however, to the love of the Good Shepherd who laid down His life for the sheep. The apostle takes the self-humbling of the Lord in 'obedience unto death, even the death of the cross', Phil. 2. 8, as the pattern for us: 'Let this mind be in you, which was also in Christ Jesus', v. 5.

These are surely lessons for us: that in our repentance God can use even *failure* to mould us after His pattern, for David's selfless disregard is a measure of his greatness. The marred vessel can indeed be 'made again another vessel, as seemed good to the potter to make it', Jer. 18. 4. We learn too that sacrifice, like failure, can be costly, for he says, 'I will not take that which is thine for the Lord, nor offer burnt offerings without cost', 1 Chr. 21. 24. What price are we prepared to pay for His 'sheep'?

> Saviour, Thy dying love Thou gavest me,
> Nor should I aught withhold,
> My Lord from Thee;
> In love my soul would bow, my heart fulfil its vow,
> Some offering bring Thee now,
> Something for Thee.

SYLVANUS PHELPS

November 7th

1 Chronicles 22-23; Ezekiel 20. 45 – 21. 32; **John 7. 31 – 8. 11**

HIS UNIQUENESS

The story of the woman taken in adultery is, sadly, a parable for our modern times. Yet, like a gem against a dark background or a star against the night sky, so Christ stands out as 'the light of the world', v. 12, a beacon of holiness in a dark world. What a testimony to His lovely manhood that, when challenged to let him 'that is without sin . . . first cast a stone', v. 7, we read, 'They went out one by one' until 'Jesus was left alone', v. 9. Well might His enemies confess that 'never man spake like this man', 7. 46, and the people exclaim, 'We never saw it on this fashion', Mark. 2. 12, and that 'he doeth all things well', 7. 37. The response of the Shulamite to the challenge 'What is thy beloved more than another?' is surely apposite: 'His speech is the very perfection of sweetness! And Himself – the concentration of loveliness', S. of S. 5. 9, 16 HELEN SPURRELL. Those closest to Him were moved in reverential fear to say, 'What manner of man is this! for he commandeth even the winds and water, and they obey him', Luke 8. 25.

But the greatest testimony, and the only verdict that ever mattered, was recorded at the Jordan, its banks teeming with sinful humanity, when Heaven declared, 'This is my beloved Son, in whom I am well pleased', Matt. 3. 17. After years of retrospect, and with the authority of an eyewitness, Peter affirms that He 'did no sin neither was guile found in his mouth', 1 Pet. 2. 22. And when calling to mind another night scene when He was transfigured before them in raiment that was 'white as the light' and with face shining 'like the sun', Matt. 17. 2, he attests, 'We were eyewitnesses of His majesty', 2 Pet. 1. 16. Well might John say, 'We beheld his glory, the glory as of the only begotten of the Father, full of grace and truth', John. 1. 14. He is indeed 'the chiefest among ten thousand', S. of S. 5. 10. Would that today, amidst the darkness, we too might get a glimpse of Him!

> Without a trace of Adam's sin,
> As Man unique in origin,
> All fair without, all pure within,
> Our blessed Lord!

I. EWAN

November 8th

1 Chronicles 24-25; **Ezekiel 22;** John 8. 12-30

STAND IN THE GAP!

To stand for what is right in a day of wrong is never easy. Here, Ezekiel is challenged to confront Jerusalem with 'all her abominations'. Instead of being a testimony as God had intended, they had become 'a reproach to the heathen, and a mocking to all', v. 4. Sadly, leaders who should have taken a stand for what was right themselves embodied the worst of failure; priests made no 'difference between the unclean and the clean', v. 26; princes set themselves 'to destroy souls', v. 27 and prophets prophesied falsely, v. 25, 28. No wonder, then, that the people also acted 'wrongfully', v. 29.

Yet, just when everything seems lost, God calls for 'a man among them, that should make up the hedge, and stand in the gap before me for the land', v. 30. Ultimately, only one man is able to answer that challenge; six centuries later Messiah himself appeared, 'and he saw that there was no man, and wondered that *there was* no intercessor: therefore his arm brought salvation unto him', Isa. 59. 16.

In dark days of testimony, God has always had His man, or His woman. In the days of Eli, He had a Samuel; in the days of the judges, a Deborah; in the days of captivity, a Daniel, and after the exile, a Haggai – 'the Lord's messenger in the Lord's message', Hag. 1. 13. As a result of Haggai's lonely stand, a prince, a priest, and then 'all the remnant of the people', v. 14, set themselves to work.

Who will take a stand for Him today? And who can tell the result if we do?

> Stand up, stand up for Jesus!
> The trumpet call obey;
> Forth to the mighty conflict
> In this His glorious day!
> Ye that are His, now serve Him
> Against unnumbered foes;
> Let courage rise with danger,
> And strength to strength oppose.
> GEORGE DUFFIELD

November 9th

1 Chronicles 26-27; **Ezekiel 23;** John 8. 31-59

PRIVILEGE AND RESPONSIBILITY

Contrasting with the world which 'hath not known thee', the Lord Jesus, when praying to the Father, said of His own, 'This is life eternal, that they might know Thee the only true God, and Jesus Christ whom Thou hast sent', John 17. 3, 25. His own 'are not of the world, even as I am not of the world' v. 14. Intimacy with Him should effect how we live, and mark us out as different – in order 'that the world might know', v. 23.

Tragically, in our chapter that wasn't so. Here, toward the end of Old Testament history, Jerusalem and Samaria are depicted in parable as two sisters, Aholibah and Ahola; they were daughters of one mother, the Kingdom of Judah. 'Aholibah' means 'my tent is in her', a reminder of Jerusalem's great heritage as the place of God's sanctuary. Tragically, instead of this making a difference, we learn how they defiled themselves by forming alliance with the nations around them and thus incurring God's displeasure. The historical parallels, in the days of King Ahaz, can be read in 2 Kings chapter 16.

The New Testament challenges us time and again as to whether our relationship with the Lord really makes a difference to our lives. It certainly should! Peter says that 'as he which hath called you is holy, so be ye holy in all manner of conversation'; James challenges us, 'Know ye not that the friendship of the world is enmity with God?' Jas. 4. 4. John warns, 'Love not the world, neither the things that are in the world. If any man love the world, the love of the Father is not in him', 1 John 2. 5.

How, otherwise, will the world ever know Christ, unless they see Him first in us? Of the blessed man who 'walked not in the counsel of the ungodly' the psalmist said, 'In his law doth he meditate day and night', Ps. 1. 2. If we want to be like Him, we need to spend much time in His presence.

> Take time to be holy, the world rushes on;
> Spend much time in secret, with Jesus alone.
> By looking to Jesus, like Him thou shalt be;
> Thy friends in thy conduct His likeness shall see.

W. D. LONGSTAFF

November 10th

1 Chronicles 28; Ezekiel 24-25; **John 9. 1-17**

HIS WORK IN US

The problem of sickness and suffering has perplexed many. In the case of this blind man they asked, 'Who did sin?' The Lord's answer is most instructive; it was not Who, but Why? It was in order that 'the works of God should be manifest in him', v. 3. One of the greatest lessons for Christian living is that God has a work to perform *in* us, and not just through us. The writer's prayer for the suffering Hebrew Christians was that the Great Shepherd of the sheep would 'make you perfect in every good work to do his will, working in you that which is well pleasing in His sight', Heb. 13. 21. In the midst of suffering, the Philippians are assured with confidence that 'he which hath begun a good work in you will perform it', Phil. 1. 6. And Paul explains that God's ultimate work in us is that 'Christ be formed in you', Gal. 4. 19.

If we allow God to do His work in us then our appreciation and worship of Him will increase day by day. This was certainly the experience of the man whose eyes were opened in John chapter 9. He first describes the Lord as just *'a man called Jesus'*, v. 11; then as 'a *prophet'*, v. 17; until finally we read that he confesses his belief in Him as the *Son of God,* 'and he worshipped him', v. 38. The work of God in him changed him forever. The change was so radical that 'they which before had seen him' were forced to ask, 'Is not this he that sat and begged?' v. 8.

There is a lesson here for us: it is as we allow the Lord to perform His work in us that He is able to work through us. Because of what they saw they asked, 'How were thine eyes opened?' v. 10, and he was able to tell them about 'a man that is called Jesus' and a place called Siloam where, he said, 'I received sight', v. 11! What greater privilege could we have today than to be asked by our neighbours to explain the difference in us, and to be able tell them about Christ and the place where we received our 'sight'?

> Have Thine own way Lord, have Thine own way;
> Hold o'er my being absolute sway!
> Fill with Thy Spirit till all shall see
> Christ only, always, living in me!

ADELAIDE A. POLLARD

November 11th
1 Chronicles 29; **Ezekiel 26;** John 9. 18-41

HIS CONTROL

In an awesome display of God's sovereign control over the circumstances of life, in response to what Tyrus 'hath said against Jerusalem', v. 2, the prophet foretells its judgement and ultimate obliteration. We read, 'Therefore thus saith the Lord God; Behold, I am against thee, O Tyrus', v. 3, and 'Though thou be sought for, yet shalt thou never be found again, saith the Lord God', v. 21. Besieged first by Nebuchadnezzar, history later records its final and complete destruction by Alexander the Great some 750 years later, exactly fulfilling the prophecy given.

Yet, we should not be surprised, for He who made the ages directs and controls all things, upholding them, and carrying them on to their appointed end 'by the word of his power', Heb. 1. 3. Mighty kings might lift their hand against God's people, but only as He allows. Although Israel suffered as slaves in Egypt, we discover that God had already told Abraham all about it some two centuries earlier, including that it would last for four hundred years, Gen. 15. 13. Later when the nation was taken captive by king Nebuchadnezzar, we discover that God had determined exactly how long it would last, just seventy years, Jer. 25. 11. Truly, He controls the ages! In respect of the Lord Jesus, 'they sought to take him; but no man laid hands on him, because his hour was not yet come', John 7. 30. And we can be just as sure that 'God has appointed a day, in the which he will judge the world', Acts 17. 31, for by His sovereign will He directs all things!

So, whatever our circumstances, remember that God is in control! If even one sparrow can't fall to the ground without our Father knowing, then Christ assures us that 'ye are of more value than many sparrows' and that 'the very hairs of your head are all numbered', Matt. 10. 30-31.

> My times are in Thy hand;
> Why should I doubt or fear?
> My Father's hand will never cause
> His child a needless tear.
> WILLIAM LLOYD

November 12th
2 Chronicles 1-2; Ezekiel 27; John 10. 1-18
THE HALF HAS NOT BEEN TOLD

'Ask what I shall give thee': what an opportunity! Yet, instead of asking for riches, honour, or long life, Solomon seeks wisdom to judge the people. Then, in a remarkable display of generosity, God granted him all of it – wisdom, riches, wealth, and honour. In his subsequent exaltation and glory there were none to compare, before or after! The Queen of Sheba testified, 'The one half of the greatness of thy wisdom was not told me: for thou exceedest the fame that I heard', 2 Chr. 9. 6.

Yet we are sure that 'a greater than Solomon is here', Matt. 12. 42. Described as 'the brightness of God's glory', Heb. 1. 3, He Himself spoke of the pre-existent 'glory that I had with thee before the world was', John 17. 5. When He was on earth He 'manifested forth his glory' in the signs that He performed, 2. 11. John was a witness of Christ's glory', John 1. 14. Yet to this glory is added even more for, looking beyond the grave, Peter affirms that God 'raised him up from the dead, and gave him glory', 1 Pet. 1. 21. Further, the writer of the Epistle to the Hebrews declares, 'We see Jesus, made a little lower than the angels . . . crowned with glory and honour', Heb. 2. 9.

One day that glory will be manifest to men, for 'they shall see the Son of man coming in the clouds of heaven with power and great glory', Matt. 24. 30. Yet, we His beloved believing people will see it first for, did He not pray, 'Father, I will that they also, whom thou hast given me, be with me where I am; that they might behold my glory', John 17. 24? How wonderful it is that He will share that glory with us then, for He also prayed 'the glory which thou gavest me I have given them', v. 22. One day His prayer will be answered and we will be glorified, but until then, just as He did, we can anticipate that glory as being already ours and manifest it to men by the lives that we live.

> We share Thy joy in Him who sitteth there;
> Our hearts delight in Thy delight in Him;
> Chiefest of thousands, fairer than the fair;
> His glory naught can tarnish, naught can dim.
>
> W. B. DICK

November 13th
2 Chronicles 3-4; **Ezekiel 28;** John 10. 19-42
HIS EXAMPLE
Typical of our race, twice over we read of the Prince of Tyrus that 'thine heart is lifted up', vv. 2, 5. However, although in sinful pride he had set his heart 'as the heart of God', the Lord says 'yet thou art a man, and not God' v. 2. The King of Tyrus was 'in Eden the garden of God' v. 13, and his attitude is certainly reminiscent of Satan's own downfall, 'for thou hast said in thine heart, I will ascend into heaven, I will exalt my throne above the stars of God', Isa. 14. 13.

Such rebellious pride has marked the history of man ever since. It was true of the first man. It was in response to the serpent's claim that 'thou shalt be as gods, knowing good and evil' that Eve took the fruit, Gen. 3. 5. Similarly, at the end of the age the man of sin will sit 'in the temple of God, shewing himself that he is God', 2 Thess. 2. 4.

Thank God, then, for the Second Man! He is altogether different! Of Him we read, 'Who, being in the form of God, thought it not robbery to be equal with God: but made himself of no reputation, and took upon him the form of a servant', Phil. 2. 6-7. Thus, in utter humility in the Upper Room, the man who was their Lord and Master took a basin and a towel and began to wash His disciples' feet. Later that same night the One who was the great 'I AM' allowed men to bind Him and lead Him away, in fulfilment of Isaiah's prophecy that He would be led 'as a lamb to the slaughter', Isa. 53. 7.

In response to Peter in the Upper Room, the Lord Jesus also said, 'if I then, your Lord and Master, have washed your feet; ye also ought to wash one another's feet', John 13. 14. Paul adds, 'Let this mind be in you, which was also in Christ Jesus', Phil. 2. 5. Imagine how different it would be if we followed His example! Imagine the grace and submissiveness of Christ!

> None but Thyself, O God, could estimate
> His riches vast, His condescension great,
> His stoop from glory's sphere in grace sublime,
> To move in servant form through scenes of time.
> W. KIRKPATRICK

November 14th
2 Chronicles 5. 1 – 6. 11; Ezekiel 29-30; **John 11. 1-27**

DOUBTS AND DELAYS

Its precious metals, glorious hangings, and seal skin covering were from an altogether different place. Yet, although never appreciated by the casual passer-by, how their glory must have caught the eye of those who entered those tabernacle courts! So here, earth's sombrest landscape was but a backdrop 'for the glory of God, that the Son of God might be glorified thereby', v. 4. Here, He would be revealed as being from an altogether different place, the great 'I am' of resurrection and of life, v. 25.

The glory of God is one of John's great themes. It was so here in John's last sign of Jesus' ministry, just as it was in his first, at the marriage in Cana, where also we read that 'he manifested forth his glory', John. 2. 11. What a lesson for us that whether in life's gladdest or saddest moments, His glory must come first.

John also delights to trace the development of faith and does so here where Martha's exclamation 'yea, Lord: I believe that thou art the Christ, the Son of God', v. 27, follows days of doubt and delay. The apparent reproach of both Martha and Mary, 'Lord, if thou hadst been here, my brother had not died', vv. 21, 32, is echoed later by the Jews who ask, 'Could not this man, which opened the eyes of the blind, have caused that even this man should not have died?' v. 37. How reminiscent of the disciples in the storm, 'Master, carest thou not that we perish?' Mark 4. 38. In both cases their reproach was prompted by the apparent delays of Christ. Here 'he abode two days still in the same place', v. 6. So, why the delay? In the first case the delay was not His, but theirs! Lazarus had been dead four days by the time He arrived, having waited two days to depart, so they must have delayed until the very day Lazarus died before sending for Him! But in His gracious overruling the delays of the journey only heightened His glory, and 'many of the Jews ... believed on Him', v. 44.

> O what peace we often forfeit,
> O what needless pain we bear,
> All because we do not carry
> Everything to God in prayer.
>
> JOSEPH SCRIVEN

November 15th
2 Chronicles 6. 12-42; Ezekiel 30. 20 – 31. 18; **John 11. 28-54**

THE EMOTIONS OF CHRIST

Think of the wonder of a weeping Christ! Here we read, 'When Jesus saw her weeping . . . Jesus wept', John 11. 33, 35. Twice more at least he wept: in sorrow at what could have been, He wept over the City, as He descended Mt. Olivet for the last time. Luke tells us that 'He beheld the city and wept over it', Luke 19. 41. He also wept in the Garden in sorrow at what was yet to be, offering up supplication and prayer 'with strong crying and tears', Heb. 5. 7. Those tears were precious and never will they be forgotten: the psalmist assures us, 'Thou tellest my wanderings: put thou my tears into thy bottle: are they not in thy book?' Ps. 56. 8.

Think too of the wonder of a troubled Christ! John tells us here that in sympathy with Mary He 'groaned in the spirit, and was troubled', v. 33. Twice more we read, 'Now is my soul troubled . . . Father, save me from this hour; but for this cause came I unto this hour', 12. 27, and again, 'he was troubled in spirit, and testified and said . . . one of you shall betray me', 13. 21. How assuring it must have been to those disciples that it was One who had Himself been troubled who twice tells, 'Let not your heart be troubled, 14. 1, 27!

He still feels for His own for 'in all things it behoved him to be made like unto his brethren, that he might be a merciful and faithful high priest', Heb. 2. 17. Referring to the tender emotions of her beloved, the Shulamite said, 'His belly is as bright ivory overlaid with sapphires', S. of S. 5. 14. Obtained through suffering and death, that ivory is now covered with the blue of heaven! For upon the throne He still identifies with His own and 'in all their affliction, he was afflicted', Isa. 63. 9. Be assured, as will the remnant of Israel in a future day of tribulation, that whatever the experiences of the day, 'He that toucheth you toucheth the apple of his eye', Zech. 2. 8.

> It tells of One whose loving heart
> Can feel my deepest woe,
> Who in my sorrow bears a part
> That none can bear below.
>
> FREDERICK WHITFIELD

November 16th
2 Chronicles 7; Ezekiel 32; **John 11. 55 – 12. 19**

WORSHIP

As the Lord enters the final week before the cross it begins with two contrasting acts of worship. First, Mary anoints Him, and then the crowds hail His entry to Jerusalem. While the entry foreshadows His second coming, it also provides a contrast to Mary's act of devotion for which she is always remembered, Matt. 26. 13.

Mary's act was personal, while the other was public. What she did is surrounded by hostility, with Christ threatened before it, John 11. 57, and one of His own after it, 12. 10-11. The entry to Jerusalem by contrast was popular, but only superficially. This is similar to the world today, where many profess Christianity but know nothing of Christ's Lordship, or true worship. The latter is often to be found in small, seemingly insignificant places, where those who truly love Him serve like Martha, enjoy fellowship like Lazarus, and worship Him as Mary did. The first mention of worship, Gen. 18. 2, where Abraham 'bowed himself', the Hebrew word elsewhere translated 'worship', and when the wise men worshipped, Matt. 2. 2, 11, are similar. In both cases the surroundings are humble and the worshippers are few, but Christ is in the midst, and what is given is costly and appreciated.

What Mary brought was also costly, approximately a year's wages. The crowds, by contrast, only laid down garments to take them up again and palm branches which were supplied by nature. Her worship was *sacrificial,* she withheld the ointment from her brother's burial, and his body stank, 11. 39, but she bestowed it on her Saviour. For Mary the experience was *humbling* as she used her hair, given for glory, to wipe His feet. What she did was also *intelligent* and *prophetic*; she recognized that He would need burial preparation and would soon leave them.

Finally her worship was lasting and *appreciated*. She is not recorded as being present at the cross, but the effect of what she did was in the aroma of her sacrifice. By contrast, the crowds would soon turn from crying 'Hosanna' to 'Away with him'. The Lord knew this, and pointed out that their rejoicing would soon turn to sorrow, Luke. 19. 42-44, but Mary's sorrow, and ours, will soon be turned to joy, John. 16. 19-24.

November 17th
2 Chronicles 8-9; Ezekiel 33; John 12. 20-50

A GREATER THAN SOLOMON

The achievements and greatness of Solomon are brought to a climax in today's chapters. They start with a summary of his great **works** and finish with a statement of his great **wealth**. In between in the first half of chapter 9 is the visit of the Queen of Sheba, and confirmation of his great **words** and **wisdom**. Having tried him with hard questions, and having observed his household and his servants 'there was no more spirit in her', and she declared that 'the half . . . had not been told'.

In the New Testament there are few references to Solomon. In fact, apart from genealogies or buildings, Matthew and Luke both record the only two direct references. In one the Lord Jesus affirms that He is 'a greater than Solomon'. In the other He tells us that Solomon 'in all his glory' was not arrayed like one of the lilies, which He created. Perhaps an even more wonderful description of Solomon's reign is found in Psalm 72. Yet even here the psalmist, under divine inspiration, seems to extol a greater than Solomon. He tells us of one who is both King and the King's son, no doubt picturing the King of kings. He goes on to extol the great character of His kingdom, righteousness and peace. Sadly, Solomon's righteousness was limited, and he is remembered for his failure, Neh. 13. 26. In contrast, the 'greater than Solomon' not only established the basis of righteousness and peace at the cross, the greatest work ever accomplished, but will also rule on this basis in a coming day, displaying infinite wisdom. Solomon's wealth is seen in that he ruled from 'the river to the end of the earth', and from 'sea to sea'. In his day this meant from the Euphrates to the tip of Sinai, and from the Dead Sea to the Mediterranean, but in Christ's day it will be from a new living river in Jerusalem and literally extend worldwide, Zech. 14. 8-9. Solomon's words were exceeded by the Lord Jesus as He 'spoke the words no other man could speak' causing men to proclaim 'never man spake like this man'. Among those words was His prayer, 'Glorify me with the glory that I had with thee before the world was'. No doubt this has been answered, and one day we shall behold His glory and proclaim, 'The half has not been told'.

November 18th
2 Chronicles 10-11; **Ezekiel 34**; John 13. 1-30

GODLY SHEPHERDING

Shepherding is one of the great themes of scripture. God has always looked favourably on those who look after sheep. In Genesis alone we see the examples of Abel, Abraham, Jacob, and Joseph, amongst others. The two greatest leaders of God's people in the Old Testament, Moses and David, both spent much of their formative years as shepherds. In a world where leadership is often associated with strong personality, authority, and assertiveness, it is important that God's people do not unwittingly follow the world's concepts. Moses is described as 'the meekest man in all the earth'. David, a 'man after God's own heart', while fierce in battle with his enemies, is gentle with his flock, in contrast to his nephews who, he says, are 'too hard for me', 2 Sam. 3. 39.

As Ezekiel prophesies, God's people are in the final throes of being taken into captivity. Like many of the prophets, Ezekiel seeks to explain how and why this has occurred. Repeatedly, he focuses on the leaders of the nation as having failed. This chapter, more than any other, lays the blame firmly at the door of the shepherds rather than the sheep! Their failure includes failing to feed the sheep, vv. 2-3, and not tending to them, v. 4. As a result, the sheep are spoiled and scattered, vv. 5-6. God will judge the shepherds, vv. 7-10. In the remainder of the chapter God Himself promises to provide true shepherding like that of David.

Sadly, among God's people today similar circumstances can be found. Many have been allowed to drift away, having experienced a lack of care, attention, and spiritual sustenance. It appears that there is no shortage of those who want to be elders or overseers, but not so many genuine shepherds. Perhaps this is because true shepherding is costly, as seen in John chapter 10, where we have the supreme example of 'the Good Shepherd' who 'gives His life for the sheep'. Peter, a natural leader, is taught this lesson and the need to 'feed' and 'tend' the 'lambs' and the 'sheep', John 21. The lesson is then passed on in 1 Peter chapter 5, where he emphasizes the need for true shepherds and 'examples', not 'lords'. Just as in Ezekiel chapter 34, the 'Chief Shepherd' will appear to gather all His sheep safely into His fold.

November 19th

2 Chronicles 12-13; Ezekiel 35. 1 – 36. 15; **John 13. 31 – 14. 14**

I WILL COME AGAIN

John chapters 13 to 17 is the **private** section of the Gospel, recorded only by John, often called 'the Upper Room ministry'. It is preceded by a **public** section which revolves around seven wondrous signs, five of which are unique to John. The Gospel concludes with a **personal** section where Jesus is alone. Like the other Gospels, this records the Lords' arrest, trial, crucifixion, and resurrection, but finishes with a chapter recording events not described elsewhere. John's Gospel is radically distinct from the others. In Matthew, Mark, and Luke the disciples are largely seen as a remnant of a failed earthly people, Israel, and the Lord's discourses with them concern His coming earthly kingdom, conditions within it, and judgement on their enemies. These are not recorded by John whose emphasis is on the Lord going to heaven and those who will follow Him to His Father's house. The disciples are now seen as the nucleus of a heavenly people, the church, rather than the remnant of an earthly people, Israel. The Upper Room ministry concentrates on the giving of the Holy Spirit at the commencement of the church age, and the need to 'love one another' which should characterize the period. Now John gives us the first direct announcement of the event which will conclude the church age, the removal of God's people from earth to heaven.

This is not an event previously prophesied, as can be seen from the Lord's teaching in chapter 5 where He speaks only of the final resurrection and judgements of all the living and dead as revealed by Daniel, vv. 28-29. However, He does perhaps also indicate another more imminent event in verse 25 when 'they that hear shall live'. This event is illustrated in chapter 11 when a dead man, Lazarus, is raised in response to Christ's loud cry, and the Lord speaks not only of the dead living, but of the living never dying. Now, in chapter 14, the Lord Jesus promises His disciples such an event, and seeks to focus their attention on 'His Father's house' rather than the world He is leaving behind. In chapter 17 He will make this event His final request for all of us, that we may be with Him where He is, and behold His glory. What a wonderful prospect we have – leaving this world for His Father's house!

November 20th
2 Chronicles 14-15; **Ezekiel 36. 16-38**; John 14. 15-31
ARE WE CONCERNED FOR GOD'S HOLY NAME?

Our selected text emphasizes the importance that God places on purity in our lives, and how this can impact on His holy character. Notwithstanding all the privileges that had been conferred upon Israel, they had systematically polluted the land, and this is compared metaphorically by God to a state of menstrual impurity, cp. Lev. 15. 19-30, and directly linked to unrestrained idolatry, v. 18. As a consequence, God punished Israel by scattering them throughout the nations, vv. 18-19. Notice that God's sentence upon Israel was proportionate to 'their conduct and their actions', v. 19b NIV. But this punishment led to God's holy name being impugned by these other nations. They simply read into the exile narrative that Israel's God was not unique or different from the other gods around, and that He could not prevent their dispersion, v. 20. This now touches on Ezekiel's overall theology. If Israel was discredited amongst the nations then so was God's holy name, v. 21, cp. Isa. 52. 5; Rom. 2. 24. So the basis of Israel's ultimate restoration to the land would not be because they were deserving of blessing, but because God would reclaim and vindicate His holy name again amongst His people, v. 22, cp. Deut. 30. 3-5; Isa. 48. 11. God would reverse the wickedness of Israel, and, in so doing, demonstrate unequivocally His sovereignty over the nations, vv. 23-24, see Ezek. 38. 23.

God's transformation of Israel is both outward and inward. He firstly sprinkles His people symbolically with clean water because visibly they were unclean, v. 25, Jer. 2. 22. Then He performs a much more delicate operation, a heart transplant, and also puts a new spirit into them, because internally they had been persistently hard-hearted and lacking in faith, vv. 26-28, cp. Jer. 31. 31-34. The results of this initiative are then evident as Israel is reconciled to God, and the land is replenished to resemble the garden of Eden, vv. 28-38. As if to underscore the point, God again reminds Israel that their forgiveness is based solely on the principle of grace, v. 32. Praise God today for His grace in Christ towards us, 2 Cor. 8. 9, but let us ever be mindful that impurity in our lives can bring God's holy name into disrepute, 2 Cor. 7. 1.

November 21st

2 Chronicles 16-17; **Ezekiel 37;** John 15. 1-16

BONES, STICKS, AND LIFE FROM THE DEAD!

We may be familiar with today's passage, but seldom do we imagine the impact these prophecies must have had on the prophet himself. He firstly sees a vision of a valley filled with dry or sun bleached bones, compare pictures of the later Holocaust, vv. 1-2. The scene was one of desolation, and Ezekiel must have reflected on the demise of his nation. He is then asked a seemingly rhetorical question, 'Can these bones live again?' Humanly speaking, this was impossible, but Ezekiel had learnt from childhood that he served the God of the impossible, Deut. 32. 39. Being instructed to prophesy over the dead, Ezekiel sees a miracle take place before his very eyes, vv. 4-10. 'Ezekiel must have felt many times in the past that he was preaching to the dead' CRAIGIE.

The miracle is in two parts. Initially, the bones are reconstituted with sinew, flesh, and skin, but with no apparent life, vv. 7-10. The deafening noise of the operation is complemented by the staggering precision of matching bones coming together, v. 7. Ezekiel is then instructed to prophesy for the breath or Spirit of God to infuse life into these bodies, and a vast company of people miraculously comes alive again, v. 10. Despite the lack of hope evident amongst God's exilic people, v. 11b, cp. Ps. 137. 1-4, the imagery represents their restoration from what was tantamount to death to new (resurrection) life in their homeland again, vv. 11-14, cp. Psalm 126. The prophet then has a second vision where he is commanded to write on two separate sticks, the names of the tribes of the southern and northern kingdoms, vv. 15-17, cp. Num. 17. 16-26. The sticks are then fused together, symbolizing the future reunification of Judah and Israel, vv. 18-22, ultimately under a Davidic king, vv. 22-28. God's sovereignty is emphasized by the repetition of the personal pronoun 'I' in verses 21-23, culminating with 'I will be their God', v. 23b. This reunification has not yet taken place, so the fulfillment is yet future. God will perform this miracle, a nation re-born and reconciled to Himself, Rom. 11. 15, 25-31, and Christ, David's greater Son, Mark 12. 35-37, reigning, Rev. 11. 15. Praise God today for His faithfulness in fulfilling His promises, Rom. 11. 29.

November 22nd
2 Chronicles 18-19; Ezekiel 38; **John 15. 17 – 16. 15**
IT IS EXPEDIENT FOR YOU THAT I GO AWAY
In this section the Lord contrasts the love that must be found among His own with the hatred they will experience from the world. This hatred is seen in its extremity later that night when the Lord is taken, abused, tried, and crucified. That, however, is viewed by Him as 'going to His Father', v. 5, and He declares, 'It is expedient for you that I go away', v. 7. These are remarkable words, for they indicate that the disciples (and we who follow on from them) are going to be better off after He has gone. The reason why is found in His repeated promise of another 'Comforter', the Holy Spirit.

There are four reasons why this age of the Spirit brings great privileges to the child of God. Firstly, there is the provision of eternal security. The Lord has intimated that the Comforter will 'abide with you forever', 14. 16. What a contrast to the events of that night, when the Lord Jesus would be taken from them! The Spirit is called the 'earnest' or guarantee of our full and final salvation, Eph. 1. 14; 2 Cor. 1. 22. He will never be taken from us.

Secondly, in chapter 15 verses 26-27, Christ affirmed, 'He shall testify of me', and 'Ye also shall bear witness'. This stands in stark contrast to the six trials of the Lord that followed, with nobody testifying for Him, no witnesses for His defence, and when He 'opened not His mouth'. But now the Holy Spirit exposes sinners. His coming makes us living witnesses of man's sin, Christ's righteousness, and judgement on 'the prince of this world', 16. 8-11.

Thirdly, vv. 12-13, the Lord explains that they cannot take in what He would like to tell them now, but the Spirit will bring them into 'all truth', and show them 'things to come'. Thus He educates saints through the completed word of God.

Finally, vv. 14-15, we find that the Spirit exalts the Saviour. That night, Christ would be humiliated and dishonoured, but henceforth the Spirit will glorify Him by producing resemblance in us.

The Comforter secures and educates His people, exposes sinners, and exalts the Saviour. How true the Lord's teaching: 'It is expedient for you that I go away', v. 7!

November 23rd
2 Chronicles 20; **Ezekiel 39;** John 16. 16-33.

WILL I . . . HAVE MERCY UPON THE WHOLE HOUSE OF ISRAEL

The beginning of this chapter concludes the judgements of God on the nations, while its end prophesies Israel's return to Him and to their land. This introduces the final chapters which are taken up, amongst other things, with this future day of restoration. The judgements on Gog and Magog, like much of Ezekiel, are paralleled in Revelation, where the destruction of earthly armies culminates in chapter 19 and is followed by a thousand year reign of Christ on earth, ch. 20. These enemies are from the north and cannot be easily identified with the enemies found in Ezekiel's day and may refer to more modern foes, such as Russia, who invariably support Israel's opponents. Clearly, Israel still has a huge significance today. It features in the news almost daily, is the subject of more United Nations resolutions than any other state, and its people have been subjected to continued oppression and opposition, including the Holocaust seventy years ago. Jews are targeted all over the world and even in Christian circles many deny that they have any future, with their blessings and promises now transferred to the church.

This flies in the face of Ezekiel, and, indeed, almost all the prophetic books of our Old Testament, which demand literal fulfilment of God's many promises to Israel. The covenant God made with Israel through Moses was dependent on them keeping the law, in which they failed miserably. This resulted in the disasters which overtook them in Ezekiel's day, and explains their situation today. However, before the covenant with Moses, God made one with Abraham concerning the land and its dimensions which was not conditional, Gen. 12. 1-3; 15. 18-21, and confirmed in Genesis chapter 17. Later, God made another unconditional covenant with David concerning the throne, not only in respect of his son, but his descendants for ever, 2 Sam. 7. Ezekiel confirms this in chapter 37 verse 25. Now in chapter 39 he makes clear that the entire nation will be restored to their land. Today, despite their unbelief, God preserves the Jewish people, but following their recognition of Christ, Zech. 12. 10, and repentance, Isa. 53, God will restore them both spiritually and literally, vv. 28-29.

November 24th
2 Chronicles 21-22; **Ezekiel 40;** John 17

THE GLORY OF THIS LATTER HOUSE SHALL BE GREATER

The above quotation from Haggai chapter 2 verse 9 refers to the temple being built by the exiles returned from the captivity of Ezekiel's day. This remnant were being encouraged by Haggai even though in verse 3 he agrees that their house is 'as nothing' compared to 'this house in her first glory', referring to Solomon's temple built to God's instruction, but destroyed by the Babylonians. The rebuilt temple never achieved the promise, and suffered desecration at the hands of Antiochus Epiphanes. It was rebuilt for the Jews by Herod, taking forty-six years, John 2. 20. This temple during the Lord's time on earth, though clearly a magnificent structure physically, never achieved moral or spiritual glory, and was also destroyed in AD 70. The books of Daniel and Revelation indicate that a temple will be built again in Jerusalem, but it will be defiled by the Antichrist, as prophesied by the Lord Jesus in the Gospels, and so can also never be filled with glory. However, as we have already seen in chapter 39, all God's promises must be fulfilled.

The remaining chapters of Ezekiel describe in detail a magnificent temple in Jerusalem, its system of administration and worship, and the city and land in which it is found. These descriptions are so detailed containing measurements, materials, and instructions which have enabled plans to be produced. In order to have any real meaning or value, these chapters must describe a literal temple in Jerusalem. It has always been God's desire to dwell among His people. This is seen with Adam in the garden before the fall. It is seen again in the tabernacle, a temporary dwelling with no foundations, or even a floor, typifying the Lord Jesus who temporarily 'dwelt', among us, John 1. 14. It is seen again in the more permanent temple built by Solomon, and its successive iterations outlined above. This will culminate in the return of the Messiah for a thousand year reign centred in Jerusalem and with this 'house' achieving its 'latter glory'. Even this wonderful millennial kingdom will pass and the eternal New Jerusalem will need no temple, for God and the Lamb will be the temple, Rev. 21. 22.

November 25th
2 Chronicles 23-24; Ezekiel 41; John 18. 1-27
FAILURE WHEN GOOD INFLUENCES HAVE GONE
The reign of Joash follows a dark period in Israel's history. Joash was the last survivor of the royal line after his father was killed by Jehu, and his grandmother Athaliah destroyed the rest of the royal seed. As an infant he was hidden by his aunt, Jehoshabeath, and raised by her and her godly husband, Jehoiada the priest. At seven years of age he was raised to the throne, and Athaliah was killed at Jehoiada's command. God's providential care over the young king is seen not only in preserving his life and giving him godly guardians, but also by allowing Jehoiada's influence to persist during an unusually long life, 24. 15, which included more than half of the young king's forty-year reign.

Chapter 24 verse 2 tells of a good reign until the death of the priest. He paid great attention to the repair of the temple and the restoration of proper worship. Sadly, like many individuals, and indeed nations, things started to decline badly when spiritual influence was gone. This is a stark lesson for Christian families, and even western countries today which are rejecting their Christian heritage, resulting in ruination. The departure culminated in the murder of Jehoiada's son (or grandson) Zechariah, whom God sent to reprove the king. The Lord Jesus refers to this, along with the murder of Abel, as an example of the wicked killing the just all the way from Genesis to 2 Chronicles (the last book in the Hebrew Bible), Matt. 23. 35. The Lord locates the incident between 'the temple and the altar', thus perhaps shedding light on the book of Joel which unlike most prophetic books, is hard to place historically. In Joel a nation in ruins is called to repentance at the same spot where this murder took place, Joel 2. 17. God's mercy is still available if there is true repentance, and a return to where things went wrong. The calamities of Joel, and of nations and individuals today, can still be rectified if there is a return to where sin occurred and genuine repentance. However, God is not mocked, and all must reap what they sow, Gal. 6. 7.

Notice that Jehoiada has the great honour of burial with the kings, though not a king, v. 16, while Joash does not, even though he was a king, v. 25.

November 26th
2 Chronicles 25; Ezekiel 42; **John 18. 28 - 19. 16**
I FIND IN HIM NO FAULT AT ALL
The unashamed hypocrisy demonstrated in these verses by the Jewish authorities almost beggars belief! They had orchestrated the arrest of a perfectly innocent man, convened an illegal, night-time arraignment, and gathered witnesses whose only qualification to testify was that they were false! Having laid charges which, to their mind, justified a death sentence, they brought the Lord Jesus before Pilate to sanction their decision. But then, with an overwhelming weight of iniquity on their shoulders, we read 'they themselves went not into the judgment hall [Gentile territory], lest they should be defiled; but that they might eat the passover', while at the same time rejecting the Lamb of God!

Pilate, not in the best of humour having been called upon so early, at first dismissed this untimely intrusion. Hearing, however, that a capital sentence was being demanded, he no doubt felt that some interrogation was required. The dialogue between the Lord and Pilate was an exchange of searching questions and weighty responses resulting in a three-fold acknowledgement by the judge of the innocence of the accused. That should have been the end of the matter, but scripture must be fulfilled and 'His hour' was fast approaching. The despising and rejection, the low esteem in the eyes of the nation, the scourging and the smiting, the shame and the spitting would bring Old Testament prophecies to life.

Pilate, in a dilemma, made one last appeal to any vestige of pity which may have remained in the hearts of the Lord's accusers, all to no avail. Their cry was now not simply that He ought to die, but a clamour for the most painful, the most shameful, the most agonisingly drawn out form of execution, 'Crucify him, crucify him'. Fear finally gripped the heart of the superstitious Roman as a fresh accusation was heard above the uproar, 'he made himself the Son of God'. Again, Pilate questioned the Lord Jesus and 'sought to release him'. Yet, doubtless energized by the adversary himself, political expediency was brought to bear upon Pilate, and, with a final cry of derision, 'Behold your king', he delivered Him 'unto them to be crucified'.

November 27th
2 Chronicles 26; Ezekiel 43; John 19. 17-42
PRIDE COMES BEFORE DESTRUCTION!

The long reign of Uzziah over Judah was exceeded in duration only by that of Manasseh the son of Hezekiah. It must, however, have seemed a daunting task which lay before this young man of only sixteen years, when he was placed on the throne by the people of Judah.

Nevertheless, his age proved to be no obstacle to his energy and zeal, as he sought the Lord and prospered, doing 'that which was right in the sight of the Lord'. No sooner had Amaziah his father passed off the scene, than Uzziah commenced a building programme which strengthened and improved the defences of Jerusalem, reclaimed territory and raised the profile of Judah in the eyes of their ancestral enemies. He was not only monarch, but builder, farmer, military engineer, campaign strategist and soldier, 'marvellously helped' and strengthened by his God.

Not content with all this, however, he wanted something more. He set his sights on the one area denied to him, the temple sanctuary, reserved exclusively for the sons of Aaron. The Spirit of God records his motive: Uzziah's 'heart was lifted up'. Pride, that deadliest of sins, had risen to the surface. No doubt with all he had achieved he felt invincible and unassailable. We read of Uzziah's 'host of fighting men', his 'mighty men of valour' and his army of 307,500 that made war. However, among the bravest men in Uzziah's kingdom were the eighty priests, deemed to be 'valiant men', who withstood the king in his intention to offer incense on the altar. Uzziah's father, Amaziah, had presumed on his military capabilities and challenged Joash the king of Israel, 2 Chr. 25. 17, only to suffer ignominious defeat. Uzziah's folly was much more serious; he had challenged God!

Sadly, the man with so much ability, whose reputation and name had 'spread far abroad', was 'thrust out' by the men whose office he sought to usurp. His pride put him not only out of the temple, but outside of the city, 'a leper unto the day of his death'.

The united offices of king and high priest are reserved alone for the One who, in millennial glory, will sit as 'a priest upon His throne', Zech. 6. 13.

November 28th
2 Chronicles 27-28; Ezekiel 44; John 20. 1-18
WHO IS MY NEIGHBOUR?
The reading today in 2 Chronicles brings before us two kings of Judah, with sharply contrasting characters. The two men were of similar age, both reigned for the same number of years, and both had godly fathers as examples. Yet Jotham 'did that which was right', while Ahaz 'did not that which was right'. Jotham, in fact, rose above the later deeds of his father, while Ahaz sank lower in his idolatry than most of the kings of Judah before him! Chapters 6 to 14 of Isaiah's prophecy cover the reign of these two kings, and should be read in order to understand the prevailing moral conditions of the day.

The record of Jotham's reign is brief. He exhibited many of his father's practical qualities and 'became mighty, because he prepared his ways before the Lord his God', a sure path to spiritual blessing.

When Ahaz assumed the throne, freed from the restraints of his father, he plunged headlong into a cesspool of idolatry. Once again, as often before, a holy God brought retribution upon the nation. A confederacy of the kings of Syria and Israel invaded from the north, with devastating results. It was at this time that the prophet Isaiah met Ahaz with a word of assurance from God that the adversaries would not prevail, and with a prophecy of Israel's fast-approaching captivity, Isa. 7. 1-9.

Such gracious guarantees were lost on Ahaz. Granted the opportunity to ask a sign of confirmation, he refused, claiming with mock piety that he would not 'tempt the Lord'. He then promptly turned to the king of Assyria for help; a futile exercise as we read, 'he helped him not'.

The brightest ray of light in this chapter is seen in the actions of the rulers of Ephraim, men of Samaria, encouraged by the prophet Oded. Instead of allowing the captives of Judah to be treated as spoils of war, these commendable 'princes' demanded their release, clothed, cleansed, and fed them, and then returned them to Jericho. We are reminded of another occasion on the Jericho road when a man from Samaria became a neighbour to one who, through no fault of his own, needed help and healing.

November 29th
2 Chronicles 29; Ezekiel 45; John 20. 19-31
THE WORK OF THE LORD WITH PASSION
This is a remarkable chapter for 'this chapter and those that follow bring out the character of Chronicles . . . Kings does not speak of the re-establishment of the worship, of the purification of the temple, or of the reorganization of the Levitical priesthood; Chronicles, by contrast, presents these measures as the only condition by which the kingdom of the son of David, and Judah itself, as a people, could subsist', writes H. L. ROSSIER.

The priority of his life, v. 3
As a relatively young man, it is pleasing to see Hezekiah start so well. Equally, it is important to see the standard to which he worked, 'that which was right in the sight of the Lord, according to all that David his father had done', v. 2. What a contrast with Ahaz! The doors of the house of the Lord that he had shut up and left to fall into ruin, Hezekiah opened and repaired.

The purification of the priests, v. 5
It is one thing to prepare the building but it is just as important to prepare the people who will serve within the building. The service of the Lord demands a sanctified priesthood, and that became Hezekiah's second task.

The passion of the king, v. 10
As the doors are opened and repaired and the Levites sanctified, the work gathers pace. What started in Hezekiah's heart is brought to fruition quickly. The last verse of the chapter tells us 'the thing was done suddenly', v. 36. But as we read through the chapter we see Hezekiah's hand in it all: 'he commanded the priests', v. 21; see also verses 24 and 27; 'he set the Levites', v. 25. His passion swept through the people present, and caused others to get involved; 'the king and all that were present with him bowed . . . and worshipped', v. 29. See the impact, vv. 31-32!

This chapter records how Hezekiah's rule *started*. It finished just as well: 'so that after him was none like him among all the kings of Judah, nor any that was before him', 2 Kgs. 18. 5. The secret of such a testimony is found in our headings. We must make the Lord's work the priority in our life, make purity the goal of our life, and be engaged in the work of the Lord with passion!

November 30th
2 Chronicles 30; Ezekiel 46; **John 21**

FEED MY SHEEP

Chapter 21 forms the epilogue to John's Gospel, and tells much of Peter and his future role. Most appropriately, it sits between the Gospels and the Acts, in the first twelve chapters of which Peter features prominently. Peter was a fisherman, and having already been told of one transformation in his life when he would become a 'fisher of men', he is now going to be told of another, which will result in him being a shepherd of the Lord's flock. Interestingly, the Lord often uses the animal kingdom to teach Peter lessons. The most common lessons are from **fish** to demonstrate dependence whether in catching a shoal of fish, Luke 5 and John 21, or a single fish, Matt. 17. The Lord uses other creatures, like the **cock** following his denial, the **unclean creatures** let down in a net in Acts 10, and the **sheep** here in our passage.

Peter is clearly a leader. He is often the first to speak or act, and others then follow. This can be for good or bad, and so such people are often the target of satanic attack, Luke 22. 31. Peter has been attacked, resulting in his denial, but is still very much the man others follow, John 21. 3. It is necessary for the Lord to complete Peter's recovery so that his future leadership will be improved. The Lord questions him three times, just as Peter denied Him three times in response to questions. He draws Peter's attention to the love, suffering, and hard work that will be required to shepherd God's flock. Sheep wander and fail, just as Peter had. They need to be fed and restored, like Peter. This will require the shepherd to love them, and suffer for them. These are vital lessons for all who would lead the Lord's people today. Worldly thinking suggests that ideally leaders should be assertive, commanding, and project themselves, but in the spiritual realm this is not to be so. Those who will 'tend' and 'feed' His 'lambs' and 'sheep' must love the Lord and His flock. They must suffer for them and, above all, be examples to them. It has been said 'an ounce of example is worth a ton of preaching'. How appropriate that Peter expounds these lessons, 1 Peter 5. 1-4, and that the Saviour recovers a man who made mistakes to shepherd His people, just as with David in the Old Testament.

December 1st

2 Chronicles 31; Ezekiel 47; **1 John 1. 1 – 2. 11**

'IF . . . SIN': SELF-DECEPTION OR SOLACE?

In this opening section of John's First Epistle, four times we read a conditional statement on the subject of sin, each beginning, 'If . . .'. The first two that we will consider depict the self-delusion of unbelievers; the latter two provide comfort for saints.

First, in chapter 1 verse 8, we read, '*If we say that we have no sin, we deceive ourselves, and the truth is not in us*'. Here we have the **principle** of sin. In the world today many deny that sin exists; others accept the reality of its existence, but think it is not in them. As the verse says, they are fooling themselves, and demonstrating that it is the truth, rather than sin, that is not in them.

The reference in chapter 1 verse 10, '*If we say that we have not sinned, we make him a liar, and his word is not in us*', is distinct from that in verse 8, which concerned the principle of sin; now we have the **practice**. The first refers to the root; the second to the fruit. Yet they are linked, for the practising of sins is the outcome of the sinful nature that we all have as human beings.

Unlike the deniers of God's Word, believers acknowledge the reality of sin within. However, we must not be content in that position. John says, 'These things write I unto you, that ye sin not', 2. 1. We are not expected to sin. Yet, sadly, when we do sin, there is a blessed reality: '*If any man sin*, we have an advocate with the Father, Jesus Christ the righteous'. The word for 'advocate' is the same word in Greek for 'comforter', which is used of the Holy Spirit, John 14. 16, 26; 15. 26; 16. 7. What an encouragement this is! If we sin, we have the Advocate, who is alongside the Father. He is the Righteous One, and He has already dealt fully with the matter of sins, 2. 2.

Hence we have the **promise**, 1. 9: '*If we confess our sins,* he is faithful and just to forgive us our sins, and to cleanse us from all unrighteousness'. This is not the forgiveness we received when we were saved; it was once-for-all, never needing to be repeated. Nothing can break our *union* with God, but sinning affects our *communion* with Him, and we need forgiveness, so that fellowship can be restored. Here we are assured that, upon honest confession, we have His forgiveness and cleansing.

December 2nd
2 Chronicles 32; **Ezekiel 48**; 1 John 2. 12-29

'THE LORD IS THERE'

In the final chapter of his prophecy, Ezekiel describes the future time, when the glory of God will be in residence on earth. And so the closing words of the book are 'The Lord is there', v. 35 – one of the lovely compound names of our God – *'Jehovah-Shammah'*. What a blessed day it will be when His presence will be so real that this divine title will be the name of the city of Jerusalem.

It is interesting to observe some of the conditions that will prevail in that millennial day, when 'the Lord is there':

Three times we read that the sanctuary 'shall be in the midst', vv. 8, 10, 21, and, associated with it, the oblation that shall be offered unto the Lord, v. 9. Evidently the presence of the Lord, and the offerings to be made to Him, will be of central importance.

In verse 14, we see that what is offered is not to be sold, or parted with in any other way – 'it is holy unto the Lord'. The people will not be free to treat lightly that which is His.

The description of what is 'in the midst' is in verses 8 to 22. Before this, vv. 1-7, and after it, vv. 23-29, the portion of each tribe is delineated. In that day, there will be a portion for every one of the people of God; none will be excluded.

We also observe that each of the gates of the city is identified, vv. 30-34. As well as providing a protected way into and out of a city the gate was the place of government. This shows that there will be orderliness, watchfulness, and divine government.

In verse 11, special honour is given to those priests 'which have kept my charge, which went not astray when the children of Israel went astray'. Faithfulness to God will be recognized by Him.

These things are future, but can be applied today to an assembly, of which the Lord says, 'There am I in the midst', Matt. 18. 20. In each such gathering, His presence, and spiritual sacrifices to Him, should be of central importance. Nor should our spiritual heritage be traded away, as if it were of little value. If things are as they ought to be, there will be a portion for every saint. There will be order, watchfulness, and godly government. Each believer should be faithful to God, knowing that this will honour Him. Happy the assembly where it is evident that 'the Lord is there'!

December 3rd
2 Chronicles 33; **Daniel 1**; 1 John 3
AN EXEMPLARY YOUNG MAN
What a delightful character we are introduced to in this chapter! Right from the beginning we can observe admirable traits in Daniel; qualities that we would all do well to emulate.

We see his **convictions**. Here is a young man, snatched away from his homeland, and placed in an environment where there is every temptation to compromise on his principles: he is both attractive physically and able mentally, v. 4, thus one whom his heathen captors would dearly love to have following their ideas. Moreover, the king is not one to take refusal to conform lightly, and Daniel is made aware that if he follows his principles, he could be putting others' lives in danger, v. 10.

However, he is undeterred. Why? Because of his **confidence** in God. So sure is he that God will honour his stance, and that there will be no danger either to himself or his friends or the king's servants, that he gives a test to prove God's faithfulness. And, of course, God fully vindicates Daniel's stance, vv. 12-15.

In his dealings with those who do not know the true God, we cannot fail to be impressed by his **courtesy**. He does not ride roughshod over those who are in ignorance, but, on the contrary, he deals with them sensitively. To be faithful to the truth, yet treat those who differ with us in a considerate way, is not easy, and Daniel is a good example of how to do it.

We also note Daniel's **company**. How important it is for believers to be together, and to encourage each other, especially when all around is contrary to us in our walk with God. Four young men are named, vv. 6, 11, 19, but clearly Daniel is the leader; for example, he is the one who 'purposed in his heart that he would not defile himself with the portion of the king's meat', v. 8. Doubtless his good influence strengthened the others in their convictions; so much so that, in chapter 3, when Daniel was not with them, they stood for God, in most trying circumstances.

It is also heartening to see Daniel's **consistency**. Here was no young man who was zealous in his youth, but who faded out of the picture in later life. No! as the chapter closes, we are told that he 'continued even unto the first year of king Cyrus', v. 21.

December 4th
2 Chronicles 34; Daniel 2. 1-23; 1 John 4
JOSIAH – A BRIGHT LIGHT IN A DARK DAY
As we near the end of 2 Chronicles, the picture is increasingly bleak as far as the kings of Judah are concerned. How refreshing it is therefore to come upon one last 'good' king – Josiah. In this chapter, we observe four pivotal years in his reign:

First we have the year when **'he began to reign'**, v. 1. Humanly speaking, circumstances were not promising: his predecessor, his father Amon, had been as wicked as they come, and lasted only two years on the throne before being murdered by his servants, leaving Josiah as king at only eight years of age. How refreshing it is to read that Josiah 'walked in the ways of David his father', v. 2. He did not follow the example of his father Amon, but of his father David, he got back to first principles, to the benefit of himself and his people. It is good to see that a person can rise above a disadvantaged start, and be mighty for God.

Secondly, our attention is drawn to **'the eighth year of his reign'**, v. 3, which gives us the secret of his good reign: he 'began to seek after the God of David his father'. In his mid-teens, when it is likely that most of his contemporaries were seeking worldly pleasures, he was seeking after God. How worthy an example this is for teenagers today, in a similarly godless environment.

Thirdly, in **'the twelfth year'**, v. 3, he began to purge out idolatry. Verses 3 to 7 indicate how comprehensively he did it. He realized how harmful idols and all associated with them were, and was uncompromising in his efforts to get rid of them. Probably few of us are guilty of bowing down to images, but we would have to confess that there are those things in our lives that so easily can take the place of God in our affections. These are idols, and Josiah's diligence in removal of idols is a commendable example.

Finally, we read of **'the eighteenth year'**, v. 8, which is described in the remainder of this chapter and up to verse 19 of the next. This year is characterized by two worthy actions: repair of God's house, vv. 8-13, and response to God's word, vv. 14-33. Once again, here is a pattern for us to follow: seeking to have godly order in the assemblies of which we form a part, and being convicted by the scriptures, resulting in repentance and recovery.

December 5th
2 Chronicles 35; Daniel 2. 24-49; **1 John 5**

'BORN OF GOD'

The phrase 'born of God', or 'begotten of God', occurs only in 1 John. In this final chapter, it is in three verses, and each of them has a practical lesson for us.

The first reference is in verse 1: 'Whosoever believeth that Jesus is the Christ is born of God: and every one that loveth him that begat loveth him also that is begotten of him'. The One 'that begat' is God; the one 'that is begotten' is my fellow-believer. Verse 2 confirms that this is so, as it speaks of loving God and loving the children of God. The teaching is clear: if I really am a child of God, then I will love my Father, and I will also love my brother – my fellow-believer. Putting it the other way round, if I do not love fellow-Christians, it puts a very big question mark over my profession to be a child of God.

The second is in verse 4: 'For whatsoever is born of God overcometh the world: and this is the victory that overcometh the world, even our faith'. The world is contrary to us, but all who are true believers have victory over it. The means of this triumph is 'our faith', because the object of our faith is the Lord Jesus Christ, as the following verse confirms: 'Who is he that overcometh the world, but he that believeth that Jesus is the Son of God?'

The third verse containing this phrase is verse 18: 'We know that whosoever is born of God sinneth not; but he that is begotten of God keepeth himself, and that wicked one toucheth him not'. That is, a true child of God does not live a life of habitual sinning. The phrase 'keepeth himself' does not mean that a believer knows preservation from a life of sin by his own strength – the testimony of scripture makes it clear that it is the Lord who preserves – but it does indicate that the child of God does have a responsibility to avoid a life of sin, and he can do this by divine help. Thus the adversary does not succeed in his claims upon the children of God nor can he do them any harm.

So, here are three tests to help me know if I really am 'born of God': Do I love other children of God? Is my constant faith in Him giving me victory over the world? And is my life characterized by seeking to please God, rather than by thraldom to sin and Satan?

December 6th
2 Chronicles 36; Daniel 3; 2 John
'TO FULFIL THE WORD OF THE LORD'
What a sorry picture is before us, as we reach the final chapter of 2 Chronicles, as far as the nation of Judah is concerned!

It is a pathetic scene as we view the *kings*, vv. 1-13: four evil kings quickly followed each other, vv. 1, 4, 8, 10, being at the mercy of foreign rulers, who could remove and replace them at will, and who carried them and their relatives away, vv. 4, 6, 10.

It is also a sad sight as we look at the *priests*, v. 14. The chief ones among them, who ought to have set an example, 'polluted the house of the Lord which he had hallowed'. That which was holy in the sight of God was desecrated, by the introduction of abominable heathen practices.

Against such a bleak background, we admire the faithfulness of the *prophets*, vv. 15, 16, and yet here we have an unhappy picture too, for the people mocked and misused these godly men, whom God in His compassion had sent to seek to turn them back to Himself. The nation, including the kings and priests, 'despised his words', arousing His wrath 'till there was no remedy'.

And so Nebuchadnezzar came without mercy, vv. 17-20, destroying the city, removing the temple treasures, killing many people, and transporting the survivors to Babylon.

On the face of it, it would appear that all was confusion. Yet, wonderfully, the book ends with mentions of two powerful Gentile kings, Nebuchadnezzar, vv. 20, 21, and Cyrus, vv. 22, 23, viewed, not as having total hegemony over God's people, but as instruments used in the hand of a sovereign God, to carry out His purposes. We are told that Nebuchadnezzar's destruction of the city and his carrying away of the people was 'to fulfil the word of the Lord by the mouth of Jeremiah', v. 21. And in the following verse we are told that it was in fulfilment of the same prophecy of Jeremiah, Jer. 25, that years later divine discipline having been carried out, Cyrus gave an edict to the very opposite effect: for the people to return to Jerusalem and rebuild the temple.

Yes, even when the picture, from a human perspective, could not be bleaker, we can rejoice to know that God is over all, and His prophecies will be fulfilled!

December 7th
Ezra 1-2; **Daniel 4**; 3 John

TWO KINGDOMS

In Daniel 4, our attention is drawn to two contrasting kingdoms: the kingdom of men, and the kingdom of the Most High God.

Nebuchadnezzar's attitude typifies that of the leaders in the kingdom of men: a smug sense of wellbeing, v. 4, and pride in one's own position and achievements, v. 30. God gives him opportunity to repent: He sends a vivid dream, vv. 5-18, interpreted by Daniel, vv. 19-26, and Daniel, in conclusion, warns him to change his ways, v. 27, but to no avail. And so God has to act, and He humbles him, by making his kingdom depart from him, v. 31, and causing him to live like a wild animal for seven years, vv. 32-34.

From this experience Nebuchadnezzar learns two very important lessons – one concerning each of the two kingdoms.

As far as the kingdom of *men* is concerned, he learns the sobering lesson that 'the most High ruleth in the kingdom of men', vv. 17, 25, 32. He gives it to 'whomsoever he will' – thus ruling out Nebuchadnezzar's boast, 'Is not this great Babylon that I have built', and He 'setteth up over it the basest of men', thus negating Nebuchadnezzar's reference to the 'honour of my majesty'. Humbled, he acknowledges the nothingness of man, and his powerlessness before the God of heaven, v. 35.

He also learns a very important lesson concerning *God's* kingdom, affirming that His 'kingdom is an everlasting kingdom, and his dominion is from generation to generation', vv. 3, 34. Having been forcibly shown how fragile was his own hold on his kingdom, clearly Nebuchadnezzar is impressed by the permanence of God's hold on His own kingdom. It is no wonder that he decides to 'praise and extol and honour the King of heaven', v. 37.

This is a salutary lesson to us, as we see proud men, often base men, in positions of power in today's world. Let us not be discouraged – God is over all. He still rules in the kingdom of men, and His kingdom – to which, by grace, we belong – will never end.

> So be it, Lord! Thy throne shall never,
> Like earth's proud empires, pass away;
> Thy kingdom stands and grows for ever,
> Till all Thy creatures own Thy sway.   JOHN ELLERTON

357

December 8th
Ezra 3-4; Daniel 5; **Revelation 1**
PAST, PRESENT, AND FUTURE

In the magnificent opening to this climactic book, the Holy Spirit, through John, uses three tenses to bring to our attention some glorious truths about our God.

In both verses 4 and 8 we see His eternity, represented by the use of the *present* – 'which is'; *past* – 'and which was'; and *future* – 'and which is to come'. He is the ever-living One.

Looking at our Lord Jesus Christ, in verse 18, we are reminded, looking back, that the One 'that liveth' became dead, but is now alive, and, looking to the future, He is 'alive for evermore'.

In verse 5 we are given three glorious offices that are His: all three are true at present, but the reference to Him as 'the faithful witness' may emphasize particularly the faithful testimony He bore when on earth, John 8. 14; and certainly He is now 'the first begotten of the dead' – the One who has priority in resurrection; and His designation as 'the prince of the kings of the earth' would point to His future manifestation, to reign over all.

Then, we see our privileged position in relation to Him, once again in three tenses, vv. 5, 6: He who 'loved us' has already 'washed us from our sins in his own blood'; now we are 'a kingdom, priests to his God and Father', as a result of which there will be to Him 'glory and dominion for ever and ever'.

Finally, in verse 19, which gives us the structure of the book, there is a similar pattern: 'Write the things which thou hast seen' – past, which John does in chapter 1; 'and the things which are' – present, which are recorded in chapters 2 and 3; 'and the things which shall be hereafter' – future, which, as chapter 4 verse 1 confirms, are written in chapters 4 to 22. Amid the debates about the interpretation of Revelation, it is good to remember that, as this division of the book shows, it is primarily about the future.

What a glorious God and Saviour we have! One who has ever been, and who has already done so much for us; who continues ever and does all for our benefit; who will for ever be, and in whose glorious future we will eternally share! And how gracious of Him to give us 'the Revelation of Jesus Christ', v. 1, that we may know more of Him and of God's purposes in Him.

December 9th
Ezra 5; **Daniel 6**; Revelation 2. 1-17
'THE GOD OF DANIEL'
In this, one of the most famous chapters in the Bible, we see God as a personal God – a God who was real to Daniel. This is testified to by Daniel's enemies, by the king, and by Daniel himself.

Four times in the chapter, God is referred to as *'his* **God'**, vv. 5, 10, 11, 23. His enemies acknowledged this, when they said, 'We shall not find any occasion against this Daniel, except we find it against him concerning the law of his God', v. 5. These men, though hostile to Daniel, nevertheless had to concede that he was obedient to his God, and that their only hope of finding anything to get him into trouble was the fact that they knew he would not contravene the principles of God. What a testimony!

Twice, the king when addressing Daniel, calls God *'thy* **God'**, vv. 16, 20. In both references, it is in connection with Daniel's service for God: 'Thy God whom thou servest continually', v. 16, and 'O Daniel, servant of the living God, is thy God, whom thou servest continually, able to deliver thee from the lions?', v. 20. Daniel was a faithful servant of the king, but the king knew that there was One whom Daniel served even more devotedly, a greater King.

Finally, in verse 22, Daniel calls Him *'my* **God'**: 'My God hath sent his angel, and hath shut the lions' mouths, that they have not hurt me'. We are given the reason: 'no manner of hurt was found upon him, because he believed in his God', v. 23. Daniel knew that this God, who was worthy of his obedience and service, could be trusted to preserve him, in the most perilous of circumstances; and, of course, preserve him He did.

In the light of all this, it is not surprising that King Darius called Him **'the God of Daniel'**, v. 26. However, he did more – he acknowledged Him as being not only Daniel's God, but 'the living God', and did all that he could to ensure that all people everywhere would fear Him, vv. 25-27.

This same God is our God. May we be so obedient to Him, so diligent in His service, and prove His preserving power so much in our lives, that those around us would see not only that He is our God, but that He is the only true God; and, like those people in Daniel's day, that they may come to know and to fear Him.

December 10th
Ezra 6; Daniel 7; Revelation 2. 18 – 3. 6
BUILDING FOR GOD

In chapter 3, the returned remnant had begun to rebuild the temple in Jerusalem, but there were obstacles; the work was hindered, and, for a time, halted, 4. 24. Now, in chapter 6, the project finally reached completion. How this came to be is instructive to us, as we seek to build for God in the spiritual sense.

Firstly, we see that their labour was according to the **will of God**. In chapter 5, men had written to King Darius, to ascertain if the children of Israel had authority to build this house. This was, humanly speaking, a threat to the work. Yet God over-ruled in a wonderful way: not only did the king find the records that showed that it was according to the command of King Cyrus, vv. 1-10, but in his response to the questioners he made it clear that there would be dire consequences for anyone who interfered with the work, vv. 11, 12. The recipients of his decree got the message, and speedily facilitated the continuation of the building project. So, when the people were working according to His will, God, in His sovereignty, ensured that the work would succeed.

Secondly, we observe the importance of the **word of God**. We read, in verse 14, that 'they prospered through the prophesying of Haggai the prophet and Zechariah the son of Iddo'. Thus, the builders were encouraged to build; knowing that they were obeying the words of those whom God had sent to bring His word to them.

Thirdly, the house was completed, because the **work of God** proceeded. Twice in verse 14 we read that they 'builded'. That God was for the work was vital, and that the prophets were exhorting them from His word was also necessary, but, in order for the work to be finished, His people had to work. And work they did, with the happy outcome that the work was completed, v. 15.

It is little wonder that it was 'with joy', vv. 16, 22, that the people of God observed the dedication of the house, v. 16, the Passover, v. 19, and the Feast of Unleavened Bread, v. 22. And, today, if we labour in the work of God, according to the will of God, as instructed for us in the word of God, then the work will prosper, and the outcome will be joyous for us too.

December 11th
Ezra 7; Daniel 8; **Revelation 3. 7-22**
SHARED FEATURES OF THE SEVEN LETTERS

Today we come to the final two letters to the seven churches. The letters have many differences, reflecting the distinct conditions pertaining in each assembly; yet they have features in common. This meditation will focus on four of these points.

The **source** of each letter is indicated by the opening words: 'These things saith . . .'. The ensuing characteristics of the Speaker (mostly features already described in chapter 1) show without doubt that it is the Lord Jesus who is speaking. Before addressing local conditions, He brings before the readers His person and work. It is apt that, before we consider our own, often failing, testimony, we are pointed to Him, in all His glorious perfection.

Then the **solemnity** of each letter is impressed upon us in the statement, '*I know thy works*', which He then describes. In the case of the first letter, the ensuing comment is positive, 2. 2; in the final letter, it is negative, 3. 15, and in most others it is a mixture. But the point is this: He fully knows our true spiritual state and our actions. Nothing is hidden from Him. This is both a comfort and a warning. May our 'works' be such that His knowing them is a consolation to us; and if otherwise, let us put things right.

Then, in each, there is a word of **solace**, in the midst of difficulties and discouragements: a blessed promise to '*him that overcometh*'. Much discussion has taken place over who the 'overcomer' is. However, the references in the passage show that the overcomers are not members of a super-spiritual élite, to which very few can aspire to belong. No, they are 'ordinary' people, saved by the grace of God, who show evidence of this by their victory over their spiritual enemies, in the whole round of life. Each true believer is, and will be, an overcomer.

Finally, we are shown the **scope** of the letters, in the exhortation at the end, or near the end, of each: '*He that hath an ear, let him hear what the Spirit saith unto the churches.*' Here the fact is impressed upon us that each letter was not only for the particular assembly to which it was sent. Each message, while dealing with local conditions, was for the instruction and obedience of us all. And it is in that spirit that we should read and obey them today.

December 12th
Ezra 8; **Daniel 9**; Revelation 4

SEVENTY YEARS AND SEVENTY WEEKS

This chapter has two parts: Daniel's prayer and confession, vv. 1-19, and God's response, vv. 20-27. They are contrasting, yet complementary, illustrating God's care for His people.

After a brief explanatory introduction, vv. 1-3, the bulk of the first section consists of Daniel's words, vv. 4-19. Likewise, a few introductory words begin the second section, vv. 20-21; then the remainder of it consists of the words of Gabriel, vv. 22-27.

Daniel's prayer flows from what he had 'understood' regarding Jeremiah's prophecy of seventy years' captivity, v. 2. In response, he is given 'understanding', vv. 22, 23, 25, regarding seventy weeks (of years), v. 24. Both the seventy years and the seventy weeks relate to Jerusalem, vv. 2, 16, 24-25, and to its state: in his confession, Daniel speaks of the current desolation of both the *city*, v. 2, and the *sanctuary*, v. 17; Gabriel informs him of further desolation of the city and the sanctuary, v. 26. This is yet to happen: Jerusalem and its people still have to face much sorrow.

But that is not all; the divine response to Daniel's prayer is also one of hope. At the start of his prayer, Daniel confesses sins and iniquity, vv. 5, 16; at the outset of the response, Gabriel speaks of a programme that will 'make an end of sins, and . . . make reconciliation for iniquity', v. 24. In his prayer, Daniel acknowledges his people's *unrighteousness*, v. 18, which contrasts with God's *righteousness*, vv. 7, 14, 16; in answer, there is a divine message of bringing in 'everlasting righteousness', v. 24. How will this be brought about? Through 'Messiah' being 'cut off', vv. 25-26. Daniel is told the fact of it, and is given the timescale.

Doubtless this was a great comfort to Daniel, whose burden for his people, against the background of the timeframe God had indicated for the Babylonian Captivity, had led him to seek God's face in confession and intercession. Now God's immediate response assures him that His promise of return from captivity would indeed happen, v. 25, but also that it would be a prelude to an even greater programme – one that would involve the Christ coming and dying, with results of eternal blessedness. This great reassurance to Daniel is for us also.

December 13th
Ezra 9; Daniel 10; **Revelation 5**

THE ONE WHO IS WORTHY

In verse 2, a question is asked: '**Who** is worthy?' This is answered in verses 1 to 7. We can ask two more questions: '**Why** is He worthy?' which is answered in verses 8 to 10; and '**Of what** is He worthy?' to which verses 11 to 14 give the answer.

In verse 1, our attention is drawn to a sealed book. Subsequent chapters show that the opening of the seals of the book will bring into motion the next phase of God's programme for the world.

Who is worthy to undertake this momentous task? John, in sadness, observed that 'no man was found worthy', v. 4. However, he need not have wept, as there was One who was worthy: our Lord Jesus Christ, here depicted by two contrasting animals – the Lion, v. 5, and the Lamb, v. 6. What glorious features are juxtaposed in these: power and purity; honour and humility; sovereignty and sacrifice; dominion and death; majesty and meekness!

Why is He worthy? What qualifies Him, and Him alone, to do this? We have a clear answer: 'Thou art worthy . . . for thou wast slain', v. 9. These words are addressed to the 'Lamb as it had been slain', v. 6. The sacrifice of Himself, offered at the cross, will ever be fresh to the hearts of His people, and will be the supreme cause for which worthiness will be ascribed to Him. Moreover, the benefits that flow to His own from His sacrifice are highlighted: we have already been 'redeemed', we are 'a kingdom of priests', and 'we shall reign on the earth', vv. 9-10. His being slain was not merely a noble act: it was with a definite purpose, for our past, present and future blessing. He is worthy indeed!

Of what is He worthy? Verse 12 supplies the answer: 'Worthy is the Lamb that was slain to receive power, and riches, and wisdom, and strength, and honour, and glory, and blessing'. He is worthy of every possible honour and distinction. For how long is He worthy of these? Verse 13 tells us: 'for ever and ever'.

So, at the start of the chapter He is seen as worthy to commence the carrying out of God's purposes for the world; at the end of it we see that when those purposes will all have been carried out, He will be eternally worthy of worship and praise. We will ascribe worthiness to Him forever, and we should do so now.

December 14th
Ezra 10; Daniel 11. 1-20; Revelation 6
EZRA – MAN OF ACTION

In Ezra chapters 9 and 10, there is a sad situation, resulting from disobedience. A detailed discussion of the particular issue is beyond the scope of this meditation, yet in the story we find helpful principles on to how to deal with failure among God's people:

In chapter 10, Ezra makes several moves, which, though physical, typify the right spiritual response when a shepherd becomes aware of failure among those for whom he has responsibility.

First, we read of Ezra *'casting himself down'*, v. 1, with weeping and confession. Though he himself was not guilty of the trespass in which his fellow-countrymen were engaged, yet he felt the guilt personally. Surely this is an exemplary attitude. It is easy, when we see failure among fellow-saints, to seek to absolve ourselves of responsibility. Rather, we all ought to feel its weight.

Then the following is recorded: 'Then *arose* Ezra', v. 5, in response to the words of Shechaniah, 'Arise; for this matter belongeth unto thee'. Ezra was encouraged to get up and deal with the matter, for it was his responsibility. This is helpful to us; it is quite in order to weep and lament the presence of sin amongst us, but the time must come when overseers will get on with seeking to put the matter right.

Soon after, he *'went into* the chamber . . . and . . . *came thither'*, v. 6. Probably this was to confer with fellow-leaders and to decide before the Lord how they were to deal with the issue. There are lessons here too: he did not act unilaterally, but consulted with other spiritual men. It is still important to have the fellowship of one's brothers in these matters.

Then 'Ezra the priest *stood up'*, v. 10, and told the people what response was necessary from them. Happily, they agreed, v. 12. So, in these days too, the guides of God's people should point out the scriptural action to take; and how vital it is that those thus admonished should respond with obedience to the word.

Finally, Ezra, and others, *'sat down'*, v. 16, to deal with the matter in a careful way. With such a spiritual response, it is not surprising that the matter was resolved. May God help us to show the same spiritual response to problems among believers today.

December 15th
Nehemiah 1-2; Daniel 11. 21-45; Revelation 7
THE GREATER THINGS – THE THINGS OF GOD

As believers, we experience a tension between our relationship to the things of this world and our loyalty to the things of God. This is not new; Nehemiah faced it many years ago. These opening chapters are a master class for us in dealing with these pressures.

Nehemiah was in a favourable **place** – Shushan the palace, 1. 1. Yet that was not where his heart lay. Right from the start, v. 2, he enquires concerning *Jerusalem*. Though the people of this world did not realize it, it was a greater place.

He was in the employ of what was then the greatest **power** on earth. Yet his true allegiance was to an altogether greater power, the One to whom he attributes 'thy great power' and 'thy strong hand', 1. 10. Beside Him, he sees the power of the king of Babylon in its true light, referring to him simply as 'this *man*', 1. 11.

He was in the awesome **presence** of the great King Artaxerxes, before whom he was 'very sore afraid', 2. 2, since to even appear 'sad in his presence', 2. 1, could have cost him his life. Yet, while there, he made use of his access to the very presence of God. In 2. 4, while the king was speaking to him, he records, 'So I prayed to the God of heaven.'

In his role in the palace as the king's cupbearer, Nehemiah was no ordinary servant, 1. 11; he was in a position of great **privilege.** However, he knew that there was a greater privilege – to be in the service of God. So, by the end of chapter 2, he is doing the work that is dear to his heart – arising and building for God.

In the narrative we see some prominent **people** – Sanballat, Tobiah and Geshem – who are highly opposed to his exercise, 2. 19. Yet Nehemiah is not in awe of them, and he does not hesitate to state the true position of these opponents: 'Ye have no portion, nor right, nor memorial, in Jerusalem', 2. 20. His heart was with a greater people – 'the remnant' – God's people, 1. 3.

As the people of God we ought, like Nehemiah, to be respectful to the authorities in this world, and faithful in the responsibilities that they place upon us. Yet, like him, let us never forget that, supremely, our honour, affection, and priorities, do not lie there, but rather with God, His people, His assembly, and His work.

December 16th
Nehemiah 3; **Daniel 12**; Revelation 8
'THE END'
In Daniel 12 we read the words 'the end' six times – very fitting in a book renowned for what it reveals about end times. It is instructive to look at the contexts in which it is found.

We read Daniel's **request** regarding the end: 'What shall be the end of these things?' v. 8. This accompanies another question regarding 'the end' – 'How long shall it be to the end of these wonders?' v. 6. So we have the questions 'What?' and 'When?' Much is revealed in this book to answer these questions, indeed, in this very chapter Daniel is given fresh revelation, for example verse 2 deals with the 'What?' of resurrection, and verses 7, 11, and 12 give some answers to the 'When?' Daniel was in the good of what God had revealed, and was eager to learn more.

Then we see Daniel's **responsibility** in view of the end: 'But thou, O Daniel, shut up the words, and seal the book, even to the time of the end', v. 4, and 'Go thy way, Daniel: for the words are closed up and sealed till the time of the end', v. 9. Daniel wanted to know more, but he had to accept that his work was done. This cannot have been easy, especially when he was told that in a future day things he had not understood, v. 8, would be understood by others: 'the wise shall understand', v. 10. God would reveal more in the days ahead: another chapter in today's readings, Revelation 8, is an example of such, but that would be after Daniel was gone. This reminds us of Peter's words about the prophets, who desired to understand more about their own writings, but who were told that they were writing, not primarily for themselves, but for us, 1 Pet. 1. 10-12.

Finally, we have Daniel's **rest** at the end: 'But go thou thy way till the end be: for thou shalt rest, and stand in thy lot at the end of the days', v. 13. His rest, and the enjoyment of the inheritance, were assured. So, a chapter that starts by warning of an unprecedented time of trouble on earth ends with the promise of rest for the servant. What a comfort to this aged, faithful servant of God!

We may never find ourselves in Daniel's circumstances, but, like him, we should desire God's word, and faithfully serve Him, knowing that it will climax in a glorious inheritance, at 'the end'.

December 17th
Nehemiah 4; **Haggai 1;** Revelation 9
CONSIDER YOUR WAYS
This blunt exhortation by the prophet Haggai 2,500 years ago to the remnant of Jews returned from their Babylonian exile was the means, under the Lord's hand, by which He awakened their consciences to their responsibilities, and prompted them to restart the building of the temple at Jerusalem. They had returned from captivity in 538 BC with the full permission of Emperor Cyrus the Great of Persia to rebuild the temple of the Lord and to re-establish His worship there. However, after an enthusiastic start in laying the foundation, they had been discouraged from continuing the project by the threats and physical opposition of the surrounding Gentile nations. That had happened in 536 BC, and it was now 520 BC, a full sixteen years later. Sadly, the Lord's people had rationalized the situation, reasoning that it was not yet the time to build the Lord's house. Meanwhile, they had been building themselves elaborate panelled houses to live in, while the Lord's house lay waste and incomplete. Consequently, the Lord had been chastising His people by frustrating their business enterprises and causing their crops to fail, as only He in His sovereignty can. Then, He sent both Haggai and his younger contemporary prophet Zechariah to rectify the situation. Happily, their ministry was heeded at once, and the whole remnant responded to this exhortation with some renewed enthusiasm. Haggai reassured them that the Lord was with them and would bless them from that time onwards. The second temple was completed and dedicated on 12th March 515 BC with great rejoicing.

Sometimes we need a 'wake-up call' from our apathy concerning the Lord's work today and the needs of our local assembly's witness. Past discouragements should never deter us, nor should direct opposition frighten us from continuing in His service. We should never put our own pursuits at home or at work before the Lord's work in our assembly. He says to us, 'Them that honour me I will honour', 1 Sam. 2. 30. Remember the words of the Lord Jesus, 'Seek ye first the kingdom of God, and his righteousness; and all these [material and temporal] things shall be added unto you', Matt. 6. 33. So let us give the Lord first place in our lives!

December 18th
Nehemiah 5; Haggai 2; Revelation 10
SO DID NOT I, BECAUSE OF THE FEAR OF GOD

MATTHEW HENRY once said, 'The fear of God is the greatest antidote against the fear of man', and ALAN REDPATH wrote that, 'Reverent fear of God is the key to faithfulness in any situation'. The life of Nehemiah abundantly illustrates these statements. He demonstrated the most exemplary moral courage in a variety of difficult and threatening situations. When his enemies attempted to deter him from building the wall of Jerusalem by direct threats of death, and also by more subtle opposition and temptation to avoid personal danger, he refused to be moved from the task to which he believed his God had called him, and to which the Persian king Artaxerxes had commissioned him. In chapter 4 of his book, he replied to all their approaches with a very firm 'No'.

Now, in chapter 5, Nehemiah is not opposed from outside the circle of his fellow-Jews, but faces serious opposition from within his own people. This could easily have ruined the whole project on which he was engaged, and also could have dishonoured the name of God. He became aware that some of the wealthy Jews were exploiting their poorer brothers and sisters, and even enslaving them. Nehemiah, therefore, demanded that these injustices be corrected at once. He feared neither his enemies, nor his influential nobles, but acted in the fear of his God alone.

The final verses of the chapter indicate that his fear of God kept him from exploiting his own people, even when it would have been possible for him to do so with impunity. The Persian governors before him had levied both money and food from their subject people, even though they themselves had plenty to live on. Nehemiah refused to take advantage of his position as governor in this way, because he feared God. Instead of exploiting his subjects, he regularly entertained a large number of them at his table entirely at his own expense. He even included some of the heathen peoples around him. He made this additional sacrifice all the time he was supervising the building of the wall. In return, he simply prayed that his God would think on him favourably for all that he had done for his people. This was the practical effect of his fear of God. What an example to us!

December 19th
Nehemiah 6; Zechariah 1; **Revelation 11**
MY TWO WITNESSES
In Acts chapter 14 verse 17, the apostles Barnabas and Paul asserted concerning God that 'he left not himself without witness'. Mankind has always had some kind of revelation from God, as a result of which men are responsible to worship Him alone, whether it has been the light of creation, conscience, or the fuller knowledge of Him in the scriptures and the Christian gospel. There have been godly men who have upheld the truth in every age of human history, no matter how dark the times have become. Enoch and Noah witnessed for God before the Flood, Abraham and Moses afterwards, while Elijah and Elisha prophesied to the apostate nation of Israel, and were followed by a succession of other true prophets of the Lord. During the present age of grace the Lord has raised up many Christian missionaries, and every believer is responsible to witness to his or her fellowmen on a daily basis. This is how the church of Christ is growing today.

It will be no different during the darkest days of the coming tribulation, when the Beast will attempt to stamp out all knowledge of the true God and claim deity himself. God will send into the world His two special witnesses to oppose him with the truth, and to bring judgement on all God's enemies by supernatural means. We do not yet know their exact identity, whether Moses and Elijah, or two future believers, but they will have a huge impact on the world for three and a half years. Their witness will be adequate, since there will be two of them. It will be energized by the power of the Holy Spirit; they will be a partial fulfilment of Zechariah's vision of the lampstand supplied by two olive trees in chapter 4 of his prophecy. They will be divinely protected until their ministry has been fulfilled successfully, as is true of every Christian witness today. After the Beast has been permitted to kill them, God will raise them from the dead and rapture them to heaven in the sight of the whole world, thus vindicating their witness and honouring their self-sacrifice, which will be great. In their ministry we see many lessons concerning witness to God which we can apply to ourselves today: its power; its cost; its victory; and its reward. Believer, be encouraged in your witness!

December 20th
Nehemiah 7; Zechariah 2-3; **Revelation 12**
WAR IN HEAVEN

In this chapter the Apostle John is given a fascinating and sobering vision of a cosmic war which has been raging from the beginning of creation between God and His adversary, Satan, who was once His privileged, anointed cherub in His immediate presence. Here are described two main phases of this heavenly conflict, a phase now past, and a phase still future. A clear understanding of the main issues involved in this war will help us to understand very much of what has already happened in human history and what will yet happen.

This scripture indicates, uniquely, that a third of the angelic hosts fell into sin with Satan. He himself is described as 'a great red dragon', v. 3, cruel and murderous. In Old Testament times, his main objective was to prevent Christ being born through God's people Israel, who are here represented by a woman in labour. When her 'man child' was born, v. 5, he tried to kill Him, but He was caught up to God's throne and escaped his clutches. Christ's pathway there via the cross and resurrection is omitted here. He is destined to rule the nations with a rod of iron in His millennial kingdom. So Satan failed to frustrate God's plan.

The future phase of this conflict will reach a critical point in the middle of the tribulation. Then there will be a great war in heaven between Michael, Israel's guardian archangel, and his angels and Satan, the dragon, and his demons. God's forces will win, and Satan will be cast out of heaven forever down to the earth. Here he will severely persecute the remnant of Israel, the woman in the vision, who will flee to the wilderness of Transjordan for safety. God will supernaturally protect her there for three and a half years against all Satan's attempts to kill her. Frustrated again, Satan will turn in his anger to persecute all believers elsewhere.

Although Satan is a defeated foe, he is still very powerful and will attack us in many ways today as believers witnessing for God. In Christ, we are vitally involved in this continual warfare 'in the heavenlies', and need to put on the whole armour of God to stand against our spiritual enemies there, see Eph. 6. 10-20. But be encouraged, we are on the victory side and will overcome!

December 21st
Nehemiah 8; **Zechariah 4;** Revelation 13
NOT BY MIGHT, NOR BY POWER, BUT BY MY SPIRIT
This statement, made by the Lord of hosts to Zerubbabel, can be taken both as a timely warning and also as a reassuring promise. The leader of the Jewish remnant had returned from Babylonian exile with permission from Cyrus, the Persian emperor, to rebuild the temple at Jerusalem. It tells us, as the Lord's servants, how the task to which He has called us both can and will be accomplished. FRANK HOUGHTON'S hymn speaks of those who are, 'facing a task unfinished, that drives us to our knees'. This is surely how many of the Lord's servants preaching the gospel in foreign lands to people with a different culture from that in our native land must often feel. They face difficulties which they are perhaps ill-equipped to solve, and opposition from those to whom they have been called to minister. We all surely feel totally inadequate to fulfil our role in the Great Commission apart from the Lord's direct help; we are simply His 'unprofitable servants', Luke 17. 10.

Therefore, this assertion in Zechariah's fifth vision was a warning to Zerubbabel not to rely on his natural ability and strength, his own resources, but rather on the help and sovereign working of God's Holy Spirit. Zerubbabel faced a mountain of *opposition* to his assigned project from the surrounding Gentiles, and also, sadly, a mountain of *apathy* concerning it from his own people. This mountain of obstacles would, however, be removed, if he relied upon God's Spirit to move in the hearts both of his opponents, and also of his fellow-workers. The Lord thus also reassured him that he would be able to finish the rebuilding of the temple, even if it was not to be as magnificent as Solomon's Temple had been. God's 'day of small things', Zech. 4. 10, such as this was, can be used by Him to humble our natural pride in what has been accomplished with God's help. Let the glory be His alone!

Today, as we all labour in our Lord's harvest field, we sometimes wonder whether souls are going to be convicted of sin and converted from darkness to embrace the truth of the gospel. But this is the work of God's Holy Spirit alone. Our part is simply to continue preaching the gospel to them, to pray that He will bless His own word, and then to praise Him for any results.

December 22nd
Nehemiah 9; Zechariah 5-6; Revelation 14
THOU ART A GOD READY TO PARDON
Daniel chapter 9, Ezra chapter 9, and Nehemiah chapter 9 all contain very moving prayers of confession and contrition by godly men on behalf of the children of Israel for their many sins against the Lord, their faithful covenant-keeping God. They are models of reverence and piety, and were heard by the Lord, because they expressed sincere repentance and a genuine desire to live henceforth in a radically different way. Daniel, Ezra, and the godly Levites in Nehemiah's day all identified themselves with their guilty people, and confessed their people's sins as their own in due humility. None of them took a proud 'holier-than-thou' attitude towards them, recognizing that they themselves were sinners like them by nature and by practice. All of them accepted that the Lord had been absolutely righteous to judge His earthly people, and made no excuses for them. These prayers are fine examples to us of true, heartfelt intercession for our brethren.

As a result of Daniel's prayer, the Lord revealed to him the unique panoramic prophecy of the seventy weeks' further discipline which Israel must suffer, before their sin and rebellion is fully dealt with. As a result of Ezra's intercessory prayer, the returned remnant rectified their sins of adultery and intermarriage with the nations around them. In Nehemiah chapter 9, the Levites rehearsed Israel's continual breaking of the Mosaic covenant, which they had originally promised to keep, and made another 'sure covenant', v. 38, with the Lord to keep it henceforth. They recognized the longsuffering of the Lord with them throughout their long history of rebellion and failure. They acknowledged that He is a God more ready to pardon them than they were to confess their sins and to repent of them. He never delights in judging His people, but longs to be able to bless them instead. He takes no pleasure in the death of the wicked, however well-deserved. He is 'gracious and merciful, slow to anger, and of great kindness', nor does He finally forsake His redeemed people, v. 17. To such a loving God and Father we should not fear to confess our failures, if we are conscious of having committed particular sins, because He will abundantly pardon us for Christ's sake.

December 23rd

Nehemiah 10-11; Zechariah 7; **Revelation 15**

THEM THAT HAD GOTTEN THE VICTORY OVER THE BEAST

In chapter 14, the Apostle John had seen the 144,000 Jewish witnesses standing with Christ on the earthly Mount Zion quite unharmed by all their experiences of persecution by the Beast and his followers, and ready to enter the millennial kingdom. This was a victory through the Lord's special protection. However, in chapter 15, John sees another large company of believers in heaven standing on a sea of glass. These are martyrs of the Beast, who were not protected from suffering death at his hands. Yet they are said to have gained the victory over him. God is sovereign in the lives of His saints, and some are allowed to live all through their lives unharmed by their enemies, while others are asked to make the supreme sacrifice for Christ in this life, but to win the martyr's crown of life in eternity. Are we today prepared to leave the choice to Him? Both options are costly!

We can, perhaps, see how martyrdom for Christ is a real victory over the enemy of our souls, not a defeat at all, when we consider the long-term results of some believers' martyrdoms during the present age of grace. For example, the Christians during the first three centuries were bitterly persecuted by the Roman authorities, yet the church grew in numbers so much that CONSTANTINE made Christianity the official religion of his empire in AD 313. TERTULLIAN said that, 'the blood of the martyrs is the seed', and the church was much purer in both doctrine and practice during those early centuries. WILLIAM TYNDALE'S martyrdom in 1536 was not in vain either; soon afterwards the whole Bible was published in English. The martyrdom in 1956 of the five young American missionaries by the Auca Indians in Ecuador eventually resulted in the conversion of many of their killers.

We are to love our enemies, and to leave all vengeance to God alone. Christ left God His Father to vindicate Him. Chapter 15 prepares for the bowls of God's wrath in chapter 16. Let us not fear those who can only kill the body. JIM ELLIOT, the pioneer missionary, said: 'He is no fool who gives what he cannot keep to gain that which he cannot lose'. Are we willing to make this self-sacrifice for our Saviour's sake?

December 24th

Nehemiah 12; **Zechariah 8;** Revelation 16

I WAS JEALOUS FOR ZION WITH GREAT JEALOUSY

Jealousy in us is usually a sin, and very similar to envy, which the Concise Oxford Dictionary defines as 'a discontented or resentful longing aroused by another's possessions, qualities, or luck'. Envy of Christ's influence over the common people led the Jewish religious leaders to deliver Him to Pilate for crucifixion, Matt. 27. 18. Very rarely can we be rightly jealous, in the sense of fiercely protective of our rights or possessions, such as our relationship with our divinely given wedded wife or husband. This is because we have so few genuine rights and exclusive possessions.

Jealousy in God's character, however, is always good and justifiable, because He is God over all and owns everything and everyone. For this reason He can rightly demand our absolute faithfulness to Him, and our exclusive worship of Himself alone. Several times in scripture the Lord God of Israel proclaims that He is a jealous God, who will tolerate no rivals to our affections and worship. This is why He condemns all idolatry throughout the Bible, especially in the Old Testament. We Christians can also have idols, people or things which displace God from first place in our hearts. These we should guard against, 1 John 5. 21. Even covetousness is called idolatry, Col. 3. 5.

In Zechariah's prophecy, God's jealousy for His own redeemed earthly people Israel is seen in two distinct ways. First, it made Him very angry with Israel for their unfaithfulness to their covenant with Him at Sinai. Eventually, it led Him to allow their enemies, the Assyrians and the Babylonians, to remove them from their Promised Land and to enslave them in prolonged exiles. Then, once this severe discipline had removed from them the desire to continue in their sins, and had thus brought them to repentance, He says that He is now jealous for them in a positive way to achieve their eternal blessing in the Land again, Zech. 1. 14. Because the Lord made many unconditional covenant promises to Israel's patriarchs, He restored them to their land. This is why He will also, in His sovereign grace, yet bless them with peace and prosperity in Christ's millennial kingdom, as this chapter abundantly predicts. Yes, Israel has a glorious future.

December 25th
Nehemiah 13; Zechariah 9-10; Revelation 17
REMEMBER ME, O MY GOD, FOR GOOD

Nehemiah's significant ministry was commenced, continued, and concluded here in an atmosphere of fervent prayer to the God whom he had come to know personally. His prayer life throughout his book is exemplary, and was surely the secret of his success. It led him to do the will of God at the right time and in the right way. Do we let God control every part of our lives like this?

Although Nehemiah was a man of vigorous action and great courage, he did not act hastily, but always prayed to God for His blessing on the work to which He had called him. When he first heard about the sad state of Jerusalem's ruined wall and the distress of his Jewish brothers who had returned there, he first turned to the Lord in an earnest prayer of confession for his people Israel's sins. Then he prayed for opportunity to broach the matter with the Persian king, his master, since he realized that he might well have opportunity as his cupbearer to ask him to assist in the situation. He waited patiently for four months, but then the king asked why he was sad in his presence. Despite natural fear in the presence of the great king, he prayed briefly for help before making his request for permission to go to Jerusalem to rebuild its wall. The king was led to grant him all his request, and more. God always answers our prayers in ways much better than we can ask or even think, Eph. 3. 20.

When Nehemiah faced opposition from his enemies during the building of the wall, he turned to God in urgent prayer that He might requite them justly for their spiteful reproach, Neh. 4. 4-5. Likewise, when he had rectified the injustice of his own people, and had shown them kindness in hospitality, he simply prayed that God would think upon him for good, 5. 19.

In chapter 13, after Nehemiah had returned from a period away in Babylon, he discovered that the returned remnant had fallen into sin again, defiling the temple, neglecting the Levites, breaking the Sabbath, and intermarrying with the Gentiles. He vigorously corrected the abuses at once, because it was the time for urgent action, not prayer, but three times prayed again to God alone for blessing and reward. What a good example to us!

December 26th
Esther 1; Zechariah 11; Revelation 18
LET THE KING GIVE HER ROYAL ESTATE UNTO ANOTHER
The book of Esther does not include the name of God, but His providential protective care for His chosen earthly people Israel is everywhere evident. It records for us the circumstances in which the Jewish feast of Purim originated during their exile in the Persian Empire. Here we can clearly see God's timely preparation of His people to meet and solve a serious threat to their very existence. Although there are no supernatural miracles in the book, the remarkable timing and natural coordination of events and people in the story reveal God's overruling hand on matters of state in the empire to achieve His sovereign purposes for Israel, who remain 'the apple of His eye', Zech. 2. 8.

How, then, did a beautiful young Jewish maiden called Esther come into a position in which she could intercede with the mightiest Persian Emperor of all time to save the lives of her doomed people at the last possible moment? Chapter 1 gives us the answer. Ahasuerus, or Xerxes I, who ruled Persia from 486-465 BC, decided to hold a magnificent feast in his winter palace at Shushan, or Susa, to display his wealth to all his nobles. During it he probably discussed with them his plans to invade Greece, a venture which later resulted in his ignominious defeat in 480-479 BC. Wine flowed freely both at the men's feast and that of his queen, Vashti, for the womenfolk. All seemed to be happy at first.

However, under the influence of drink, the king decided to call for Vashti, in order to show the men her natural beauty, possibly in an indecent display of her body. Vashti, understandably and rightly, refused to comply with this request by the king. She had a due sense of modesty and faithfulness to her husband. Ahasuerus became very angry with her, and, after consulting his counsellors, decided to divorce her for disobedience. He feared that she might influence all the ladies in his empire to disobey their husbands. One of his close counsellors, Memucan, then advised him to choose another queen in Vashti's place. This is how Esther, a lovely young virgin, became involved in a very morally dubious selection process, and was Ahasuerus' immediate choice to succeed Vashti. Thus the scene was set for the unfolding of the story.

376

December 27th

Esther 2; Zechariah 12. 1 – 13. 6; **Revelation 19. 1-10**

THE MARRIAGE OF THE LAMB IS COME

The opening words of our passage, 'after these things', dates its main subject after the final judgement of the world's commercial centre, Babylon the Great, at the very end of the great tribulation. Babylon the Great will be both a false religious system and a city. The Beast will destroy *the religious system* at the mid-point of the tribulation, in order to establish himself as the only object of worship. God will destroy *the city* in one hour by the great earthquake of the seventh bowl judgement. So the false church will be destroyed before God announces the wonderful event of the marriage of His Son, the Lamb of Calvary's cross, to His true bride, the church. The false must make way for the true.

The marriage of the Lamb, the only perfect marriage of all time, will be made in heaven one day between Christ and all true Christians, who form the church. It will be preceded by a four-fold 'hallelujah chorus', as heaven's citizens celebrate Christ's triumph in the tribulation judgements, and announce His imminent reign on earth in the very place where He was rejected and crucified. Christ 'must reign', 1 Cor. 15. 25, and we will reign with Him.

Christ the Bridegroom's name, the Lamb, will forever remind us of His vicarious sacrifice on Calvary for our sins. His bride is the church of redeemed sinners who have trusted in Him for salvation. He, not His bride, will be the focus of attention in that day, unlike in present weddings. He will be seeing in us the results of 'the travail of His soul' Isa. 53. 11, and will be satisfied.

We are now being allowed to make our own wedding dress for that occasion; for the fine linen in which we will be clothed is said to be 'the righteous acts of the saints', v. 8 RV. Our present service for Christ is preparing us to honour our heavenly Bridegroom then. How well are we making our wedding garment?

We shall have a wonderful wedding reception after our marriage to Christ in heaven, probably on earth during the millennial kingdom, rather than in heaven. To this all believers from other ages will be invited to share Christ's joy in us, including the Old Testament saints and the tribulation saints, both the martyrs and the still living believers. Will you be there?

December 28th
Esther 3-4; **Zechariah 13. 7- 14. 21;** Revelation 19. 11 – 20. 6
THE LORD SHALL BE KING OVER ALL THE EARTH
Zechariah's prophecy rises to a crescendo of triumph in its last chapter. Christ, the Lord's true Shepherd of Israel, will return from heaven to deliver His people Israel from annihilation by their besieging enemies at the last possible moment, and then will establish His divine rule over the whole earth as King of kings. The same Man whom the Lord smote on Calvary with the sword of His justice to atone for our sins, as well as Israel's, will take over the government of this world from the Gentile kingdoms and establish a kingdom characterized entirely by holiness. There will be no idolatry, and every nation that has survived the tribulation judgements will be required to worship the Lord with the appropriate sacrifices at the annual feasts. Many geographical changes will take place at the beginning of the millennium, which will be one of peace and righteousness.

But why must there be such a millennium? Why could not this present age be concluded simply by a final general judgement of all mankind? Why must Christ reign? Firstly, Christ must be vindicated in the very place where He was humiliated and crucified. Secondly, Christ must reclaim the earth for God from Satan, who must be finally defeated. Thirdly, God's unconditional promises of blessing to Israel must all be fulfilled in Christ. Fourthly, God will fulfil His original purpose for man that he should rule the earth for Him through Christ. Finally, the millennial kingdom is mankind's final test under perfect government and ideal conditions to see if he will obey God. It is the seventh and final dispensation in God's programme for the ages. When mankind fails this test at the end of the millennium through Satan's renewed temptation, it will prove that the heart of man is so incurably wicked that God must destroy the present heavens and earth, and replace them with the new heaven and earth, in which righteousness not simply reigns with a rod of iron, but dwells eternally. The millennium will be the antechamber to eternity, but not the final state of things.

During the millennial kingdom, Christ will give varying administrative responsibilities to saints of this church age according to our faithfulness to Him now. How ready are we all for this?

December 29th
Esther 5-6; Malachi 1. 1 – 2. 9; Revelation 20. 7 – 21. 8
THE MAN WHOM THE KING DELIGHTETH TO HONOUR

Today we rejoin the story of the book of Esther at a critical moment. Haman the Agagite, an Amalekite and enemy of the Jews, has ingratiated himself with the king and received preferment over other nobles in the kingdom. When Esther's older cousin, Mordecai, who had brought her up, refused, on conscientious grounds, to acknowledge Ahasuerus' new favourite, Haman was mortally offended and sought means to retaliate against not only him, but all Jews throughout the Persian Empire. He persuaded the king to pass a law condemning all Jews in the empire to death on a day near the end of that year. Mordecai was mortified at the result of his stand for God, but realized that Esther could turn the situation around, and rescue her people from their fate by interceding with her royal husband. Bravely, Esther agreed to approach the king, despite exposing herself to danger in so doing. She invited the king and Haman to a banquet, and then repeated the invitation for the following day, intending to expose Haman as a traitor then. The latter had already prepared a gallows on which to hang Mordecai the next day. The drama is now intense!

Here God steps in and gives the king a sleepless night, during which he reads his chronicles and discovers that Mordecai had once saved his life. Concerned that nothing had been done to reward him, as soon as Haman approached him in the morning, intending to ask for the death of Mordecai, the king asked him instead what should be done to the man whom the king delights to honour. Haman, thinking that the king would honour him, gave an answer calculated to secure his own public acclaim. But the king turned the tables on him by telling him to do exactly that to Mordecai. Haman had to comply, but sensed his imminent downfall in favour of his enemy. This occurred in the next chapter, and he was hanged on his own gallows. What poetic justice!

This is how the Jews were saved from annihilation by Esther and Mordecai, and the Feast of Purim celebrates God's sovereignty in achieving their deliverance. Mordecai is a faint foreshadowing of the true Saviour of His people, the Lord Jesus Christ, who is supremely the Man whom His Father delights to honour!

379

December 30th

Esther 7-8; Malachi 2. 10 – 3. 6; **Revelation 21. 9 – 22. 5**

THE LORD GOD ALMIGHTY AND THE LAMB ARE ITS TEMPLE

According to 1 Corinthians chapter 15 verse 28, the grand objective of Christ's redemptive work on the cross and of His millennial kingdom is that 'God may be all in all'. Here in the eternal city, New Jerusalem, we see that objective finally fulfilled. Here God fills everything in every way. He is the city's glory, the city's only light, and its one object and subject of worship. Since in the new creation sin has been removed entirely, there is no longer any need to build a separate temple enclosure for God's glory, as in the previous temples on the old earth, because everything is now in perfect accordance with God's own holiness.

The names given to God and Christ His Son here indicate some of the themes of our worship of them in eternity. Lord God Almighty reminds us that God is absolutely sovereign in all He does, and able to accomplish all His purposes by His almighty power. In His sovereignty He chose us to be His own, and by His almighty power He saved us, and brought us to glory by means of the resurrection and rapture of the church. The name given to Christ, the Lamb, vividly reminds us of His sacrificial death on Calvary's cross for us, and the love of God which motivated the whole plan of redemption through Him. The word used for Lamb here actually means a young lamb, in all apparent weakness, but in chapter 5 Christ as the young Lamb is seen standing in the midst of the throne of God, though bearing mortal wounds, in resurrection power victorious and acclaimed by all in heaven as the Redeemer. We shall worship both the Father and the Son for these wonderful spiritual truths and blessings in the power of His indwelling Spirit forever. What an occupation will be ours!

The New Jerusalem will be *our eternal home.* We shall feel at home there, because we will be completely free from indwelling sin. We shall be a kingdom of priestly servants, delighting to do our Lord's will. We shall constantly see His face, and be like Him with glorified immortal bodies. Whatever God's purposes in eternity are revealed to be, we will cooperate with Him in all of them out of gratitude for His grace which saved us and brought us there. But, reader, will you be there?

December 31st
Esther 9-10; **Malachi 3. 7 – 4. 6;** Revelation 22. 6-21

THEY THAT FEARED THE LORD

Malachi lived in dark days of declension and departure from the Lord. The Jewish remnant that had returned from the Babylonian exile had begun a spiritual recovery well, but later generations had not followed their good example. They had become careless about their service to the Lord, offering Him defective sacrifices and failing to give the Levites their required tithes. Also, they had compromised in their marriage relationships. Some of them had divorced their Jewish wives and formed relationships with Gentile idolatrous women. Both the people and the priests were guilty of all these sins. Yet they seemed to have become blind to their faults. When Malachi challenged them about these matters, they reacted in surprise at his rebukes and asked in what way they had offended. Some of them, perhaps in view of their current difficulties, were even questioning the value of serving God.

Malachi's task was not only to rebuke Israel for their failures, but also to encourage them to give the Lord His rightful dues. The Lord promised that, if they did so, He would pour them out an overflowing blessing. Their Promised Land would again become a delightful land. Malachi also predicted the coming of several more divine messengers to rectify the situation in the nation: first, John the Baptist; then Christ; and finally, the prophet Elijah before the darkest days of the still future tribulation.

There were, however, even in Malachi's day, some who were distinct from the majority of the nation. These humble folk feared the Lord with due reverence and gave Him His rightful place in their lives. They meditated on the Lord's name, and then spoke often about Him to their fellow-saints. They had happy fellowship with one another. The Lord promised to reward this faithful remnant when He came again into this world. They would be His special treasure, and exempt from judgement.

Faithful believers today are like this remnant in Malachi's day. We are saddened by all the sin and departure around us, but we continue to fear the Lord and to encourage one another with thoughts about His name. He promises to reward us too at His future coming.